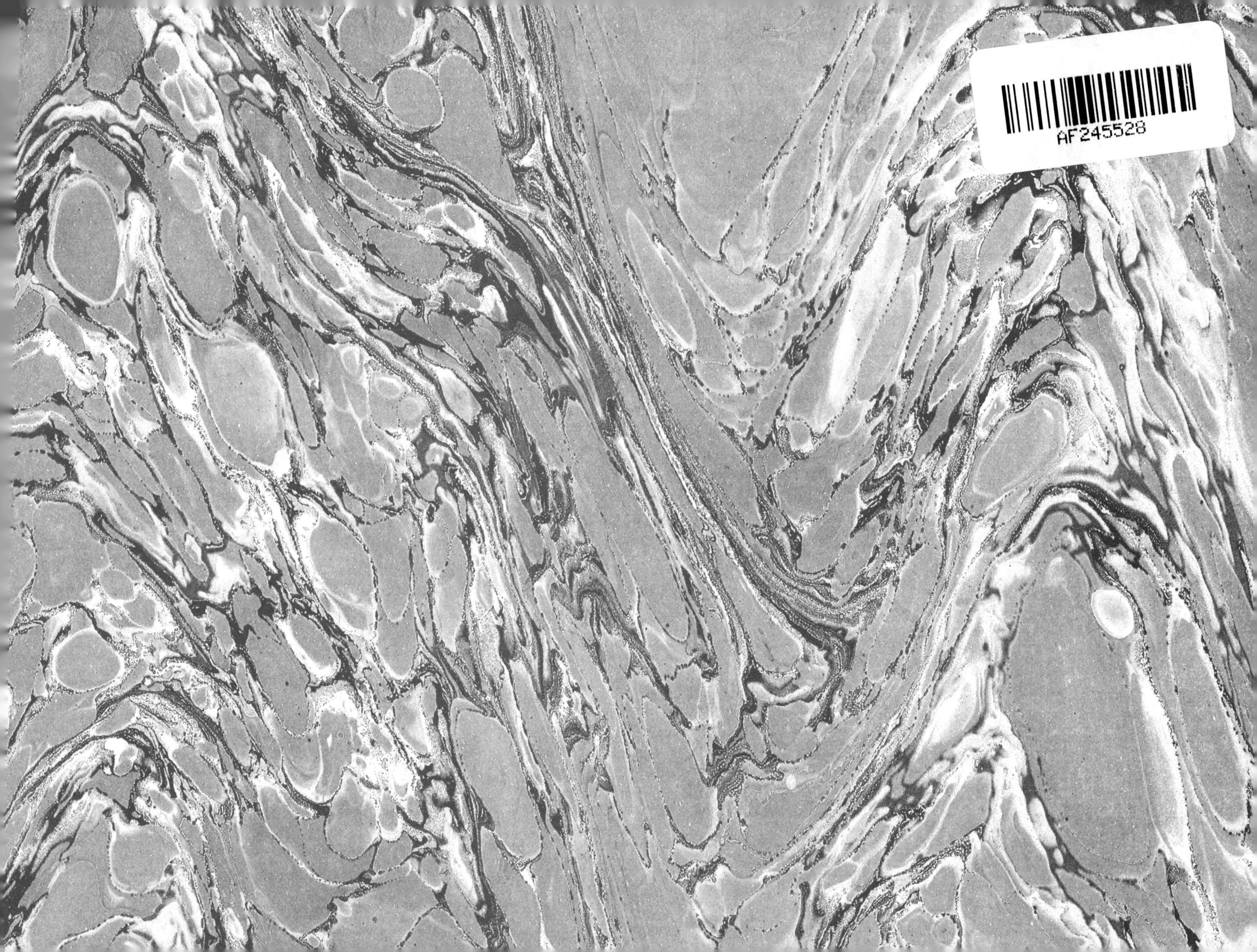

THE VICTORIAN CATALOGUE

OF

TOOLS FOR TRADES AND CRAFTS

PHILIP WALKER

STUDIO
EDITIONS

*The Victorian Catalogue of
Tools for Trades and Crafts*

This edition published in 1994 by Studio Editions
Ltd, Princess House, 50 Eastcastle Street, London
W1N 7AP, England

ISBN 1 85891 120 6
Printed in India

INTRODUCTION

THE BOOK

The catalogue of about 1845 reprinted in this book is a very different thing from the type of catalogue, often produced by mail-order firms and distributed in millions of copies, which we are familiar with today. Yet it is a direct ancestor and is worth considering for its part in the history of advertising as well as for the interest of the objects which it illustrates.

For most of human history the craftsmen who produced goods relied for their sales on customers coming to their workshops. These customers may have been simply neighbours, buying retail, as we would say, or merchants who bought in quantity in order to retail at the local market or wholesale into the mercantile network which, even in prehistoric times, resulted in certain goods being distributed far and wide. At least as early as the 15th century these merchants had sought ways of ensuring their resale market before committing capital to the purchase of stock. Apart from making financial arrangements like factoring or selling on commission, they had sought to get firm orders by showing samples, models or patterns. The practice probably started in textiles where, of course, it still exists in the form of the swatches or colour cards which are obtainable from fabric and thread manufacturers. However, in the middle years of the 18th century the great complex of developments constituting the Industrial Revolution began and gave birth as an essential part of the process to the trade catalogue.

The defining characteristic of the Industrial Revolution was a huge increase in production by the industrialising areas for which correspondingly enlarged markets had to be found. The existing neighbourhood markets would absorb some part of the extra production thanks to the increases in general prosperity and in population which the revolution brought about, but for the bulk of the new production the market area itself had to be widened. Whether or not the initial pressure came from the merchants who hitherto had been content to carry actual samples, manufacturers adopted the idea of having printed illustrations of the goods they could produce. The prints could easily be carried much further afield, shown to potential customers and used as the basis for obtaining orders. These copperplate prints were still thought of more in terms of the samples which they replaced – they were called 'pattern books', suggesting that goods could be made to the designs shown, rather than 'catalogues' with the implication of a list of goods just waiting to be handed off the shelves.

The process of printing with copperplates involved cutting the outlines and any shading into the surface of a smooth copper plate using special engraving tools. The cuts and scratches were then loaded with ink, the uncut surface being wiped clean, and a sheet of paper was pressed onto the plate. Great pressure was applied through a felt mat by a pair of steel rollers. The inking and rolling process had to be repeated for each impression taken. The pressure exerted through the flexible mat ensured that the whole of the design was picked up even if the surface of the copper was slightly uneven and this meant that it was possible to erase parts of a design and add new bits by scraping, burnishing and re-engraving areas of an old plate. Since the engraving of a complete new plate was quite an expensive process such alterations were frequently resorted to for later editions of a catalogue. To take Plate 112, for example, there are at least three different engraved scripts, and it is clear that the French Pattern Mincing Knife and the Potato Masher were added after the original items. Plate 154 is another case in point where the ghost of the earlier trowel handle can be seen through the added Modellers Tools. The presence of a number of such alterations in this catalogue allows one to assume that many of the plates were originally engraved considerably earlier than 1845, the presumed publication date of the present book. The leading authority on this catalogue, K. D. Roberts, who has examined minutely all the evidence, including watermarks, and established 1845 as its most probable publication date, is of the opinion that many of the engravings date from about 1820 or even earlier in the 19th century.

Each printing of a pattern book at that time would have been quite small, probably about 50 copies at a time. They were therefore costly to produce but were valuable property to the chosen agents who got copies and who almost certainly had to bear part of the cost. Most modern catalogues are, of course, printed in much greater quantities and are designed to advertise the firm which puts them out as well as the actual goods offered for sale. In contrast, most early pattern books did not even bear the manufacturer's/publisher's name. This was to protect the interests of the agents or merchants who would run the risk of being cut out if the customers to whom they showed the book saw a chance of buying directly from source. The title page of this book does not appear to have survived, so we do not know whether it showed the name of the firm, Richard Timmins, which in any case does not appear on the individual plates. However, it was the period in which the modern type of catalogue was emerging and certainly by the time of the Great Exhibition of 1851, Richard Timmins, like other firms, was only too pleased to announce its name, products and exhibition awards to the public at large. One cannot make hard-and-fast generalisations and just as today there are exceptions where the distribution of certain products is carefully controlled through selected agents or franchises, so there were exceptions to the general rule of anonymity. In fact, the earliest known tool catalogue, that of John Wyke of Liverpool dating to about 1760, has 'Made by Iohn Wyke' engraved on most of the individual plates.

The Firm

Although the individual plates bear no manufacturer's name and the original title page has not survived, we know that this catalogue was produced by the firm of Richard Timmins & Sons of Birmingham because many of the same plates, albeit in some cases altered, were used in subsequent editions which were clearly identified. Moreover, there is in existence a named Richard Timmins price list which relates all the items to the same plate numbers as appear in this publication. Richard Timmins started his business in the last decade of the 18th century and the firm continued trading, after a number of mergers, under the name of Wynn, Timmins & Co. up to 1969. This was not the first catalogue or pattern book produced by the firm. There is evidence of one in 1826, although no copy appears to have survived, and in the light of the prominence of Timmins in the Birmingham trade, it is highly probable that they had issued books even earlier in the century. Plates engraved for these early editions continued to be used with or without amendments in the 1840s and for many years after.

Birmingham

Birmingham had no great natural resources of coal, water power or iron, but the inhabitants of the area had long shown skill and ingenuity in producing small metal items with a large element of design and work in relation to a relatively small input of raw material and power. Such things as buttons, buckles, nails, needles, locks and firearms were staples of the area by the 18th century. With the enormous growth of a money economy accompanying the Industrial Revolution, the whole category of products known locally as toys experienced a boom in demand. This term 'toy' covered a great variety of small products but they were essentially metal items incorporating novelty, decoration or ingenuity – just the sort of thing to appeal to the huge new middle class who for the first time had money to spend on attractive gadgets in addition to the basic essentials of life. In addition to the tradesmen's hand tools (which in some cases were also attractions for the 'impulse buyers'!) this catalogue shows a range of the sort of merchandise which contributed to Birmingham's phenomenal growth and prosperity in the 19th century.

THE CONTENTS

This range of tools and Birmingham 'toys' commercially available when Queen Victoria had been on the throne less than ten years provides much detailed information, particularly on questions of nomenclature and dating, for the technical historian. However, the non-specialist reader too may find that a glance through the contents prompts intriguing reflections. Is it surprising to find tin-openers (Plate 130, Knives for opening meat Cases) in a catalogue which still offers a whole range of Fire Steels (Plates 91 and 100) and a Tinder Box (Plate 115)? What sort of need can there have been for a lockable Dog Collar (Plate 133) or long Steel Tobacco Pipes (Plate 91)? What kind of people bought the various sets of tools which would have had little appeal to the normal craftsman who would have acquired everything necessary for his trade piecemeal during a long apprenticeship? Some kits, such as the Deal Chests of Tools for Carpenters, Joiners, etc. and the Shoe Makers' Sets of Tools (Plate 2) do seem quite practical for men hoping to earn their livings at a trade, so one recalls the large–scale emigration to the USA, Australia and elsewhere which took place in the 19th century, emigration which was encouraged and often financed by charities offering the sea passage and a set of tools to suitable emigrants. Some other sets, such as the tools for repairing shoes or cleaning and adjusting guns, could have been useful to non-professional users, but sets such as those on Plates 8, 10 & 11, where one handle has to serve a whole range of chisels and other implements and where the hammer comes in three parts, were hopelessly impractical. The fact that they were evidently saleable and worth advertising is a clear indication of the enormous social changes accompanying the Industrial Revolution. Although these upheavals did, of course, leave many struggling to survive in appaling conditions, even more were quitting a background of subsistence labour and entering the burgeoning middle classes. These people were conscious of their new prosperity and could be tempted by neat and intriguing gadgets. One can easily imagine that the Japan'd Box with 24 interchangeable tools (No.2292 on Plate 10) would be equally satisfactory as a Christmas present for the factory foreman or City clerk who received it as for the wife and children who gave it to him.

On the question of the names given to tools no great significance should be attached to apparent eccentricities. Tool names were largely established in the vernacular, often by men who had never seen them in writing, and they varied from area to area and from trade to trade. Clerks and storemen tended to write down just what they heard workmen say. The Acking Knife on Plate 61 no doubt lost its initial H in this way. In other cases the description was simply a response to the advertiser's perennial problem: what to call the product to make it sound different, superior and attractive. Regional attributions like London Pattern or words such as Warranted and Improved were doubtless descriptive originally but even by this date had become largely promotional. Using a qualifying word instead of the substantive is another way in which names become established, e.g. Bevel Gauges are, on Plate 28, simply called Bevils, just as Butt Hinges are nowadays referred to by tradesmen as Butts. Similarly, inconsistencies in spelling (Sets or Setts, Guage or Gauge and the continued use of the long 'S') are quaint but not altogether surprising in the context of a catalogue like this. The fact that an 1886 edition from the same firm has generally orthodox spellings probably owes more to the printer than to the manufacturer who drew up the list.

Prices on all the copperplate engravings are marked in shillings and pence, e.g. 5/9 or 178/- Only in the typeset text to Plates 1 & 2 are the prices in pounds, shillings and pence, e.g. £5 18s 6d (£1=20s, ls=12d). It should be noted that the prices marked are usually per dozen, but some items are priced individually. Sometimes this is made clear, particularly where there are cheaper or more expensive options, e.g. 'Without handles 2/- Pr. Doz. less' or 'If 3 holes 4d pr. pair extra'. Items priced individually are usually marked '6/6 each' or '7/- ea' but there are many cases where one must assume that the price is per dozen unless common sense and a comparison with other prices suggest otherwise.

The great majority of the objects in this pattern book were engraved at full size (although each plate has been reduced to half size in the present reproduction). Presumably the life-size pictures were thought to give potential buyers a more immediate idea of what was on offer and this is another reminder of the evolutionary stage which the book represents. Showing a full-size drawing can be seen as halfway between putting an actual sample into the customer's hands and the modern advertisement photograph where scale is automatically understood or, occasionally, indicated by a single dimension.

It should be noted that since the c.1845 publication was made up using some or even all plates which had been used before, they do not form a complete numbered sequence. Some of the earlier plates will have been altered and updated, some were simply rejected. So the absence of a Plate No.41, for example, does not indicate a defect in the present publication!

THE PLATES

(All plates are reduced to half original size)

PLATES 1, 2, & 4. Sensible sets of tools. Just as today, the beginnings of DIY for many and of a skilled and satisfying hobby for a few.

PLATE 5. Plumbers' Turn Pins were for opening out the mouth of a lead pipe in order to joint another into it. Dressers were for beating down folds and flanges in lead sheet.

PLATE 9. The feathers were probably intended for lightly applying oil. The large claw hammer is a mystery. It is not the type of hammer one would expect to find with gun tools. It ill fits the box and its very unusual shaping closely resembles hammers advertised for export by the German firm of Schürhoff in about 1842. One can speculate that the copperplate engraver, having been sent many basketfuls of tools to copy, may have forgotten his precise instructions as to grouping and decided to put this hammer in the gun box, partially cutting away a partition to accommodate it.

PLATE 10. The central item at the bottom is for compressing the lock spring of a flintlock gun.

PLATE 13. The cranked tool tied down with a tape is of interest. It is a kind of chisel called a Butteris or Buttress (*see also* Plate 33) used for paring hooves with a pushing motion. At the date of this catalogue it had already been outlawed by many British farriers as being dangerous in comparison with the paring knife (three examples shown in the centre loops) which is drawn towards the user and thus easier to control.

PLATE 15A. The term Tower as here in New Pattern Tower compasses occurs in several places. Its significance is not certain but a number of standards were kept by the Tower of London, e.g. the Tower Pound weight and Tower Arsenal Proof for gunpowder, so it may indicate a pattern approved for government service.

PLATE 17. The considerably more expensive Box Joint tools have one arm of the tool passing right through the other and inextricably locked into it. This is a skilful hot forging technique which often mystifies laymen. Nippers are to shoemakers what pincers are to woodworkers, tools for extracting nails, etc.

PLATE 18. Shoe Pincers are designed to grip the leather upper and strain it over the last, using the hammer-like projection as a fulcrum. The projection is also a convenient hammer for tacking the stretched upper to the last.

PLATE 19. Blocking Pincers are similar to Shoe Pincers but for working on the front of boots. Shoe Stamps are used to close and conceal the holes left by nails which held the insole to the last. Shoe Punches cut lace holes.

PLATE 22. Many kinds of 'sticks' or 'bones' are used in finishing handmade leather shoes. There appears to have been even less uniformity and consistency in the naming of leather-working tools than was the case in other trades, however the word 'ran' or 'rand' usually meant much the same as welt. The Ran Key therefore was for rubbing down the stitch marks in the welt of a shoe.

PLATES 23, 25 & 26. Shoemakers' files were mainly Kit Files intended for maintaining and reshaping Kit Tools (see Plates 25 & 26). The Kit Tools are now usually known as edge irons. They are used for 'setting' or shaping the edges of sole and welt. The Boot Lace Drawer has sharp-edged circular holes through which a square-edged lace cut from a hide can be drawn to round it off.

PLATE 27. Woodworkers' gauges for marking or cutting lines parallel to the edge of a workpiece. The Mortice Gauges mark the double line which defines the edges of a mortice joint.

PLATE 28. Just as the noun 'square' is generally used to mean a square gauge (i.e. a right-angled one) so bevel gauges are here simply called Bevils.

PLATE 29. The Pads are handles to take narrow replaceable saw blades. Such a saw complete is thus called a pad-saw.

PLATE 33. For the Buttress (No.1515) see note to Plate 13. Just as women sometimes had their hair singed as an alternative to cutting, so it was customary to singe the coats of horses with the Instrument (No.2390) which incorporated a box into which coals were put to keep it hot.

PLATE 34. Sheeps Ear Plyers were used before the introduction of a suitable dye to identify flocks of sheep by punching a distinguishing combination of shaped holes in the animals' ears. Cow Knob Pincers were used to screw brass or lead knobs (latterly known as horn trainers) onto the horns of cattle. A bar or cord could then be fixed between the two horns so as to train them to grow at a more desirable angle for show purposes (*see also* Plate 35). The Cattle Probe is a sharp dagger carrying round its blade a flanged tube. The probe is thrust into the animal's belly and then withdrawn leaving the tube (its penetration limited by the flange which rests against the animal's hide) to vent a dangerous accumulation of stomach gas. Cattle Holders have rounded claws which can be locked onto the septum in a beast's nose and thus provide a temporary ring for leading the animal.

PLATE 35. Combination tools although seldom part of a regular tradesman's kit are, of course, valuable for occasional and emergency use as, for instance, when travelling. Thus, when most travelling was done by horse, a small and compact tool which could save the animal from going lame by picking a stone out of its hoof or drawing and resetting a nail – which might also involve filing (both Horse Picks illustrated incorporate a file although this is not mentioned in the caption) – was as handy as a motor breakdown organisation is today. The tapered slot in the combined Hammer Bed Key would get sufficient grip on square or hexagonal nuts of various sizes to adjust the tension of the wire mesh beds which were then popular. A lead or brass Cow Knob is illustrated inside the combination Key used for screwing the knob onto a horn.

PLATE 36. Most hammer combination tools intended for packing and unpacking in warehouse work, where they had to stand up to being thrown about and dropped, were made entirely of metal. An exception was the Orange Chest Hammer which, equipped with an adze blade and a wooden handle, was evidently intended for more careful work. Why this should be so remains a mystery although it is also notable that the traditional forging of these tools tends to be fine and decorative. Compare this special treatment of the tool with that of the Glazier's Hammer (Plate 67) which, by ancient tradition, was also often made with elaborate decoration.

PLATE 37. The twists in the blade of some of the smaller screwdrivers (the more usual name for these tools used to be turnscrew) may be purely decorative. However, at least one example has been seen where the blade was double-ended, i.e. had a bit at each end of slightly different sizes, and the twist afforded a grip for pulling the blade out of the handle in order to reverse it. If the screwdrivers in the catalogue did possess this feature it is curious that the captions fail to mention it, but it would not be the only example of a lack of perfect liaison between the manufacturer and the engraver of the plates.

PLATE 40. The Rimer is a tool for enlarging holes, nowadays called a reamer. The significance of 'to shift', engraved over two of the blades, is not clear. However, amongst woodworkers such forked screwdrivers are only used for the nuts and screws which hold saw blades into their handles, so possibly it had been intended to add the words 'saw screws' after 'to shift'.

PLATE 45. The Slaters Hatchet and the Slaters Hammer each have a sharp spike for knocking small holes in slates through which copper nails can be driven into the roof battens. The Slaters Ripper is used for pulling these nails out when slates need replacing. The Shingling Hatchet is an exception to the rule that regular tradesmen don't use combination tools. When up on a roof it is clearly an advantage to have a single tool which can trim shingles to size, nail them on and pull nails out rather than having to manage three separate tools.

PLATE 48. Veneering Hammers are used to press down veneer and squeeze out excess glue. It is interesting that such tools were available commercially as most cabinet-makers seem to have preferred to make their own entirely of wood, apart from an inset strip of zinc or copper to avoid the risk of rust stains from iron.

PLATES 49,50,51,52 & 53. Saw-sets are for bending the teeth of saws alternately to left and right. It is very important that each tooth should have the same degree of bend and ensuring this, using the simple 'gate' tools, required considerable skill and judgment. The slides fitted to the last three saw-sets enabled a limit to be set to the angle of bend whilst the American or Patent Saw-set, which was quite a new invention in 1845, also controlled the depth at which the teeth were bent.

PLATE 54. It is curious that this plate which was evidently designed originally to show four sizes out of a range of screw-adjustable wrenches not so very different from today's adjustable spanners has had added to it a more primitive type of adjustable, the Wedge or Slip Wrench. Moreover, the artist who added the Improved Wedge Wrench appears to have misunderstood the mechanism (and misjudged the space required to illustrate it) with the result that the wedge does not appear at all.

PLATE 60. The later addition of items for archers and for use with muzzle-loading guns to this plate originally devoted to tailors' implements results in an odd miscellany. The Gun Charges are small, double-ended cases with sprung lids, easily held and pushed open with one hand. They would contain two charges of gunpowder previously measured out to enable a muzzle-loading gun to be reloaded rapidly. As with the Spectacle Cases these powder cases were available in soft or hard versions, the hard being slightly more expensive. It seems likely that the material was leather since, hard or soft, it was cheaper than the brass option. After the powder had been poured down the gun barrel it had to have a wad rammed down on top of it followed by a second wad after the shot. These wads were cut from felt or other suitable fabric with a

Wadding Punch. The fact that these punches were sold in (as)sorted sizes reflects the lack of standardisation in the bore measurements of older guns. The Mattress Punch was used to cut the leather rosettes which commonly anchored the stitching through horsehair mattresses.

PLATE 61. Glaziers acking knives have stout blades as they are struck with a hammer in order to chop out old glass and putty. The initial 'h' of hacking cannot be dispensed with in orthodox English but this is no doubt a case where a clerk wrote down exactly what he heard.

PLATE 62. These saddler's tools include Rowels, spiked wheels to mark out stitch holes regularly spaced and parallel to the edge of a workpiece; Palms, the saddler's equivalent of a thimble but held in the hand rather than being worn on a finger; a Seat Iron for pushing stuffing into saddlery and various tools for edging and creasing to finish and decorate straps, etc.

PLATE 63. These Pincers, like the shoemaker's variety, serve to strain or stretch material (*see* Note to Plate 18).

PLATE 64. The Punches are illustrated as though the cutting edges are viewed face-on whilst the shanks present a side view. This, of course, does not mean that the tools were bent through ninety degrees but was simply a device to convey information economically. This device has been employed by artists since at least the 13th century and was easily intelligible to the contemporary viewers, although a later generation expressed surprise when seeing Picasso's use of it.

PLATE 65. The terms 'Ladies' and 'Gentlemens' did not imply that the use of the tool was limited by the gender of the user. It had simply become a conventional way of indicating sizes smaller than those of the normal tradesman's tools.

PLATE 66. Sailors Palms, for use when stitching sails and other canvas work, were attached to a sort of half-glove (*see* Plate 152) unlike the leather-working palms which were held in the hand. The Trimmers Hammers were intended for upholstering the interiors of coaches and carriages.

PLATE 67. Note that the Glazier's Hammers still carried extra decorative features, a tradition which dates back to the 17th century and very possibly earlier. It may well have started when glass for ordinary windows was a new and precious commodity giving the specialists who fitted it a particular prestige.

PLATE 70. The Square-faced Steady or Stake is one of a range of tools designed to fit into the hole in a larger anvil when the metal-worker needed a small or specially shaped surface to work on.

PLATE 73. Carpet Strainers when in use are fitted with a bulbous and padded wooden handle. The carpet fitter uses his knee against the pad to stretch the carpet forward leaving his hands free to tack it down. Counting the various sizes and tooth numbers available, there are nine different strainers on offer here. It is perhaps surprising that fitting carpets to floors was already at the date of this publication sufficiently widespread to justify such a variety in the specialised tools.

PLATE 77. The slide or ring on the Slide Plyers is a device also used on blacksmiths' tongs and in a number of other applications. By sliding the ring backwards the grip can be locked onto the workpiece. Blucher Plyers are, like other leather-workers' pliers, for straining the material. The name Blucher referred to a particular type of heavy boot.

PLATE 79. Coopers Drivers are used with a hammer to force hoops down onto the bulge of casks. The Coopers Whittles are knives for shaping wooden hoops.

PLATE 80 Crose Irons are the cutters fitted into a croze, the tool for cutting the groove in the neck of a cask to hold the head. An illustration of a complete croze, reduced to a quarter of the scale of the other tools, has been awkwardly superimposed onto the Tap Borer which, as the name implies, is for boring a tapered hole into a cask to take a tap or spigot. A Coopers Vice is simply a handle which can be screwed into a cask head in order to pull it up. A Bung Tickler serves to lever a bung out of its hole. The Coopers Fret is designed to bore a small hole into a cask, either to provide an air vent or to take a sample of the contents. Note the collar forged round the shank of the fret. This is to enable the fret itself to bung the hole and avoid wastage of the contents until a receptacle, or a small bung known as a spile, is ready to hand.

PLATE 81. The axe or hatchet, in its infinite variety of forms, has been throughout history until the last century or so the most versatile and widely used tool for working wood. Apart from the chief task of falling (felling) trees and chopping them up, the axe has been the principal tool for shaping workpieces in most trades. Today it is only the small and diminishing band of master coopers who demonstrate how an axe can be used to turn a slab of raw material (a cleft oak billet) into a highly subtle and accurate component of a watertight vessel (a stave for a cask). The edges of shaping axes are usually bevelled on one side only, i.e. they are like chisels with the side normally used against the wood left flat. Of the axes on this plate the Wheelers, Carpenters, Coopers and possibly the Boat Builders would have been single bevelled although the perspective of the engraving does not make this clear. Until around the middle of the last century most tools were made of the relatively soft but tough material, wrought (wrot) iron,with only the cutting edges being steel. Here we see that since carpenters and others used the back (the poll) of their axes as heavy hammers, the better and more expensive tools had steel polls as well as steel edges. We can assume that the Sham Polled axes simply had thick polls built up with layers of wrought iron. The Coopers Froe was a tool, pounded with a wooden maul and controlled by a handle passing through its round eye, for splitting (cleaving or riving) logs into billets suitable for shaping into staves. The skill of coopers was such that the staves fitted together to form a watertight cask without any kind of packing or sealant. However, old casks became leaky and a cooper would repair them by inserting flags (reeds) between the staves. For this purpose he used the Flagging Iron as a sort of spanner to twist adjoining staves apart. He could do this by pressing on the flattened end with his hip leaving his hands free to insert the flags. Coppering Hammers were originally intended for the work of covering the hulls of wooden ships with copper plates (as can be seen on the *Cutty Sark* at London's Greenwich dock) but became useful for any work needing a light hammer with a broad, rounded face.

PLATE 84. The Seed Taps enabling seeds to be planted well below the surface were very obviously added as later engravings on this plate.

PLATES 85 & 86. Timber Scribes, also known as race knives, were designed to cut shallow circular and straight grooves into a wooden surface. They were thus used by coopers and other tradesmen to mark their work with letters or numbers. The Bag Hook (*see also* Plate 96) was for handling merchandise when almost everything if not packed in a cask was sewn into hard-to-grip sacks or bales.

PLATES 87 & 88. There had been a long tradition, supposedly introduced to Europe by returning crusaders in the 12th century, of ladies and even gentlemen, making delicate net to be used as insertions in clothing, particularly at the top of ladies' dress fronts where it was an obvious point of attraction. The small Cases of Teeth Instruments were for home dental care – picking, scraping and even filing one's own teeth – whereas the Tooth Drawing Instruments were intended for professionals, albeit in a profession which was still largely self-taught and part-time. The possession of one or two of these instruments, ferociously efficient with the leverage they could apply against a patient's jawbone, was enough to set a man up profitably as a puller of bad teeth in the local market. It was not until 1860 that the first examinations in dental surgery were held and only in 1879 were persons advertising themselves as dentists required by law to be qualified and registered – even then an exception was made for those already practising.

PLATE 91. Tuning Hammers and Tuning Forks are, of course, for tuning pianos. Fire Steels were for striking sparks off a flint into a tinder-box which could then be blown into a flame.

PLATE 96. For Bag Hooks *see* Note re Plate 86.

PLATE 100. For Fire Steels *see* Note re Plate 91.

PLATE 102. For Wine Coopers Fret *see* Note re Plate 80.

PLATES 103 & 104. The more elegant types of men's riding boots were close-fitting and had no straps, buttons or lacing to loosen them. They therefore required considerable effort to pull on using these Boot Hooks hooked into cloth loops sewn into the inside of the boot tops. The equally smart type of trousers known as overalls were worn outside the boots and were kept pulled taut by straps passing under the instep. To dress oneself in overalls, one had first to insert the boot tops into the trouser legs and then roll the trousers down over the boots before pulling both on together. As trouser straps went under the foot they wore fast and needed replacing, hence the Plyers and Punches for cutting new buttonholes. Gloves, like boots, were worn very tight and the buttons consequently needed strenuous manoeuvring with a Button Hook.

PLATES 105, 106, 107 & 108. Elegant fashion demanded that hair as well as collars and cuffs should be waved, curled, crimped or pinched with hot irons shaped for the purpose. The mechanism of the Italian Curling Tongs on Plate 108 is not very clear from the engraving but the principle was the same as that used in box smoothing irons, i.e. detachable core elements were heated separately and placed successively inside the Tongs or Iron thus maintaining a fresh heat and avoiding any risk of soot on the ironing surface.

PLATE 110. Paste Markers decorated the edges of pastry. The Lemon Racer produced thin and even slivers of rind.

PLATES 112 UP TO 124, where relevant. Sugar was sold in the large conical lumps (called sugar loaves) into which it had crystallised in the vat. Hence the various Cleavers, Hatchets and Nippers for breaking it down into usable quantities.

PLATE 113. Larding Pins served to thread thin strips of fat bacon under the surface of meat or game in order to provide extra fat when roasting.

PLATE 114. Steel Cats and Dogs were so designed that whichever way they were put down they would stand firmly. They were placed on the hearth in front of the fire so that toast, dishes, etc. could be left on them to keep warm.

PLATE 115. For Tinder Box *see* Note re Plate 91.

PLATES 127, 128 & 129. For Bed Keys *see* Note re Plate 35.

PLATE 130. The offer of several patterns of tin-opener (Knives for opening Preserved meat Cases) at this early date has already been commented on. The Door fastener is an interesting security device which has now been reintroduced in the form of a wedge which both jams the door and sounds an electric alarm when pressure is applied. This simple mechanical gadget, when once its wedge had been pushed under the door and its pointed bolt screwed firmly down, must have been very reassuring to travellers obliged to stop at the more dubious inns and hostelries.

PLATES 131 & 132. The Sportsmans Turnscrews, particularly the double ones which fitted into each other to produce a rounded dumb bell shape, were handy pocket tools when firearms needed frequent adjustment and cleaning. Several of them carried prickers, as well as screwdrivers, for poking out the touch hole or nipple on muzzle-loading guns. The Bullet Mould caption is interesting as a reflection of the origin of the modern system of describing shotguns as 12-, 16-, or 20-bore (gauge, in America). Solid lead spheres made, for example, 12 to the pound weight would exactly fit a 12-bore gun. So the higher the number the smaller the gun.

PLATE 133. The Worms, sold as part of Military Turnscrews, would have had to be fixed to the end of a ramrod in order to extract the wads from a muzzle-loading gun after a misfire.

PLATE 139. The inscription 'Collars to all above 12 Bitts' is mystifying. It appears also on Plates 141 and 142. A collar was a block of brass which fitted closely round a bit and guided it when boring. Collars were normally only used when boring the bars for window sashes with the parallel-sided-shank Sash Bitt (*see* No.840 on Plate 143, although this has been badly drawn and gives the appearance of having a reverse taper). Sash bits normally only came in two sizes and, in any case, most other bits with their tapering shanks would jam tight in a collar. Probably there was some misreading by the engraver here.

PLATE 140. Wire was made by pulling a bar of metal through a series of holes of diminishing size in a steel plate (*see* Plate 162 for illustration of such plates). These Wire Drawing Tongs are so designed that the greater the pull on the hooked handle the greater the jaws' grip on the wire.

PLATE 141. There has been some debate about the term Scotch as applied to this and other types of brace. Certainly it does not seem that the tool was in any way Scottish in either design or manufacture. The evidence is that the overwhelming majority of such braces originated in Birmingham or Sheffield. My own feeling is that the term probably related to the way in which the bits were held in place by a latch or catch fitting into a notch in the bit. The word scotch can mean an incision or a wedge, and to scotch a wheel means to block its movement to stop it. Perhaps these braces were described as Scotch because they had something like a scotch to prevent the bits from falling out?

PLATE 141. These four braces each exemplify a different method of holding interchangeable bits. Only the one with a spring catch is described as Scotch.

PLATE 143. It is unfortunate that this plate which could be valuable for reference is rather defective in both drawing and captions. The fact that the drawing of the Sash Bitt distorts its one essential feature has been referred to in the Note to Plate 139. As another example, only one of the illustrated Countersinks is a Rose Head. The other, on the left, is a Single Notched or Snailhorn Countersink.

PLATE 145. This is another set of tools for which it is difficult to envisage a practical use. One can imagine a Victorian lady doing a little genteel pruning or gathering fruit with the Fruit Knife, but would she really be wise to lash out with the interchangeable Billhook, a difficult and dangerous tool for an amateur at the best of times and one which in this form would inevitably start to unscrew from its handle after the first few slashes? Moreover, at 14 or 16 shillings for the set, the outlay would more than buy her a complete set of properly mounted tools as shown on Plate 146.

PLATE 159. Screw Plates are hardened steel with a series of holes each of which has a screw thread cut inside it. Screws can be made simply by twisting a piece of wire through the appropriate-sized hole. The holes are usually in pairs of the same size, one with a looser thread for the first cut, the other tight for finishing the screw.

PLATE 162. Bow drills are known from tomb paintings in ancient Egypt and the method is still used in some applications where high speed of rotation and accuracy are required in drilling small holes. Two of the three components of a complete bow drill are illustrated: the bow which will carry a cord under a slight and easily adjustable tension and the stock incorporating the chuck to hold a bit at the right-hand end with the spool around which the bow cord will pass. The user is left to provide the third component: a handle, bib or breastplate through which to apply pressure to the pointed end of the stock.

For Draw Plates *see* Note re Plate 140.

FURTHER READING

Crom, Theodore R., *Trade Catalogues 1542 to 1842*, Melrose, Florida 1989.

Dascher, Reininghaus & Kugler (editors), *Mein Feld ist Die Welt*,
   Musterbücher und Kataloge 1784–1914, Dortmund 1984.

Goodison, Nicholas, 'The Victoria & Albert Museum's Collection of Metal-Work
   Pattern Books', *Journal of The Furniture History Society*, Vol XI, 1975.

Roberts, Kenneth D., *Tools for the Trades and Crafts*, Fitzwilliam, New Hampshire
   1976. This work is largely devoted to the c.1845 Richard Timmins catalogue. It
   contains much comparative material and is the result of a great deal of research
   into tool catalogues of the period.

Salaman, R.A., *Dictionary of Woodworking Tools c.1700-1970*, revised edition,
   London 1989.

Salaman, R.A., *Dictionary of Leather-Working Tools c.1700-1950*, London 1986.

Smith, Joseph, *Explanation or Key to the Various Manufactories of Sheffield*,
   Sheffield 1816. Reprinted by Early American Industries Association in 1975

Wyke, John, *A Catalogue of Tools for Watch and Clock Makers*, Liverpool c.1760.
   Reprinted by Henry Francis du Pont Winterthur Museum, Virginia 1978.

Young, W.A. and Strange, E.F., *Old English Pattern Books of the Metal Trades*,
   Victoria & Albert Museum, London 1913.

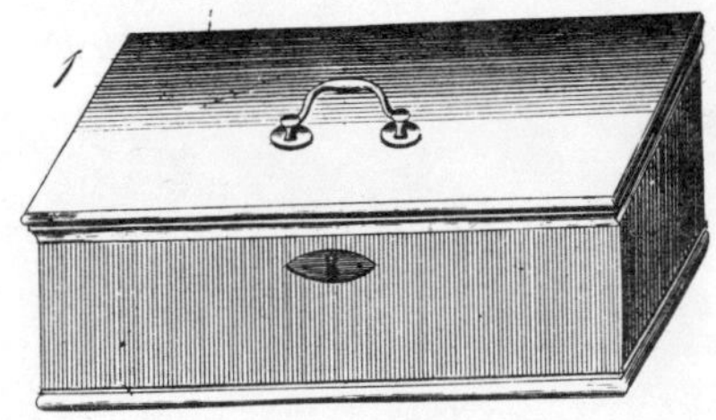

No. 1.—Contains

HAMMER, pincers, saw, hatchet, two-foot rule, mallet, turnscrew, file, rasp, brad punch, gouge, two firmers, two brad awls, and three gimlets . . . .

No. 2.—Contains

Hammer, pincers, saw, hatchet, two-foot rule, mallet, turnscrew, file, rasp, brad punch, keyhole saw, compasses, pliers, small plane, gouge, two firmers, two brad awls, three gimlets, and a wood partition, containing screws, nails, &c. . . . .

No. 3.—Contains

Hammer, pincers, saw, hatchet, two-foot rule, mallet, plane, hand vice, file, rasp, brad punch, keyhole saw, compasses, pliers, gouge, three firmers, two turnscrews, two brad awls, three gimlets, and a wood partition, containing screws, nails, &c. . . . . . .

No. 4.—Contains

Hammer, pincers, best saw, hatchet, two-foot rule, mallet, plane, hand vice, rasp, brad punch, keyhole saw, compasses, pliers, claw wrench, gouge, three firmers, two turnscrews, two brad awls, two files, four gimlets, and wood partitions, containing nails, screws, brass work, &c.

No. 5.—Contains

Hammer, pincers, two-foot rule, rasp, keyhole saw, compasses, brad punch, pliers, hand vice, bright chisel, claw wrench, gouge, three firmers, two turnscrews, two files, two brad awls, four gimlets, and wood partitions, containing an assortment of nails, screws, brass work, &c. In a drawer are contained a mallet, saw, oil stone in wood case, jack plane, smoothing plane, and hatchet . . .

	OAK.			MAHOGANY.		
	£.	s.	d.	£.	s.	d.
No. 1	1	0	0	1	4	6
No. 2	1	6	0	1	11	6
No. 3	1	11	6	2	0	0
No. 4	2	0	0	2	10	0
No. 5	2	12	6	3	3	0

No. 6.—Contains

Hammer, pincers, cutting nippers, two-foot rule, rasp, keyhole saw, compasses, brad punch, pliers, hand vice, saw set, claw wrench, chisel, three firmers, two gouges, two turnscrews, three files, two brad awls, four gimlets, and wood partitions, containing an assortment of nails, screws, brass work, &c. In a drawer are contained a mallet, saw, oil stone in wood case, jack plane, smoothing plane, and hatchet . . . .

No. 7.—Contains

Hammer, pincers, cutting nippers, two-foot rule, compasses, brad punch, saw set, chisel, claw wrench, striking knife, two pair of pliers, three brad awls, six gimlets, three turnscrews, and wood partitions, containing nails, screws, brass work, &c. In a drawer are contained a mallet, hand saw, oil stone in wood case, jack plane, smoothing plane, hatchet, and dove-tail saw. In another drawer are four firmers, two gouges, hand vice, bick iron, keyhole saw, bevil, square, line and roller, rasp, four files, and two mortice chisels . . . .

No. 8.—Contains

Hammer, pincers, cutting nippers, two-foot rule, rasp, compasses, brad punch, saw set, chisel, claw wrench, striking knife, two pair of pliers, four brad awls, six gimlets, three turnscrews, bick iron, and sundry partitions, containing nails, screws, brass work, &c. In a drawer are contained a mallet, hand saw, oil stone in wood case, jack plane, smoothing plane, hatchet, and dove-tail saw. In another drawer are three mortice chisels, two gouges, four firmers, five files, hand vice, keyhole saw, line and roller, bevil, square, brace, with eight bits, and a glue pot . . . .

	OAK.			MAHOGANY.		
	£.	s.	d.	£.	s.	d.
No. 6	3	5	6	4	0	0
No. 7	4	12	0	5	8	0
No. 8	5	18	6	6	15	0

No. 9.—Contains

In the Chest and in two drawers—The same Tools as in No. 8, with the addition of a set of Garden Tools, as follows :—A rake, saw, bill-hook, a paddle, a hoe, and a fruit-knife with hook ; these six articles are made to screw into a ferrule to fix upon a staff. Also, a pruning-knife, a pair of scissors, line and reel, a pair of shears, a fork, and some list

☞ Any of the other Chests may be had with a drawer, containing a set of Garden Tools, as in No. 9, for £2 more . . .

	OAK.			MAHOGANY.		
	£.	s.	d.	£.	s.	d.
	7	10	0	8	18	0

GARDEN CHESTS.

No. 10.—Contains

A set of Garden Tools as under :—A rake, a saw, a bill-hook, a paddle, a hoe, and a fruit-knife with hook ; these six articles are made to screw into a ferrule, to fix upon a staff. Also, a hammer, a fork, a pair of scissors, and a partition with some nails and list . .

1	10	0	1	15	0

No. 11.—Contains

A set of Garden Tools as under :—A rake, a saw, a bill-hook, a paddle, a hoe, and a fruit-knife with hook ; these articles are made to screw into a ferrule, to fix upon a staff. Also, a hammer, a fork, a pruning-knife, a pair of scissors, a pair of shears, a line and reel, a small hand-saw, and a hatchet, three gimlets, and a partition with some nails and list.

2	4	0	2	16	0

DEAL CHESTS OF TOOLS,
FOR CARPENTERS, JOINERS, &c.

From £5. 5s., to £30 and upwards.

GENTLEMEN'S
MAHOGANY GUN CHESTS OF TOOLS,
FOR CLEANING GUNS.

No. 12	13	14	15	16	17	18
25s.	31s. 6d.	35s.	42s.	48s.	52s. 6d.	57s.

YOUTH'S OAK TOOL CHESTS.

No. 1383	1384	1385	1386	1387	1388
8s.	10s.	12s.	14s.	16s.	18s.

SHOE MAKERS'
SETS OF TOOLS.

WOMAN'S MANS, No. 1.

One cramping-hammer, pair of pincers, pair of bright nippers, one hollowing stick, one long sole burnisher, one heel iron, one bone ran key, one stamp with handle, one round star stamp, one licking-stick, one rasp and file, one dozen of awl blades sorted, with six handles, three hollow punches sorted, one knife, one sand stone, one size stick . . .

MAN'S MAN, No. 2.

One pane-hammer, pair of pincers, pair of bright nippers, one shoe jigger with handle, one seat iron, one fore-part iron, one ran or back file, all with handles, one rasp and file, one dozen of awl blades with six handles sorted, three hollow punches sorted, one stamp with handle, one round star stamp, one knife, one sand stone, one size stick . .

BOOT MAN'S, No. 3.

One large pane-hammer, one cramping hammer, pair of strong pincers, pair of bright nippers, one seam setter, one jigger, one ran or back file, one seat iron, one fore-part iron, all with handles, one rasp and file, one stamp with handle, one round star stamp, one knife, one sand stone, one dozen of awl blades with handles, three hollow punches sorted, one size stick . . . .

A COMPLETE CHEST OF FOREMAN'S TOOLS, No. 4.

Pair of large clicking pincers, one half-circle knife, one best box size stick, pair of large pincers, pair of hollow punch piercing pliers, pair of bright nippers, one large pane-hammer, one cramping hammer, one steel jigger, one rasp and file, one seat iron, one fore-part iron, one ran or back file, all with handles, one knife, one sand stone, one dozen of awl blades sorted, with handles, two small hollow punches, one stamp with handle, one round star stamp . . . .

	WITHOUT CHEST.			IN DEAL CHEST.			IN OAK CHEST.		
	£.	s.	d.	£.	s.	d.	£.	s.	d.
No. 1	0	14	6	0	16	6	0	18	6
No. 2	0	16	0	0	18	0	1	0	0
No. 3	0	18	0	1	0	0	1	2	0
No. 4	1	4	0	1	7	0	1	9	0

Improved or London Pattern Gentlemen's Tool Chests.

Engraved ⅙ the size.

50/.
1621

70/.
1622

150/.
1625

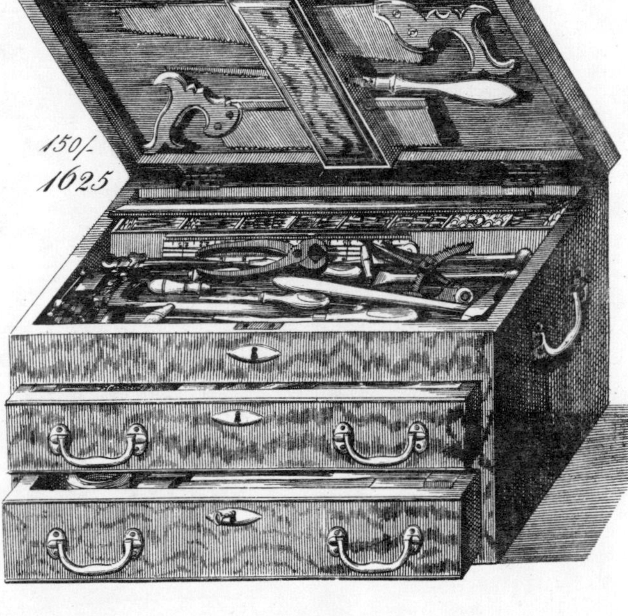

Nº1621. 50/. CONTAINS.
In the Chest a Hammer, Hatchet. Table vice. Pincers. Plyers. Rule. 6 Gimblets, 2 Brad awls. 2 Turnscrews. 2 Files. Rasp. Gouge. 3 Firmers. Brad punch, Mallet, Plane. Compasses, Claw wrench. Nails, Screws. Brass work &c. Under the Lid a Hand saw. Dove tail saw & Key hole saw.

Nº1622. 70/. CONTAINS.
In the chest. Hammer, Table vice. Pincers. Plyers. Rule. 6 Gimblets, 2 Brad awls, 2 Turnscrews. 2 Files. Rasp. Gouge. 3 Firmers. Brad punch, Compasses. Claw wrench. Nails. Screws, Brass work &c. Under the Lid a Hand saw Dove tail saw, & key hole saw. In a Drawer. a Mallet. Jack plane. Smoothing plane, Oil Stone. & Hatchet.

Nº 1623. 85/. CONTAINS.
In the Chest — Claw Hammer, Riveting Hammer, Table vice Hand-vice, Pincers, Plyers, Rule, 6 Gimblets. 2 Brad-awls, 2 Turnscrews, 2 Files, Rasp. 2 Gouges. 3 Firmers. Brad-punch, Compasses, Claw-wrench, Chisel, Sawset, Nails Screws Brass-work &c. Under the Lid a Hand-saw Dovetail saw, & Key-hole-saw. In a Drawer. a Mallet, Jack-plane, Smoothing Plane, Oil stone & Hatchet,

Nº 1624. 115/. CONTAINS.
In the Chest. Claw Hammer, Riveting hammer, Table vice, Hand-vice, Pincers, Cutting Nippers. Plyers, Rule, 6 Gimblets, 3 Brad-awls, 2 Turnscrews, Rasp, 3 Files, 2 Gouges, 4 Firmers. Brad-punch, Compasses, Claw-wrench, Chisel, Sawset, Nails. Screws. Brass work &c. In a Drawer, a Mallet. Jack-plane. Smoothing plane, Oil-stone. Hatchet. & Glue Pot. In another Drawer, Brace & 12 Bitts. Spokeshave. Line & roller, Plated Square & Plated Bevil, Under the Lid. a Hand saw. Dove tail saw. & Key hole saw.

Nº1625. 150/. CONTAINS.
In the Chest. Claw hammer, Riveting hammer, Table vice. Table Bick iron. Hand vice. Pincers. Cutting Nippers. round Plyers. flat Plyers. Rack Compasses. Rule. 6 Gimblets, 3 Brad-awls. 3 Turnscrews. Brad-punch, Compasses. Chisel. Claw-wrench, Sawset. Nails. Screws. Brass work &c. In a Drawer 4 Files. Rasp. 6 Firmers. 2 Gouges. Brace & 18 Bitts. Spokeshave. Line & Roller. Plated Square Plated Bevil, Marking guage. & 2 Mortice Chisels, In another Drawer a Mallet. Jack plane. Smoothing plane. Oil-stone. Hatchet. Glue Pot & brush. Under the Lid a Hand Saw. Dovetail saw & Key hole saw.

Nº1626. 178/. Contains the same as 1625, with addition of a Drawer, containing a set of Garden Tools, as under, viz. Rake. Saw. Bill hook. Paddle. Fruit Knife. & Hoe. (all made to screw on a staff) also a Hammer. Pruning Knife, pair of Scissors. Line & Reel. pair of Shears. Fork, Nails, & List.

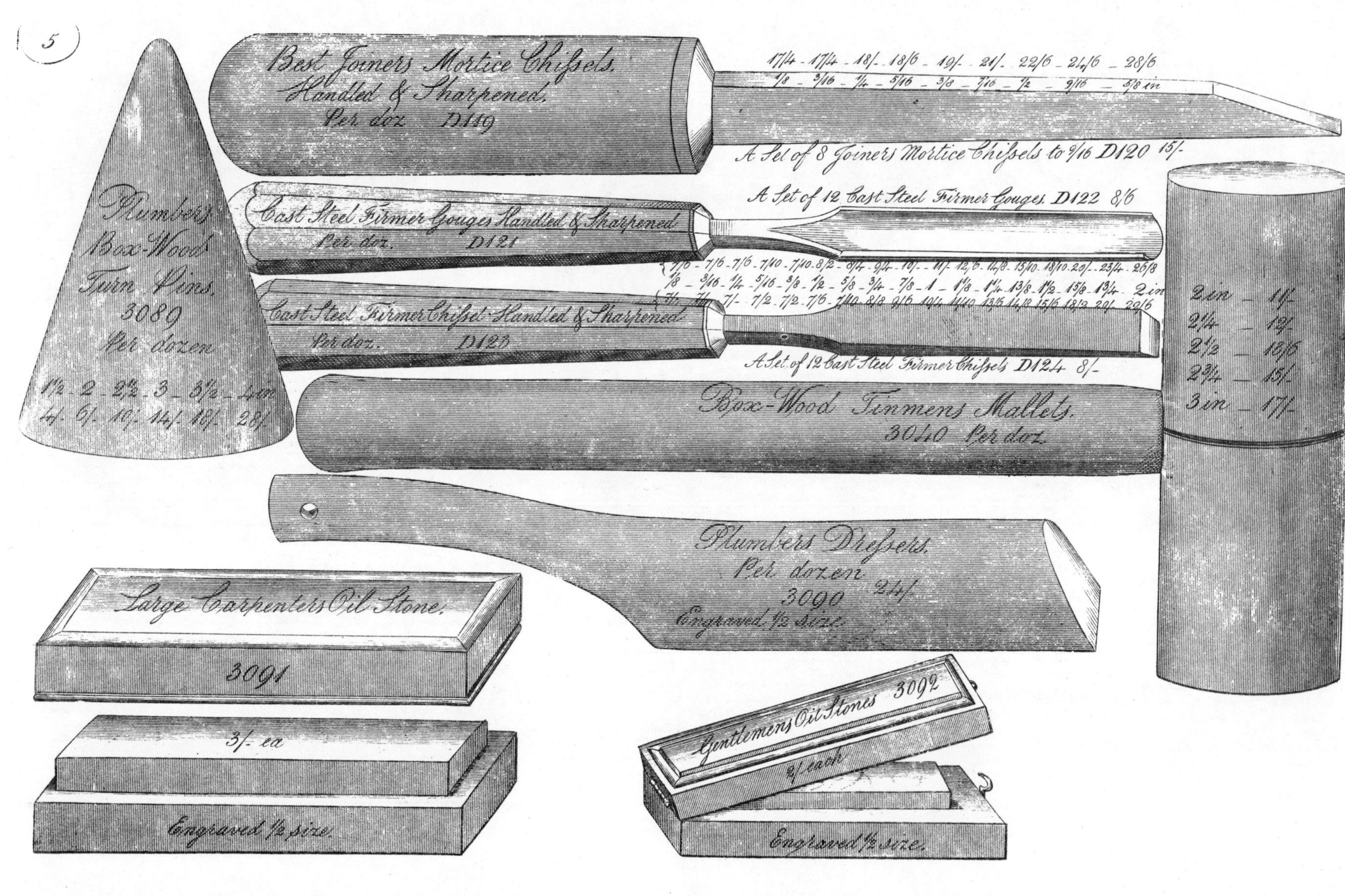

5
Best Joiners Mortice Chissels. Handled & Sharpened. Per doz D119
17/4 - 17/4 - 18/- - 18/6 - 19/- - 21/- - 22/6 - 24/6 - 28/6
1/8 - 3/16 - 1/4 - 5/16 - 3/8 - 7/16 - 1/2 - 9/16 - 5/8 in
A Set of 8 Joiners Mortice Chissels to 9/16 D120 15/-
A Set of 12 Cast Steel Firmer Gouges. D122 8/6
Cast Steel Firmer Gouges Handled & Sharpened Per doz. D121
7/6 - 7/6 - 7/6 - 7/10 - 7/10 - 8/2 - 8/4 - 9/4 - 10/- - 11/- - 12/6 - 14/8 - 15/10 - 18/10 - 20/- - 23/4 - 26/8
1/8 - 3/16 - 1/4 - 5/16 - 3/8 - 1/2 - 5/8 - 3/4 - 7/8 - 1 - 1 1/8 - 1 1/4 - 1 3/8 - 1 1/2 - 1 5/8 - 1 3/4 - 2 in
7/- - 7/- - 7/- - 7/2 - 7/2 - 7/6 - 7/10 - 8/8 - 9/6 - 10/4 - 11/10 - 13/6 - 14/8 - 15/6 - 18/2 - 20/- - 22/6
Cast Steel Firmer Chissel Handled & Sharpened Per doz. D123
A Set of 12 Cast Steel Firmer Chissels D124 8/-
Plumbers Box-Wood Turn Pins. 3089 Per dozen
1 1/2 - 2 - 2 1/2 - 3 - 3 1/2 - 4 in
4/- 6/- 10/- 14/- 18/- 28/-
Box-Wood Tinmens Mallets. 3010 Per doz
2 in — 11/-
2 1/4 — 13/-
2 1/2 — 15/6
2 3/4 — 15/-
3 in — 17/-
Plumbers Dressers. Per dozen 3090 24/- Engraved 1/2 size.
Large Carpenters Oil Stone. 3091 3/- ea Engraved 1/2 size.
Gentlemens Oil Stones 3092 2/ each Engraved 1/2 size.

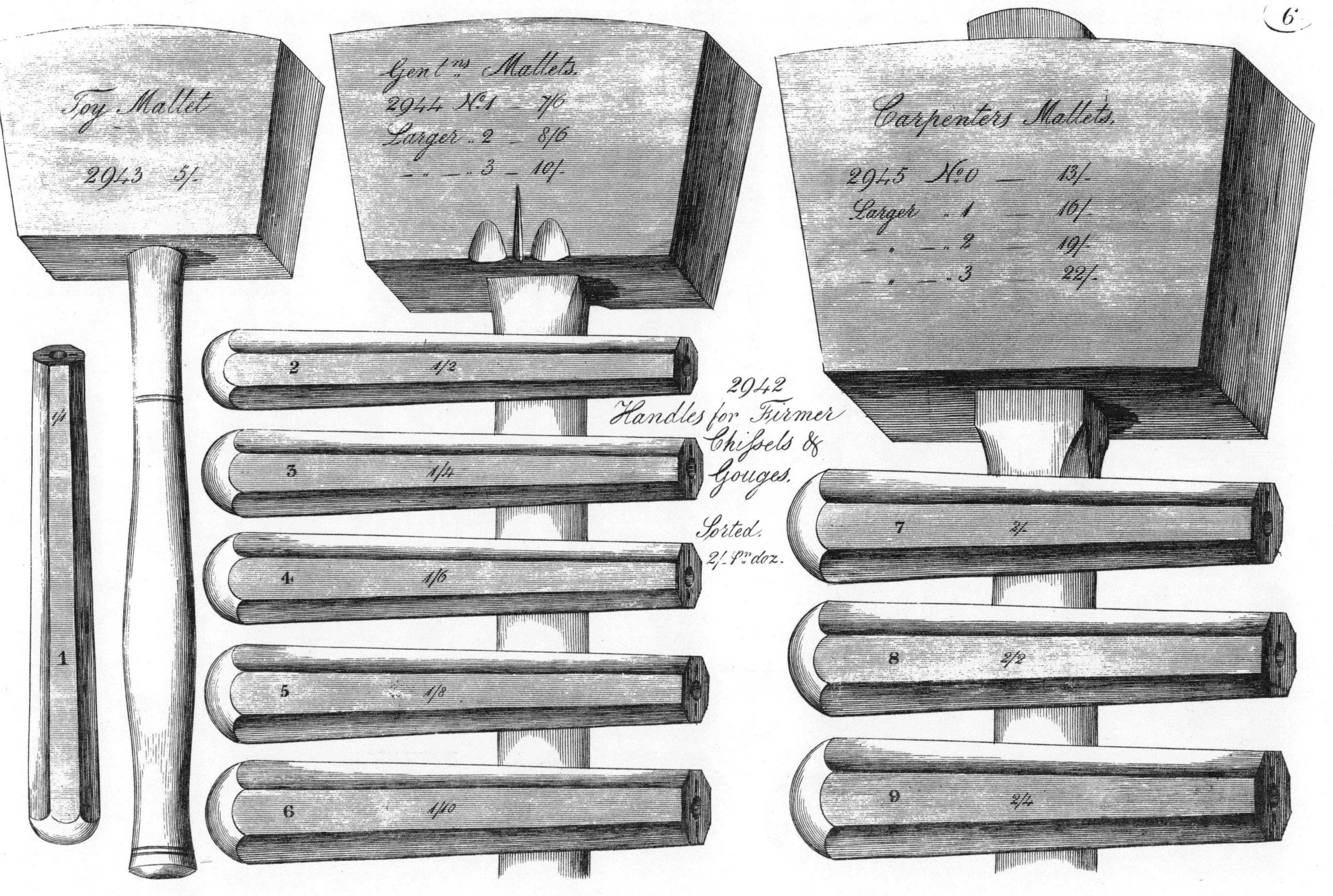

Toy Mallet
2943   5/
Gent.ns Mallets.
2944 N.o 1 _ 7/6
Larger _ 2 _ 8/6
_ _ _ 3 _ 10/
Carpenters Mallets.
2945 N.o 0 _ 13/
Larger _ 1 _ 16/
" _ _ 2 _ 19/
" _ _ 3 _ 22/
2942
Handles for Firmer
Chisels &
Gouges.
Sorted.
2/. 5.n doz.
1/4
1
2   1/2
3   1/4
4   1/6
5   1/8
6   1/10
7   2/
8   2/2
9   2/4

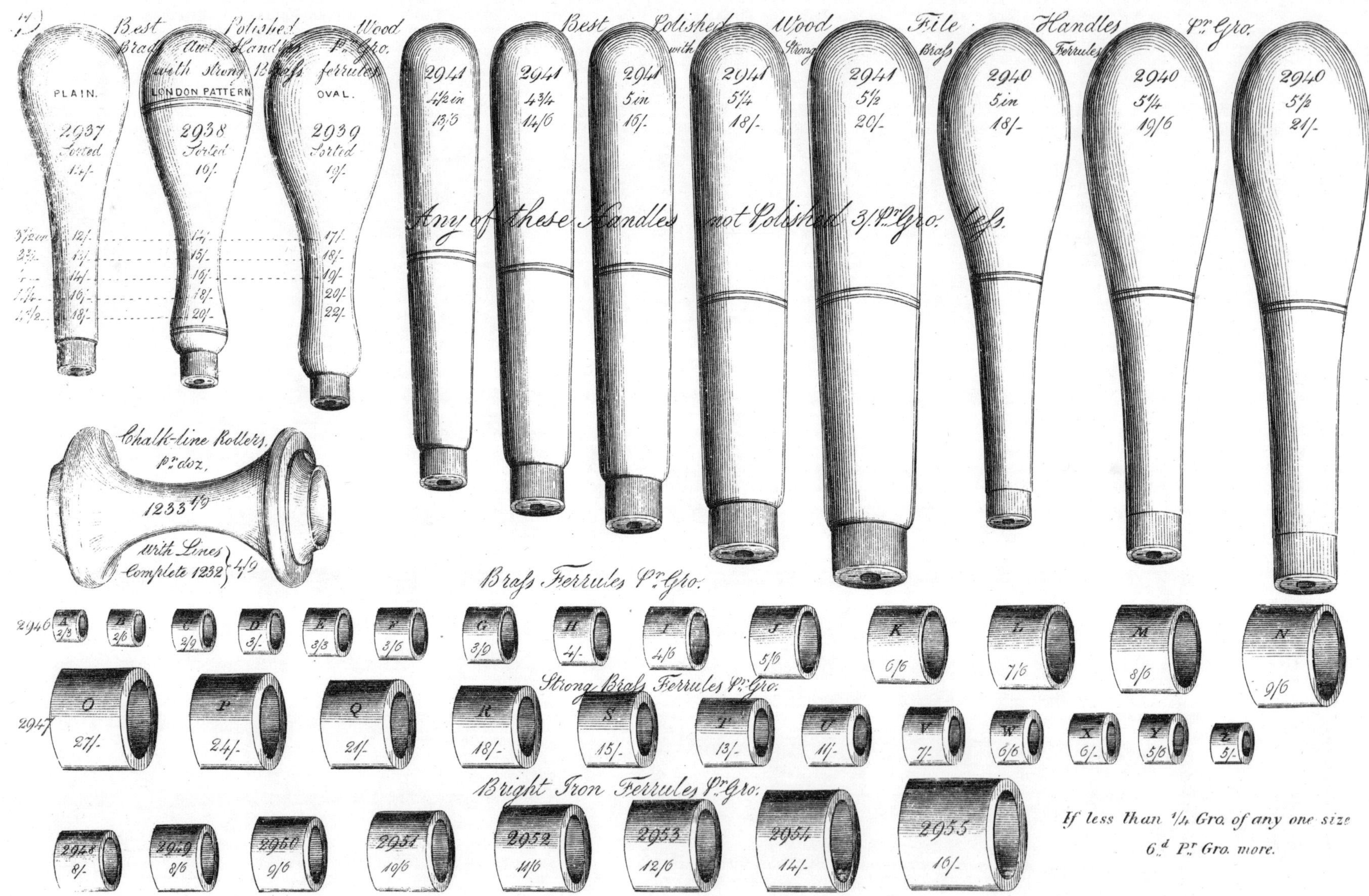
Best Polished Brass Awl Handles with strong Brass ferrules. Pr. Gro.
PLAIN.
LONDON PATTERN
OVAL.
2937 Sorted 14/-
2938 Sorted 19/-
2939 Sorted 19/-
Best Polished Wood File Handles with strong Brass Ferrules. Pr. Gro.
2941 4½ in 13/3
2941 4¾ 14/6
2941 5 in 16/-
2941 5¼ 18/-
2941 5½ 20/-
2940 5 in 18/-
2940 5¼ 19/6
2940 5½ 21/-
Any of these Handles not Polished 3/ Pr. Gro. less.
Chalk-line Rollers. Pr. doz.
1233 4/9
With Lines Complete 1232 4/9
Brass Ferrules Pr. Gro.
2946 A 2/3 B 2/6 C 2/9 D 3/- E 3/3 F 3/6 G 3/9 H 4/- I 4/6 J 5/6 K 6/6 L 7/6 M 8/6 N 9/6
Strong Brass Ferrules Pr. Gro.
2947 O 27/- P 24/- Q 21/- R 18/- S 15/- T 13/- U 11/- V 7/- W 6/6 X 6/- Y 5/6 Z 5/-
Bright Iron Ferrules Pr. Gro.
2948 8/- 2949 8/6 2950 9/6 2951 10/6 2952 11/6 2953 12/6 2954 14/- 2955 16/-
If less than ⅓ Gro. of any one size 6d. Pr. Gro. more.

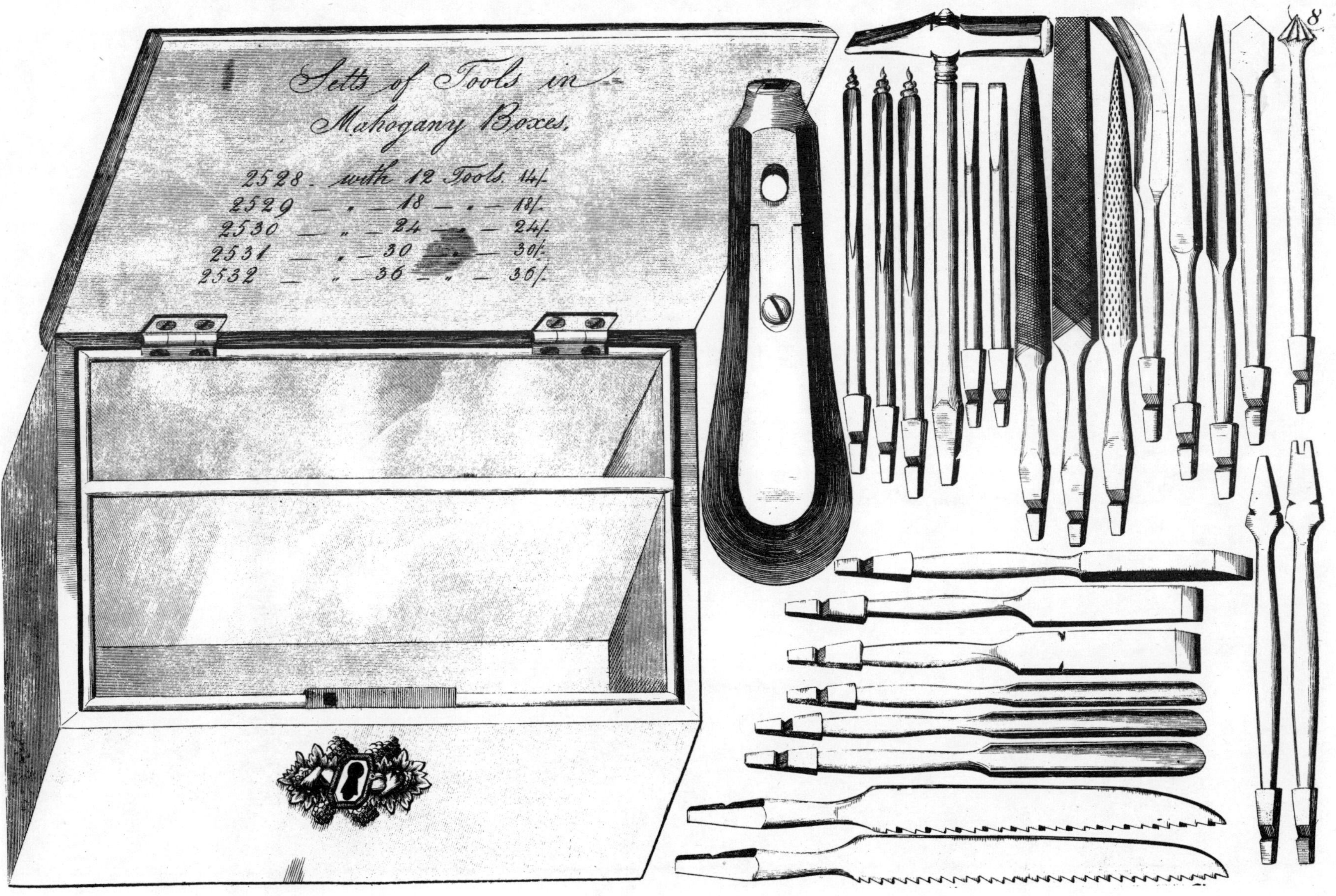

Setts of Tools in
Mahogany Boxes.
2528. with 12 Tools. 14/
2529 — „ — 18 — „ — 18/
2530 — „ — 24 — „ — 24/
2531 — „ — 30 — „ — 30/
2532 — „ — 36 — „ — 36/

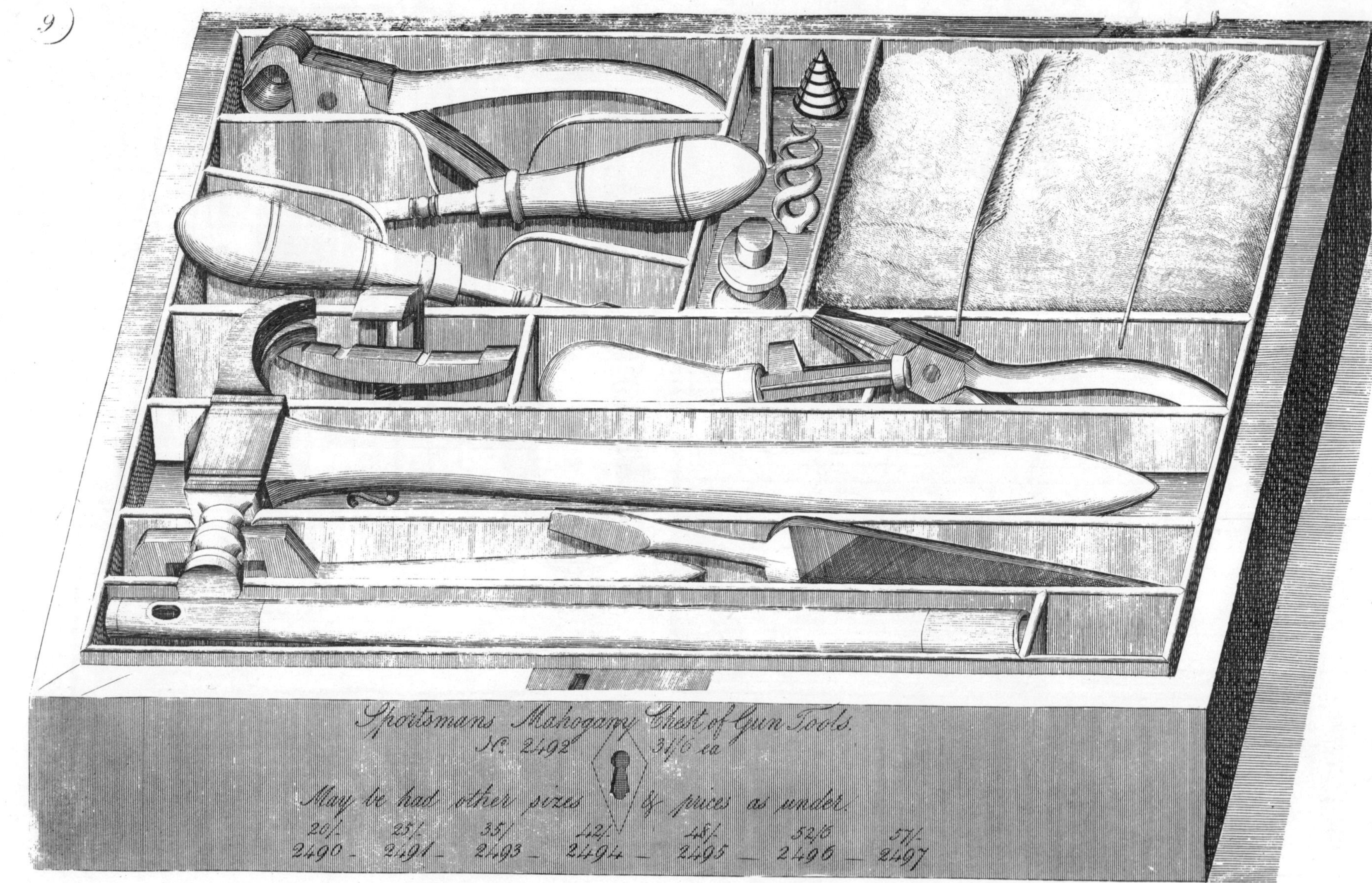

Sportsmans Mahogany Chest of Gun Tools.
Nº 2492   31/6 ea
May be had other sizes & prices as under.
20/.   25/.   35/.   42/.   48/.   52/6   57/.
2490 _ 2491 _ 2493 _ 2494 _ 2495 _ 2496 _ 2497

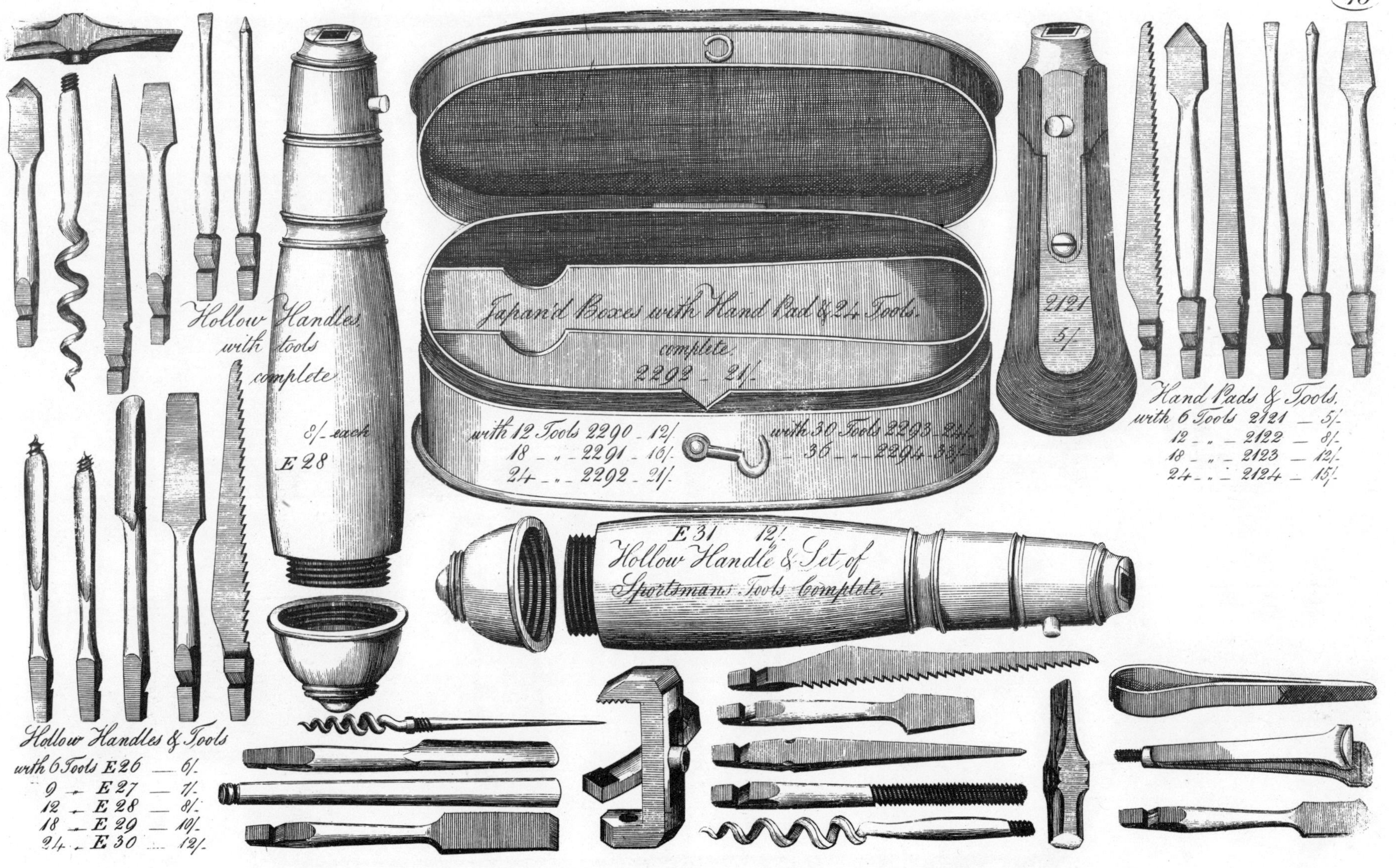

10
Hollow Handles
with tools
complete
8/- each
E 28
Japan'd Boxes with Hand Pad & 24 Tools.
complete
2292 - 21/-
with 12 Tools 2290 - 12/
18 - " 2291 - 16/
24 - " 2292 - 21/
with 30 Tools 2293 - 24/
- 36 - " 2294 - 33/
2121
5/
Hand Pads & Tools.
with 6 Tools 2121 - 5/
12 - " 2122 - 8/
18 - " 2123 - 12/
24 - " 2124 - 15/
E 31 12/
Hollow Handle & Set of
Sportsmans Tools Complete.
Hollow Handles & Tools
with 6 Tools E 26 - 6/
9 - E 27 - 7/
12 - E 28 - 8/
18 - E 29 - 10/
24 - E 30 - 12/

Best Black Leather Roller
with Pad & 12 Tools.
Nº 2434 18/.
With 18 Tools — 2435 — 22/.
" — 24 — " — 2436 — 28/.
" — 30 — " — 2437 — 35/.
" — 36 — " — 2438 — 46/.
Red Morrocco Rollers.
2/- extra. —

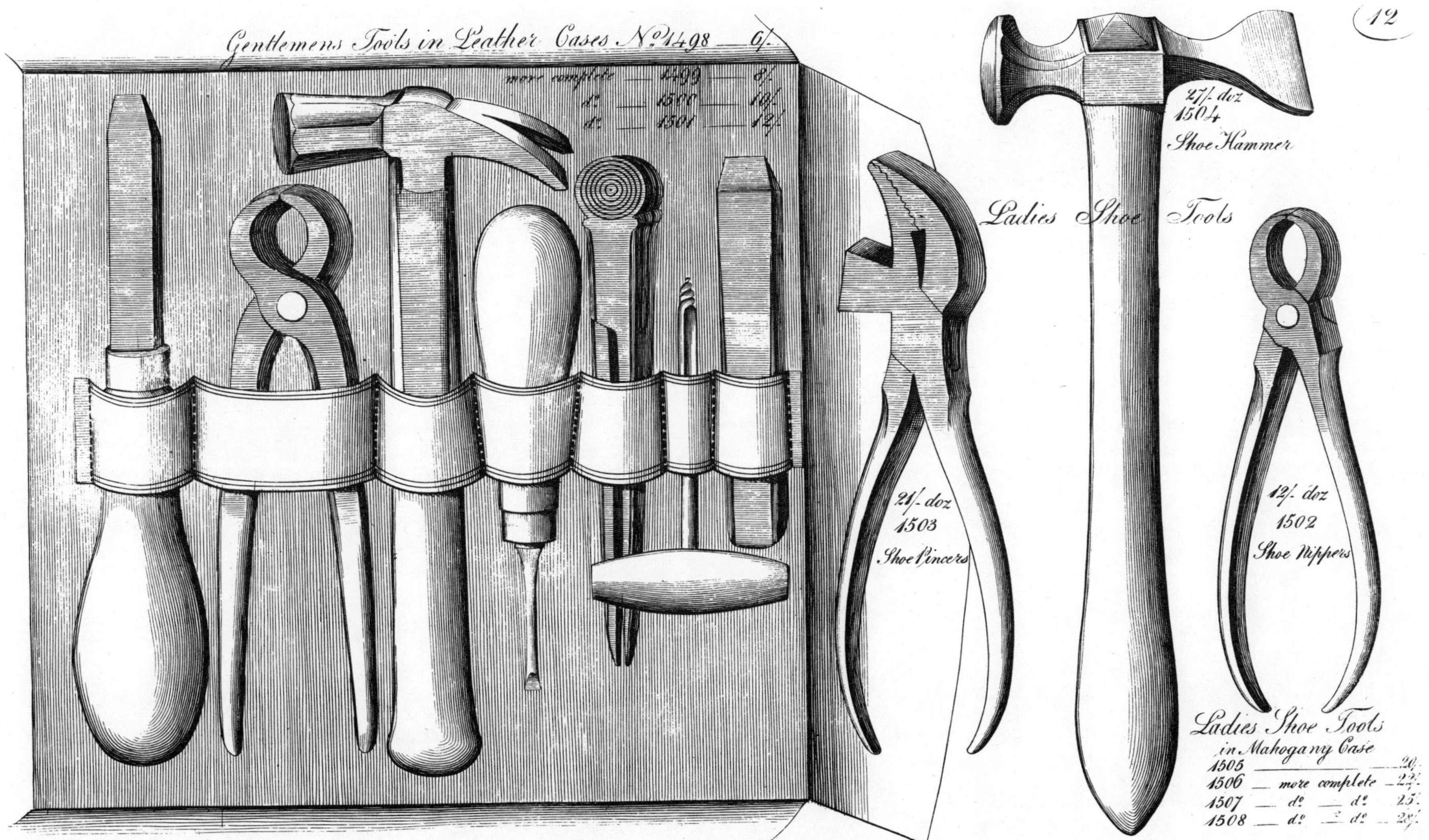
Gentlemens Tools in Leather Cases No 1498 — 6/.
more complete — 1499 — 8/.
do — 1500 — 10/
do — 1501 — 12/
27/. doz
1504
Shoe Hammer
Ladies Shoe Tools
21/. doz
1503
Shoe Pincers
12/. doz
1502
Shoe Nippers
Ladies Shoe Tools
in Mahogany Case
1505 — 20/
1506 — more complete — 22/
1507 — do — do — 25/
1508 — do — do — 28/
12

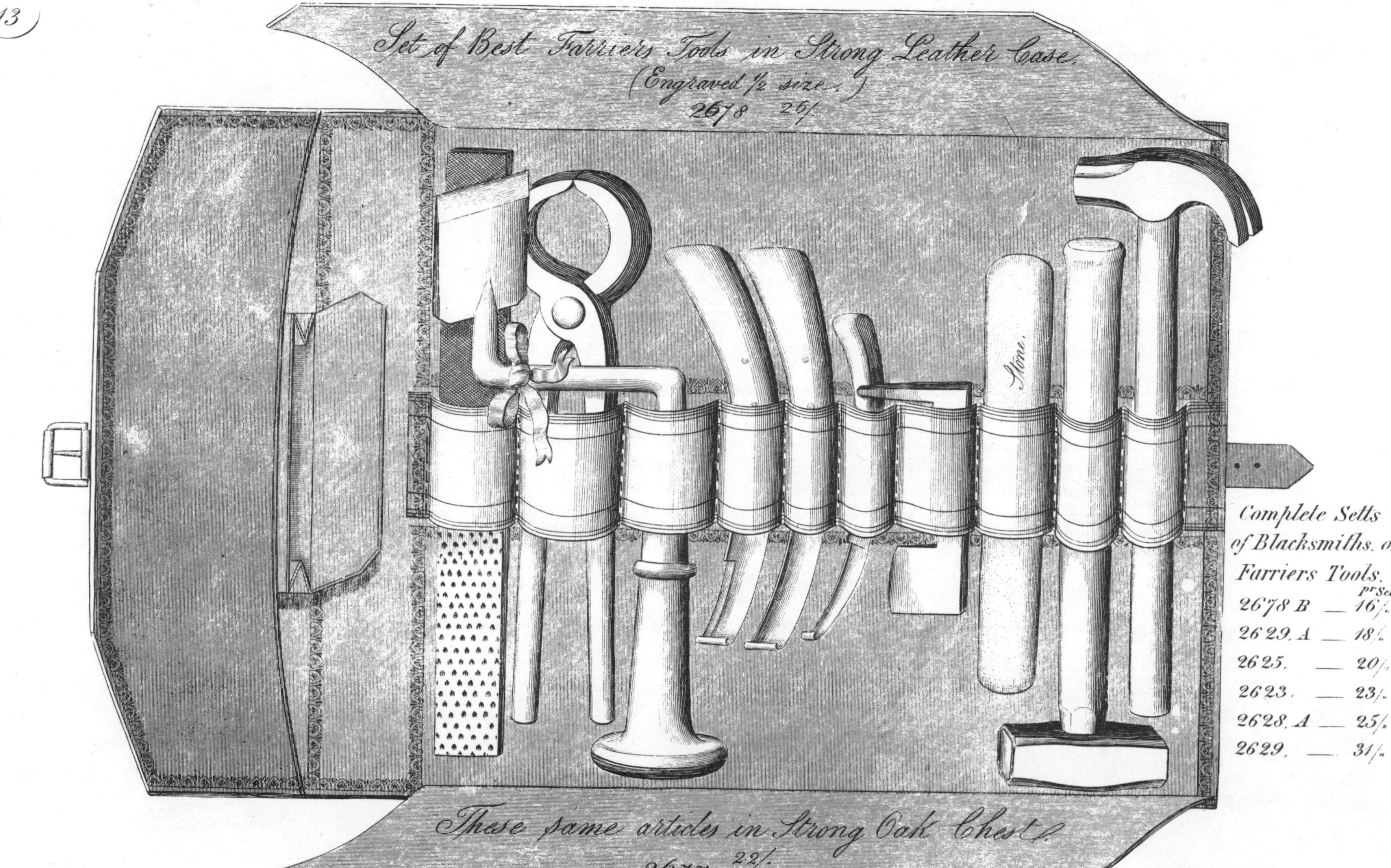

Set of Best Farriers Tools in Strong Leather Case.
(Engraved ½ size.)
2678   26/
Stone.
Complete Setts
of Blacksmiths. or
Farriers Tools.
prSett
2678 B — 16/.
2629. A — 18/.
2625. — 20/.
2623. — 23/.
2628. A — 25/.
2629. — 31/.
These same articles in Strong Oak Chest.
2677.   22/.

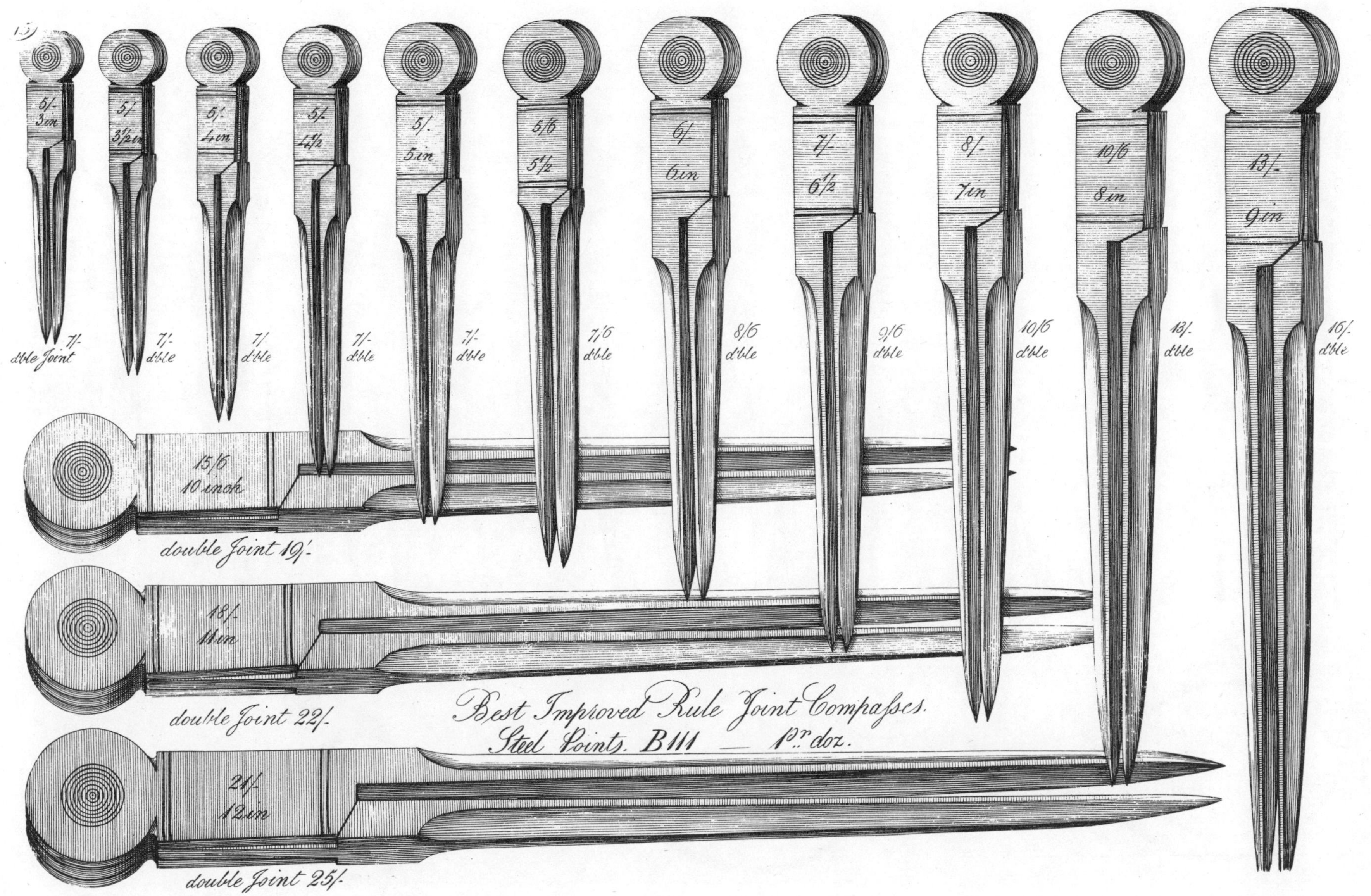

Best Improved Rule Joint Compasses.
Steel Points. B111 — Pr. doz.
double Joint 19/-
double Joint 22/-
double Joint 25/-
15/6 10 inch
18/- thin
21/- 12in
6/- 3in
5/- 3½in
5/- 4in
5/- 4½
5/- 5in
5/6 5½
6/- 6in
7/- 6½
8/- 7in
10/6 8in
13/- 9in
7/- dble Joint
7/- dble
7/- dble
7/- dble
7/- dble
7/6 dble
8/6 dble
9/6 dble
10/6 dble
13/- dble
16/- dble

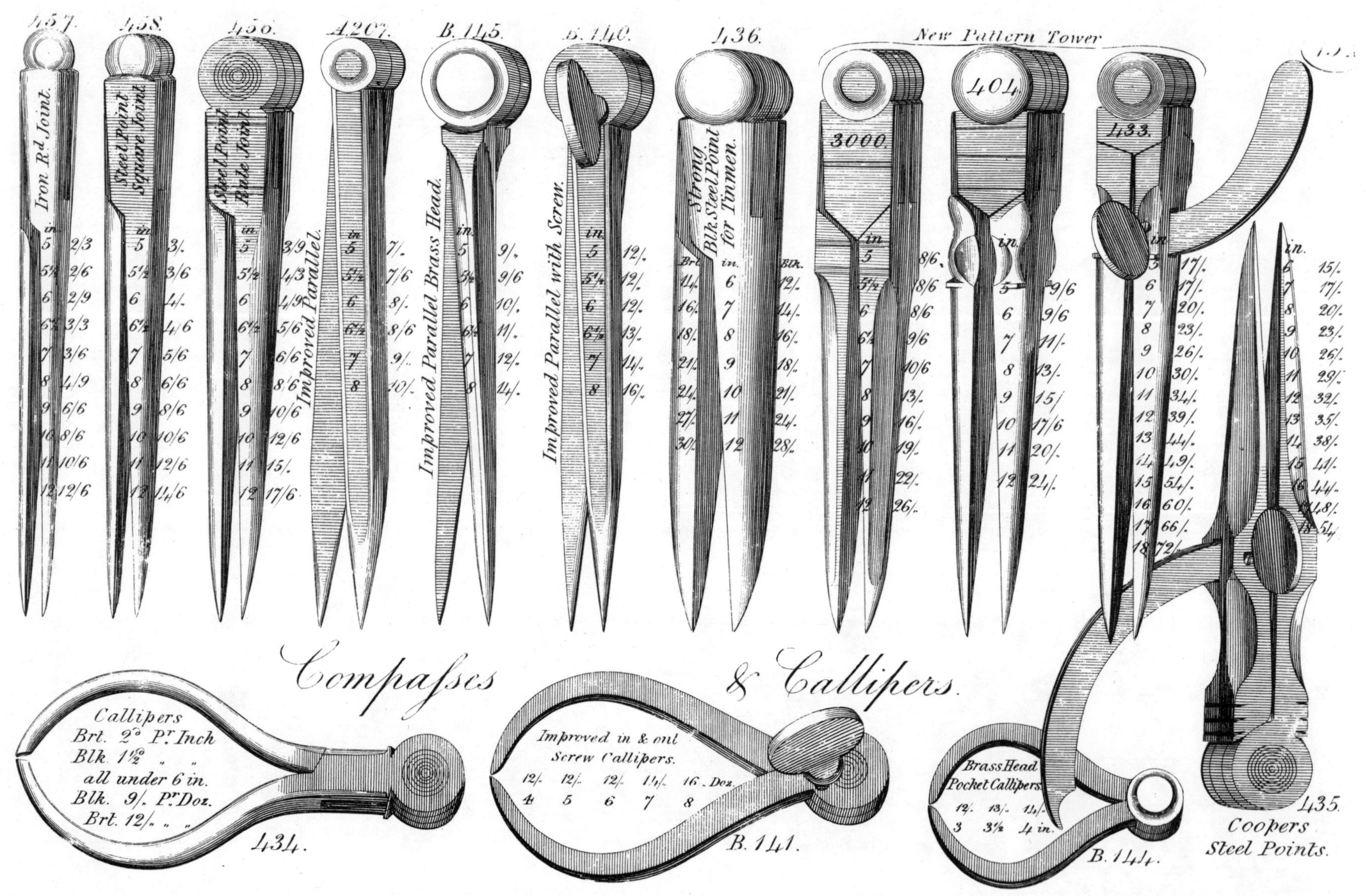

New Pattern Tower
453.
Compasses & Callipers.

457. Iron Rd. Joint.
in. 5 — 2/3; 5½ — 2/6; 6 — 2/9; 6½ — 3/3; 7 — 3/6; 8 — 4/9; 9 — 6/6; 10 — 8/6; 11 — 10/6; 12 — 12/6

458. Steel Point Square Joint.
in. 5 — 3/.; 5½ — 3/6; 6 — 4/.; 6½ — 4/6; 7 — 5/6; 8 — 6/6; 9 — 8/6; 10 — 10/6; 11 — 12/6; 12 — 14/6

456. Steel Point Bale Joint.
in. 5 — 3/9; 5½ — 4/3; 6 — 4/9; 6½ — 5/6; 7 — 6/6; 8 — 8/6; 9 — 10/6; 10 — 12/6; 11 — 15/.; 12 — 17/6

Improved Parallel. 4207.
in. 5 — 7/.; 5½ — 7/6; 6 — 8/.; 6½ — 8/6; 7 — 9/.; 8 — 10/.

Improved Parallel Brass Head. B.145.
in. 5 — 9/.; 5½ — 9/6; 6 — 10/.; 6½ — 11/.; 7 — 12/.; 8 — 14/.

B.140. Improved Parallel with Screw.
in. 5 — 12/.; 5½ — 12/.; 6 — 12/.; 6½ — 13/.; 7 — 14/.; 8 — 16/.

436. Strong Blk. Steel Point for Tinmen.
Brt. / in. / Blk.
14/. — 6 — 12/.; 16/. — 7 — 14/.; 18/. — 8 — 16/.; 21/. — 9 — 18/.; 24/. — 10 — 21/.; 27/. — 11 — 24/.; 30/. — 12 — 28/.

3000.
in. 5 — 8/6; 5½ — 8/6; 6 — 8/6; 6½ — 9/6; 7 — 10/6; 8 — 13/.; 9 — 15/.; 10 — 17/6; 11 — 20/.; 12 — 24/.

404.
in. 5 — 9/6; 6 — 9/6; 7 — 11/.; 8 — 13/.; 9 — 15/.; 10 — 17/6; 11 — 20/.; 12 — 24/.

433.
in. 5 — 17/.; 6 — 17/.; 7 — 20/.; 8 — 23/.; 9 — 26/.; 10 — 30/.; 11 — 34/.; 12 — 39/.; 13 — 44/.; 14 — 49/.; 15 — 54/.; 16 — 60/.; 17 — 66/.; 18 — 72/.

in. 5 — 15/.; 6 — 17/.; 7 — 20/.; 8 — 23/.; 9 — 26/.; 10 — 29/.; 11 — 32/.; 12 — 35/.; 13 — 38/.; 14 — 41/.; 15 — 44/.; 16 — 48/.; 17 — 54/.

434. Callipers
Brt. 2d Pr Inch
Blk. 1½ " "
all under 6 in.
Blk. 9/. Pr Doz.
Brt. 12/. " "

B.141. Improved in & out Screw Callipers.
12/- 12/- 12/- 14/- 16/. Doz.
4 5 6 7 8

B.144. Brass Head Pocket Callipers.
12/- 13/- 14/.
3 3½ 4 in.

435. Coopers Steel Points.

Brass Compasses Steel Points

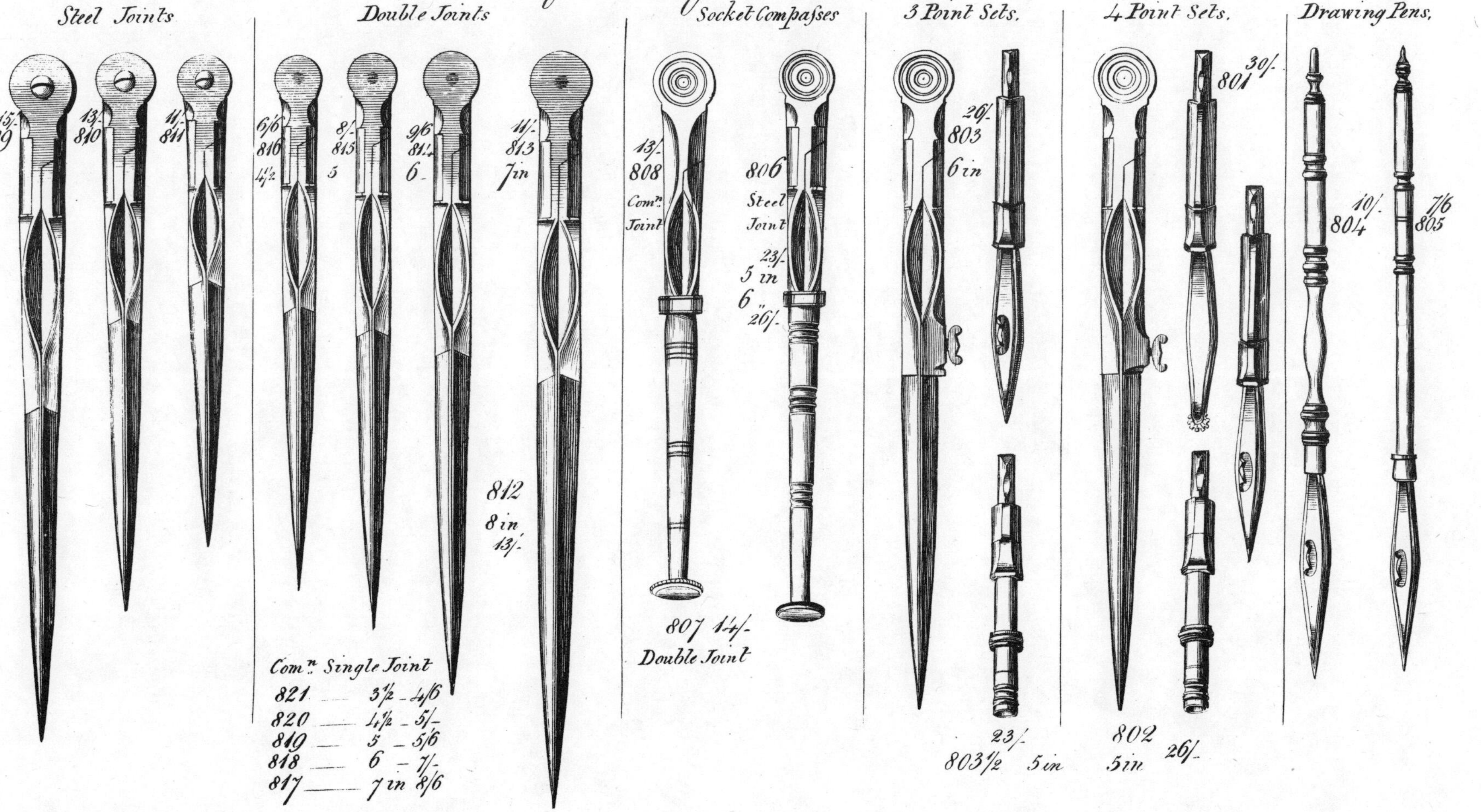

Steel Joints.

15/ 809
13/ 810
11/ 811

Double Joints.

6/6 816 4½
8/ 815 5
9/6 814 6
11/ 813 7 in
812 8 in 13/

Comn Single Joint
821 —— 3½ - 4/6
820 —— 4½ - 5/
819 —— 5 - 5/6
818 —— 6 - 7/
817 —— 7 in 8/6

Socket Compasses.

13/ 808 Comn Joint
806 Steel Joint
23/ 5 in
6" 26/
807 14/ Double Joint

3 Point Sets.

26/ 803 6 in
23/ 803½ 5 in

4 Point Sets.

30/ 801
802 5 in 26/

Drawing Pens.

10/ 804
7/6 805

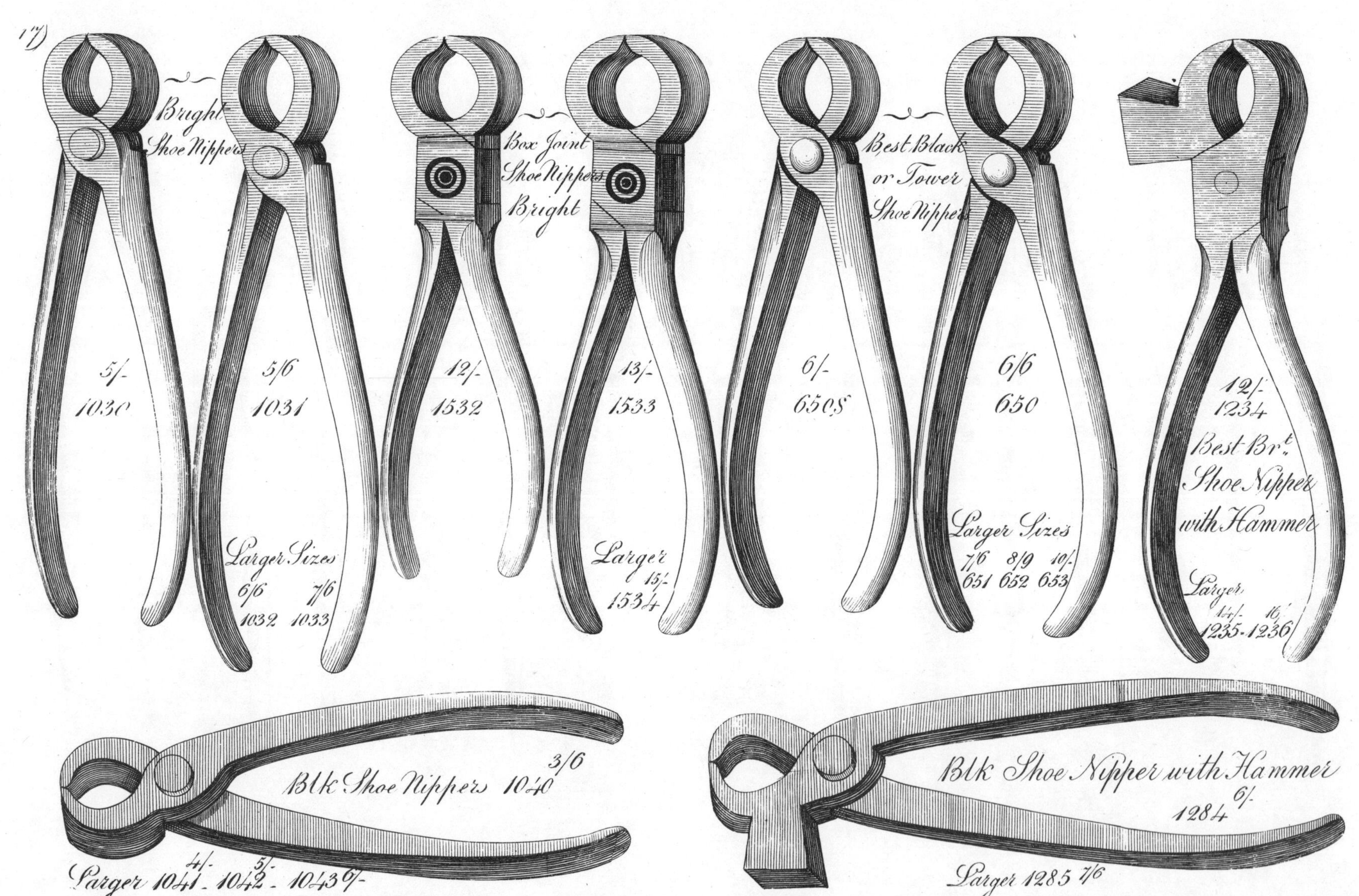
17)
Bright Shoe Nippers
5/- 1030
5/6 1031
Larger Sizes 6/6 7/6 1032 1033
Box Joint Shoe Nippers Bright
12/- 1532
13/- 1533
Larger 15/- 1534
Best Black or Tower Shoe Nippers
6/- 650S
6/6 650
Larger Sizes 7/6 8/9 10/- 651 652 653
12/- 1234
Best Brt. Shoe Nipper with Hammer
Larger 14/- 16/- 1235-1236
Blk Shoe Nipper 1040 3/6
Larger 1041 4/- 1042 5/- 1043 6/-
Blk Shoe Nipper with Hammer 6/- 1284
Larger 1285 7/6

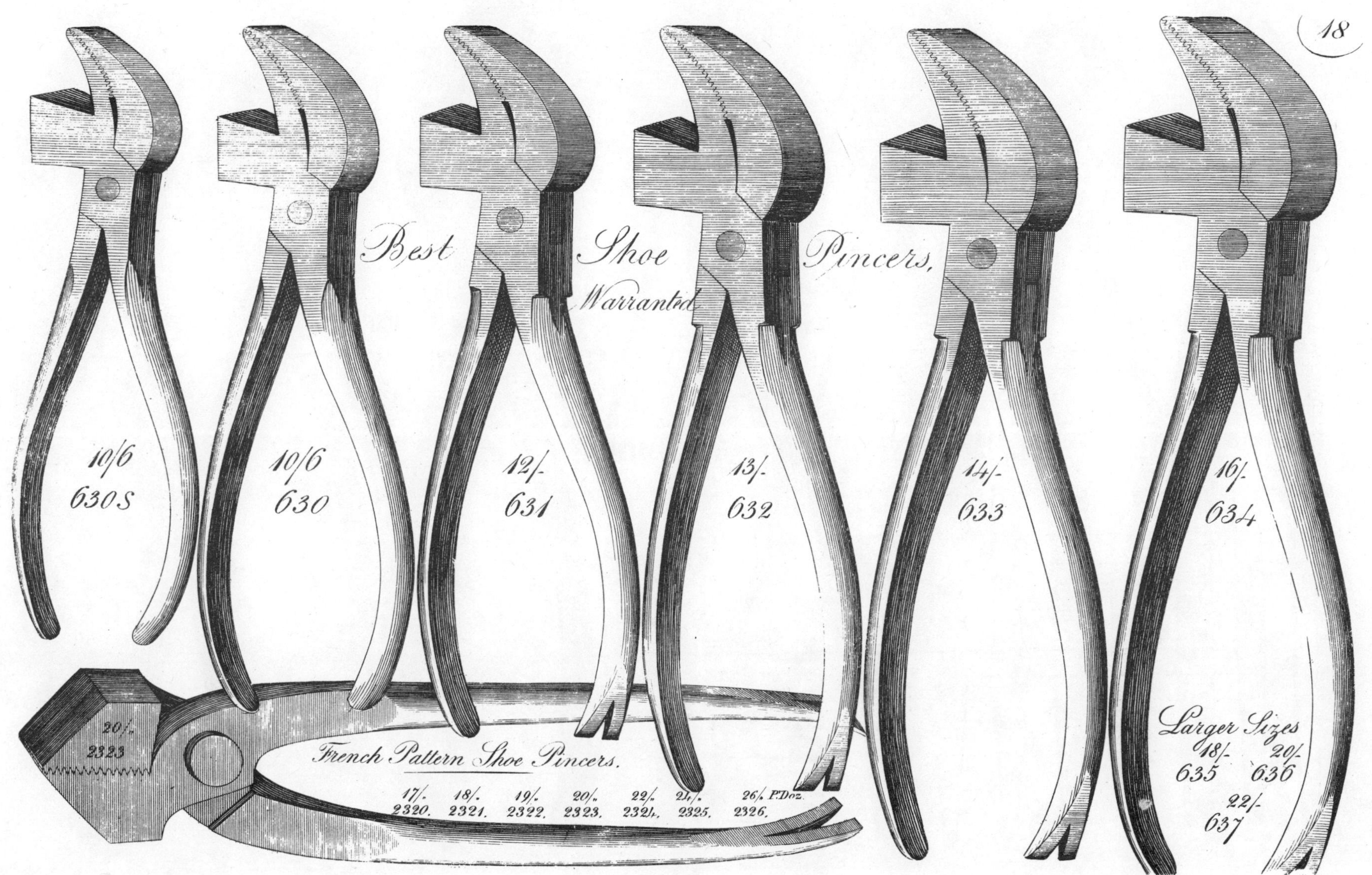
18
Best Shoe Pincers.
Warranted
10/6
630 S
10/6
630
12/-
631
13/-
632
14/-
633
16/-
634
20/-
2323
French Pattern Shoe Pincers.
17/-   18/-   19/-   20/-   22/-   24/-   26/- P. Doz
2320.   2321.   2322.   2323.   2324.   2325.   2326.
Larger Sizes
18/-   20/-
635   636
22/-
637

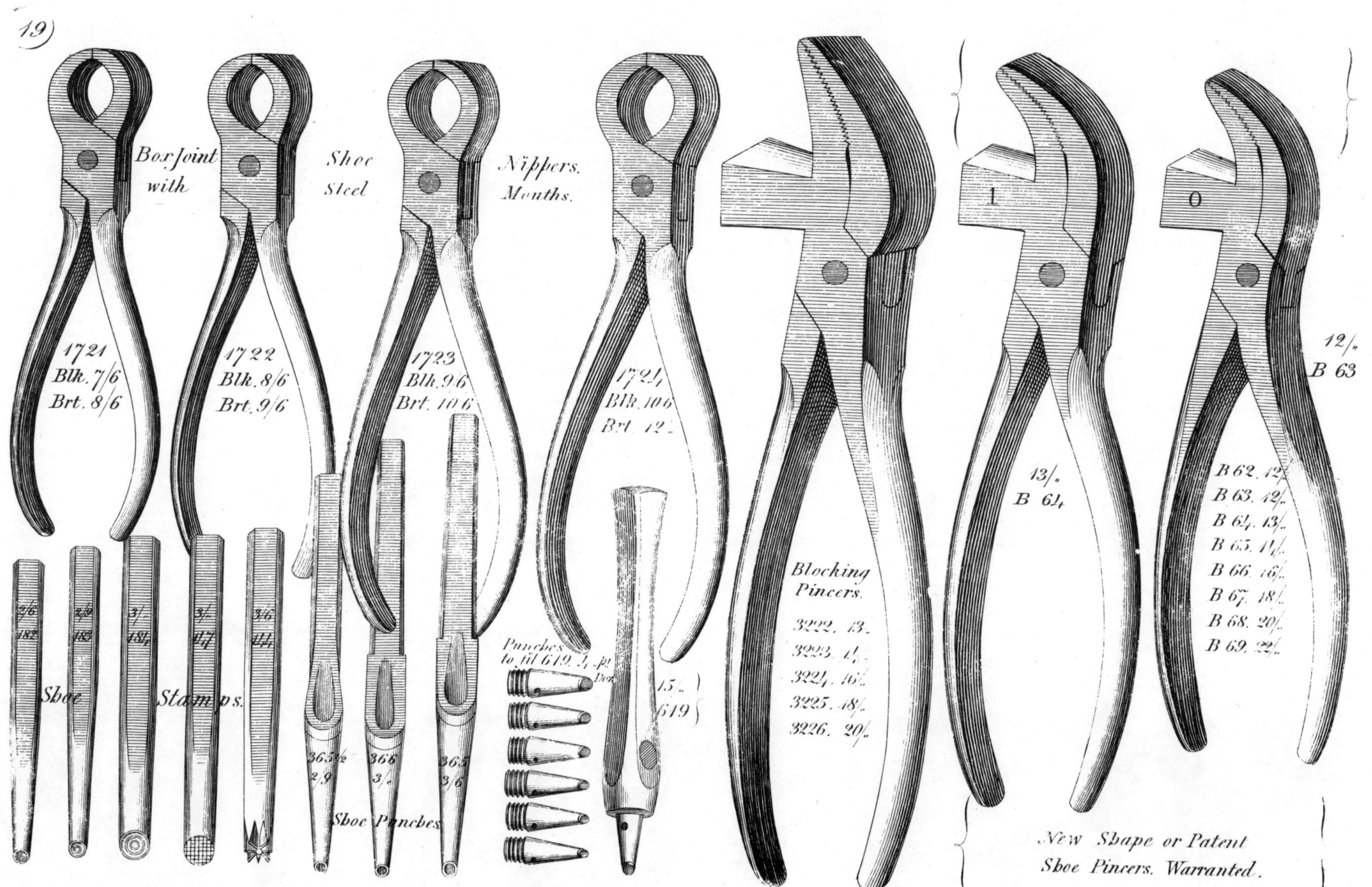
19
Box Joint with
Shoe Steel
Nippers. Mouths.
1721
Blk. 7/6
Brt. 8/6
1722
Blk. 8/6
Brt. 9/6
1723
Blk. 9/6
Brt. 10/6
1724
Blk. 10/6
Brt. 12/-
Shoe
Stamps.
Shoe Punches
Punches to fit 619.
Blocking Pincers.
3222. 13/-
3223. 14/-
3224. 16/-
3225. 18/-
3226. 20/-
1
13/-
B 64
0
12/-
B 63
B 62. 12/-
B 63. 12/-
B 64. 13/-
B 65. 14/-
B 66. 16/-
B 67. 18/-
B 68. 20/-
B 69. 22/-
New Shape or Patent
Shoe Pincers. Warranted.

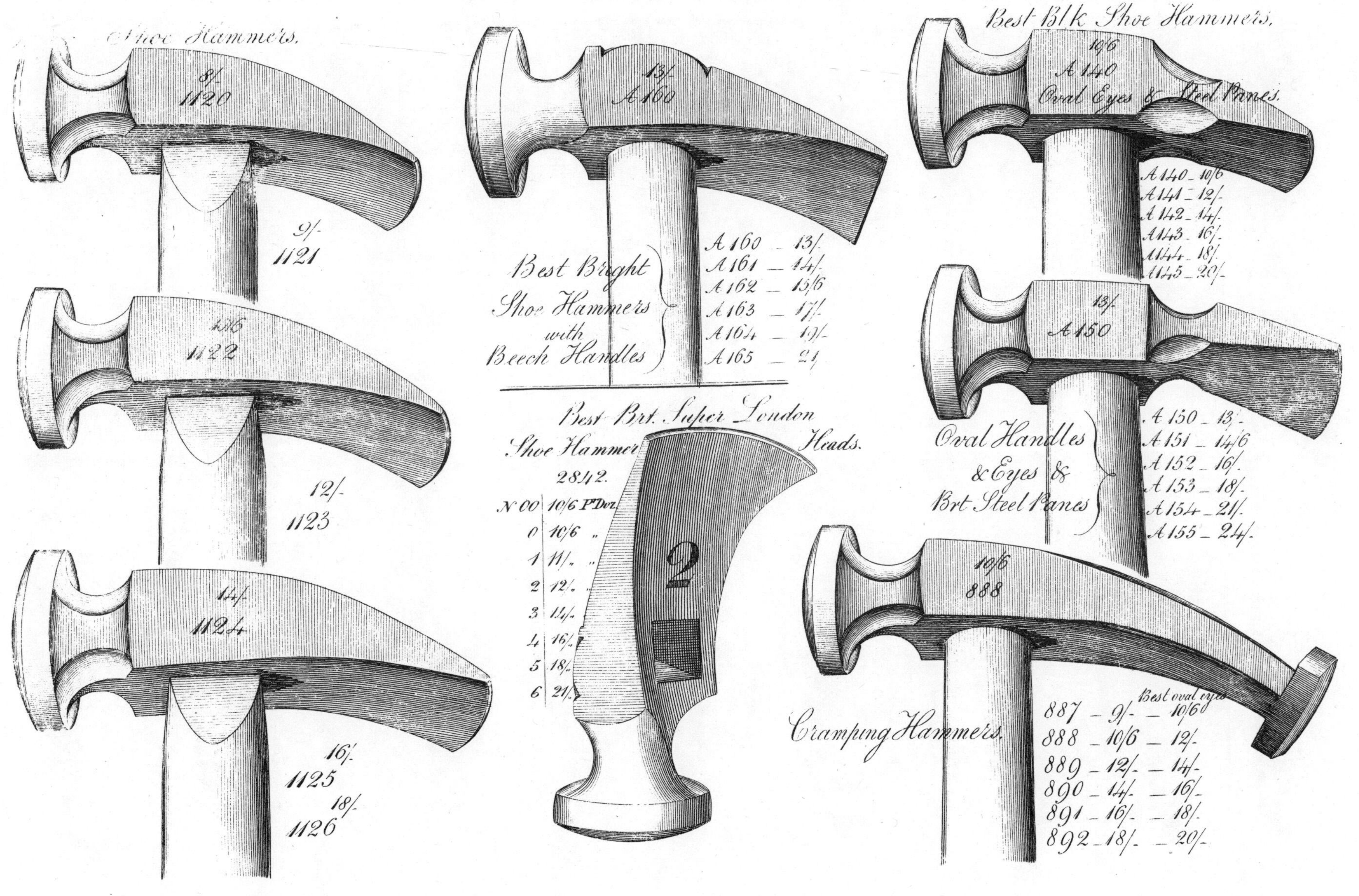
Shoe Hammers.
8/
1120
9/
1121
13/6
1122
12/
1123
14/
1124
16/
1125
18/
1126
13/
A 160
Best Bright
Shoe Hammers
with
Beech Handles
A 160 — 13/
A 161 — 14/
A 162 — 15/6
A 163 — 17/
A 164 — 19/
A 165 — 21/
Best Brt. Super London
Shoe Hammer
2842.
N OO 10/6 P Doz.
0   10/6   "
1   11/.   "
2   12/.   "
3   14/.   "
4   16/.   "
5   18/.   "
6   21/.   "
2
Heads.
Best Blk Shoe Hammers.
10/6
A 140
Oval Eyes & Steel Panes.
A 140 — 10/6
A 141 — 12/
A 142 — 14/
A 143 — 16/
A 144 — 18/
A 145 — 20/
13/
A 150
Oval Handles
& Eyes &
Brt. Steel Panes
A 150 — 13/
A 151 — 14/6
A 152 — 16/
A 153 — 18/
A 154 — 21/
A 155 — 24/
10/6
888
Cramping Hammers.
Best oval eyes
887 — 9/ — 10/6
888 — 10/6 — 12/
889 — 12/ — 14/
890 — 14/ — 16/
891 — 16/ — 18/
892 — 18/ — 20/

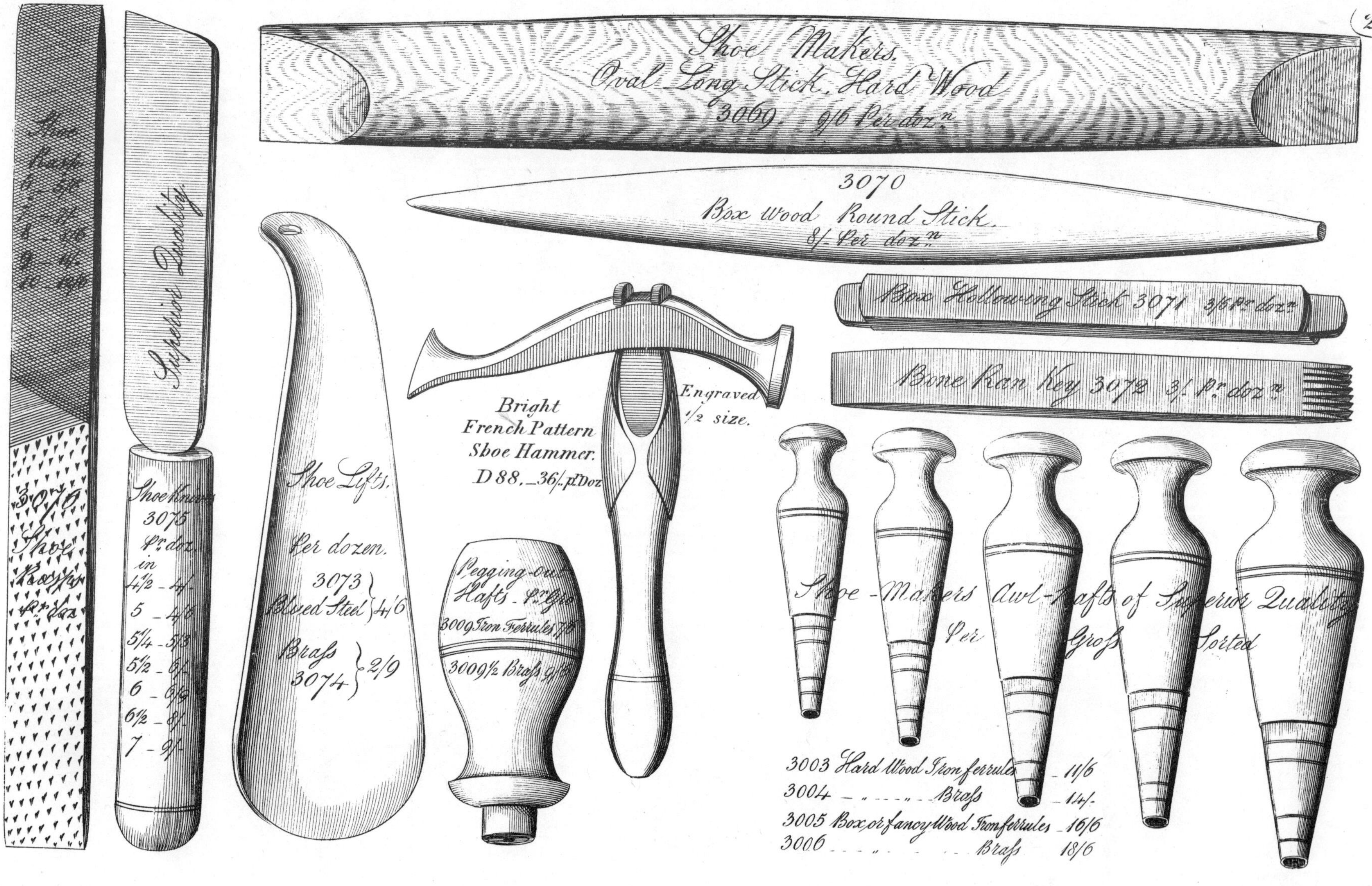

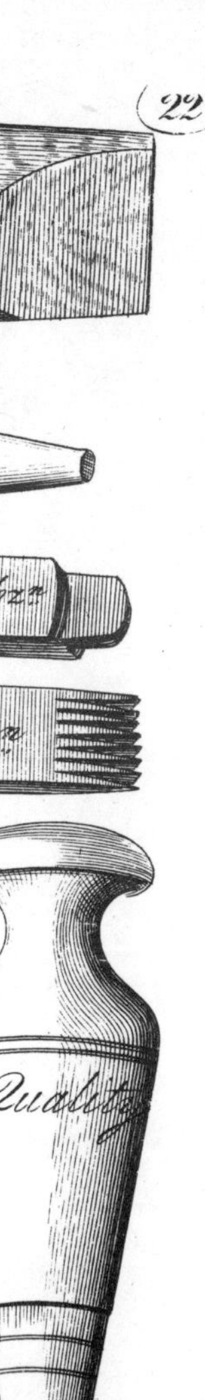

Shoe Makers.
Oval Long Stick. Hard Wood
3069.   9/6 Per dozn

3070
Box Wood Round Stick.
8/- Per dozn

Box Hollowing Stick 3071 3/6 Pr dozn

Bone Ran Key 3072 3/- Pr dozn

Superior Quality

Shoe Knives
3075
8/ Pr doz
in
4½ - 4/
5 - 4/6
5¼ - 5/3
5½ - 6/
6 - 6/6
6½ - 8/
7 - 9/

3070
Shoe
Rasps
Pr doz

Shoe Lifts.
Per dozen.
3073
Blued Steel 4/6
Brass
3074 2/9

Bright
French Pattern
Shoe Hammer.
D 88. _ 36/- p.Doz

Engraved
½ size.

Pegging out
Hafts. Pr Gro
3009 Iron Ferrules 7/6
3009½ Brass 9/6

Shoe-Makers   Awl Hafts of Superior Quality
Per
Gross   Sorted

3003 Hard Wood Iron ferrules _ 11/6
3004 _ " _ _ _ " _ _ Brass _ 14/-
3005 Box or fancy Wood Iron ferrules _ 16/6
3006 _ _ _ " _ _ _ _ _ Brass 18/6

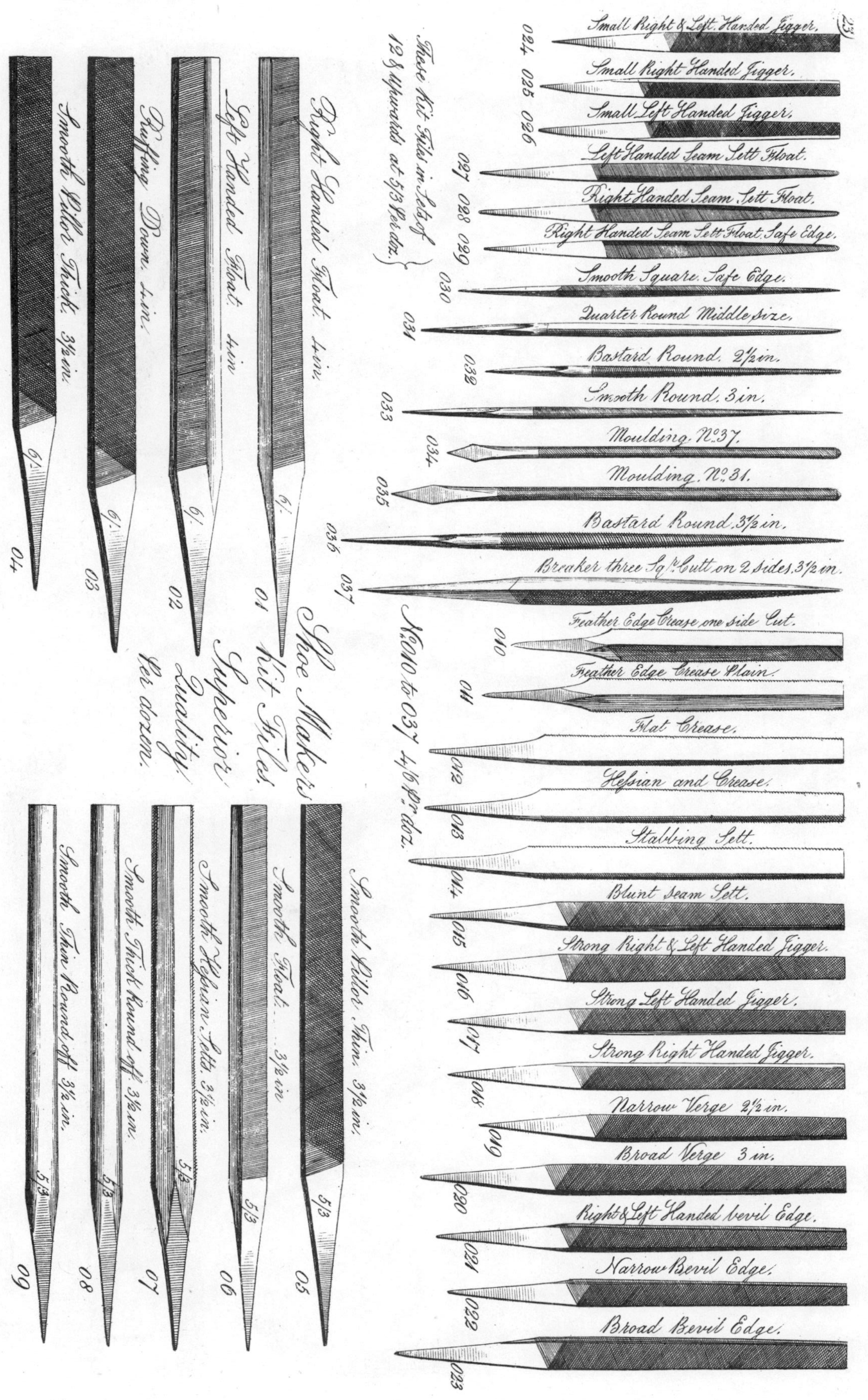

23)

Small Right & Left Handed Jigger.
Small Right Handed Jigger.
Small Left Handed Jigger.
Left Handed Seam Sett Float.
Right Handed Seam Sett Float.
Right Handed Seam Sett Float. Safe Edge.
Smooth Square. Safe Edge.
Quarter Round Middle size.
Bastard Round. 2½ in.
Smooth Round. 3 in.
Moulding. No. 37.
Moulding. No. 31.
Bastard Round. 3½ in.
Breaker three Sqr. Cutt on 2 sides. 3½ in.
Feather Edge Crease one side Cut.
Feather Edge Crease Plain.
Flat Crease.
Hessian and Crease.
Stabbing Sett.
Blunt seam Sett.
Strong Right & Left Handed Jigger.
Strong Left Handed Jigger.
Strong Right Handed Jigger.
Narrow Verge 2½ in.
Broad Verge 3 in.
Right & Left Handed bevil Edge.
Narrow Bevil Edge.
Broad Bevil Edge.

024 025 026 027 028 029 030 031 032 033 034 035 036 037

010 011 012 013 014 015 016 017 018 019 020 021 022 023

These Kit Files in Sets of
12 & Upwards at 5/3 Per doz.

No. 010 to 037 4/6 Pr. doz.

Right Handed Float. 4 in.   6/-   01
Left Handed Float. 4 in.   6/-   02
Ruffing Down. 4 in.   6/-   03
Smooth Pillor Thick. 3½ in.   6/-   04

Shoe Makers
Kit Files.
Superior
Quality.
Per dozen.

Smooth Pillor Thin. 3½ in.   5/3   05
Smooth Float. 3½ in.   5/3   06
Smooth Hessian Setts 3½ in.   5/3   07
Smooth Thick Round off. 3½ in.   5/3   08
Smooth Thin Round off. 3½ in.   5/3   09

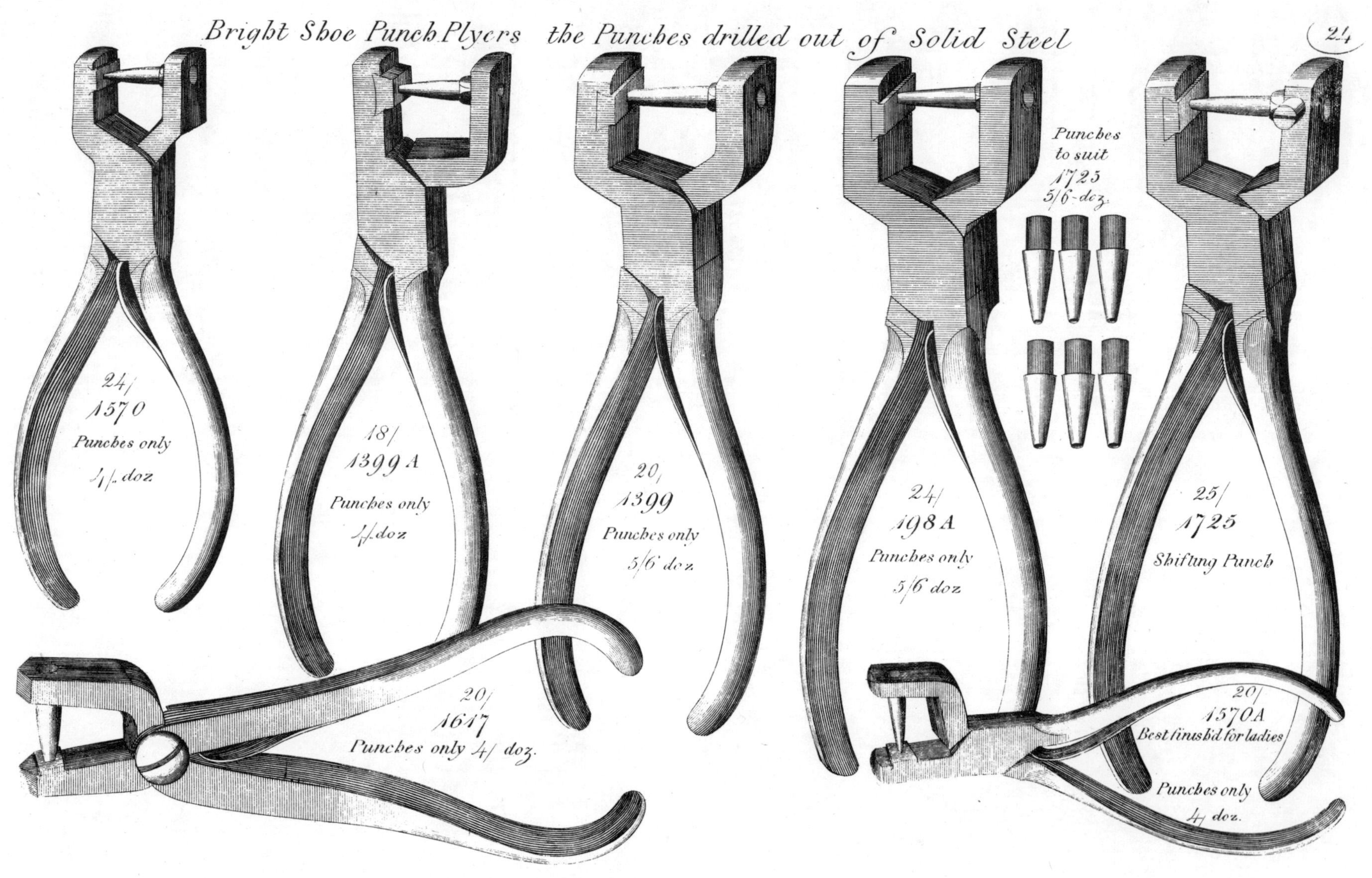

Bright Shoe Punch Plyers   the Punches drilled out of Solid Steel
24
24/
1570
Punches only
4/. doz
18/
1399 A
Punches only
4/ doz
20/
1399
Punches only
5/6 doz.
Punches
to suit
1725
5/6 doz.
24/
198 A
Punches only
5/6 doz
25/
1725
Shifting Punch
20/
1647
Punches only 4/ doz.
20/
1570 A
Best finish'd for ladies
Punches only
4/ doz.

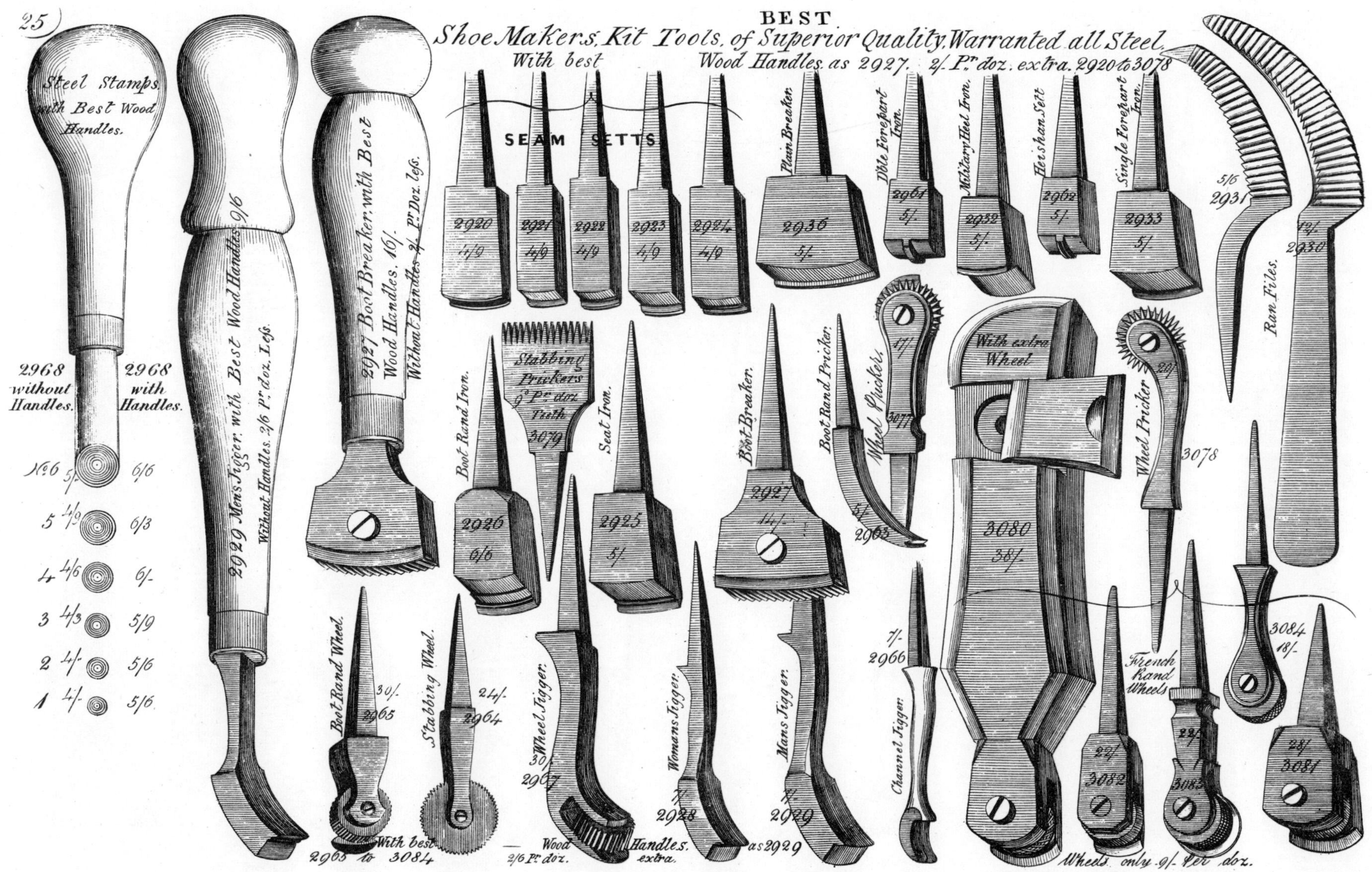

25
BEST
Shoe Makers, Kit Tools, of Superior Quality, Warranted all Steel.
With best Wood Handles, as 2927. 2/- Pr. doz. extra. 2920 to 3078
Steel Stamps with Best Wood Handles.
SEAM SETTS
Plain Breaker.
Dble Forepart Iron.
2964 5/-
Military Heel Iron.
2932 5/-
Hessian Sett
2962 5/-
Single Forepart Iron.
2933 5/-
5/6 2931
Ran.Files.
12/- 2930
2920 4/9
2921 4/9
2922 4/9
2923 4/9
2924 4/9
2930 5/-
2968 without Handles.
2968 with Handles.
2929 Mens Jigger, with Best Wood Handles 9/6
Without Handles. 2/6 Pr. doz. Less.
2927 Boot Breaker, with Best Wood Handles. 16/-
Without Handles 2/- Pr. Doz. less.
No.6 5/- 6/6
5 4/9 6/3
4 4/6 6/-
3 4/3 5/9
2 4/- 5/6
1 4/- 5/6
Boot Rand Iron.
Stabbing Prickers 9/- Pr. doz. Teeth 3079
Seat Iron.
Boot Breaker.
2927 14/-
Boot Rand Pricker.
5/- 2963
Wheel Pricker.
17/- 3077
With extra Wheel
Wheel Pricker 22/- 3078
2926 6/6
2925 5/-
3080 38/-
Boot Rand Wheel. 30/- 2965
Stabbing Wheel. 24/- 2964
Wheel Jigger. 30/- 2967
Womans Jigger. 7/- 2928
Mans Jigger. 7/- 2929
Channel Jigger. 7/- 2966
French Rand Wheels
3084 18/-
22/- 3082
22/- 3083
28/- 3081
With best
2965 to 3084
Wood
2/6 Pr. doz.
Handles. extra.
as 2929
Wheels only 9/- per doz.

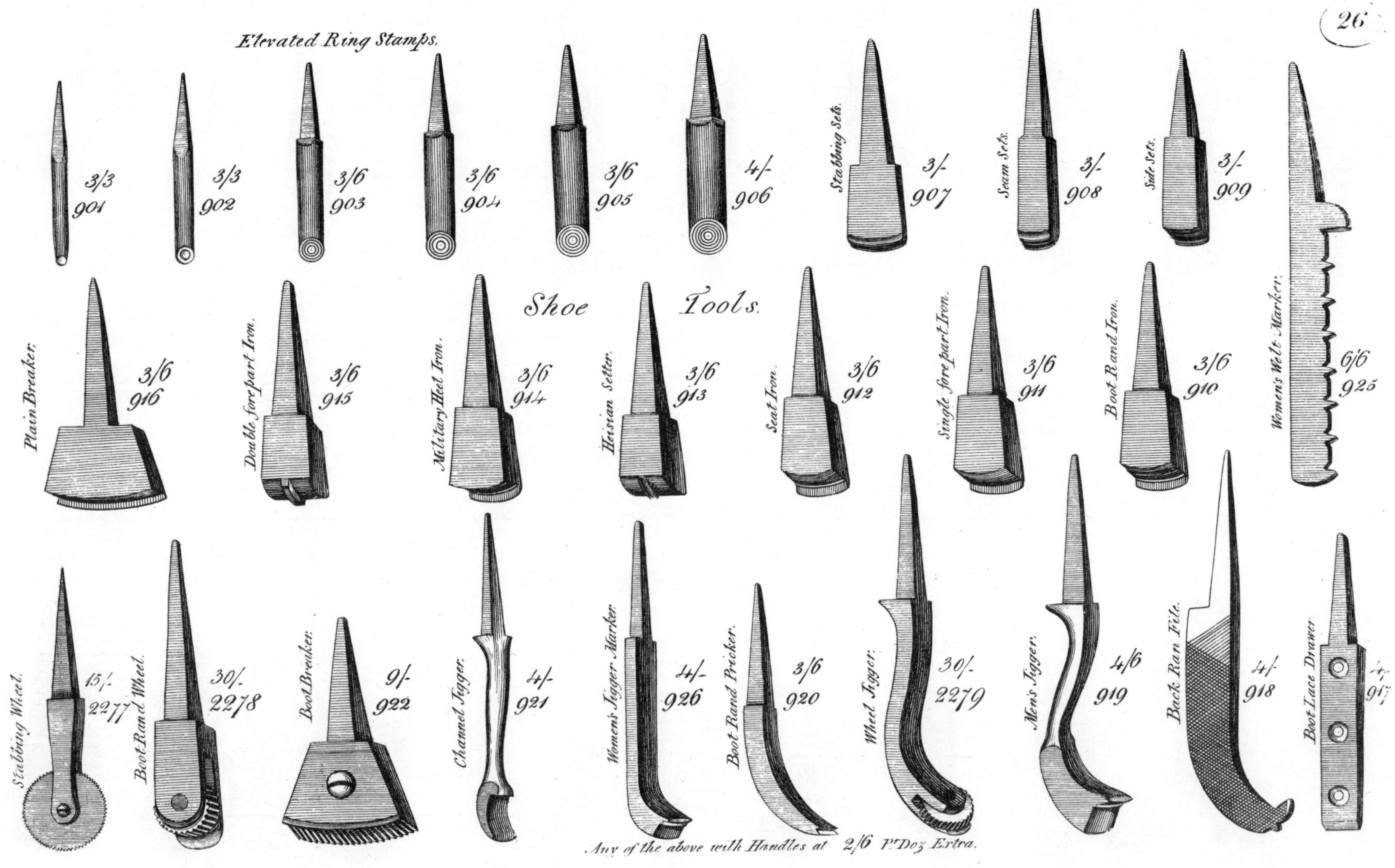
Elevated Ring Stamps.
3/3 901
3/3 902
3/6 903
3/6 904
3/6 905
4/- 906
Stabbing Sets. 3/- 907
Seam Sets. 3/- 908
Side Sets. 3/- 909
Shoe Tools.
Plain Breaker. 3/6 916
Double forepart Iron. 3/6 915
Military Heel Iron. 3/6 914
Hessian Setter. 3/6 913
Seat Iron. 3/6 912
Single forepart Iron. 3/6 911
Boot Rand Iron. 3/6 910
Women's Welt Marker. 6/6 925
Stabbing Wheel. 15/- 2277
Boot Rand Wheel. 30/- 2278
Boot Breaker. 9/- 922
Channel Jigger. 4/- 921
Women's Jigger Marker. 4/- 926
Boot Rand Pricker. 3/6 920
Wheel Jigger. 30/- 2279
Men's Jigger. 4/6 919
Back Ran File. 4/- 918
Boot Lace Drawer. 4/- 917
Any of the above with Handles at 2/6 P.r Doz Extra.

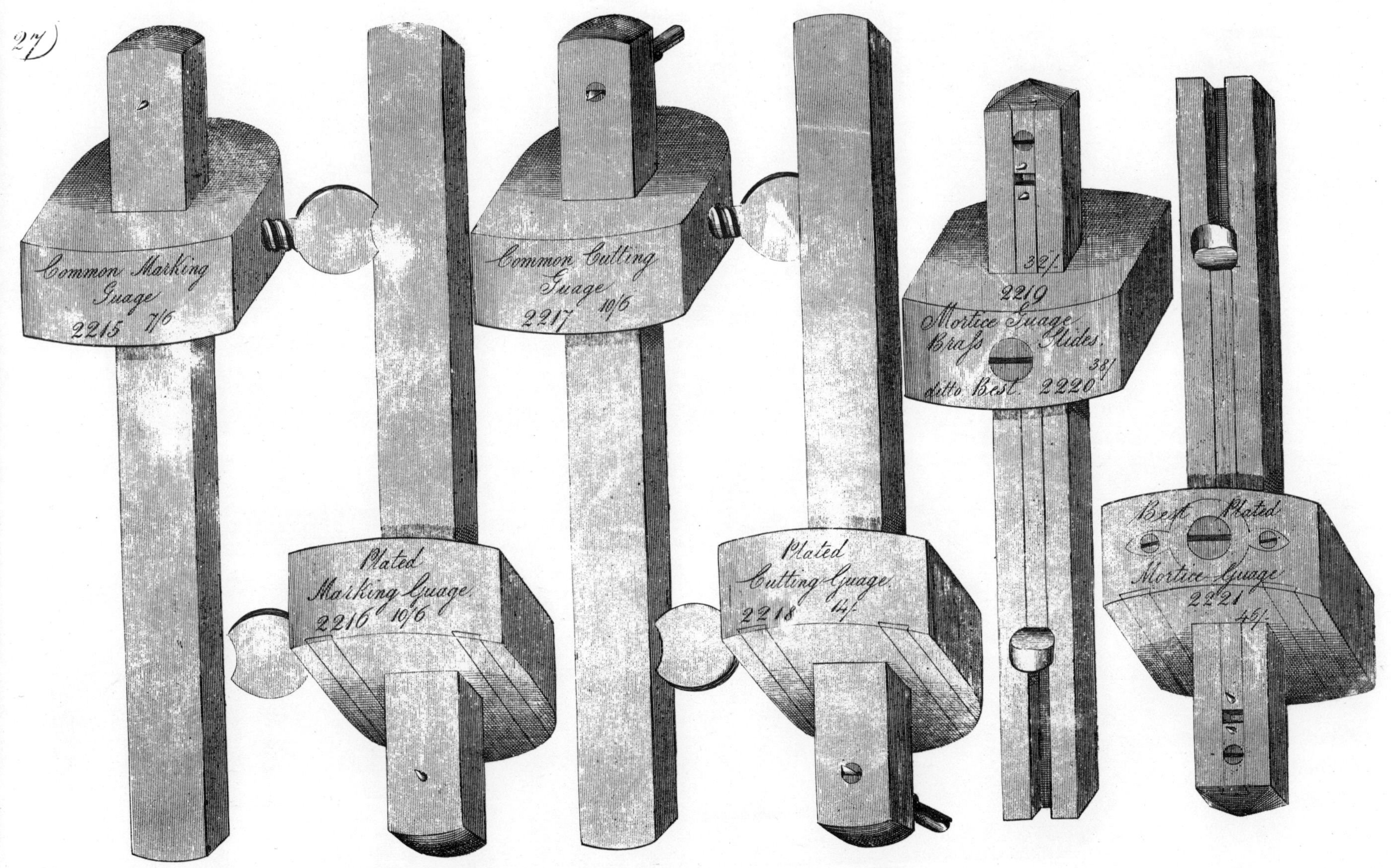

27
Common Marking Guage 2215 7/6
Common Cutting Guage 2217 10/6
32/
2219
Mortice Guage Brass Slides
ditto Best 2220 38/
Plated Marking Guage 2216 10/6
Plated Cutting Guage 2218 14/
Best Plated Mortice Guage 2221 42/

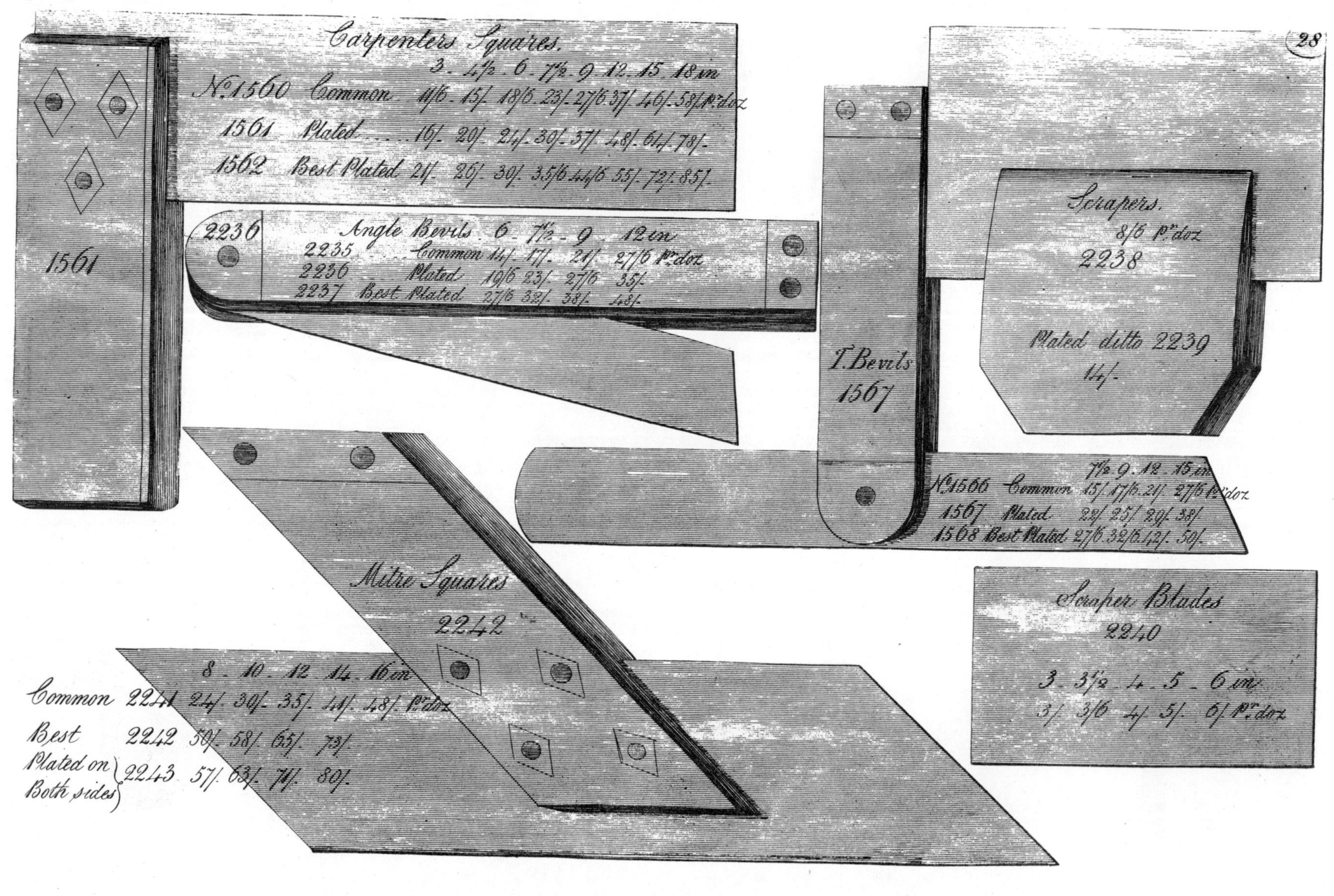

Carpenters Squares.
3. 4½. 6. 7½. 9. 12. 15. 18 in
No 1560 Common   11/6. 15/. 18/6. 23/. 27/6 37/. 46/. 58/ Pr doz
1561   Plated   16/. 20/. 24/. 30/. 37/. 48/. 64/. 78/.
1562   Best Plated   21/. 26/. 30/. 35/6. 44/6 55/. 72/. 85/.
1561
Angle Bevils   6. 7½. 9. 12 in
2236
2235   Common   14/. 17/. 21/. 27/6 Pr doz
2236   Plated   19/6 23/. 27/6 35/.
2237   Best Plated   27/6 32/. 38/. 48/.
Mitre Squares
2242
8. 10. 12. 14. 16 in
Common 2241   24/. 30/. 35/. 44/. 48/. Pr doz
Best   2242   50/. 58/. 65/. 73/.
Plated on   2243   57/. 63/. 74/. 80/.
Both sides
T. Bevils
1567
7½. 9. 12. 15 in
No 1566 Common   15/. 17/6. 21/. 27/6 Pr doz
1567   Plated   22/. 25/. 29/. 38/.
1568 Best Plated   27/6 32/6. 42/. 50/.
Scrapers.
8/6 Pr doz
2238
Plated ditto 2239
14/.
Scraper Blades
2240
3. 3½. 4. 5. 6 in
3/. 3/6. 4/. 5/. 6/ Pr doz

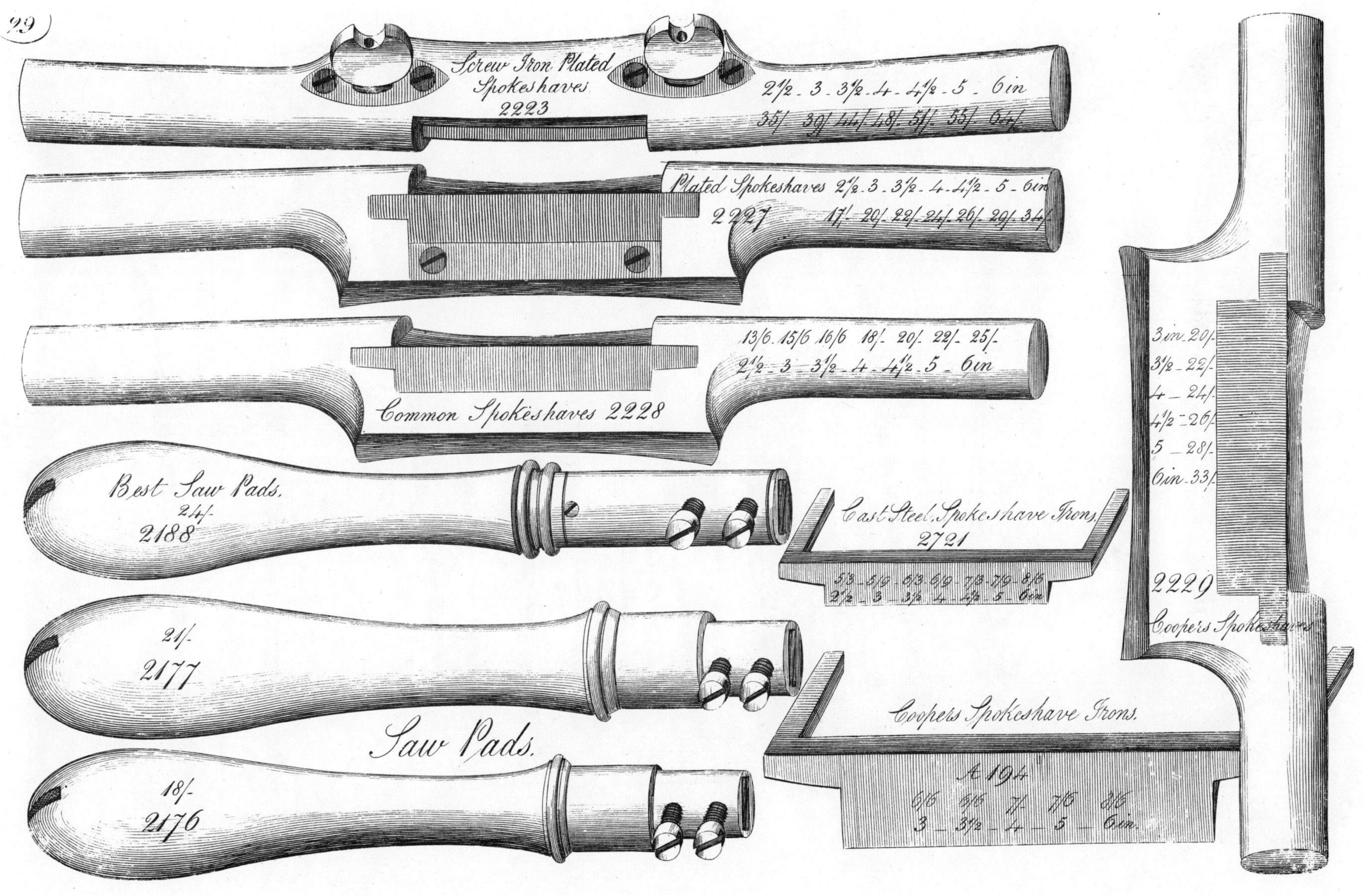
29
Screw Iron Plated Spokeshaves 2223
2½ . 3 . 3½ . 4 . 4½ . 5 . 6 in
35/ 39/ 44/ 48/ 51/ 53/ 64/
Plated Spokeshaves 2½ . 3 . 3½ . 4 . 4½ . 5 . 6 in
2227
17/ 20/ 22/ 24/ 26/ 29/ 34/
13/6. 15/6 16/6 18/ 20/ 22/ 25/
2½ . 3 . 3½ . 4 . 4½ . 5 . 6 in
Common Spokeshaves 2228
Best Saw Pads.
24/
2188
21/
2177
Saw Pads.
18/
2176
Cast Steel Spokeshave Irons.
2721
5/3 5/9 6/3 6/9 7/3 7/9 8/6
2½ . 3 . 3½ . 4 . 4½ . 5 . 6 in
Coopers Spokeshave Irons.
A 194
6/6 6/6 7/ 7/6 8/6
3 . 3½ . 4 . 5 . 6 in
3 in. 20/
3½ . 22/
4 . 24/
4½ . 26/
5 . 28/
6 in 33/
2229
Coopers Spokeshaves

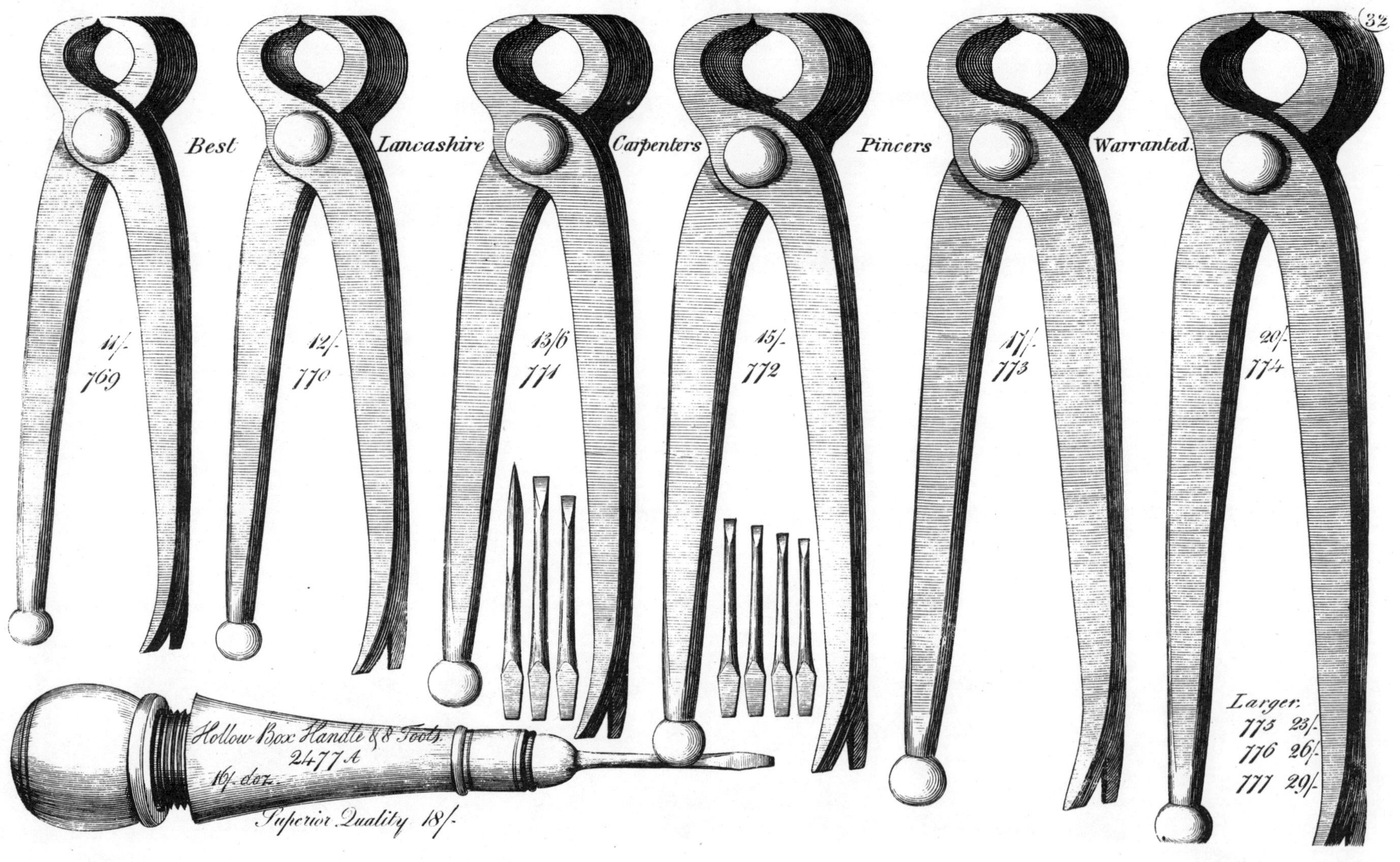

32
Best
Lancashire
Carpenters
Pincers
Warranted.
11/-
769
12/-
770
13/6
771
15/-
772
17/-
773
20/-
774
Hollow Box Handle & 8 Tools.
2477 A
16/- doz.
Superior Quality 18/-
Larger.
775 23/-
776 26/-
777 29/-

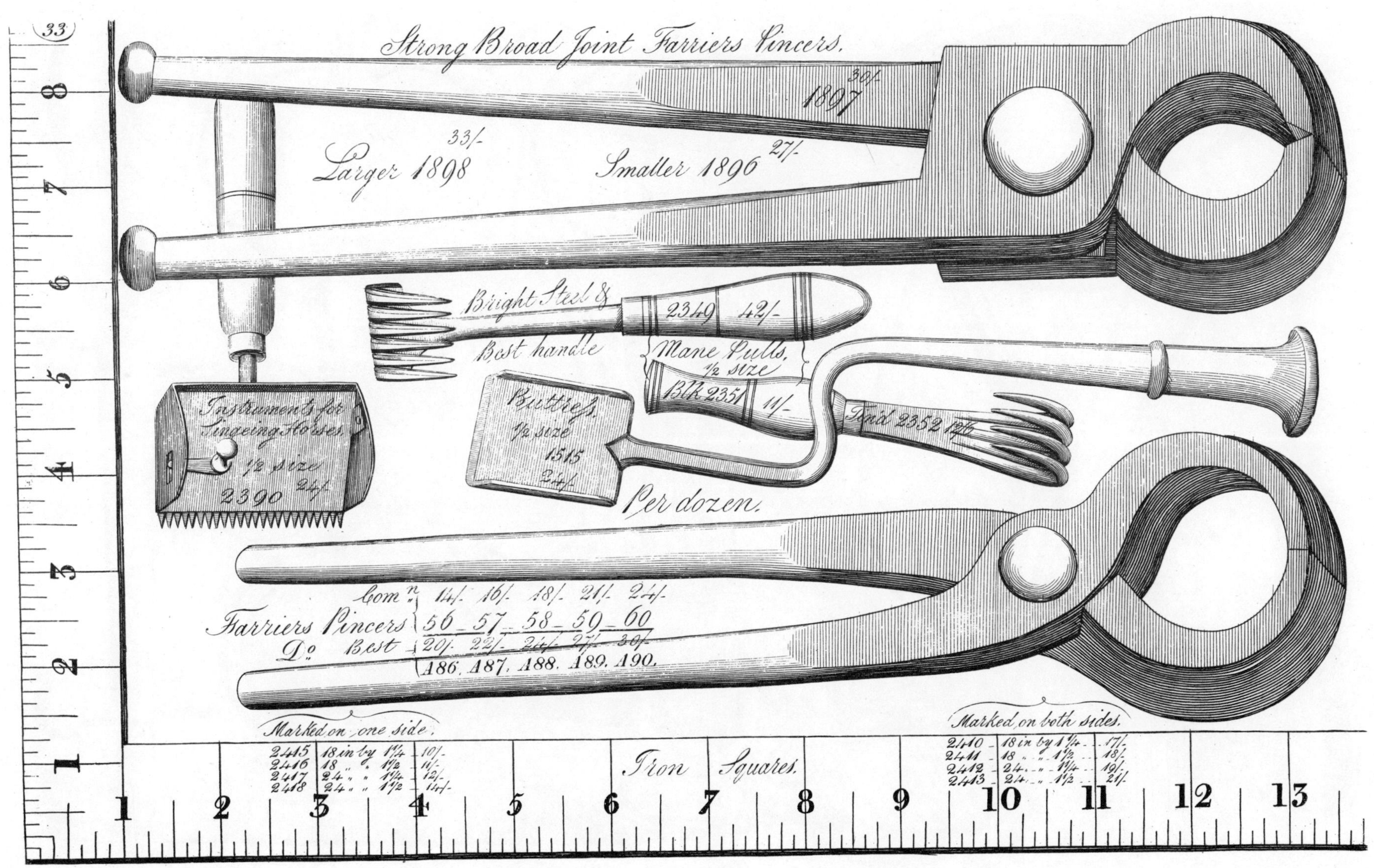

33
Strong Broad Joint Farriers Pincers.
30/
1897
33/
Larger 1898
27/
Smaller 1896
Bright Steel &
Best handle
2349 42/
Mane Pulls,
½ size
Blk 2351 11/
Tind 2352 12/6
Instrument for
Singeing Horses
½ size
2390 24/
Buttress,
½ size
1515
24/
Per dozen.
Com.n 14/ 16/ 18/ 21/ 24/
Farriers Pincers 56 57 58 59 60
D.o Best 20/ 22/ 24/ 27/ 30/
186. 187. 188. 189. 190.
Marked on one side.
2415 18 in by 1¼ 10/
2416 18 " 1½ 11/
2417 24 " 1¼ 12/
2418 24 " 1½ 14/
Iron Squares.
Marked on both sides.
2410 18 in by 1¼ 17/
2411 18 " 1½ 18/
2412 24 " 1¼ 19/
2413 24 " 1½ 21/

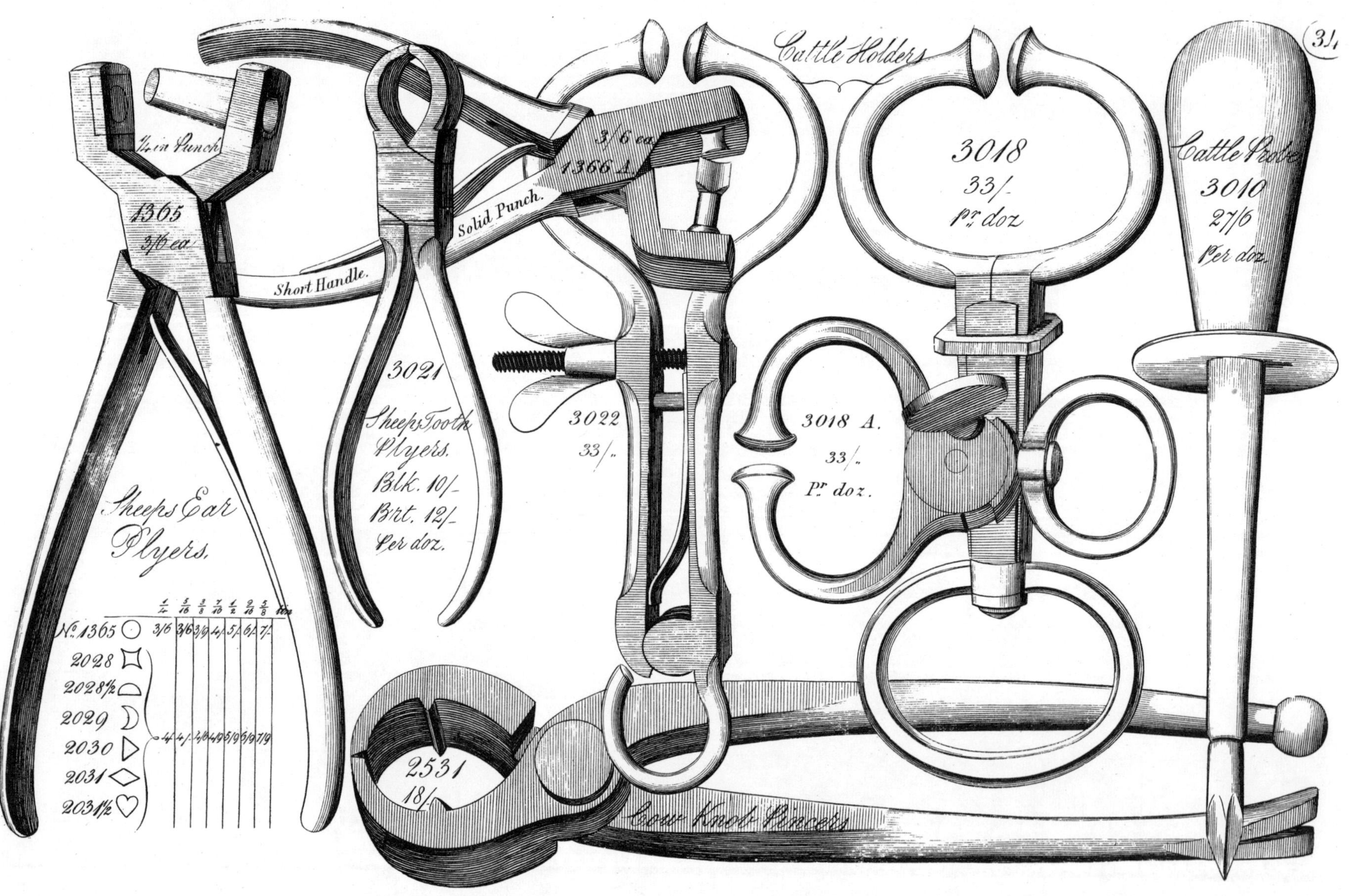
(34)
Cattle Holders
Twin Punch
1365
3/6 ea
Short Handle.
Solid Punch.
3/6 ea
1366 A
3021
Sheeps Tooth
Plyers.
Blk. 10/-
Brt. 12/-
Per doz.
3022
33/.
3018
33/.
Pr doz
3018 A.
33/.
Pr. doz.
Cattle Probe
3010
27/6
Per doz.
Sheeps Ear
Plyers.
No. 1365
2028
2028½
2029
2030
2031
2031½
2531
18/-
Cow Knob Pincers

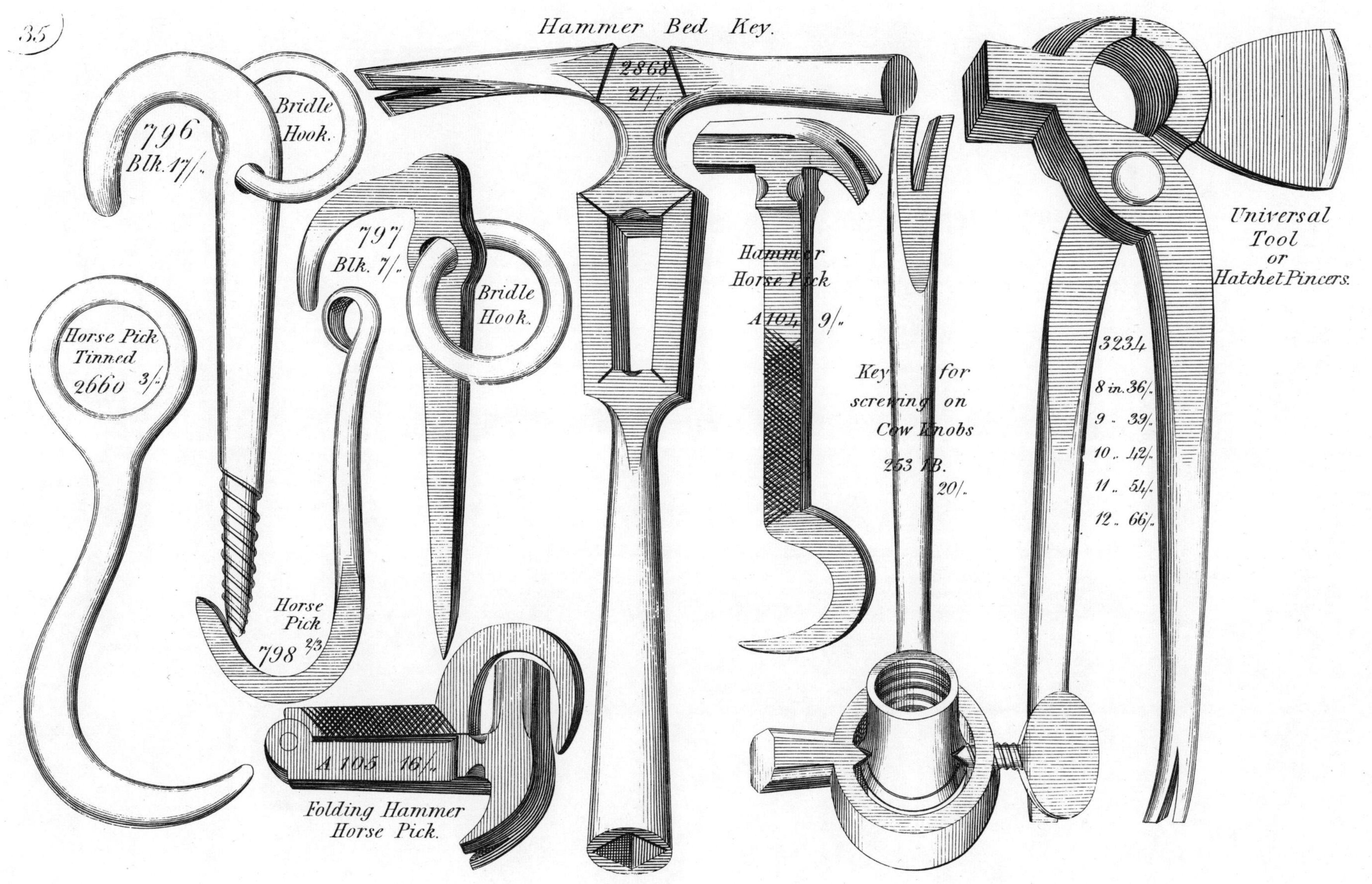
Hammer Bed Key.
796 Blk. 17/..
Bridle Hook.
797 Blk. 7/..
Bridle Hook.
Horse Pick Tinned 2660 3/.
Horse Pick 798 2/3
Folding Hammer Horse Pick.
A 105 16/.
2868 21/..
Hammer Horse Pick A 104 9/..
Key for screwing on Cow Knobs 253 B. 20/.
Universal Tool or Hatchet Pincers.
3234
8 in. 36/.
9 .. 39/.
10 .. 42/.
11 .. 54/.
12 .. 66/.

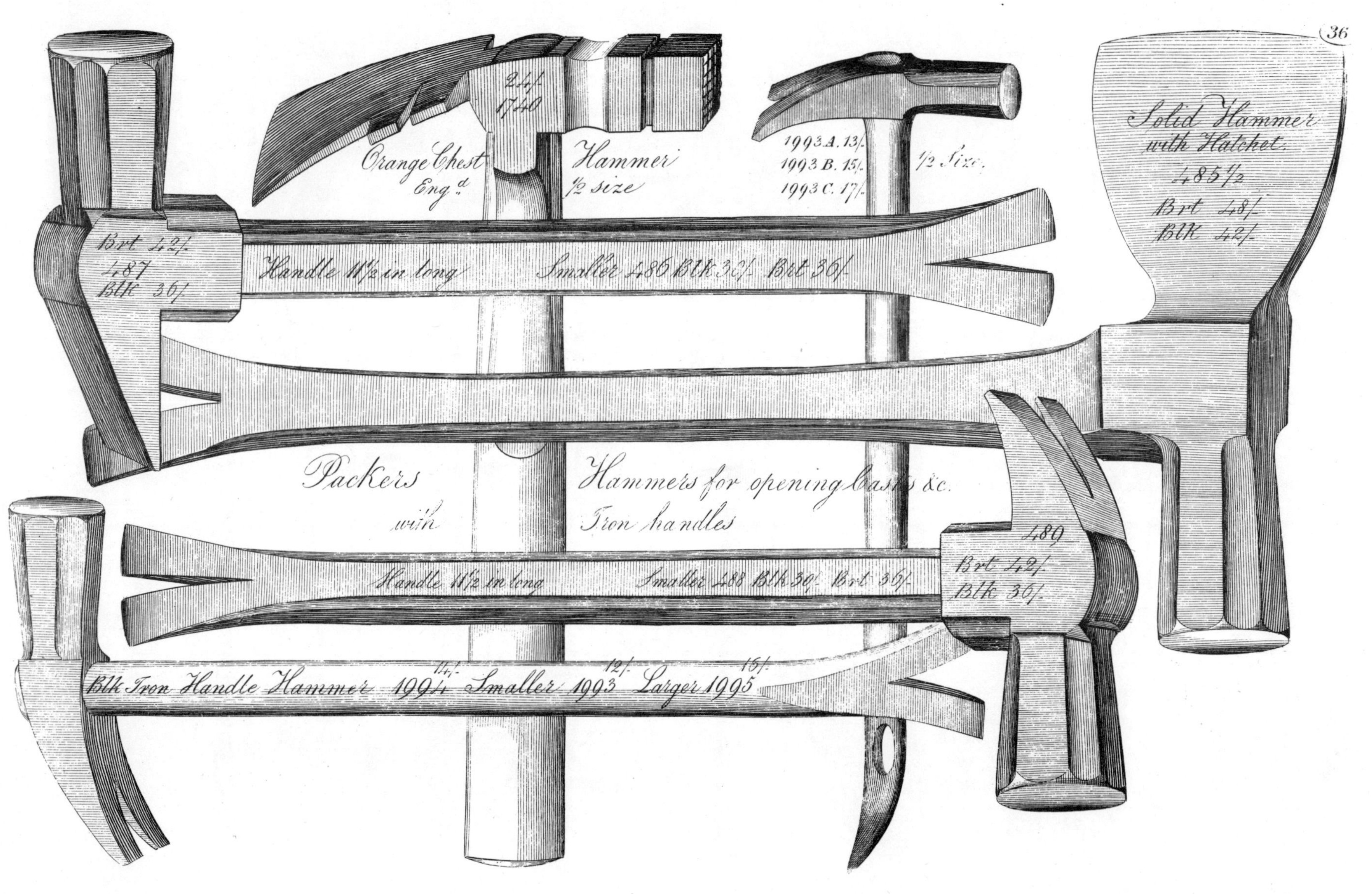
36
Orange Chest
Eng.d
24/
1740
Hammer
½ size
1993 A. 13/
1993 B. 15/
1993 C. 17/
½ Size.
Solid Hammer
with Hatchet.
485½
Brt 48/
Blk 42/
Brt 42/
487
Blk 36/
Handle 11½ in long
Smaller 486 Blk 32/. Brt 36/
Packers
with
Hammers for opening Casks &c.
Iron handles
489
Brt 42/
Blk 36/
Handle 11½ in long
Smaller 488 Blk 30/. Brt 36/.
Blk Iron Handle Hammer 1994 Smaller 1993 Larger 1995
11/
12/
16/

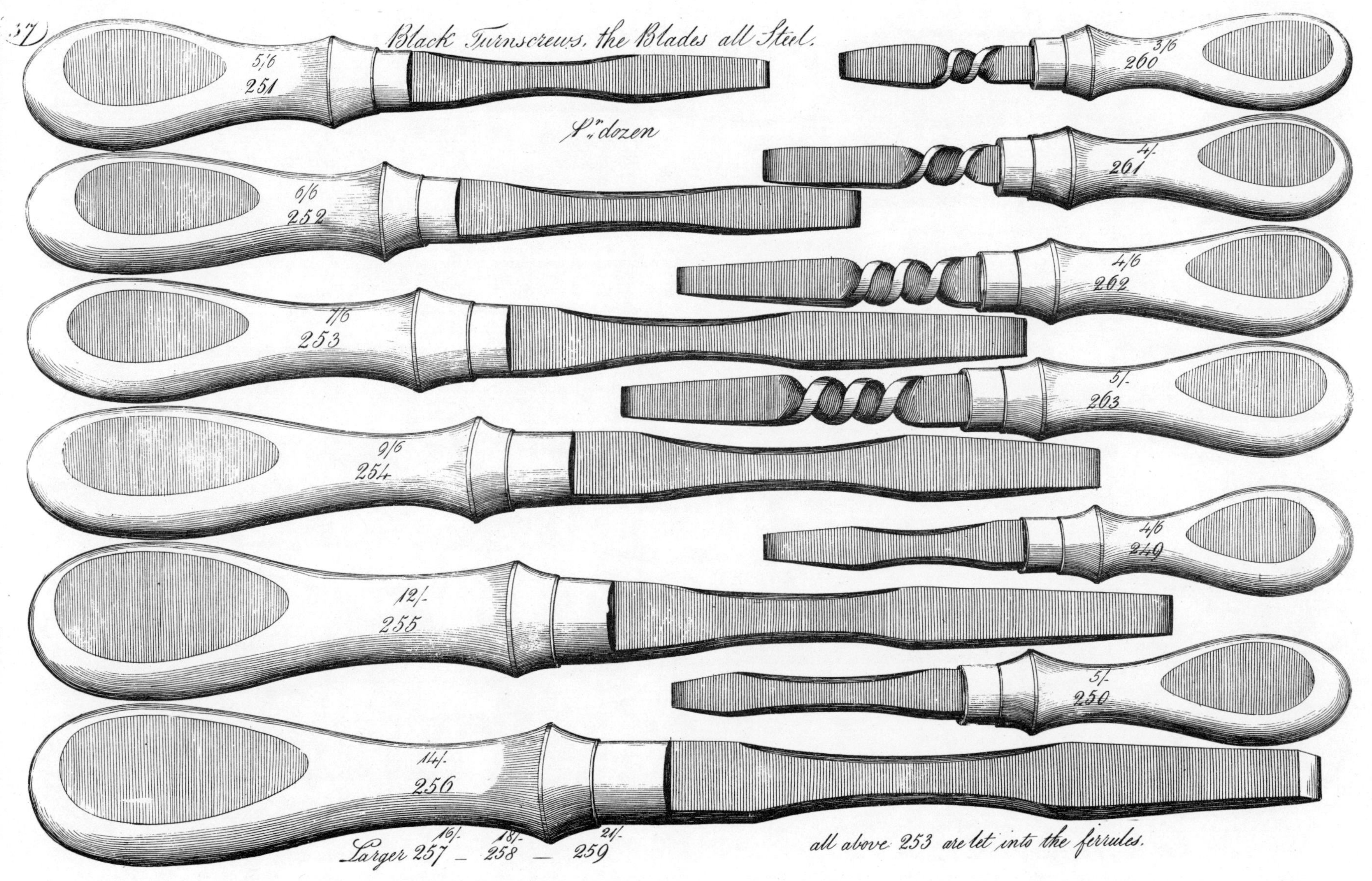
37
Black Turnscrews, the Blades all Steel.
S. dozen
5/6
251
6/6
252
7/6
253
9/6
254
12/-
255
14/-
256
Larger 257 — 16/- 258 — 18/- 259 — 21/-
3/6
260
4/-
261
4/6
262
5/-
263
4/6
249
5/-
250
all above 253 are let into the ferrules.

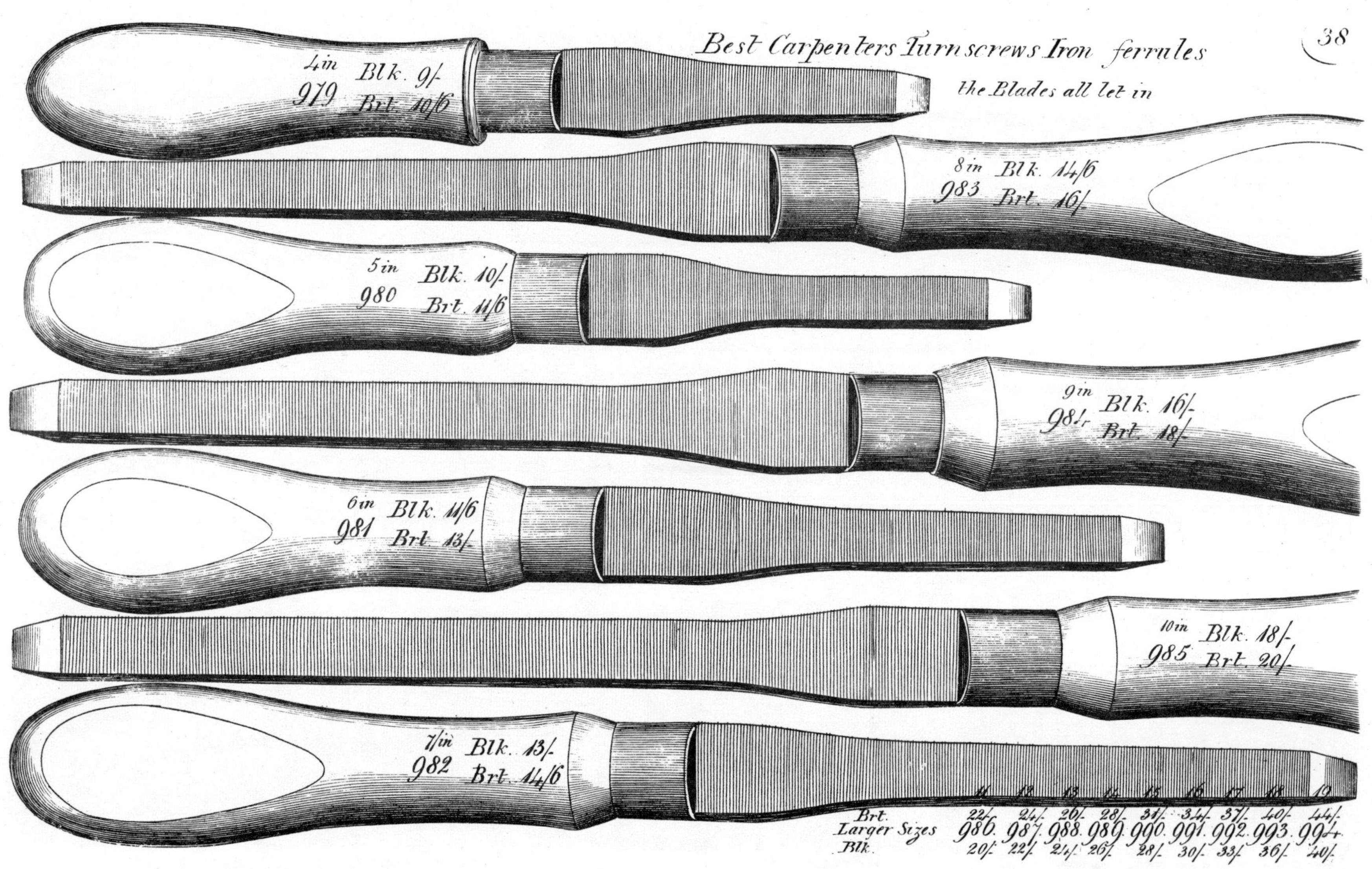
Best Carpenters Turnscrews Iron ferrules
the Blades all let in

4 in   Blk. 9/-
979   Brt. 10/6

8 in   Blk. 14/6
983   Brt. 16/-

5 in   Blk. 10/-
980   Brt. 11/6

9 in   Blk. 16/-
984   Brt. 18/-

6 in   Blk. 11/6
981   Brt. 13/-

10 in   Blk. 18/-
985   Brt. 20/-

7 in   Blk. 13/-
982   Brt. 14/6

11   12   13   14   15   16   17   18   19
Brt.   22/- 24/- 26/- 28/- 31/- 34/- 37/- 40/- 44/-
Larger Sizes   986. 987. 988. 989. 990. 991. 992. 993. 994
Blk.   20/- 22/- 24/- 26/- 28/- 30/- 33/- 36/- 40/-

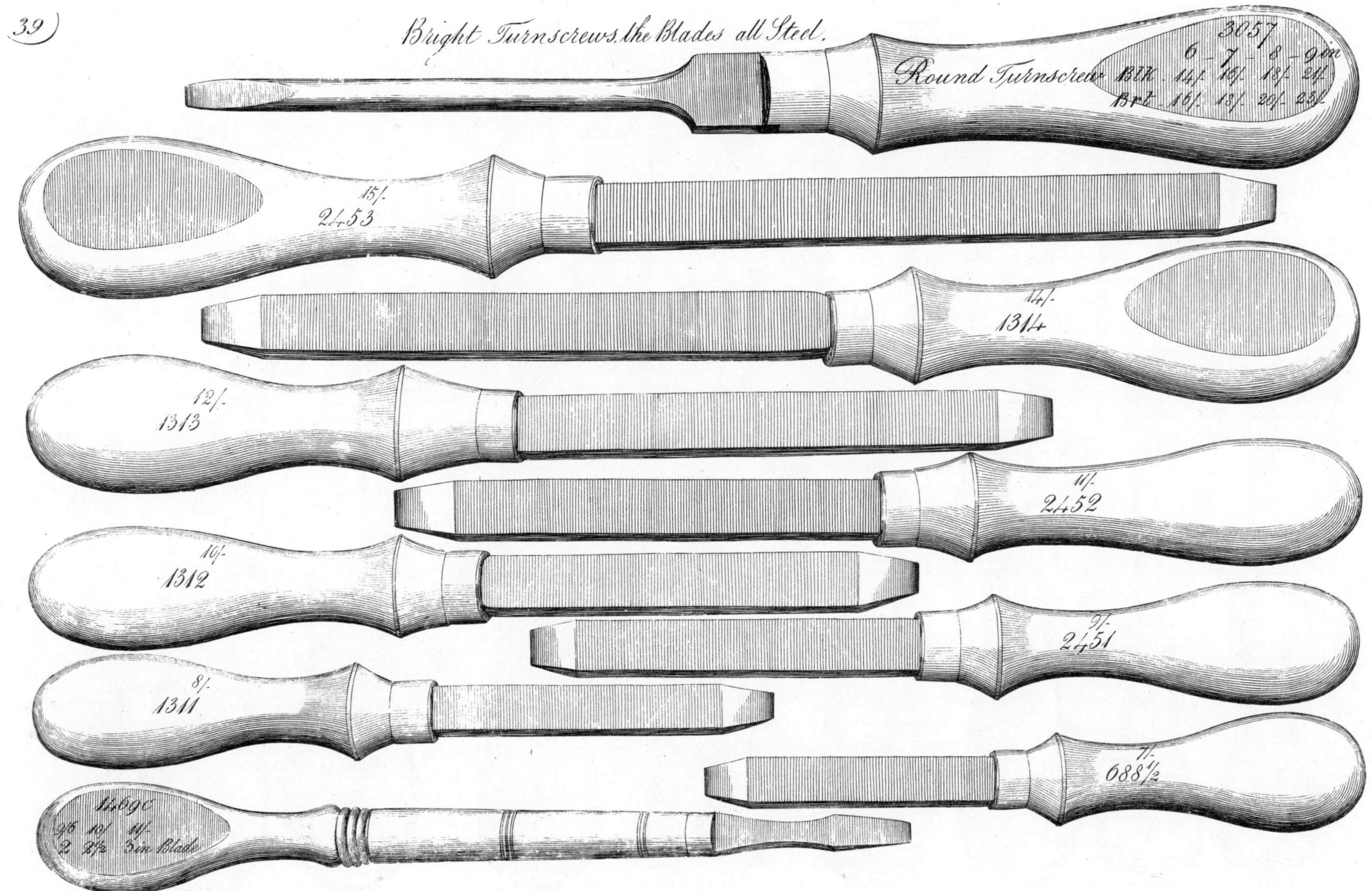
Bright Turnscrews, the Blades all Steel.
3057
Round Turnscrew Blk   14/.   16/.   18/.   24/.
6 - 7 - 8 - 9 in
Brt   16/.   18/.   20/.   26/.
15/.
2453
14/.
1314
12/.
1313
11/.
2452
10/.
1312
9/.
2451
8/.
1311
7/.
688½
1469 C
9½   10/   11/
2   2½   3 in Blade
7/.
688½

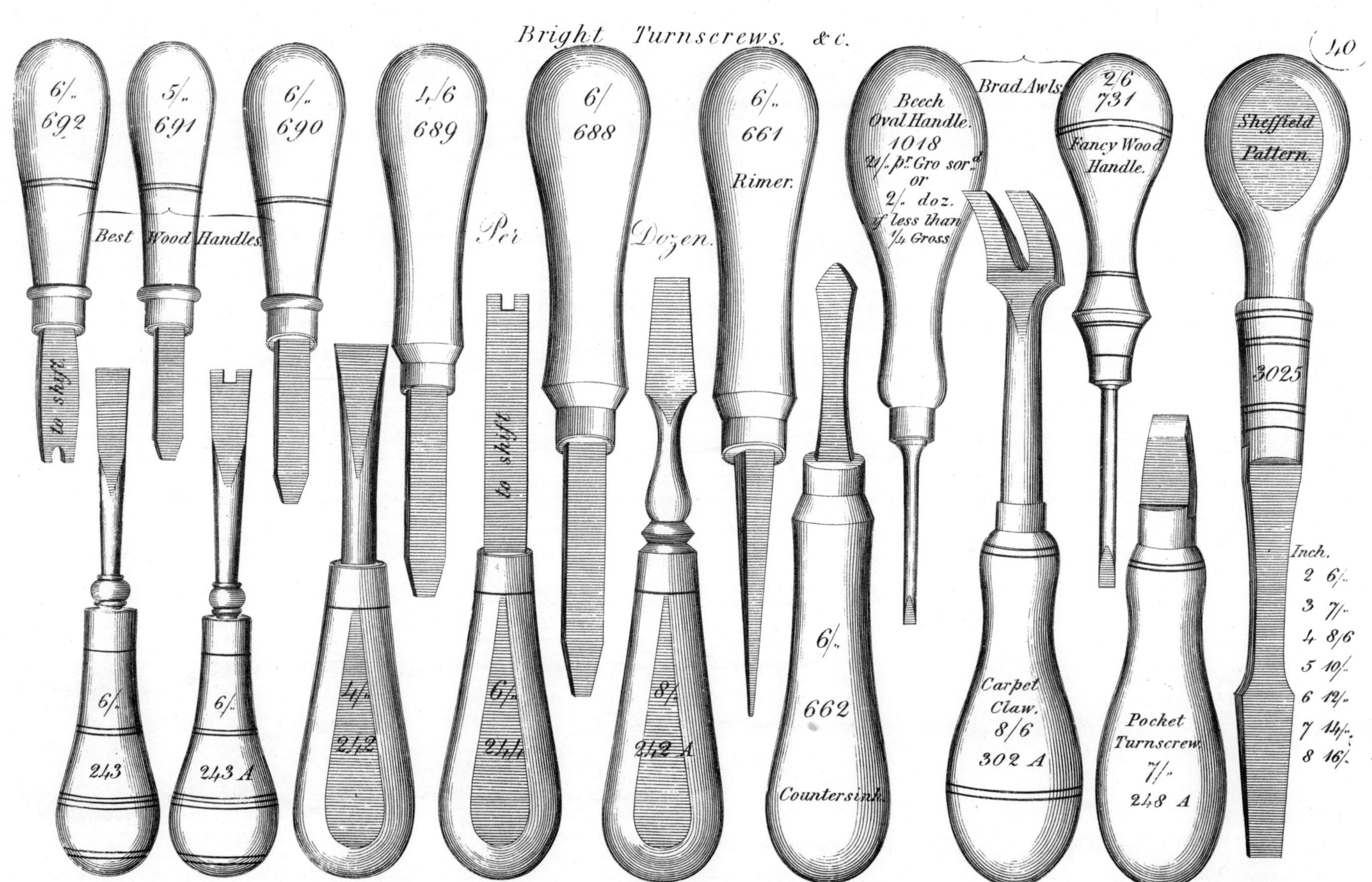

Bright Turnscrews. &c.
40
6/.. 692
5/.. 691
6/.. 690
1/6 689
6/ 688
6/ 661
Beech Oval Handle. 1018 21/. pr Gro sord or 2/. doz. if less than 1/4 Gross
Brad Awls.
2/6 731
Sheffield Pattern.
Best Wood Handles.
Per
Dozen.
Rimer.
Fancy Wood Handle.
to shift
to shift
3025
6/..
243
6/..
243 A
4/..
242
6/..
244
8/..
242 A
6/..
662
Countersink.
Carpet Claw. 8/6 302 A
Pocket Turnscrew 7/.. 248 A
Inch.
2 6/..
3 7/..
4 8/6
5 10/..
6 12/..
7 14/..
8 16/..

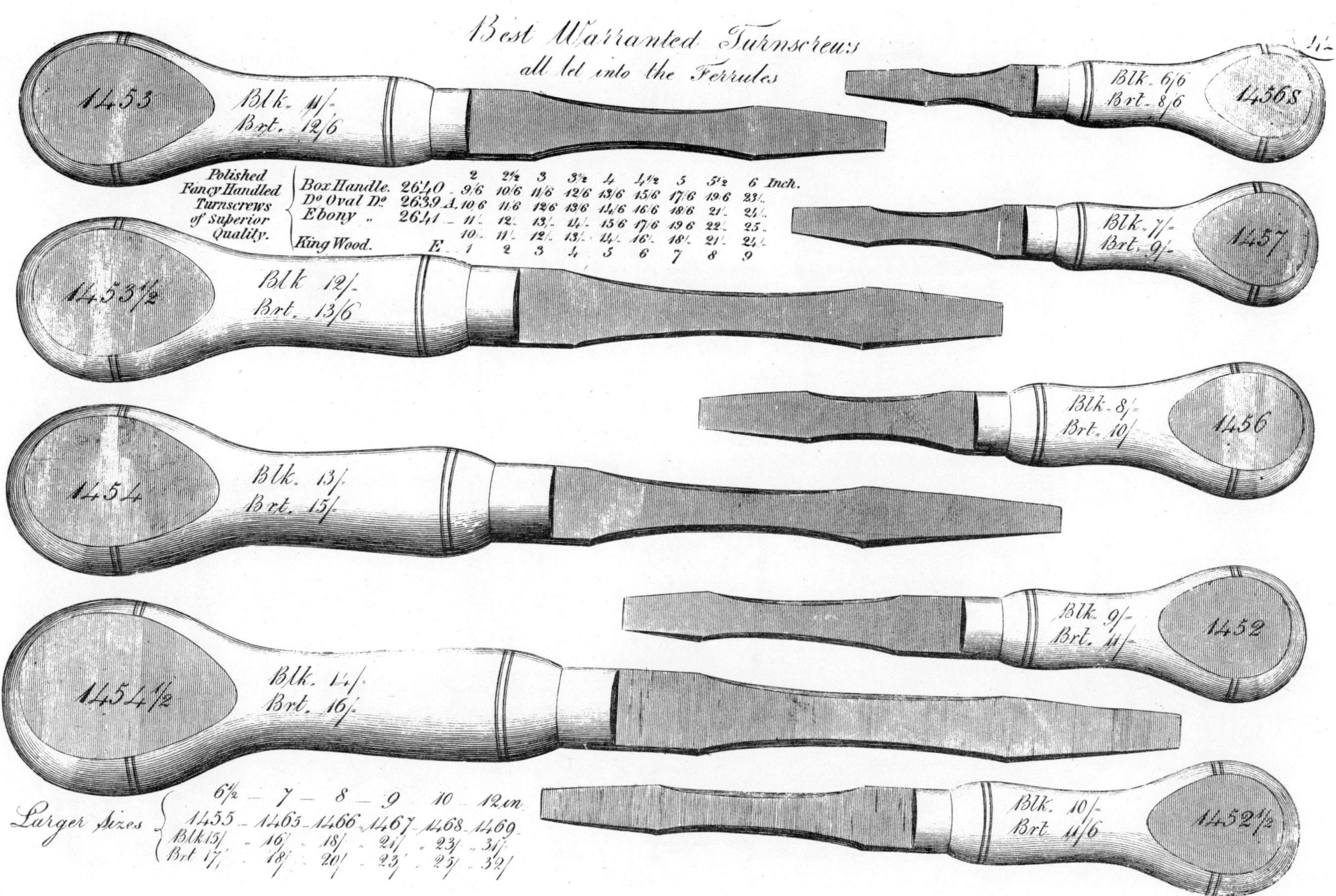

		2	2½	3	3½	4	4½	5	5½	6 Inch.
Box Handle.	2640	9/6	10/6	11/6	12/6	13/6	15/6	17/6	19/6	23/-
Do Oval Do	2639 A	10/6	11/6	12/6	13/6	14/6	16/6	18/6	21/-	24/-
Ebony "	2641	11/-	12/-	13/-	14/-	15/6	17/6	19/6	22/-	25.-
King Wood.		10/-	11/-	12/-	13/-	14/-	16/-	18/-	21/-	24/-
	E	1	2	3	4	5	6	7	8	9

	6½	7	8	9	10	12 in.
	1455	1465	1466	1467	1468	1469
Blk	15/-	16/-	18/-	21/-	23/-	31/-
Brt	17/-	18/-	20/-	23/-	25/-	32/-

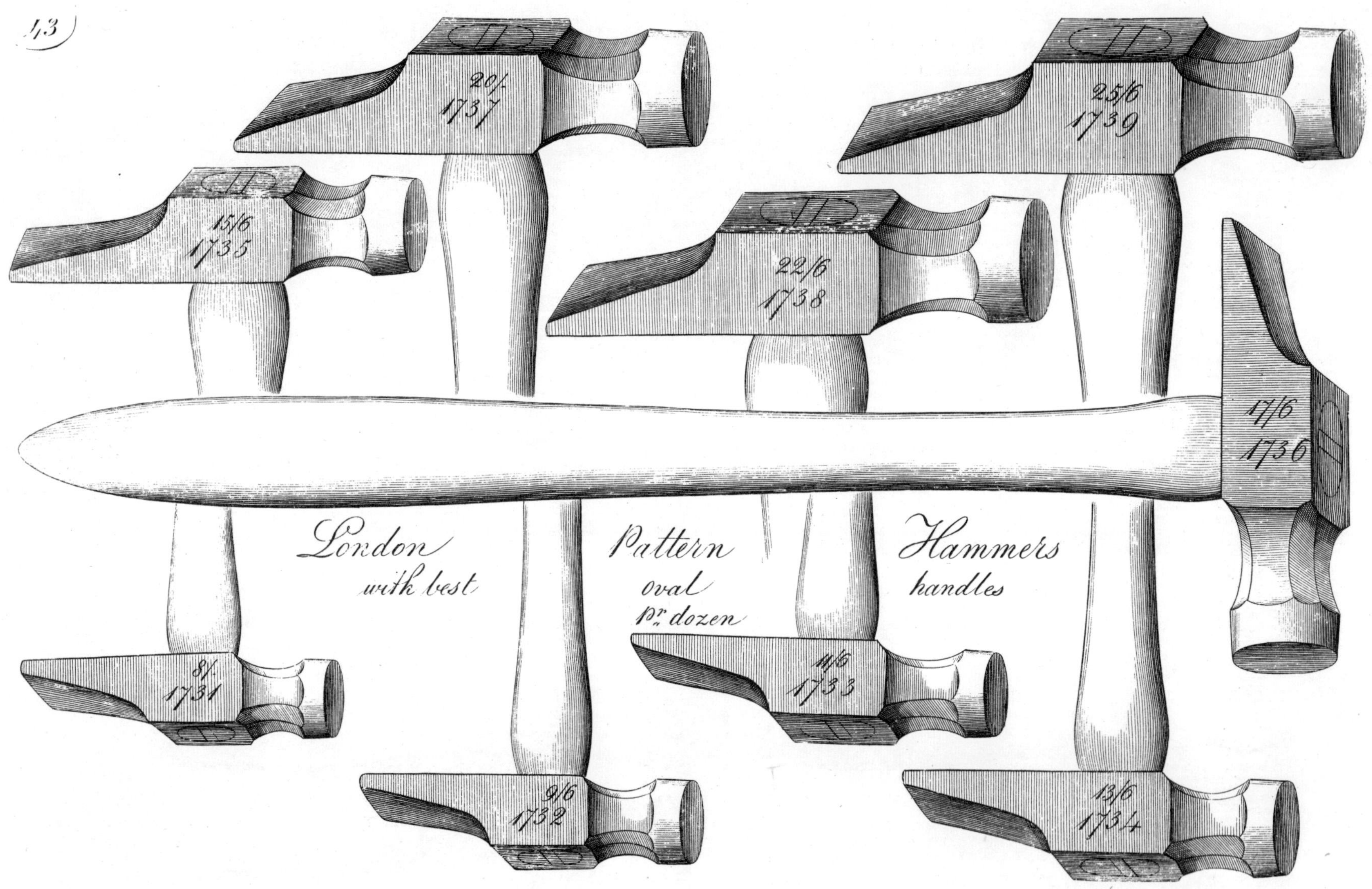
43
20/-
1737
25/6
1739
15/6
1735
22/6
1738
17/6
1736
London
with best
Pattern
oval
Pr. dozen
Hammers
handles
8/-
1731
9/6
1732
14/6
1733
13/6
1734

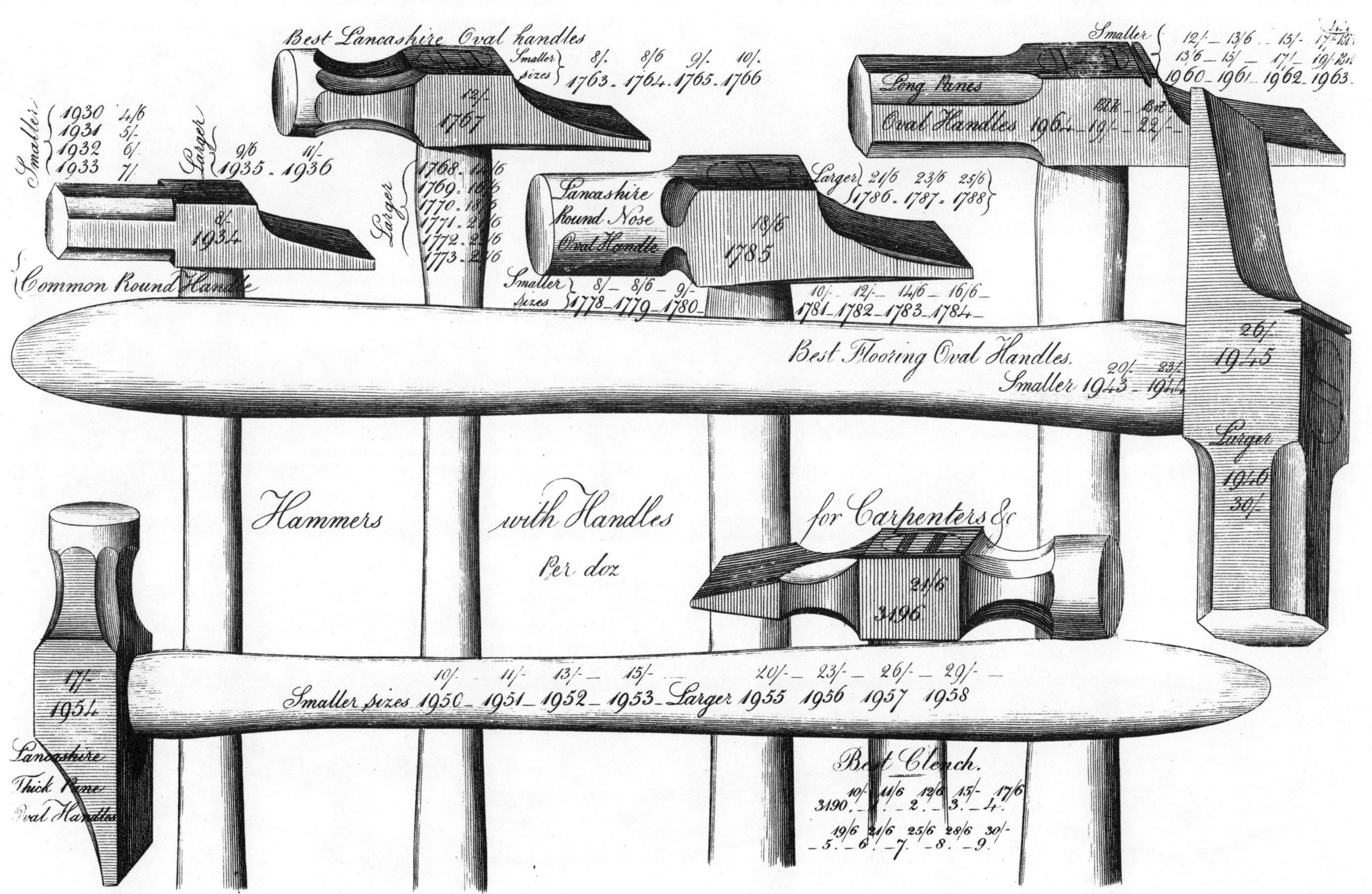

Best Lancashire Oval handles
Smaller sizes 8/. 8/6 9/. 10/. 1763. 1764. 1765. 1766
19/. 1767
Smaller 1930 4/6 1931 5/. 1932 6/. 1933 7/.
Larger 9/6 11/. 1935. 1936
8/. 1934
Common Round Handle
Larger 1768. 14/6 1769. 16/6 1770. 18/6 1771. 20/6 1772. 21/6 1773. 22/6
Lancashire Round Nose Oval Handle
18/6 1785
Larger 21/6 23/6 25/6 1786. 1787. 1788
Smaller sizes 8/. 8/6 9/. 1778. 1779. 1780
10/. 12/. 14/6 16/6 1781. 1782. 1783. 1784
Long Panes Oval Handles 1964 19/. 22/.
Smaller 12/. 13/6 15/. 13/6 15/. 17/. 19/. 1960. 1961. 1962. 1963
Best Flooring Oval Handles.
Smaller 1943 . 1944 20/. 23/. 26/. 1945
Larger 1946 30/.
Hammers with Handles for Carpenters &c
Per doz
24/6 3196
17/. 1954
Lancashire Thick Pane Oval Handles
10/. 11/. 13/. 15/. 20/. 23/. 26/. 29/.
Smaller sizes 1950. 1951. 1952. 1953. Larger 1955 1956 1957 1958
Best Clench.
10/. 11/6 12/6 15/. 17/6
3190. 1. 2. 3. 4.
19/6 21/6 25/6 28/6 30/.
5. 6. 7. 8. 9.

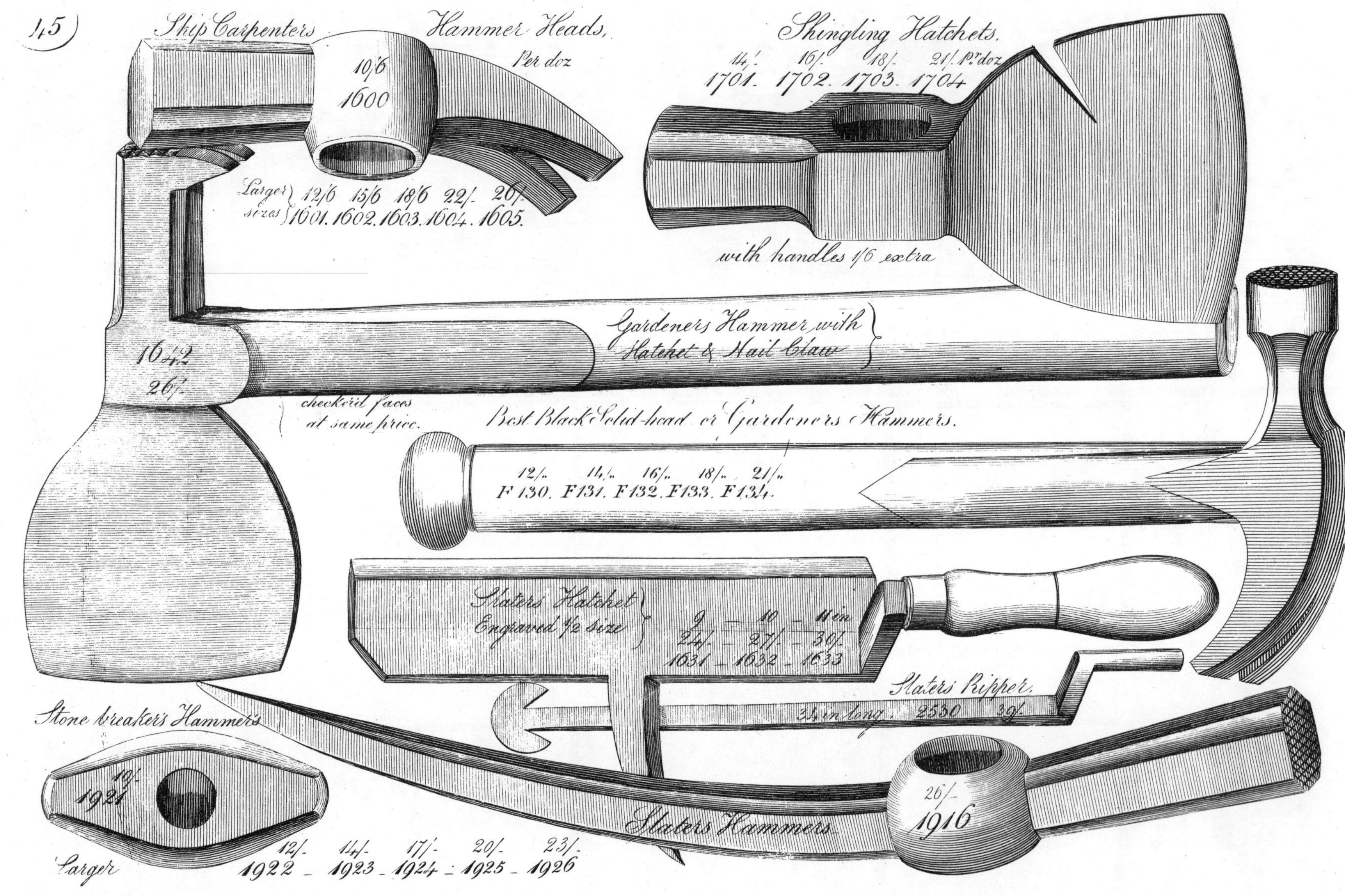

45
Ship Carpenters
Hammer Heads,
Per doz
10/6
1600
Larger sizes) 12/6 15/6 18/6 22/- 26/-
1601. 1602. 1603. 1604. 1605.
Shingling Hatchets.
14/- 16/- 18/- 21/- P.r doz
1701. 1702. 1703. 1704.
with handles 1/6 extra
1642
26/-
checkerd faces at same price.
Gardeners Hammer with Hatchet & Nail Claw
Best Black Solid-head or Gardeners Hammers.
12/- 14/- 16/- 18/- 21/-
F 130. F 131. F 132. F 133. F 134.
Slaters Hatchet Engraved ½ size
9 10 11 in
24/- 27/- 30/-
1631 1632 1633
Slaters Ripper.
34 in long. 2530 39/-
Stone breaker's Hammers
19/-
1921
Larger
12/- 14/- 17/- 20/- 23/-
1922 1923 1924 1925 1926
Slaters Hammers
26/-
1916

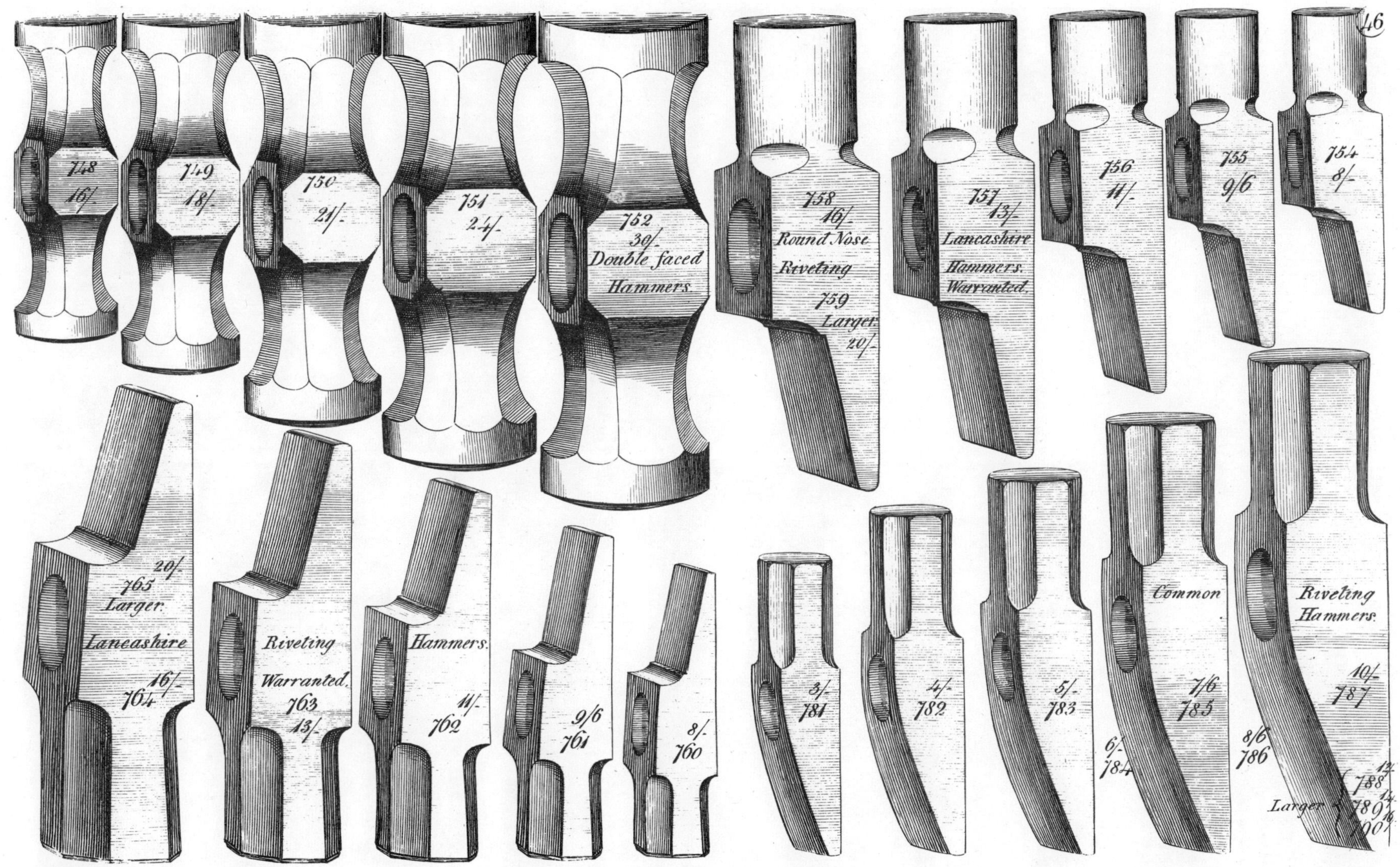
46
748
16/
749
18/
750
21/
751
2/4
752
30/
Double faced
Hammers.
758
16/
Round Nose
Riveting
759
Larger
20/
757
13/
Lancashire
Hammers.
Warranted.
756
11/
755
9/6
754
8/
20/
765
Larger.
Lancashire
16/
764
Riveting
Warranted.
763
13/
Hammers.
11/
762
9/6
761
8/
760
3/
781
4/
782
5/
783
6/
784
Common
7/6
785
8/6
786
Riveting
Hammers.
10/
787
Larger
12/
788
14/
789
16/
790

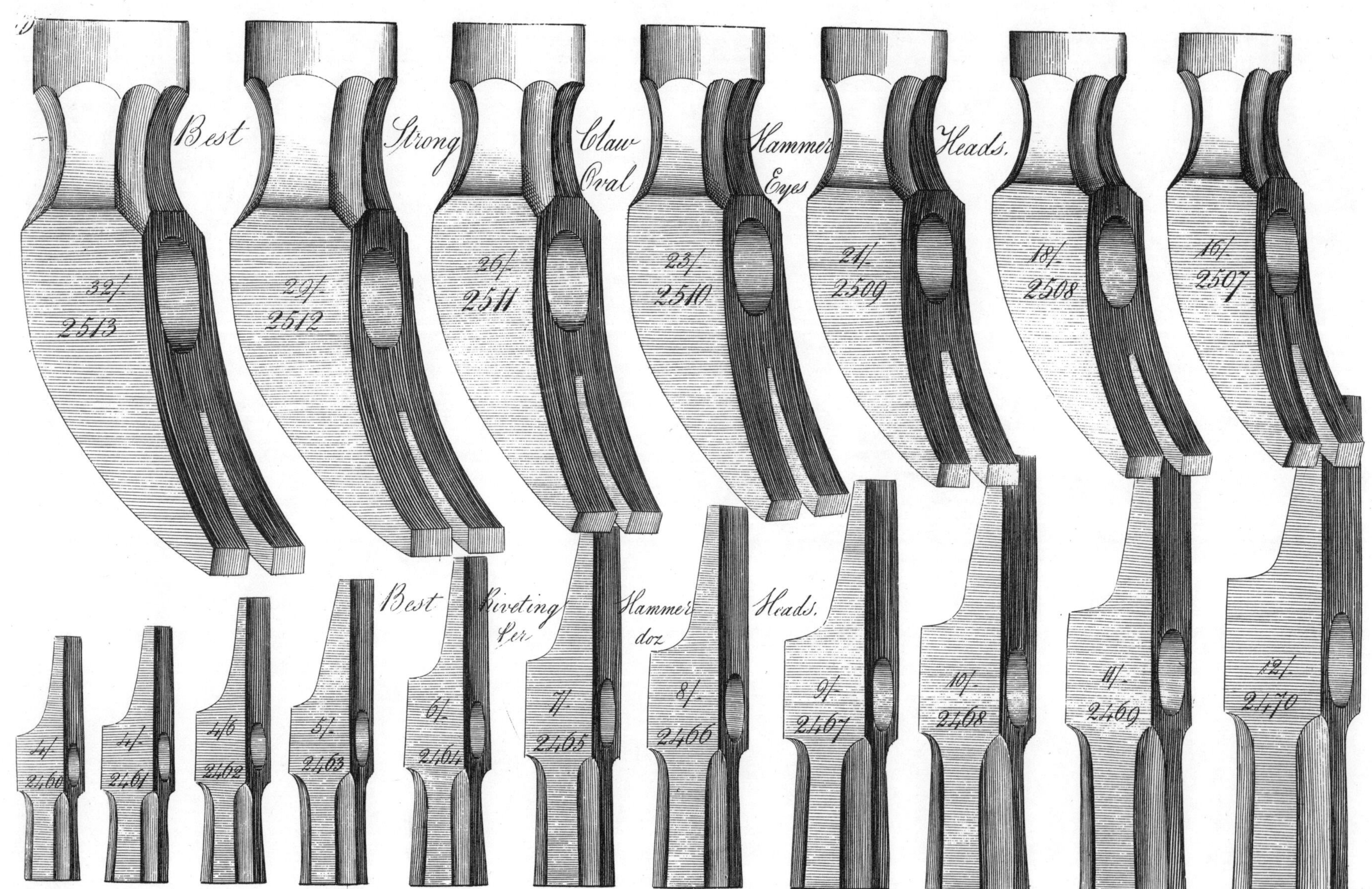

Best Strong Claw Oval Hammer Eyes Heads.
32/
2513
29/
2512
26/
2511
23/
2510
21/
2509
18/
2508
16/
2507
Best Riveting per Hammer doz Heads.
4/
2460
4/
2461
4/6
2462
5/
2463
6/
2464
7/
2465
8/
2466
9/
2467
10/
2468
11/
2469
12/
2470

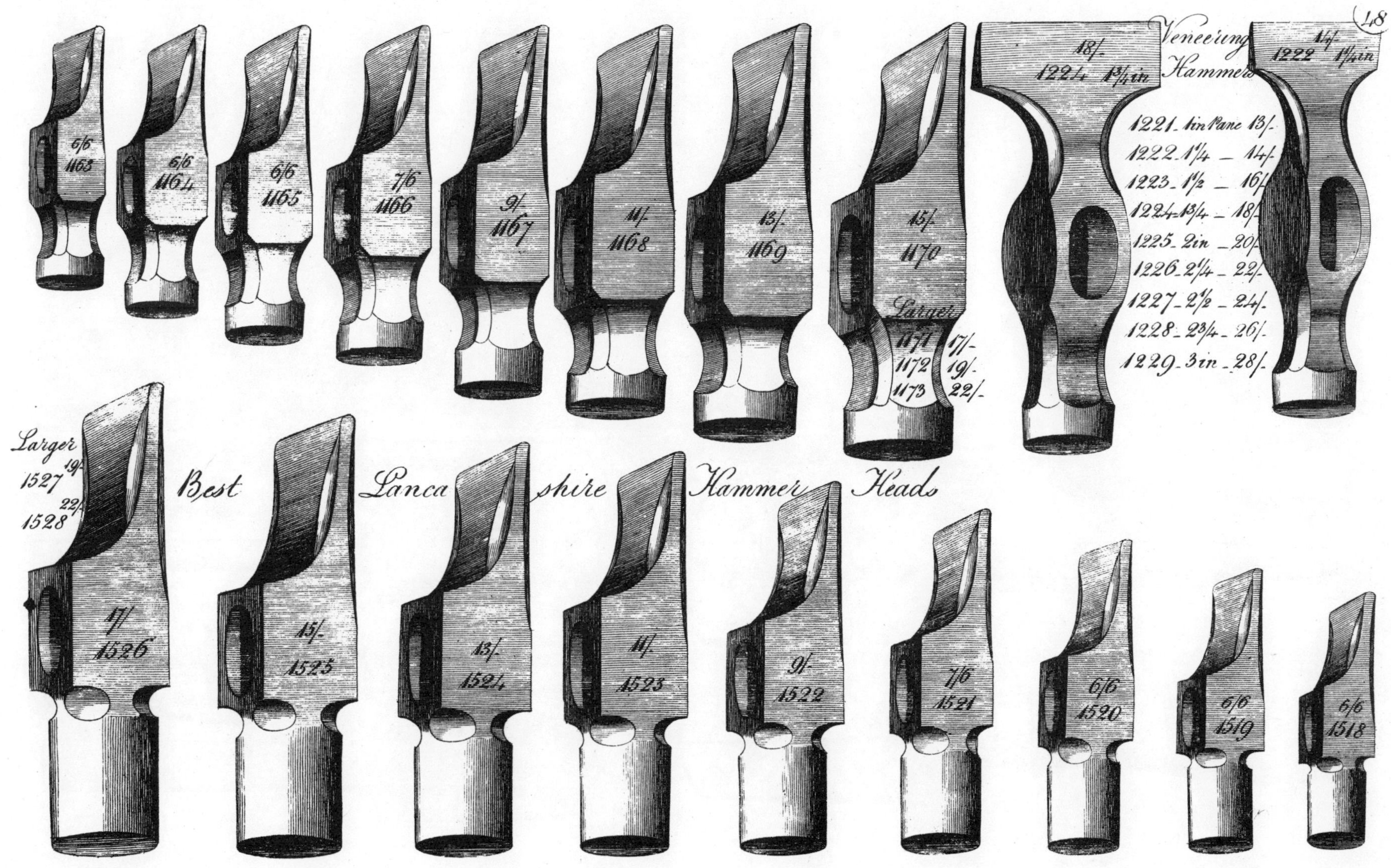
6/6
1163
6/6
1164
6/6
1165
7/6
1166
9/
1167
10/
1168
13/
1169
15/
1170
Larger
1171
1172
1173
17/
19/
22/
18/
1224 1¾ in
Veneering Hammers
1222 1¼ in
1221. 1 in Pane 13/-
1222. 1¼ — 14/-
1223. 1½ — 16/-
1224. 1¾ — 18/-
1225. 2 in — 20/-
1226. 2¼ — 22/-
1227. 2½ — 24/-
1228. 2¾ — 26/-
1229. 3 in — 28/-
Larger
1527
1528
19/
22/
Best Lanca shire Hammer Heads
17/
1526
15/
1525
13/
1524
14/
1523
9/
1522
7/6
1521
6/6
1520
6/6
1519
6/6
1518

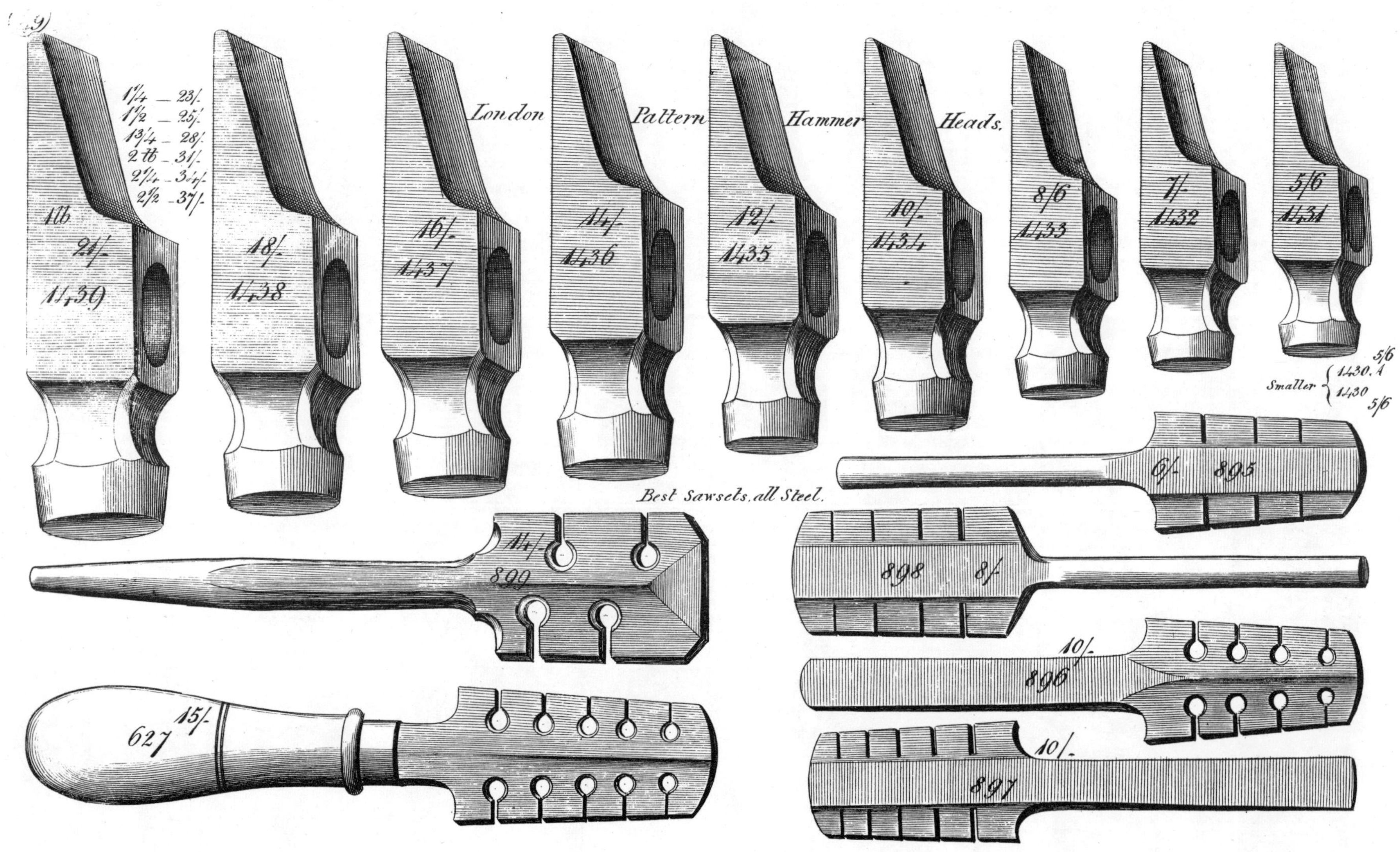

1 1/4 — 23/-
1 1/2 — 25/-
1 3/4 — 28/-
2 lb — 31/-
2 1/4 — 34/-
2 1/2 — 37/-
London Pattern Hammer Heads.
21/-
1439
18/-
1438
16/-
1437
14/-
1436
12/-
1435
10/-
1434
8/6
1433
7/-
1432
5/6
1431
Smaller { 1430. A
1430
5/6
5/6
Best Sawsets, all Steel.
6/-
895
14/-
899
898 8/-
10/-
896
15/-
627
10/-
897

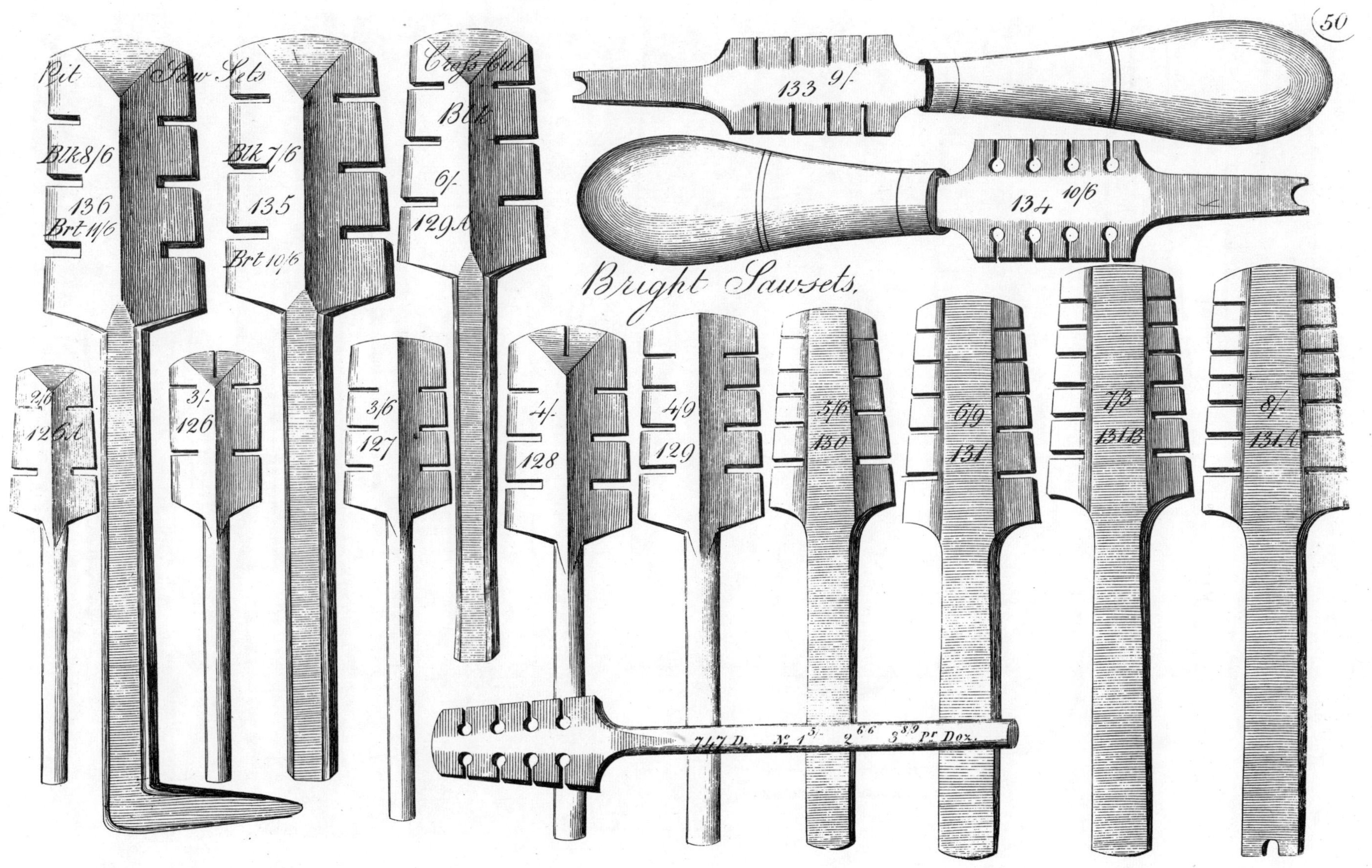

Rit
Saw Sets
Cross cut
Blk 8/6
Blk 7/6
Blt
136
135
6/-
Brt 11/6
Brt 10/6
129 A
133 9/-
134 10/6
Bright Sawsets.
2/6
126 A
3/-
126
3/6
127
4/-
128
4/9
129
5/6
130
6/9
131
7/3
131 B
8/-
131 A
747 D.   No 1 3/-   2 6/6   3 8/9 pr Doz.

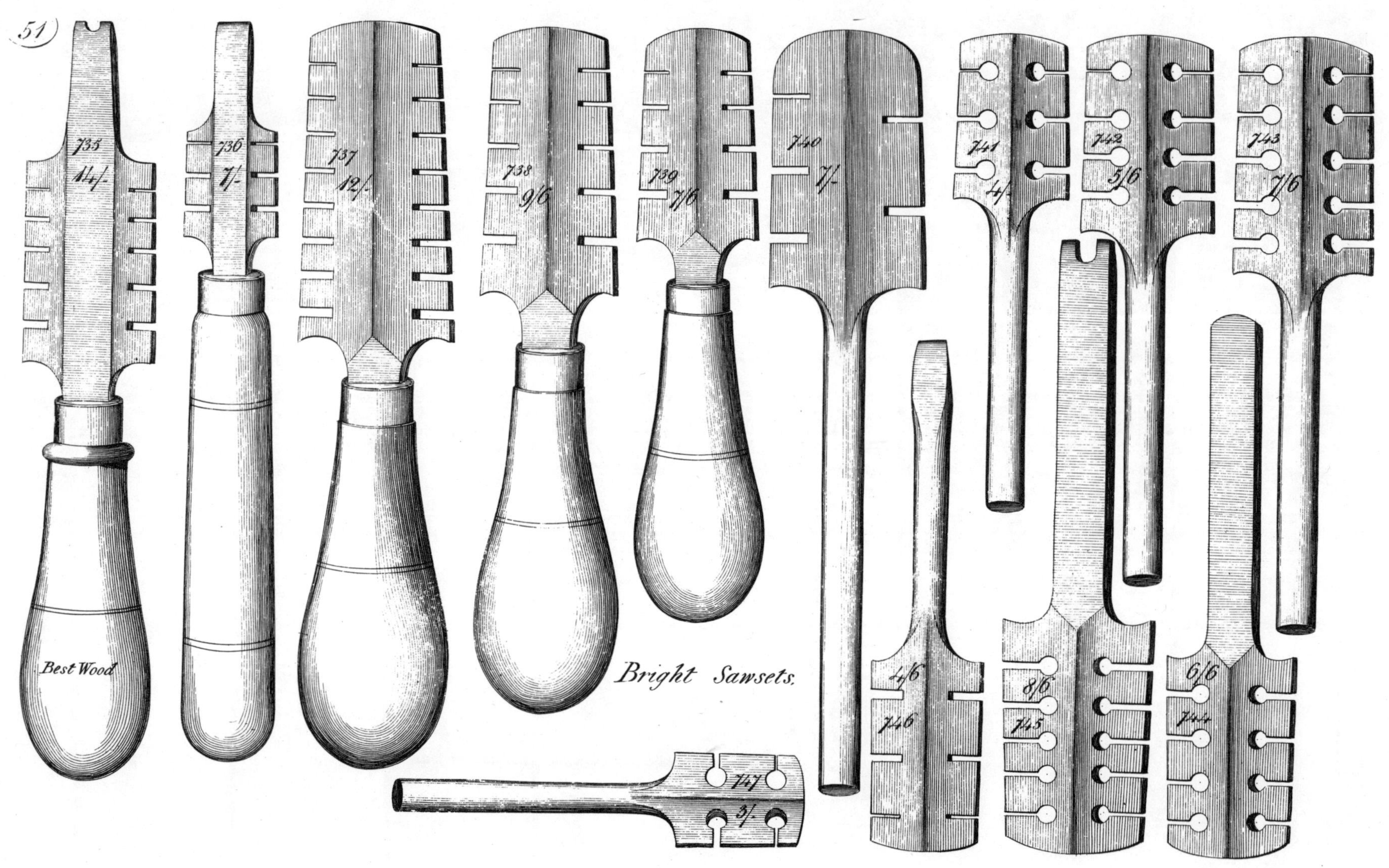

51
735
14/-
Best Wood
736
7/-
737
12/-
738
9/6
739
7/6
740
7/-
741
4/-
742
5/6
743
7/6
Bright Sawsets.
747
3/-
746
4/6
745
8/6
744
6/6

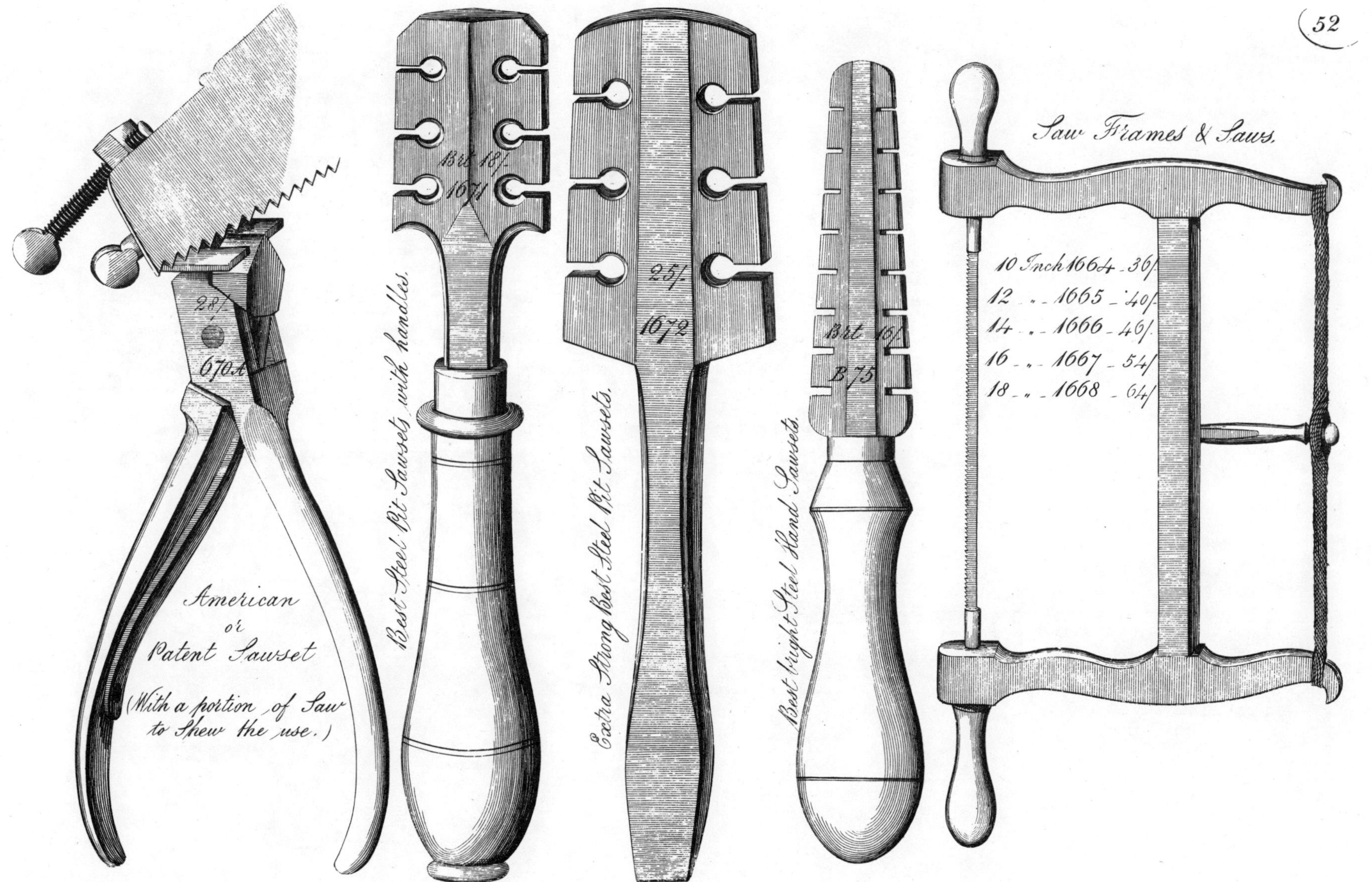
670A
28/
American
or
Patent Sawset
(With a portion of Saw
to Shew the use.)
Brt. 18/.
1671
Best Steel Pit Sawsets with handles.
25/
1672
Extra Strong Best Steel Pit Sawsets.
Brt. 16/
B.75
Best Bright Steel Hand Sawsets.
Saw Frames & Saws.
10 Inch 1664 . 36/
12 .. 1665 . 40/
14 .. 1666 . 46/
16 .. 1667 . 54/
18 .. 1668 . 64/
52

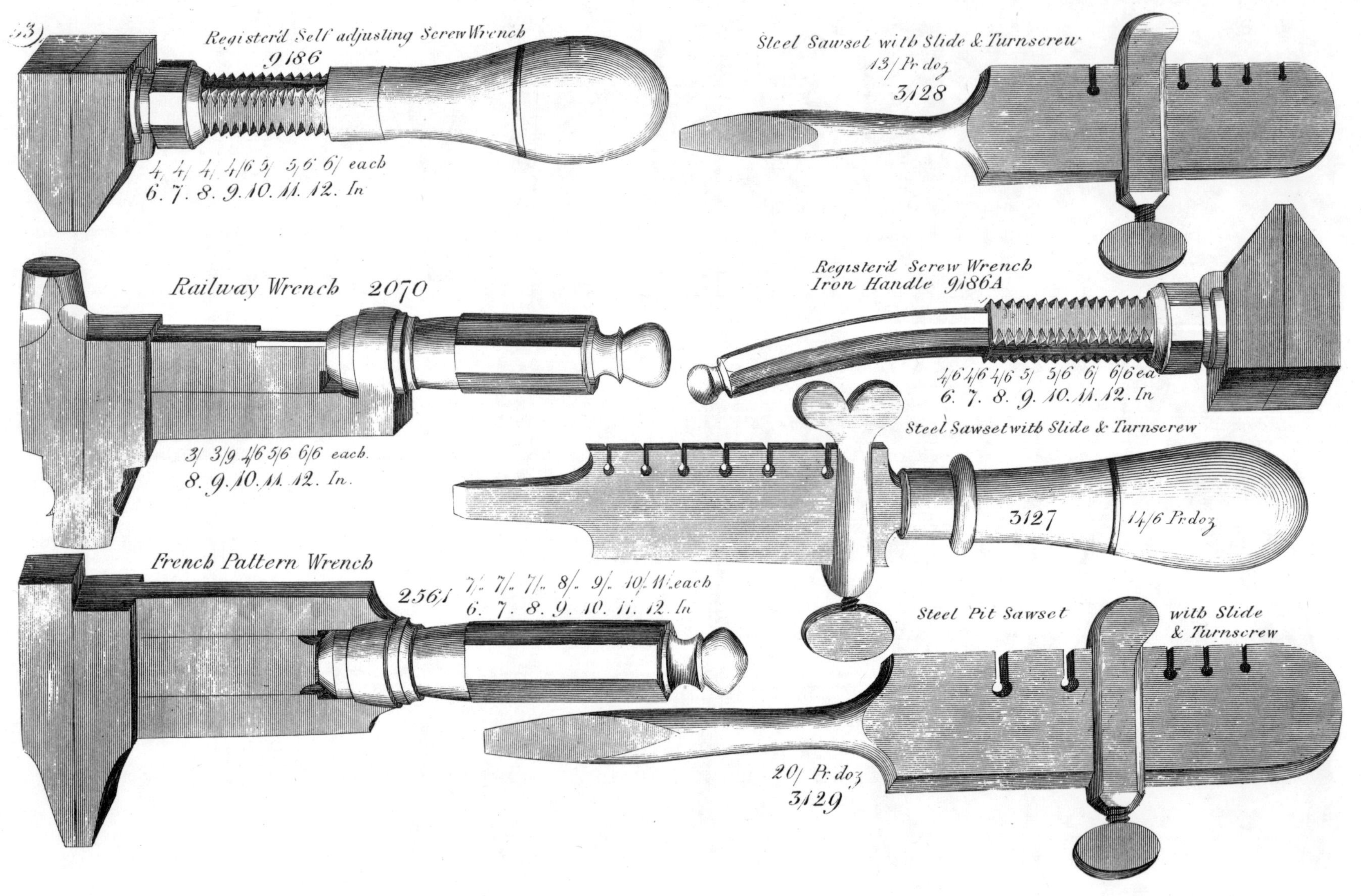
53
Registerd Self adjusting Screw Wrench
9186
4/ 4/ 4/ 4/6 5/ 5/6 6/ each
6. 7. 8. 9. 10. 11. 12. In
Steel Sawset with Slide & Turnscrew
13/ Pr doz
3128
Railway Wrench 2070
3/ 3/9 4/6 5/6 6/6 each.
8. 9. 10. 11. 12. In.
Registerd Screw Wrench
Iron Handle 9186A
4/6 4/6 4/6 5/ 5/6 6/ 6/6 ea.
6. 7. 8. 9. 10. 11. 12. In
Steel Sawset with Slide & Turnscrew
3127 14/6 Pr doz
French Pattern Wrench
2561 7/ 7/ 7/ 8/ 9/ 10/ 11/ each
6. 7. 8. 9. 10. 11. 12. In
Steel Pit Sawset with Slide & Turnscrew
20/ Pr doz
3129

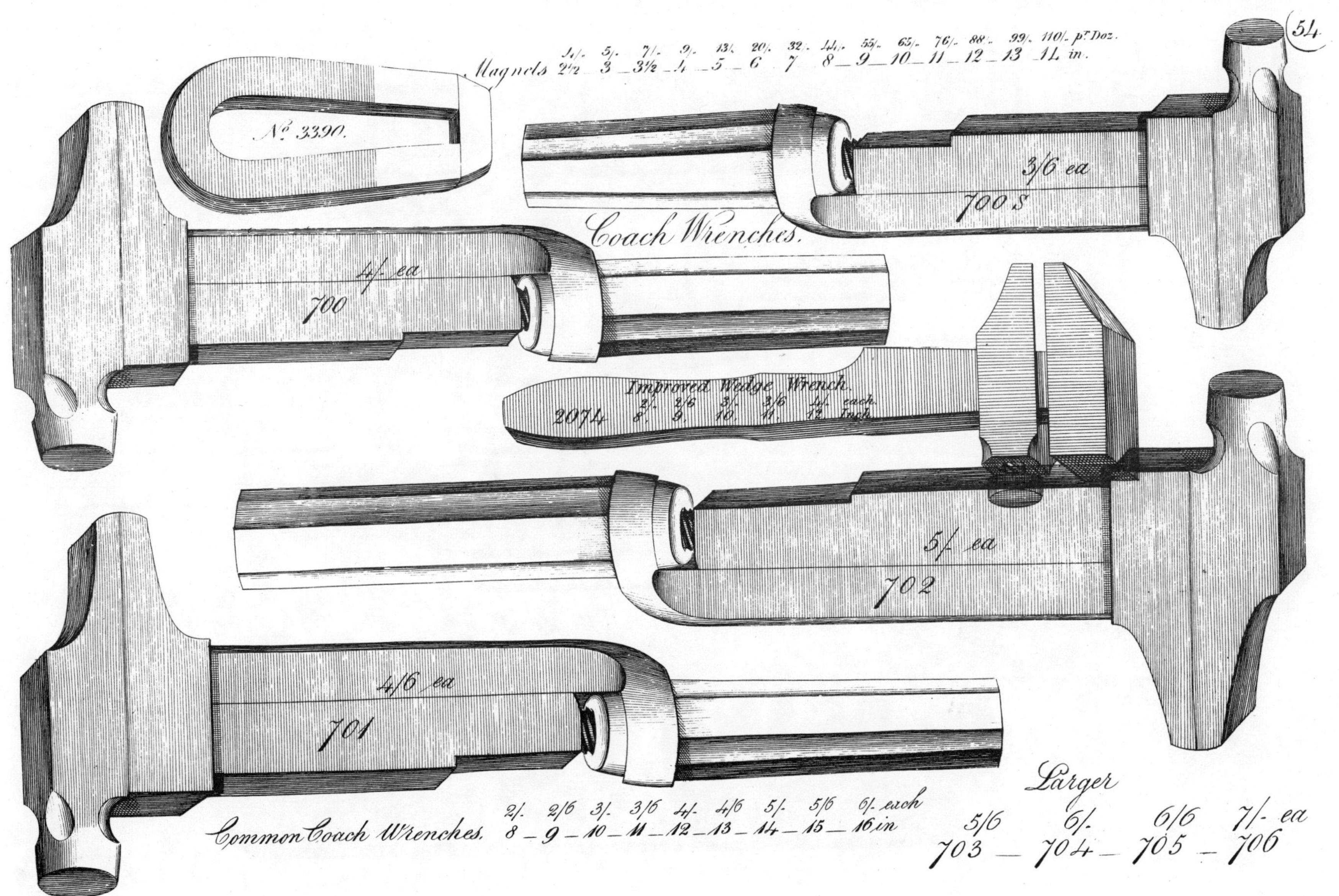
54
4/. 5/. 7/. 9/. 13/. 20/. 32/. 44/. 55/. 65/. 76/. 88/. 99/. 110/. pr Doz.
Magnets 2½ 3 3½ 4 5 6 7 8 9 10 11 12 13 14 in.
No 3390.
Coach Wrenches.
3/6 ea
700 S
4/. ea
700
Improved Wedge Wrench.
2074
2/. 2/6 3/. 3/6 4/. each
8 9 10 11 12 Inch
5/. ea
702
4/6 ea
701
Larger
Common Coach Wrenches.
2/. 2/6 3/. 3/6 4/. 4/6 5/. 5/6 6/. each
8 — 9 — 10 — 11 — 12 — 13 — 14 — 15 — 16 in
5/6 6/. 6/6 7/. ea
703 — 704 — 705 — 706

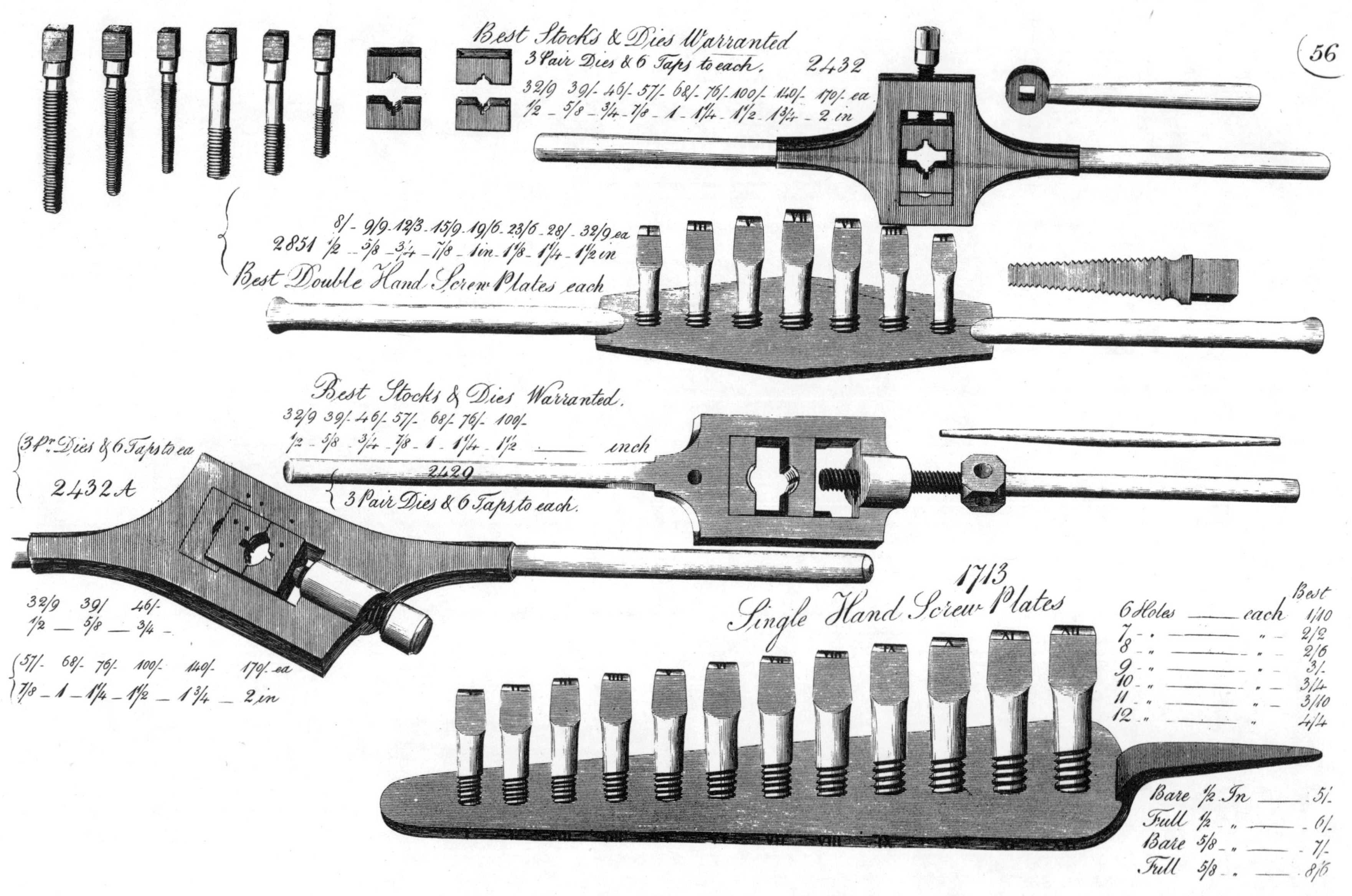
Best Stocks & Dies Warranted
3 Pair Dies & 6 Taps to each.   2432
32/9 39/- 46/- 57/- 68/- 76/- 100/- 140/- 170/- ea
1/2 - 5/8 - 3/4 - 7/8 - 1 - 1 1/4 - 1 1/2 - 1 3/4 - 2 in
(56)
8/- 9/9. 12/3. 15/9. 19/6. 23/6. 28/. 32/9 ea
2851 1/2 - 5/8 - 3/4 - 7/8 - 1 in - 1 1/8 - 1 1/4 - 1 1/2 in
Best Double Hand Screw Plates each
Best Stocks & Dies Warranted.
32/9 39/- 46/- 57/- 68/- 76/- 100/-
1/2 - 5/8 - 3/4 - 7/8 - 1 - 1 1/4 - 1 1/2 ______ inch
2420
3 Pair Dies & 6 Taps to each.
3 Pr. Dies & 6 Taps to ea
2432A
32/9   39/   46/-
1/2 - 5/8 - 3/4 -
57/- 68/- 76/- 100/- 140/- 170/- ea
7/8 - 1 - 1 1/4 - 1 1/2 - 1 3/4 - 2 in
1713
Single Hand Screw Plates
6 Holes ____ each   Best 1/10
7 "   ____ "   2/2
8 "   ____ "   2/6
9 "   ____ "   3/
10 "   ____ "   3/4
11 "   ____ "   3/10
12 "   ____ "   4/4
Bare 1/2 In ____ 5/.
Full 1/2 " ____ 6/.
Bare 5/8 " ____ 7/.
Full 5/8 " ____ 8/6

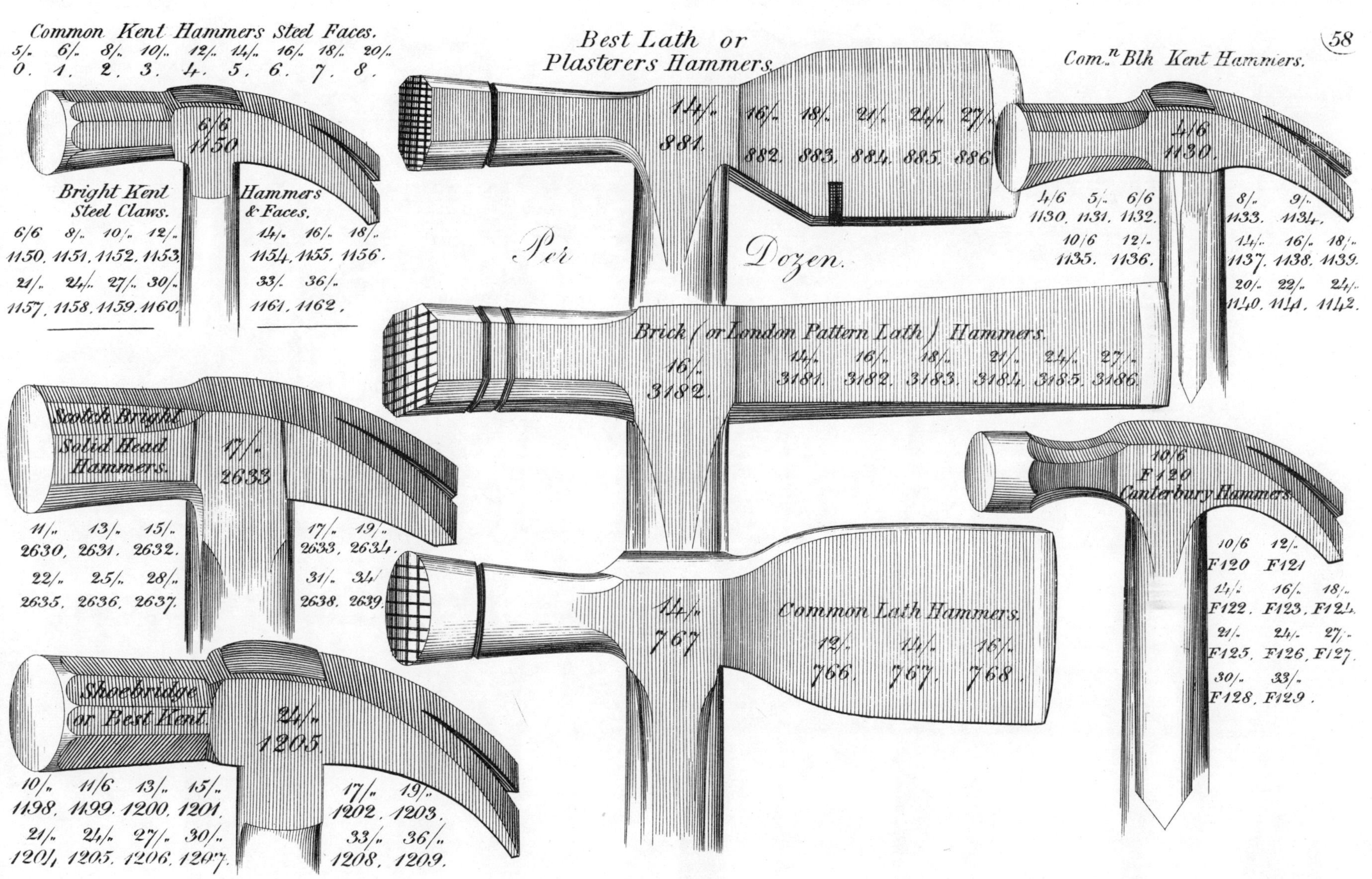

Common Kent Hammers Steel Faces.
5/- 6/- 8/- 10/- 12/- 14/- 16/- 18/- 20/-
0.   1.   2.   3.   4.   5.   6.   7.   8.

Best Lath or Plasterers Hammers.
14/-   16/- 18/- 21/- 24/- 27/-
881.   882. 883. 884. 885. 886.

Com.n Blk Kent Hammers.
6/6
1150

4/6
1130.

Bright Kent Steel Claws.
6/6   8/-   10/- 12/-
1150. 1151. 1152. 1153.
21/- 24/- 27/- 30/-
1157. 1158. 1159. 1160.

Hammers & Faces.
14/- 16/- 18/-
1154. 1155. 1156.
33/- 36/-
1161. 1162.

Per   Dozen.

4/6   5/-   6/6
1130. 1131. 1132.
10/6 12/-
1135. 1136.
8/-   9/-
1133. 1134.
14/- 16/- 18/-
1137. 1138. 1139.
20/- 22/- 24/-
1140. 1141. 1142.

Brick (or London Pattern Lath) Hammers.
16/-   14/- 16/- 18/- 21/- 24/- 27/-
3182.   3181. 3182. 3183. 3184. 3185. 3186.

Scotch Bright Solid Head Hammers.
17/-
2633

11/- 13/- 15/-
2630. 2631. 2632.
22/- 25/- 28/-
2635. 2636. 2637.
17/- 19/-
2633. 2634.
31/- 34/-
2638. 2639.

10/6
F120
Canterbury Hammers.

10/6 12/-
F120 F121
14/- 16/- 18/-
F122. F123. F124.
21/- 24/- 27/-
F125. F126. F127.
30/- 33/-
F128. F129.

Shoebridge or Best Kent.
24/-
1205.

14/-
767

Common Lath Hammers.
12/- 14/- 16/-
766. 767. 768.

10/- 11/6 13/- 15/-
1198. 1199. 1200. 1201.
21/- 24/- 27/- 30/-
1204. 1205. 1206. 1207.
17/- 19/-
1202. 1203.
33/- 36/-
1208. 1209.

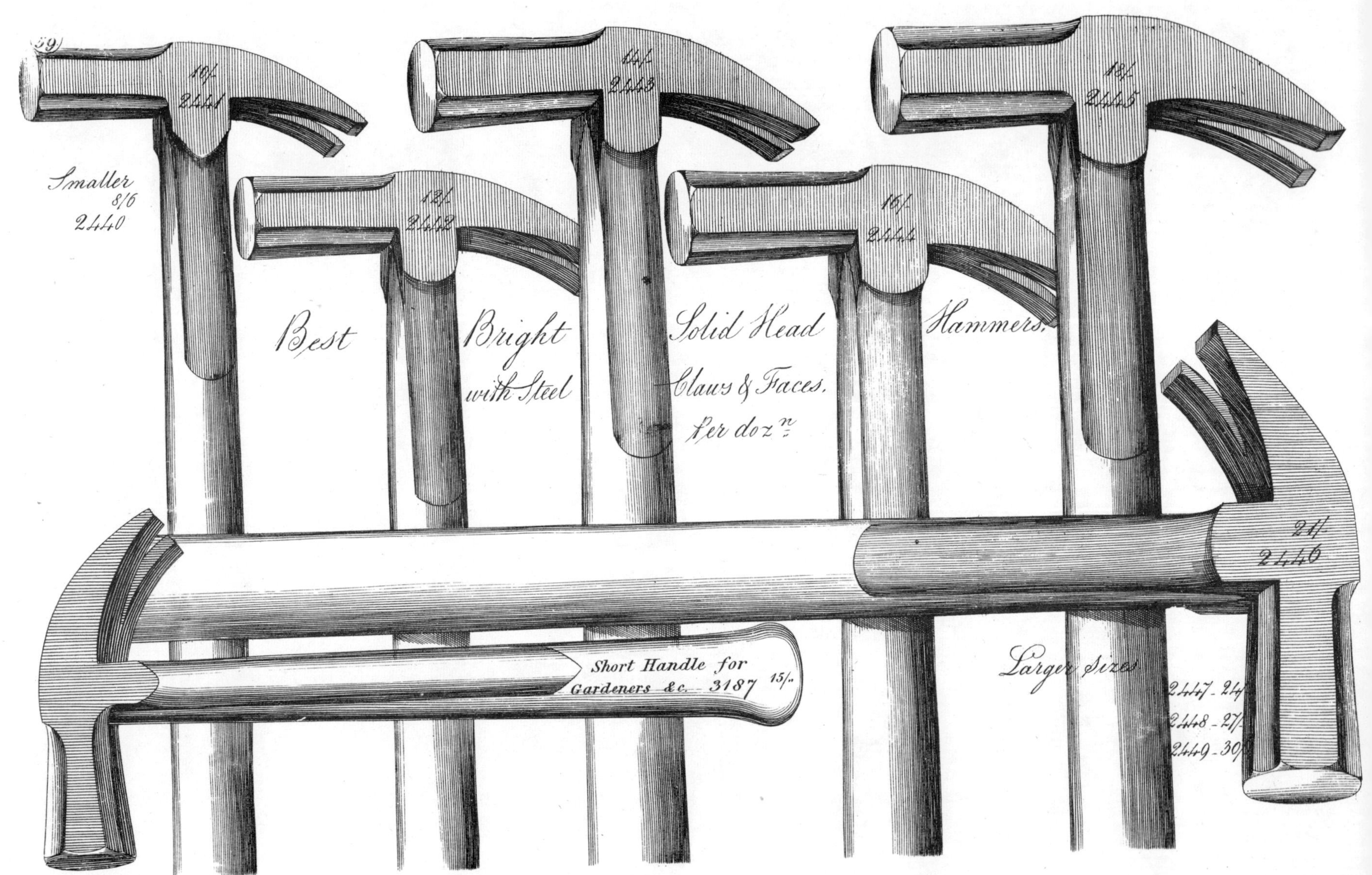
59
Smaller
8/6
2440
10/.
2441
14/.
2443
18/.
2445
Best
12/.
2442
16/.
2444
Bright
with Steel
Solid Head
Claws & Faces.
Per dozn
Hammers.
21/.
2446
Short Handle for
Gardeners &c. 3187 15/-
Larger Sizes
2447 - 24/.
2448 - 27/.
2449 - 30/.

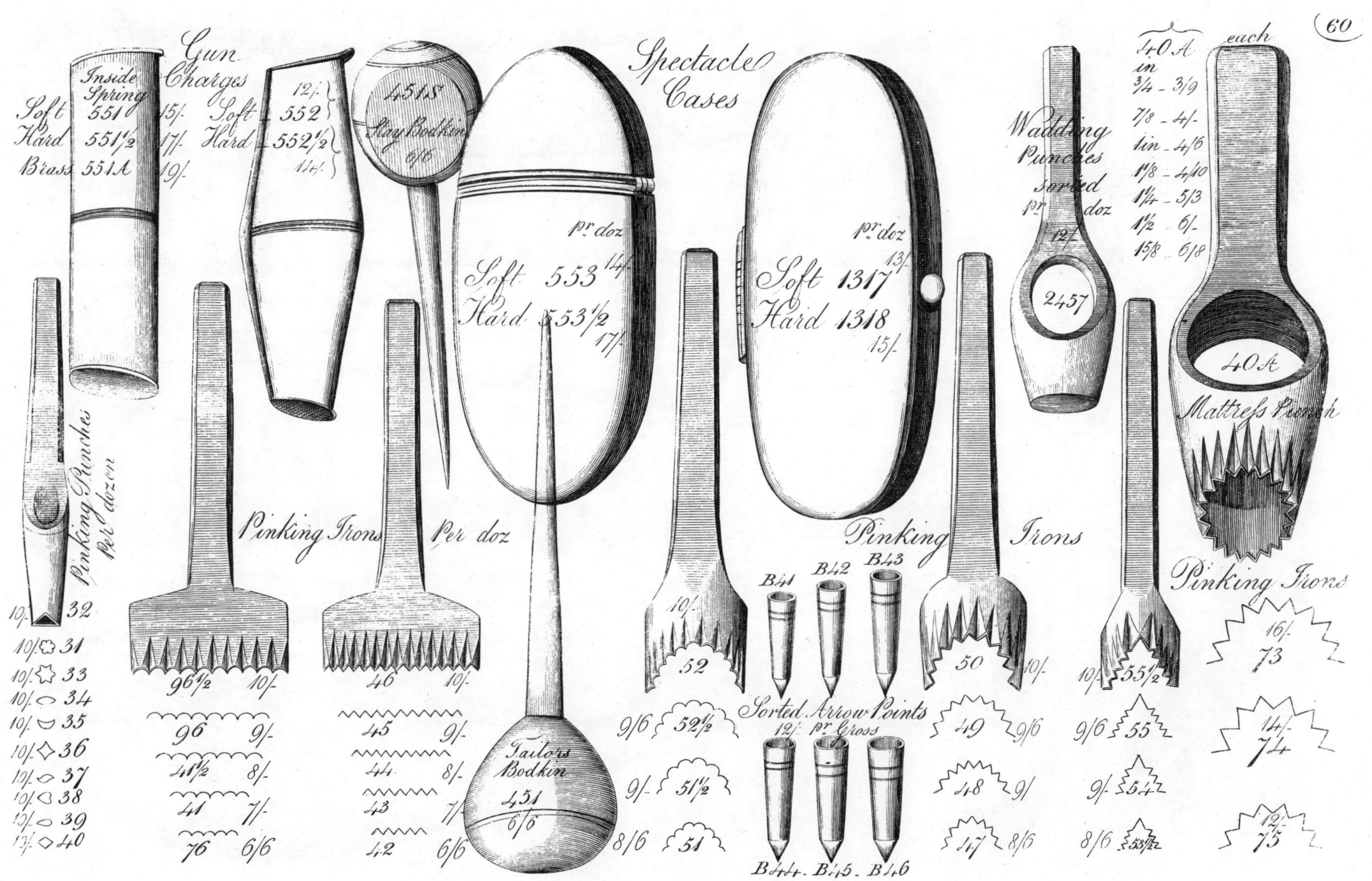

Gun Charges
Inside Spring
Soft 551 15/
Hard 551½ 17/
Brass 551A 19/
Soft 552 12/
Hard 552½ 14/
451S
Stay Bodkin 6/6
Spectacle Cases
pr doz
Soft 553 14/
Hard 553½ 17/
pr doz
Soft 1317 13/
Hard 1318 15/
Wadding Punches sorted
pr doz
12/
2457
4 O A each
in
3/4 - 3/9
7/8 - 4/
1in - 4/6
1 1/8 - 4/10
1 1/4 - 5/3
1 1/2 - 6/
1 5/8 - 6/8
40 A
Mattress Punch
Pinking Punches Per dozen
10/ 32
10/ 31
10/ 33
10/ 34
10/ 35
10/ 36
10/ 37
10/ 38
10/ 39
10/ 40
Pinking Irons Per doz
96½ 10/
96 9/
41½ 8/
41 7/
76 6/6
46 10/
45 9/
44 8/
43 7/
42 6/6
Tailors Bodkin
451
6/6
10/ 52
9/6 52½
9/ 51½
8/6 51
Pinking Irons
B44 B42 B43
Sorted Arrow Points
12/ pr Gross
B44. B45. B46
50 10/
49 9/6
48 9/
47 8/6
10/ 55½
9/6 55
9/ 54½
8/6 53½
Pinking Irons
16/ 73
14/ 74
12/ 75

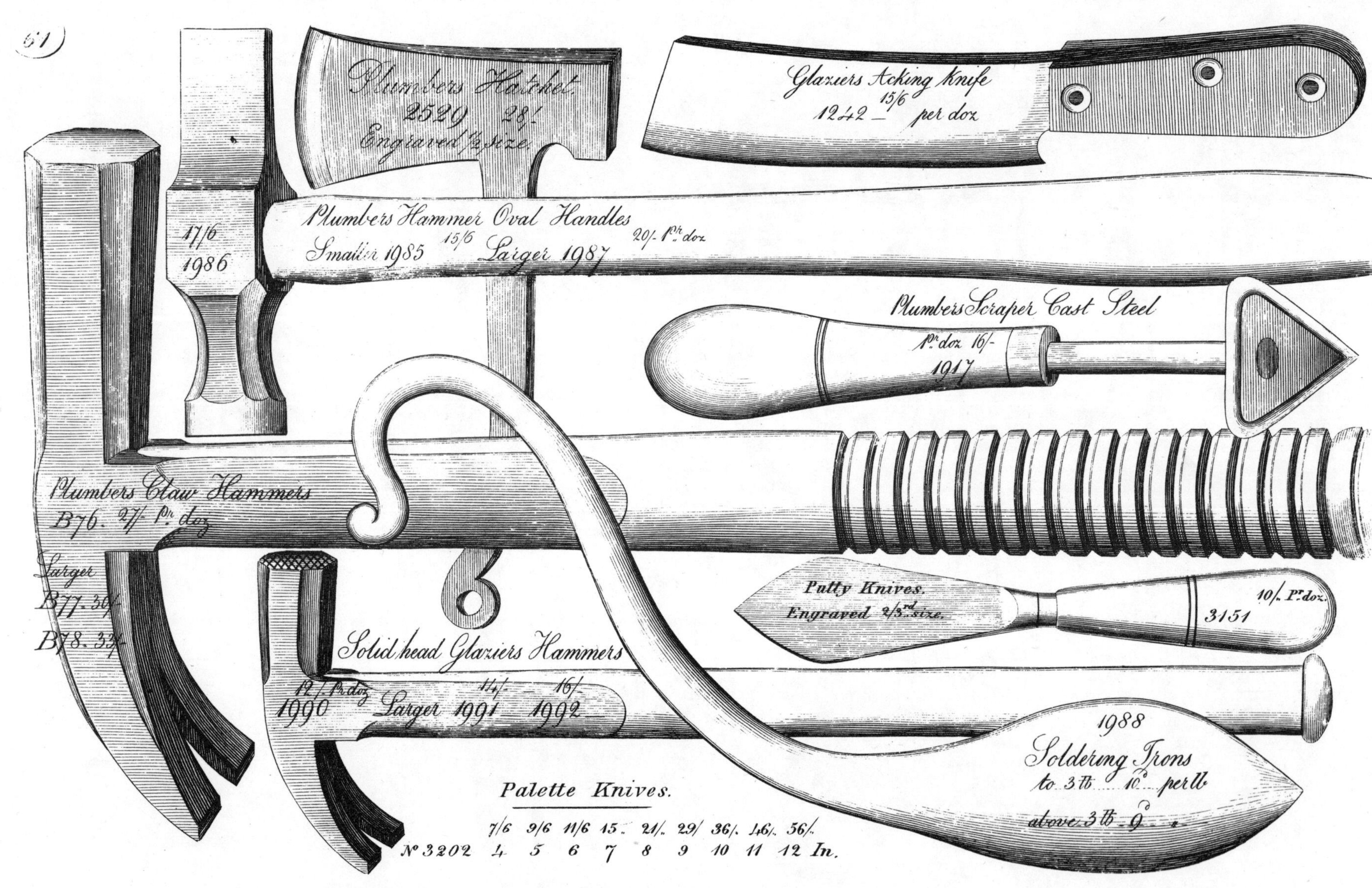
51
Plumbers Hatchet
2529   28/
Engraved 1/3 size
Glaziers Acking Knife
15/6
1242 — per doz.
Plumbers Hammer Oval Handles
15/6
Smaller 1985   Larger 1987   20/ Pr doz
17/6
1986
Plumbers Scraper Cast Steel
Pr doz 16/
1917
Plumbers Claw Hammers
B76. 2/ Pr doz
Larger
B77. 3/
B78. 3/
Solid head Glaziers Hammers
12/ Pr doz   14/   16/
1990   Larger 1991   1992
Putty Knives.
Engraved 2/3rd size.
10/ Pr doz.
3151
1988
Soldering Irons
to 3 lb 10d per lb
above 3 lb 9d
Palette Knives.
7/6 9/6 11/6 15. 21/. 29/ 36/. 46/. 56/.
No 3202   4   5   6   7   8   9   10   11   12 In.

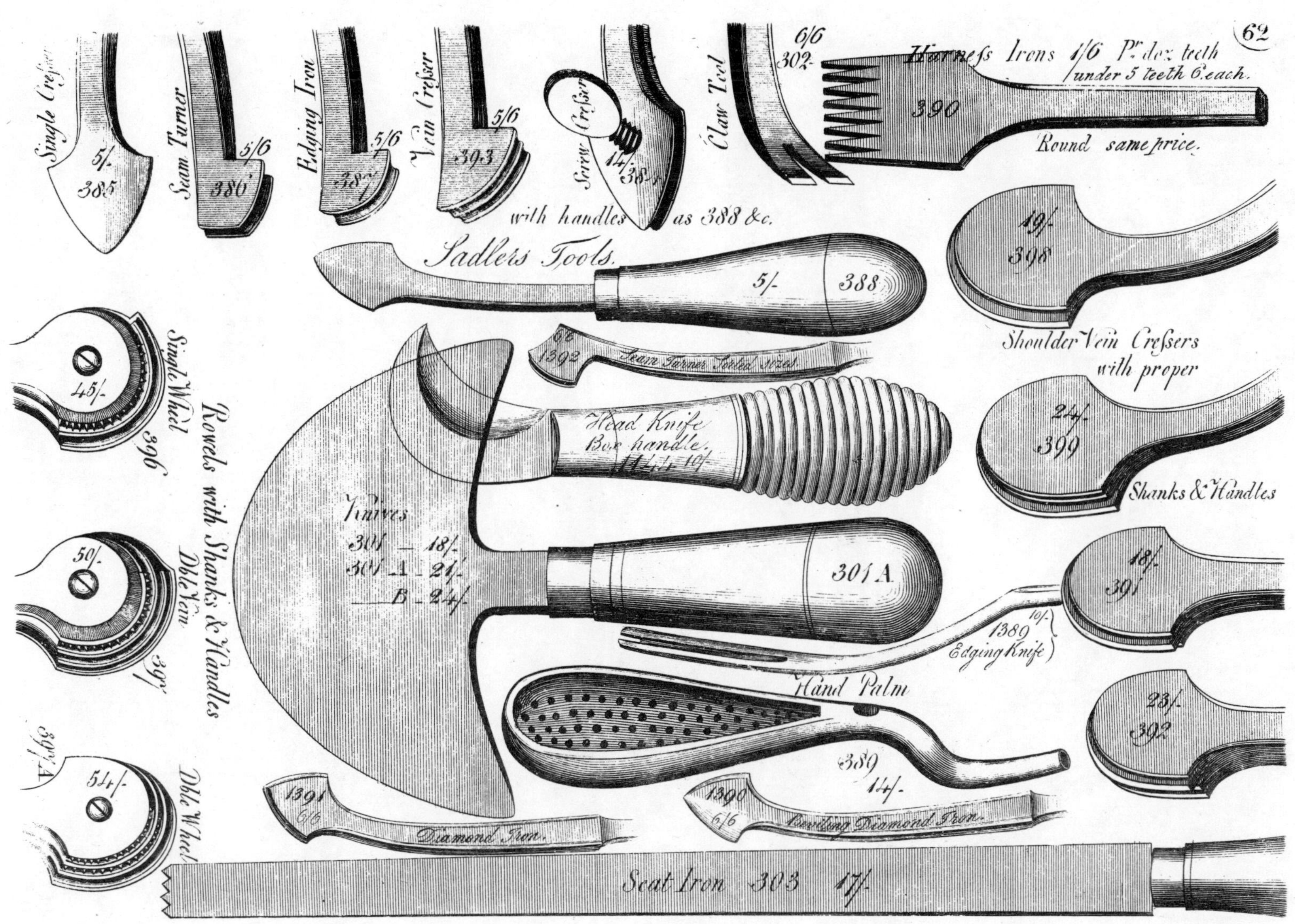

62
Single Crefser
5/-
385
Seam Turner
5/6
386
Edging Iron
5/6
387
Vein Crefser
5/6
303
Screw Crefser
14/-
388
with handles as 388 &c.
Claw Tool
6/6
302
Harnefs Irons 1/6 Pr. doz. teeth
under 5 teeth 6. each.
390
Round same price.
Sadlers Tools.
5/-
388
19/-
398
Shoulder Vein Crefsers
with proper
24/-
399
Shanks & Handles
6/6
1392
Seam Turner Tooled Steel
Head Knife
Box handle.
14, 4, 10/
Single Wheel
45/-
396
Rowels with Shanks & Handles
Knives
301 — 18/-
301 A — 21/-
B — 24/-
301 A
10/-
1389
Edging Knife
18/-
391
Dble Vein
50/-
391
Hand Palm
23/-
392
Dble Wheel
5/-
397 A
1391
6/6
Diamond Iron.
389
14/-
1390
6/6
Bevelling Diamond Iron.
Seat Iron 303 17/-

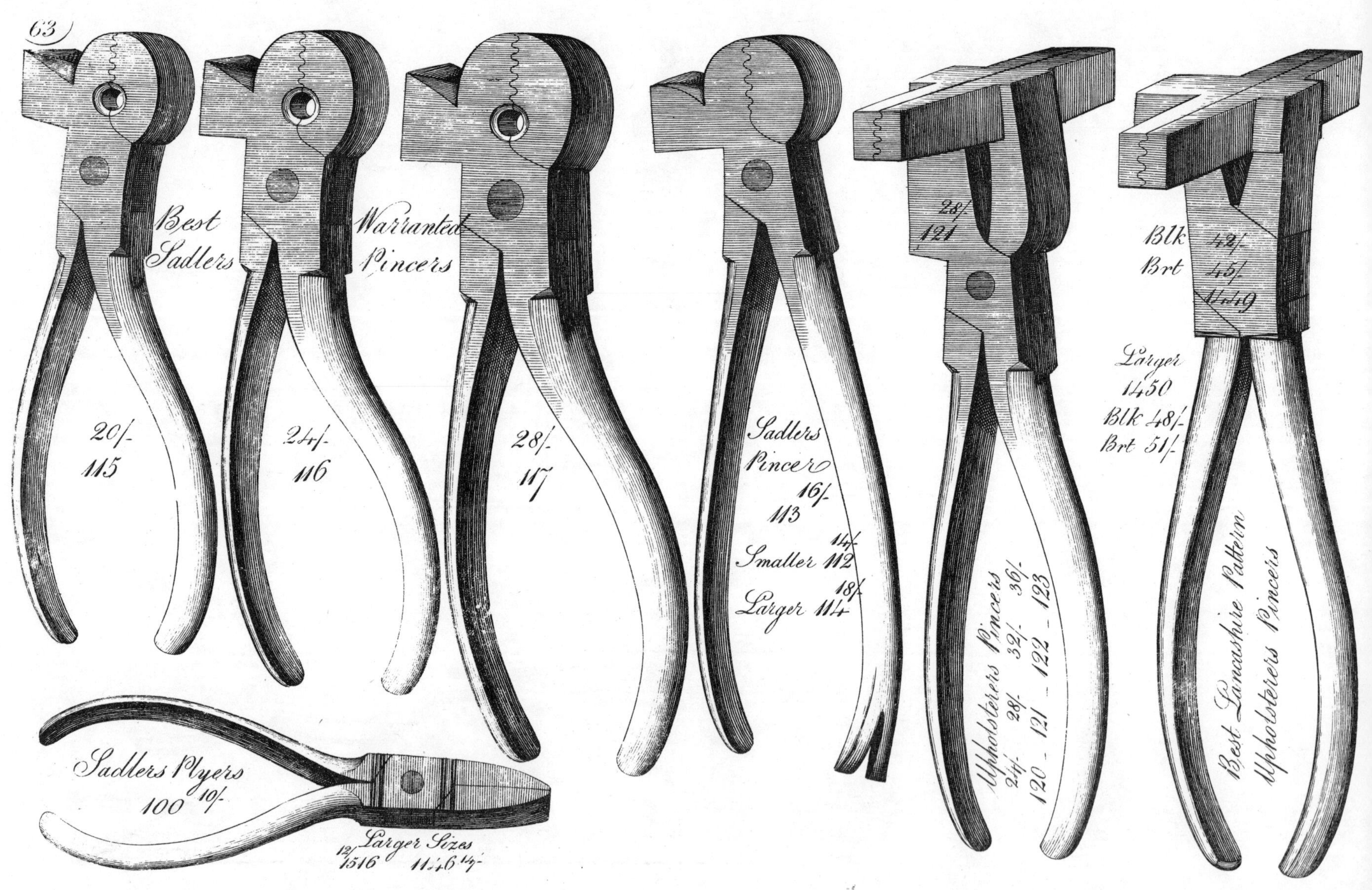

63
Best Sadlers
Warranted Pincers
20/- 115
24/- 116
28/- 117
Sadlers Pincer 16/- 113
Smaller 14/- 112
Larger 18/- 114
28/- 121
Blk Brt 42/- 45/- 1449
Larger 1450 Blk 48/- Brt 51/-
Upholsterers Pincers 24/- 28/- 32/- 36/- 120 - 121 - 122 - 123
Best Lancashire Pattern Upholsterers Pincers
Sadlers Plyers 100 10/-
Larger Sizes 12/ 1516 11/+6 14/-

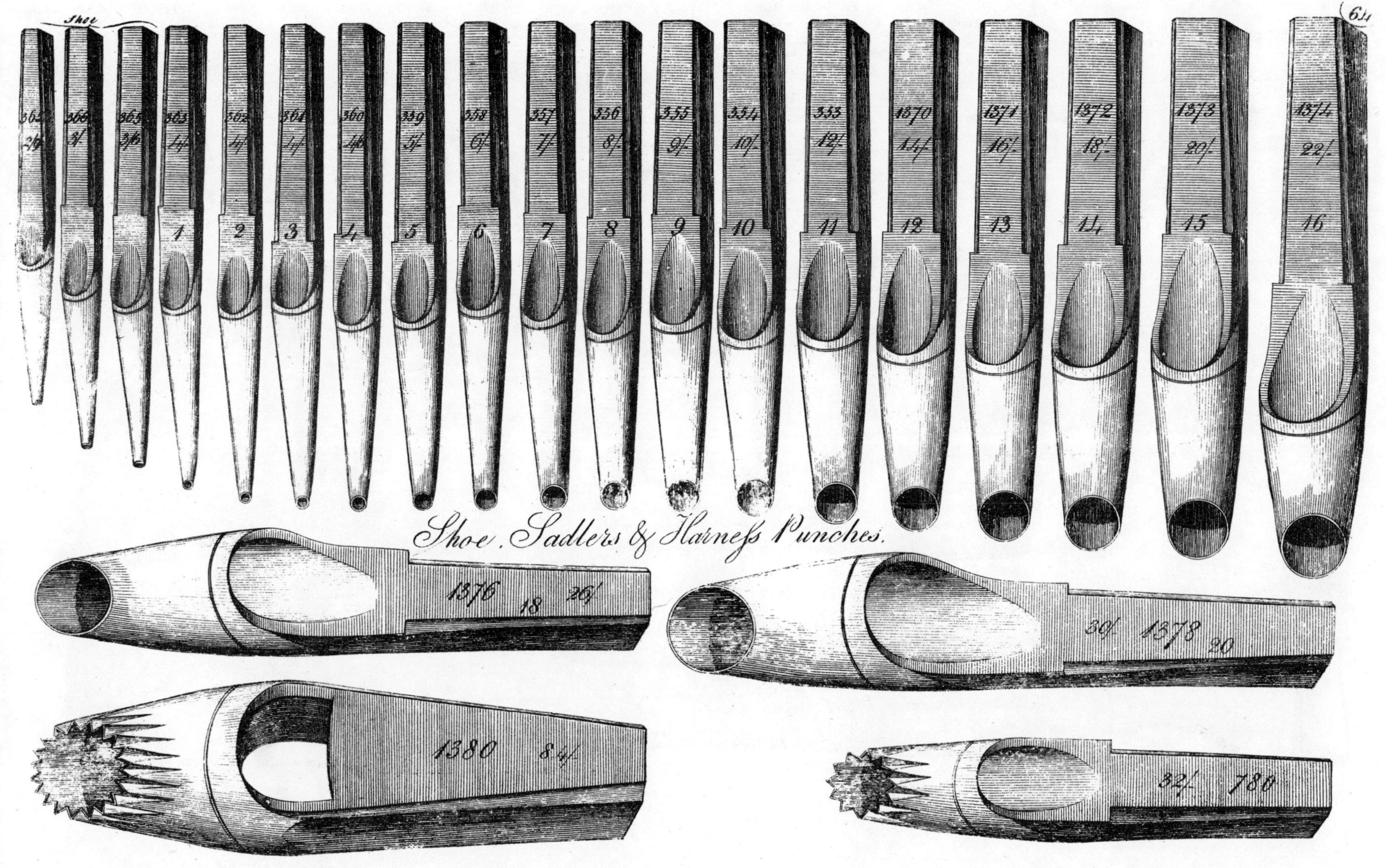

Shoe, Sadlers & Harness Punches.

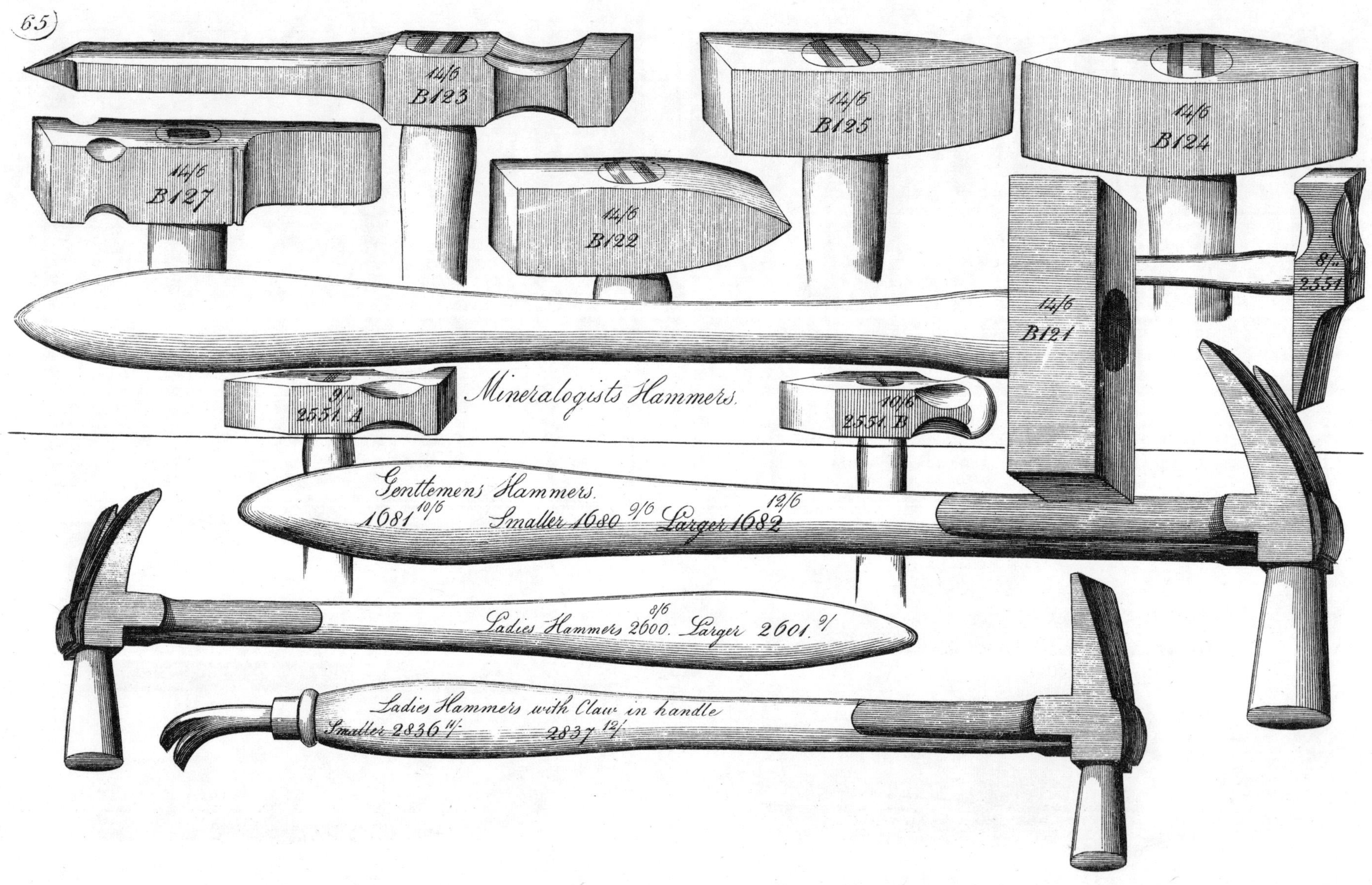
65
14/6 B123
14/6 B125
14/6 B124
14/6 B127
14/6 B122
8/.. 2551
14/6 B121
9/.. 2551 A
10/6 2551 B
Mineralogists Hammers.
Gentlemens Hammers.
10/6
1681
Smaller 1680 9/6 Larger 1682
12/6
8/6
Ladies Hammers 2600. Larger 2601 9/
Ladies Hammers with Claw in handle
Smaller 2836 11/
2837 12/

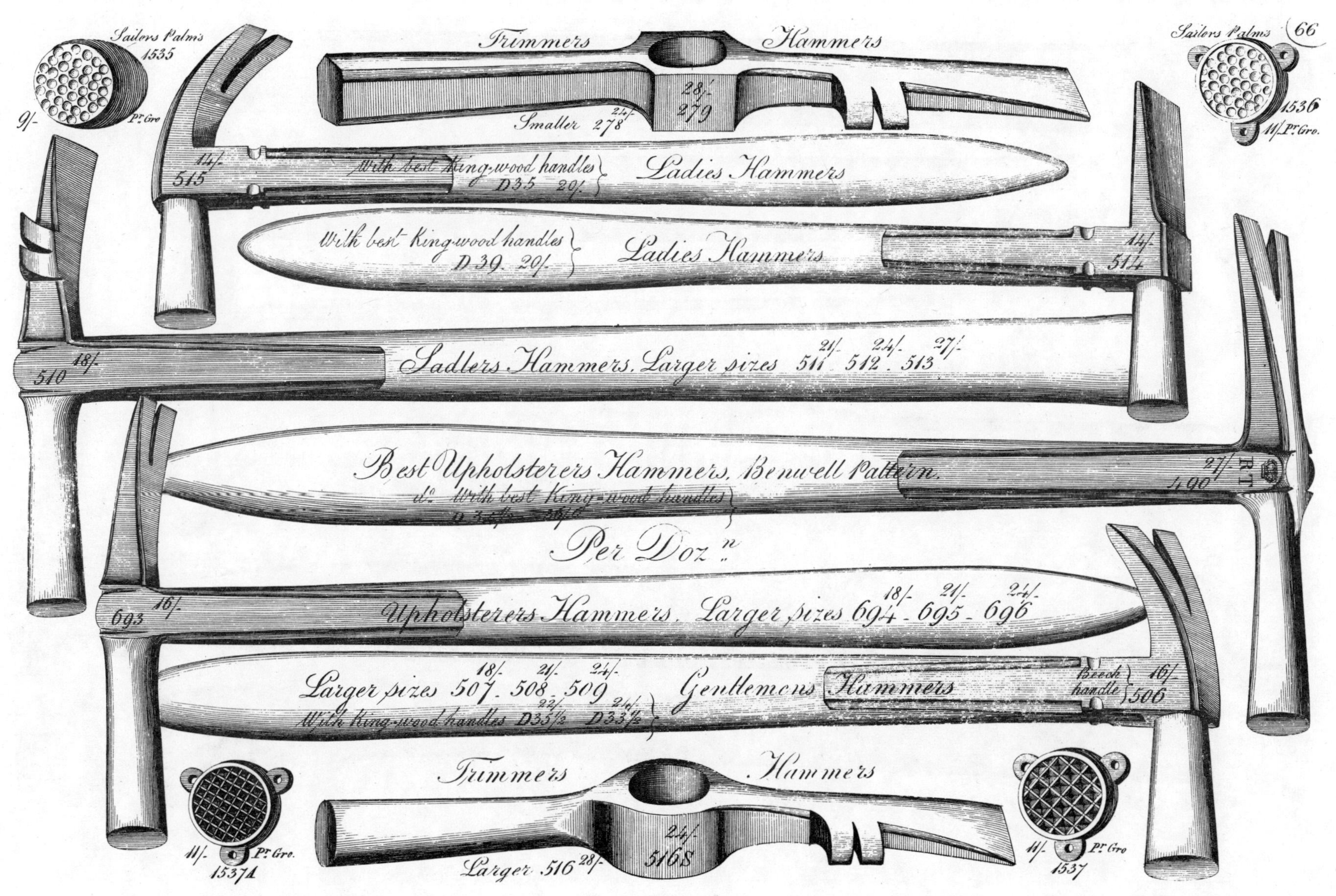

Sailors Palms
1535
9/-
Pr. Gro.
Trimmers   Hammers
28/-
279
Smaller 278 24/-
Sailors Palms
1536
11/. Pr. Gro.
66
14/-
515
With best King-wood handles
D35. 20/.
Ladies Hammers
With best King-wood handles
D 39. 20/.
Ladies Hammers
14/-
514
510 18/-
Sadlers Hammers. Larger sizes 511 21/- 512 24/- 513 27/-
Best Upholsterers Hammers. Benwell Pattern.
do. With best King-wood handles
27/-
400 RT
Per Doz.n
693 16/-
Upholsterers Hammers. Larger sizes 694 18/- 695 21/- 696 24/-
Larger sizes 507 18/- 508 21/- 509 24/-
With King-wood handles D35½ 22/- D33½ 24/-
Gentlemens Hammers
Brock handle 16/- 506
Trimmers   Hammers
24/-
516S
1537L 11/- Pr. Gro.
Larger 516 28/-
11/- Pr. Gro. 1537

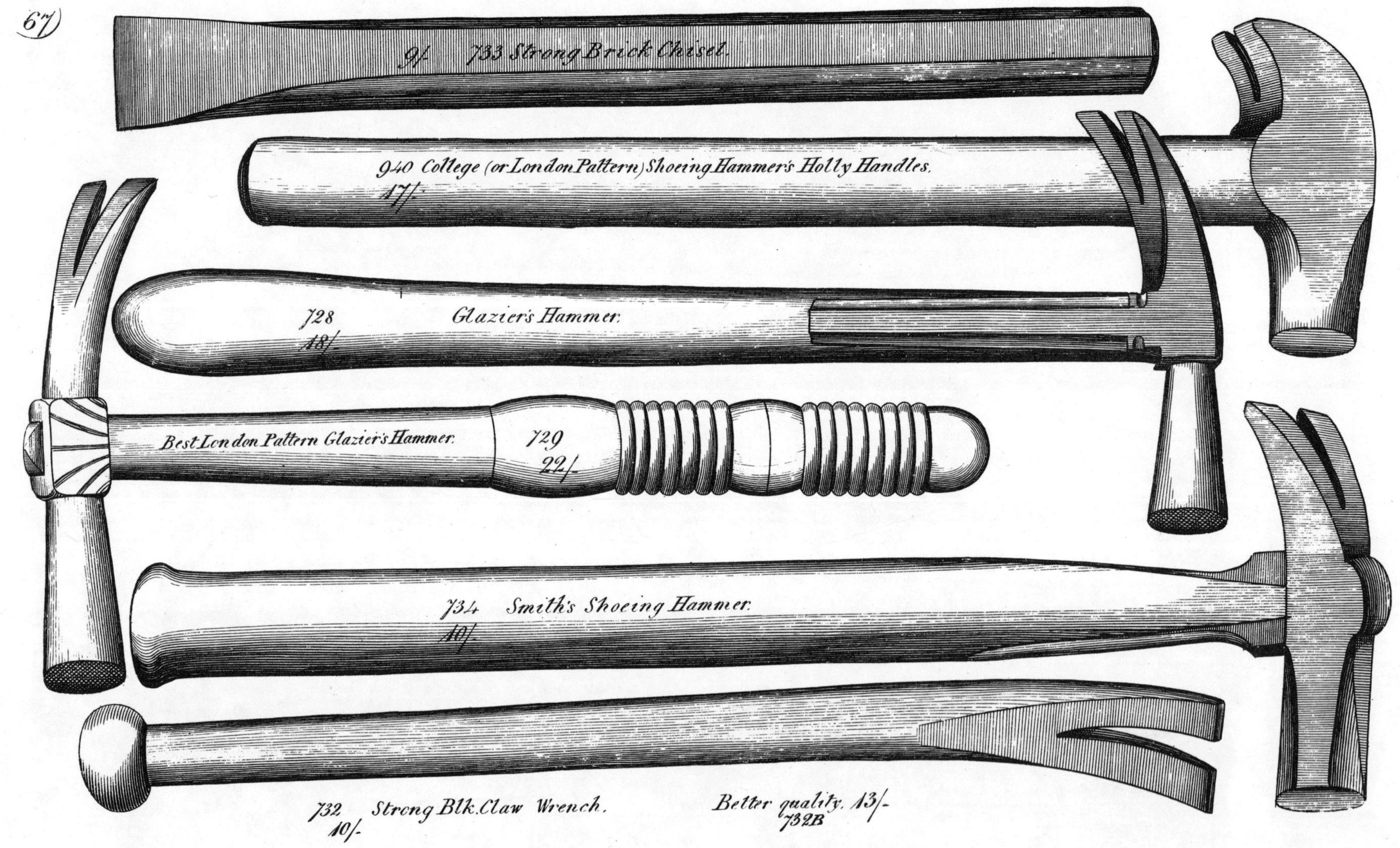
9/ 733 Strong Brick Chisel.
940 College (or London Pattern) Shoeing Hammers Holly Handles.
47/-
728 Glazier's Hammer.
18/
Best London Pattern Glazier's Hammer. 729
22/
734 Smith's Shoeing Hammer.
10/
732 Strong Blk. Claw Wrench.
10/-
Better quality. 13/-
732B

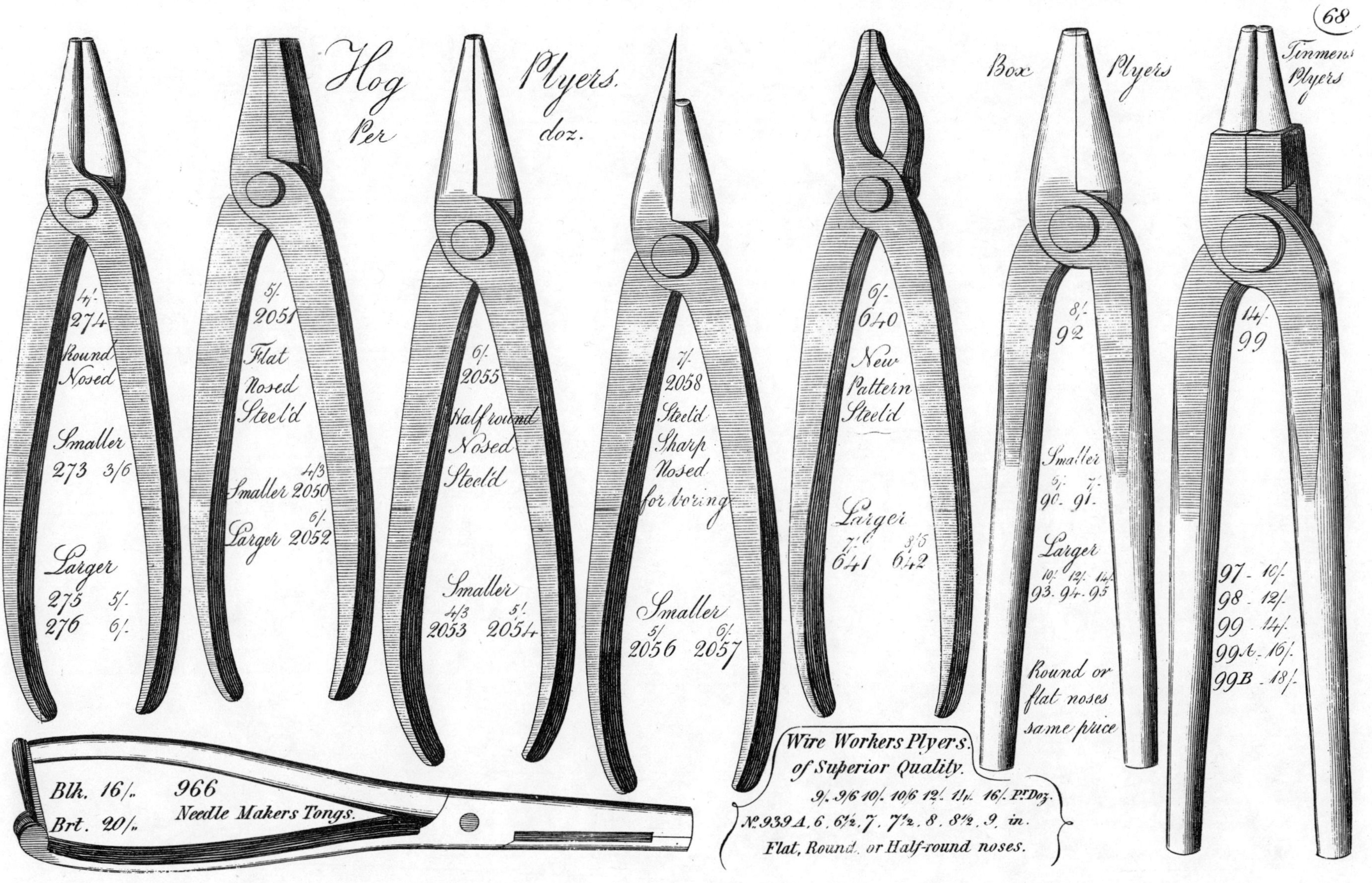

Hog
Plyers.
Per doz.
Box Plyers
Tinmens Plyers
4/ 274 Round Nosed
Smaller 273 3/6
Larger 275 5/
276 6/
5/ 2051 Flat Nosed Steel'd
Smaller 2050 4/3
Larger 2052 6/
6/ 2055 Half round Nosed Steel'd
Smaller 2053 4/3
2054 5/
7/ 2058 Steel'd Sharp Nosed for boring
Smaller 2056 5/
2057 6/
6/ 640 New Pattern Steel'd
Larger 641 7/
642 8/5
8/ 92
Smaller 90. 91 5/. 7/
Larger 93. 94. 95 10/. 12/. 14/
Round or flat noses same price
14/ 99
97 . 10/
98 . 12/
99 . 14/
99 A . 16/
99 B . 18/
Blk. 16/.
Brt. 20/.
966 Needle Makers Tongs.
Wire Workers Plyers. of Superior Quality.
9/. 9/6 10/. 10/6 12/. 14/. 16/. Pr Doz.
No 9.3.9 A. 6. 6½. 7. 7½. 8. 8½. 9. in.
Flat, Round. or Half-round noses.

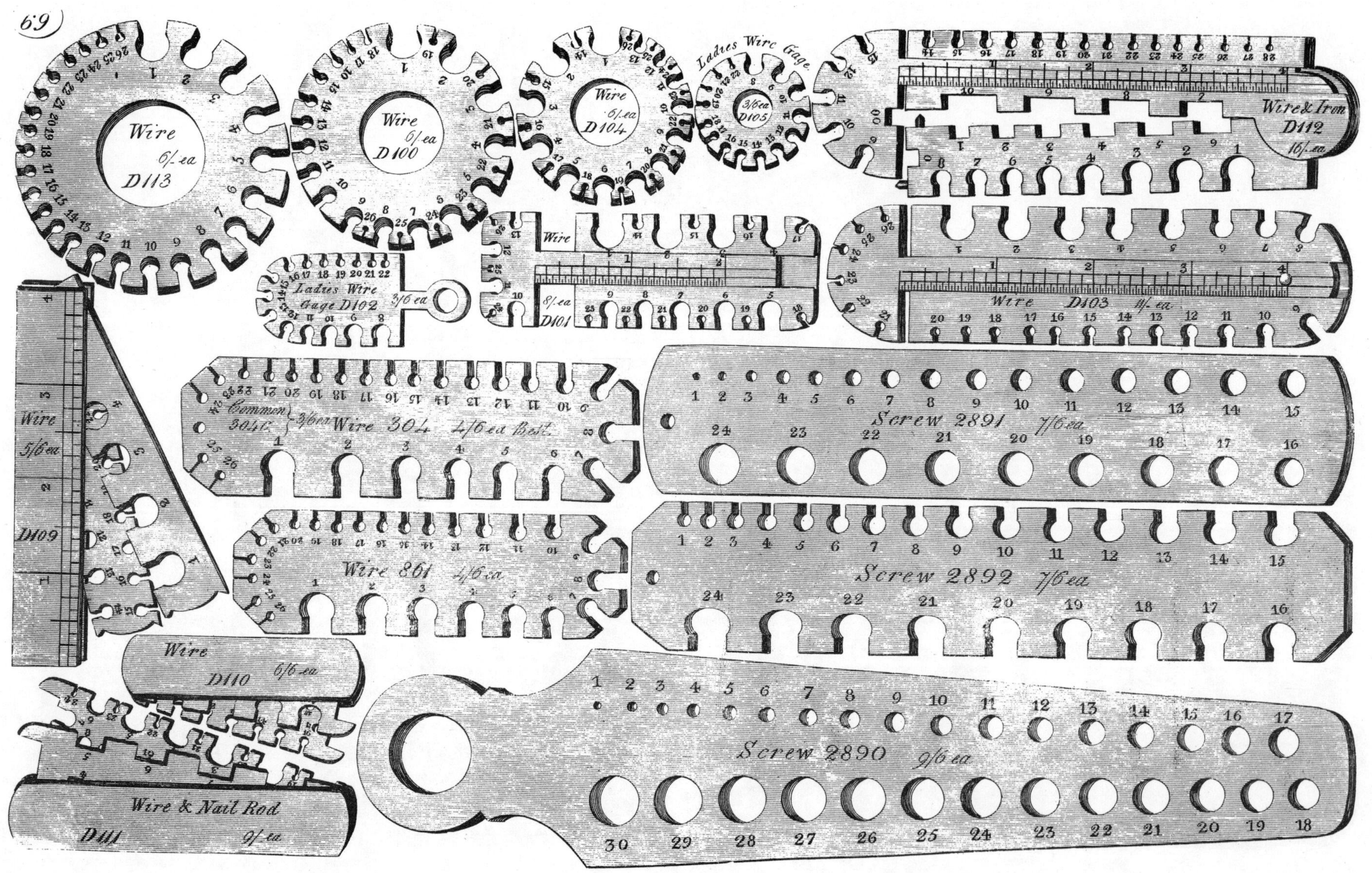
69
Wire 6/ ea D113
Wire 6/ ea D100
Wire 6/ ea D104
Ladies Wire Gage. 3/6 ea D105
Wire & Iron 16/ ea D112
Ladies Wire Gage D102 3/6 ea
Wire 8/ ea D101
Wire D103 4/ ea
Common 304 C 3/6 ea Wire 304 4/6 ea Best
Screw 2891 7/6 ea
Wire 861 4/6 ea
Screw 2892 7/6 ea
Wire 5/6 ea D109
Wire D110 6/6 ea
Wire & Nail Rod D111 9/ ea
Screw 2890 9/6 ea

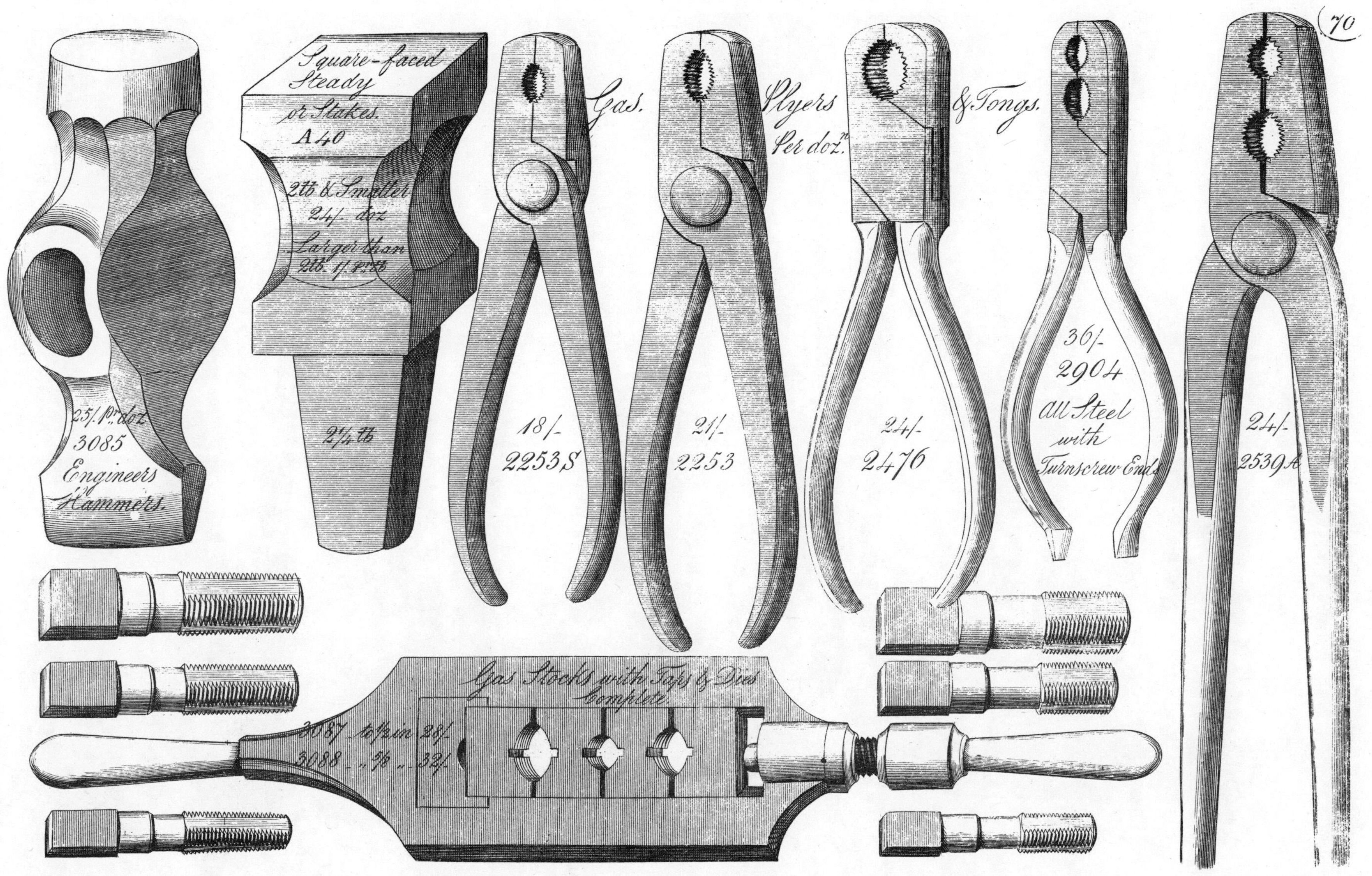
Gas. Plyers Per doz. & Tongs.
Square-faced Steady or Stakes. A40
2℔ & Smaller 24/- doz
Larger than 2℔ 1/- ℔
2¼℔
25/- Pr doz 3085 Engineers Hammers.
18/- 2253S
24/- 2253
24/- 2476
36/- 2904 All Steel with Turnscrew Ends
24/- 2539A
Gas Stocks with Taps & Dies Complete
3087 to ½ in 28/-
3088 .. ⅝ .. 32/-

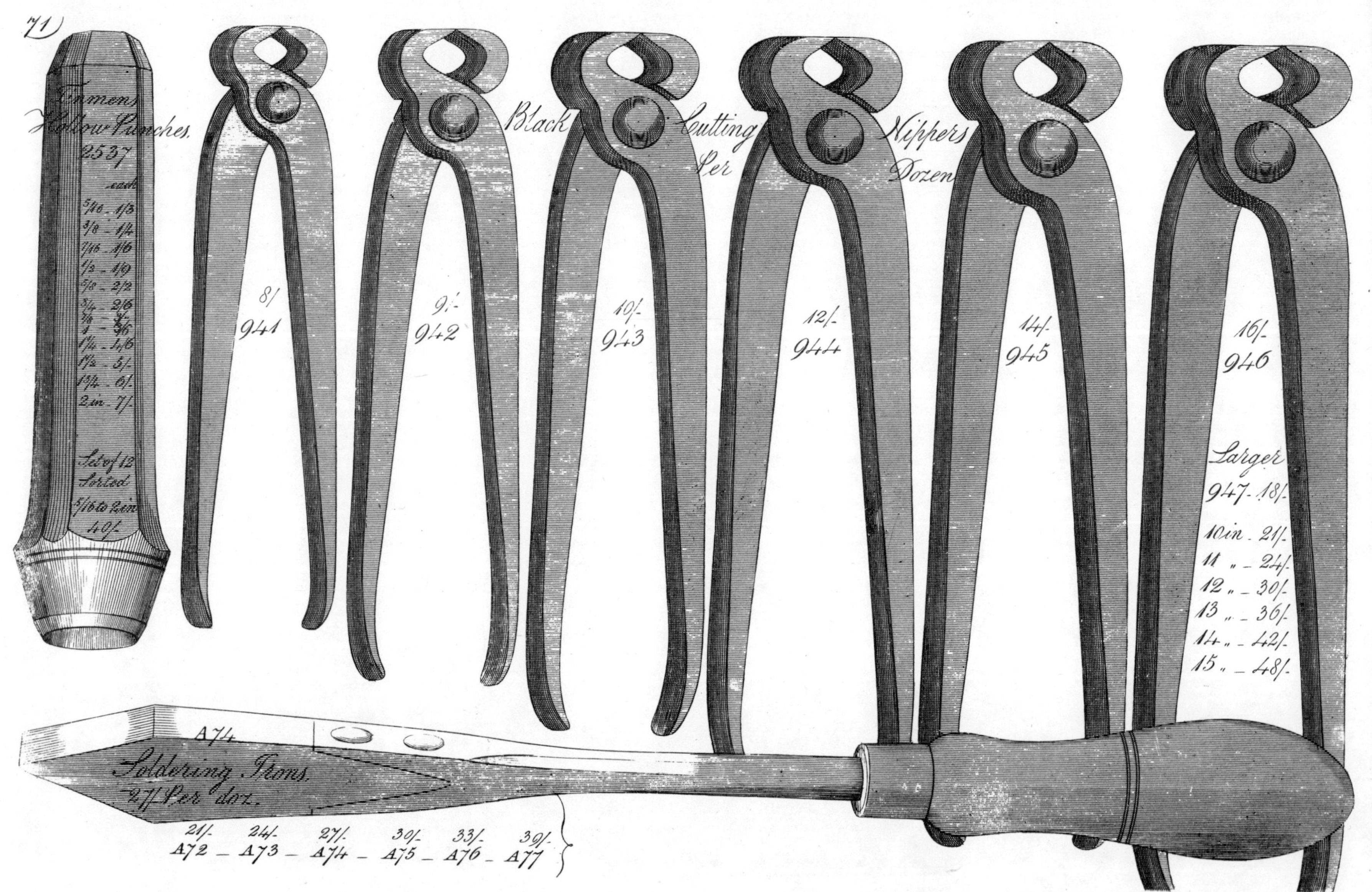

71
Tinmens Hollow Punches. 2537
each
5/16 - 1/3
3/8 - 1/4
7/16 - 1/6
1/2 - 1/9
5/8 - 2/2
3/4 - 2/6
7/8 - 3/
1 - 3/6
1 1/4 - 4/6
1 1/2 - 5/
1 3/4 - 6/
2 in - 7/
Set of 12 Sorted
5/16 to 2 in 40/
Black Cutting Per Nippers Dozen
8/ 941
9/ 942
10/ 943
12/ 944
14/ 945
16/ 946
Larger 947 - 18/
10 in - 21/
11 " - 24/
12 " - 30/
13 " - 36/
14 " - 42/
15 " - 48/
A74
Soldering Irons. 27/ Per doz.
21/ 24/ 27/ 30/ 33/ 39/
A72 - A73 - A74 - A75 - A76 - A77

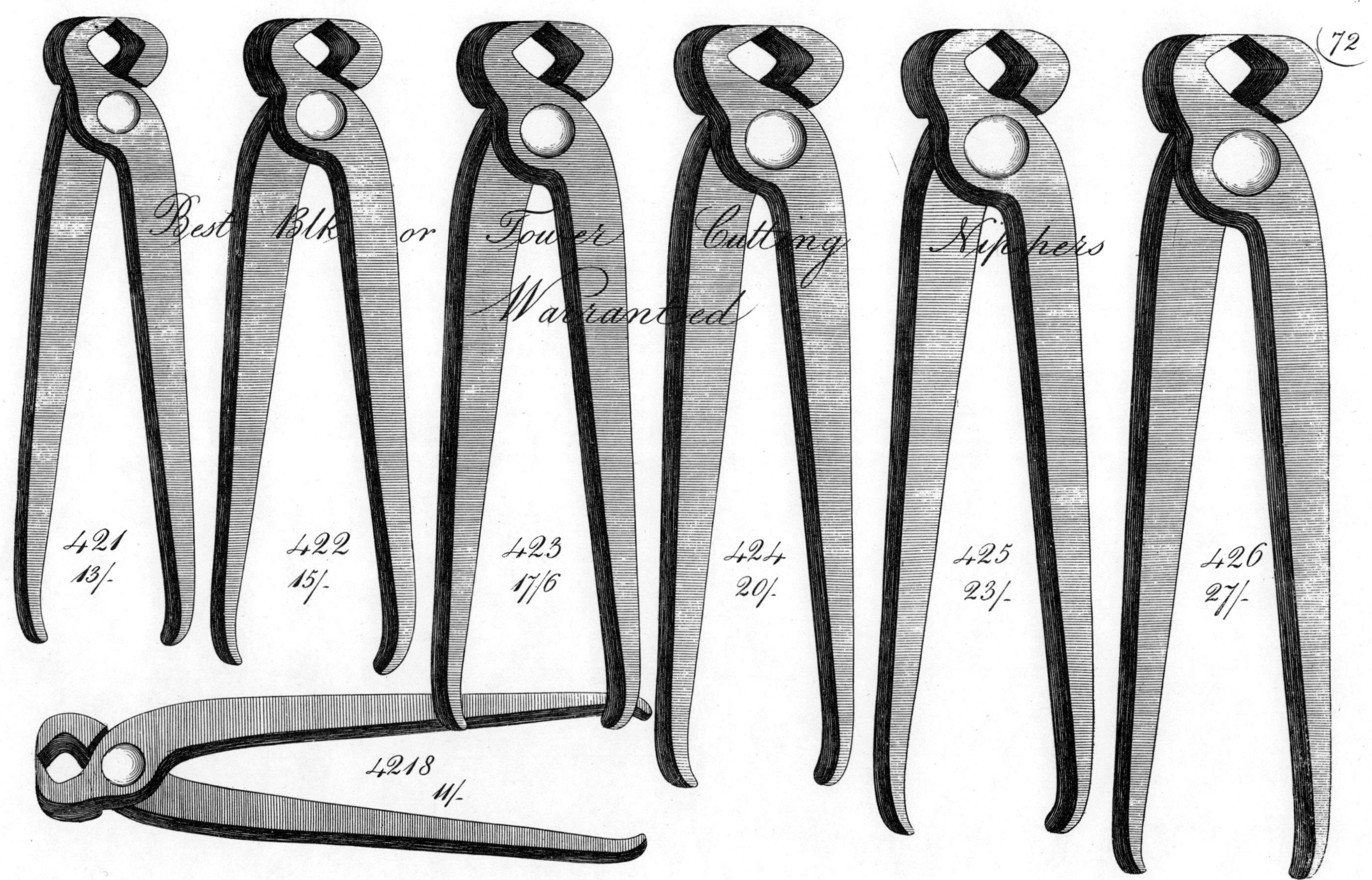
Best Blk or Tower Cutting Nippers
Warranted
421
13/-
422
15/-
423
17/6
424
20/-
425
23/-
426
27/-
4218
11/-

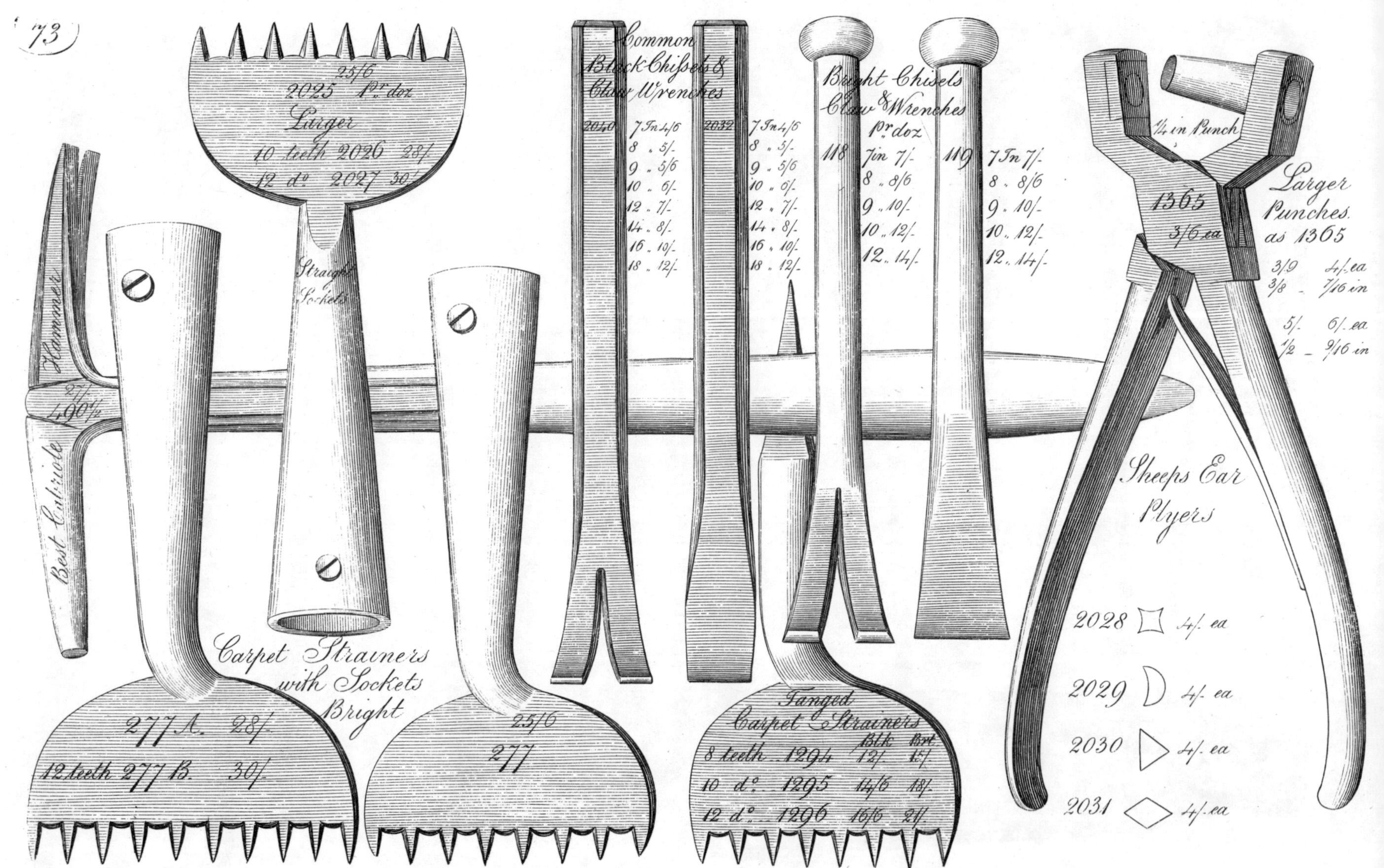
73

Best Cutirole Hammers
27/
100½

25/6
2025 Pr doz
Larger
10 teeth 2026 28/
12 do 2027 30/

Straight Sockets

Carpet Strainers
with Sockets
Bright
277 A. 28/
12 teeth 277 B. 30/

25/6
277

Common
Black Chisels &
Claw Wrenches
2040 7 In 4/6
8 ,, 5/-
9 ,, 5/6
10 ,, 6/-
12 ,, 7/-
14 ,, 8/-
16 ,, 10/-
18 ,, 12/-

2032 7 In 4/6
8 ,, 5/-
9 ,, 5/6
10 ,, 6/-
12 ,, 7/-
14 ,, 8/-
16 ,, 10/-
18 ,, 12/-

Bright Chisels
Claw & Wrenches
Pr doz
118 7 in 7/-
8 ,, 8/6
9 ,, 10/-
10 ,, 12/-
12 ,, 14/-

119 7 In 7/-
8 ,, 8/6
9 ,, 10/-
10 ,, 12/-
12 ,, 14/-

Tanged
Carpet Strainers
Blk   Brt
8 teeth 1294 12/   15/
10 do 1295 14/6 18/
12 do 1296 16/6 21/

¼ in Punch
1365
3/6 ea

Larger
Punches.
as 1365
3/9   4/- ea
3/8 - 7/16 in
5/   6/- ea
½ - 9/16 in

Sheeps Ear
Plyers
2028   4/- ea
2029   4/- ea
2030   4/- ea
2031   4/- ea

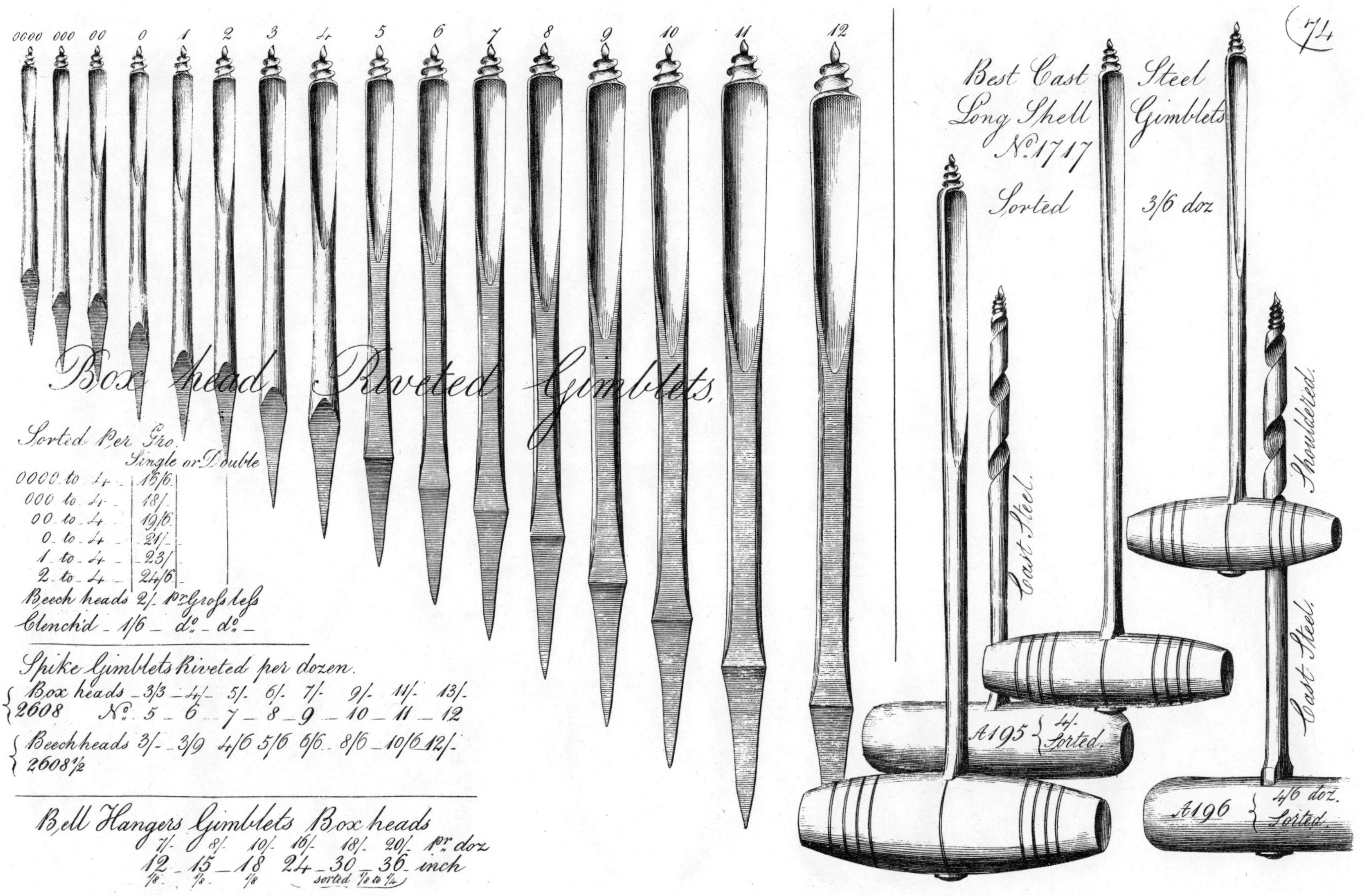
0000 000 00 0 1 2 3 4 5 6 7 8 9 10 11 12
(74)
Box head Riveted Gimblets.
Sorted Per Gro.
Single or Double
0000 to 4 — 16/6
000 to 4 — 18/
00 to 4 — 19/6
0 to 4 — 21/
1 to 4 — 23/
2 to 4 — 24/6
Beech heads 2/ Pr Gross less
Clench'd — 1/6 — do — do —
Spike Gimblets Riveted per dozen.
Box heads — 3/3 — 4/ 5/ 6/ 7/ 9/ 11/ 13/
2608   No 5 — 6 7 — 8 — 9 — 10 — 11 — 12
Beech heads 3/ — 3/9 4/6 5/6 6/6 — 8/6 — 10/6 12/
2608½
Bell Hangers Gimblets Box heads
7/ 8/ 10/ 16/ 18/ 20/ Pr doz
12 — 15 — 18 24 — 30 36 inch
1/8 1/8 1/8 sorted 1/8 to 1/4
Best Cast Steel Long Shell Gimblets No 1717 Sorted 3/6 doz
Cast Steel.
Shouldered.
Cast Steel.
Cast Steel.
A195 { 4/ Sorted.
A196 { 4/6 doz. Sorted.

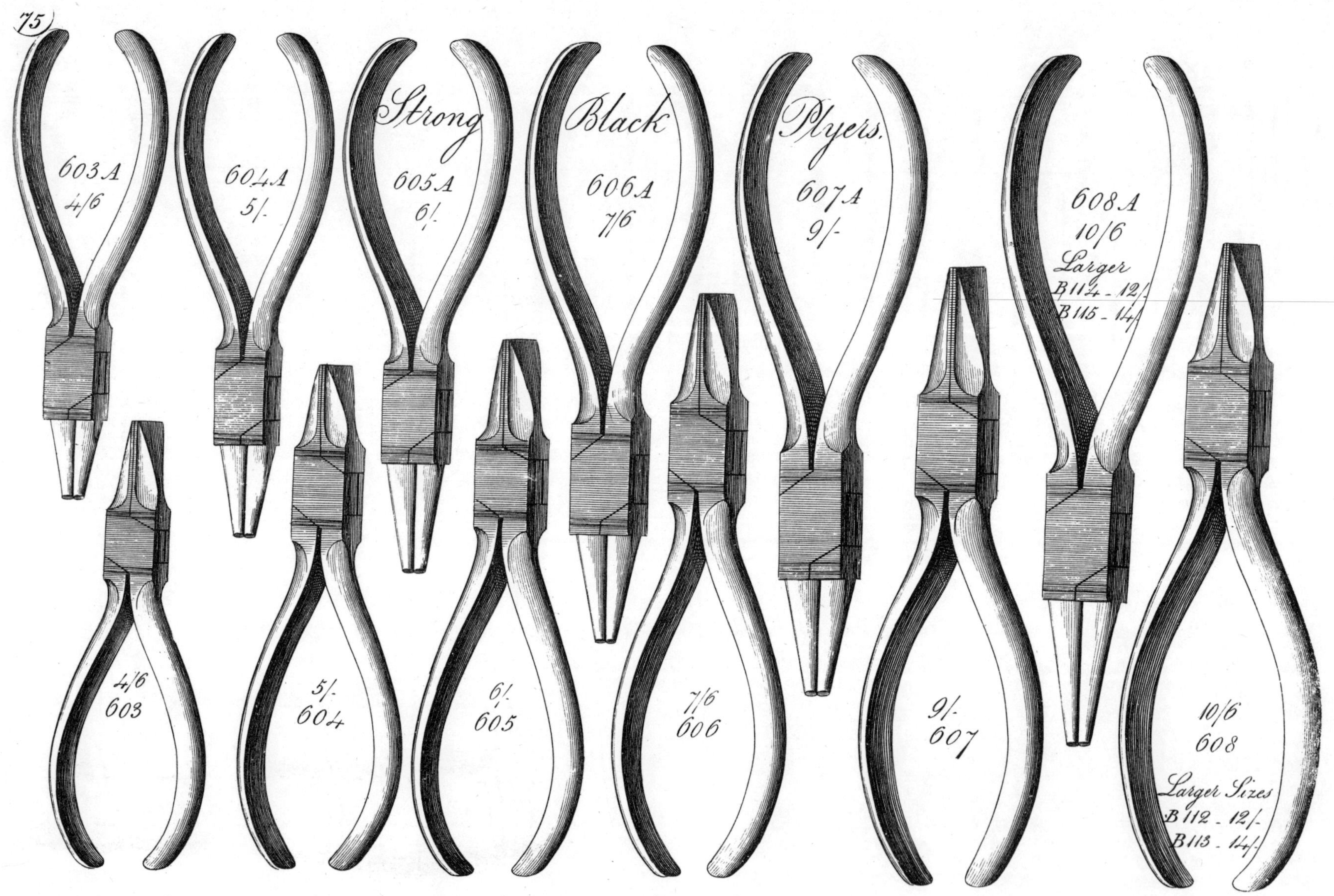

Strong
Black
Plyers.
603A
4/6
604A
5/-
605A
6/-
606A
7/6
607A
9/-
608A
10/6
Larger
B114 - 12/-
B115 - 14/-
4/6
603
5/-
604
6/-
605
7/6
606
9/-
607
10/6
608
Larger Sizes
B112 - 12/-
B113 - 14/-

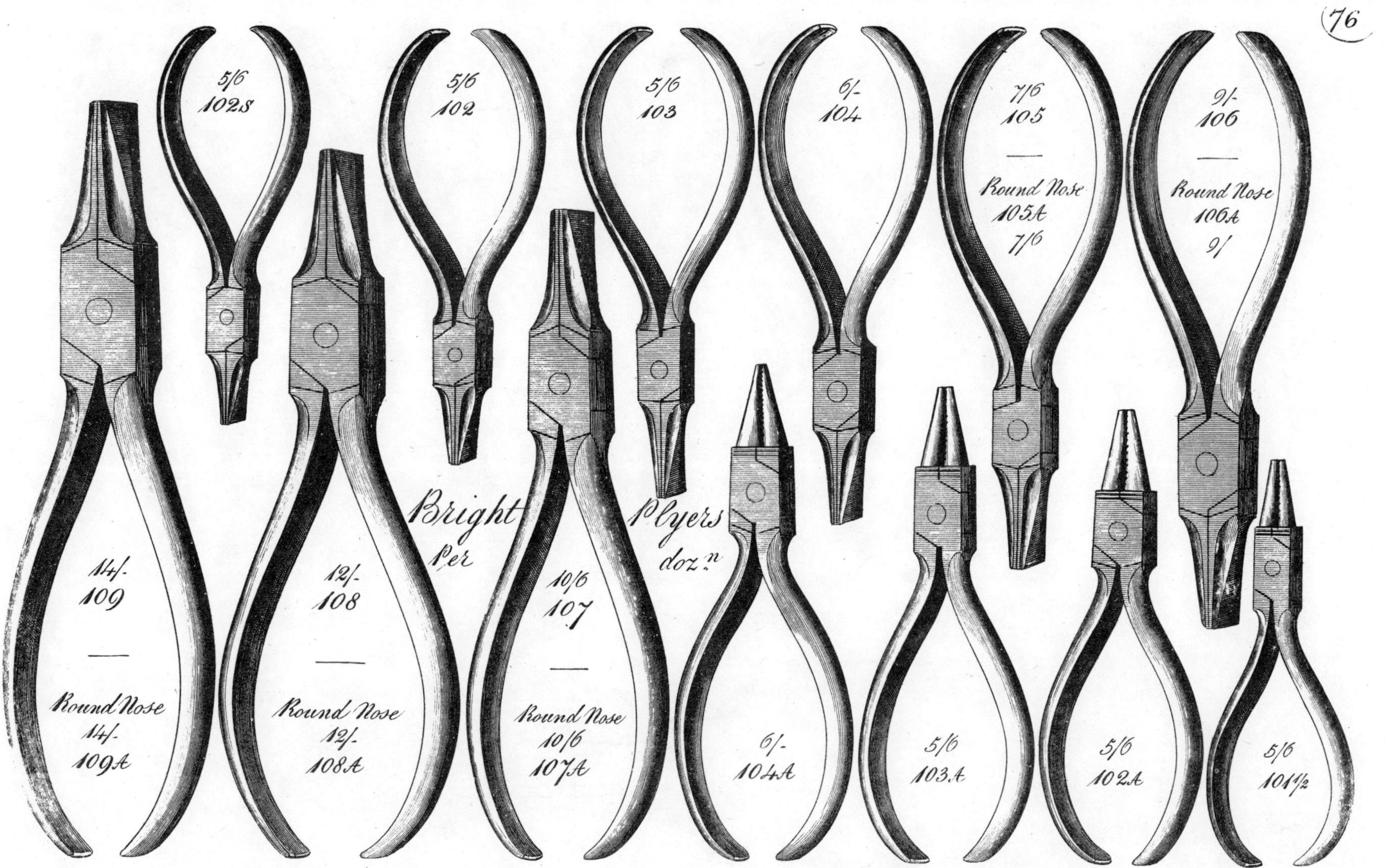
5/6
102S
5/6
102
5/6
103
6/-
104
7/6
105
—
Round Nose
105A
7/6
9/-
106
—
Round Nose
106A
9/
14/-
109
—
Round Nose
14/-
109A
12/-
108
—
Round Nose
12/-
108A
Bright
Per
10/6
107
—
Round Nose
10/6
107A
Plyers
doz.n
6/-
104A
5/6
103A
5/6
102A
5/6
101½

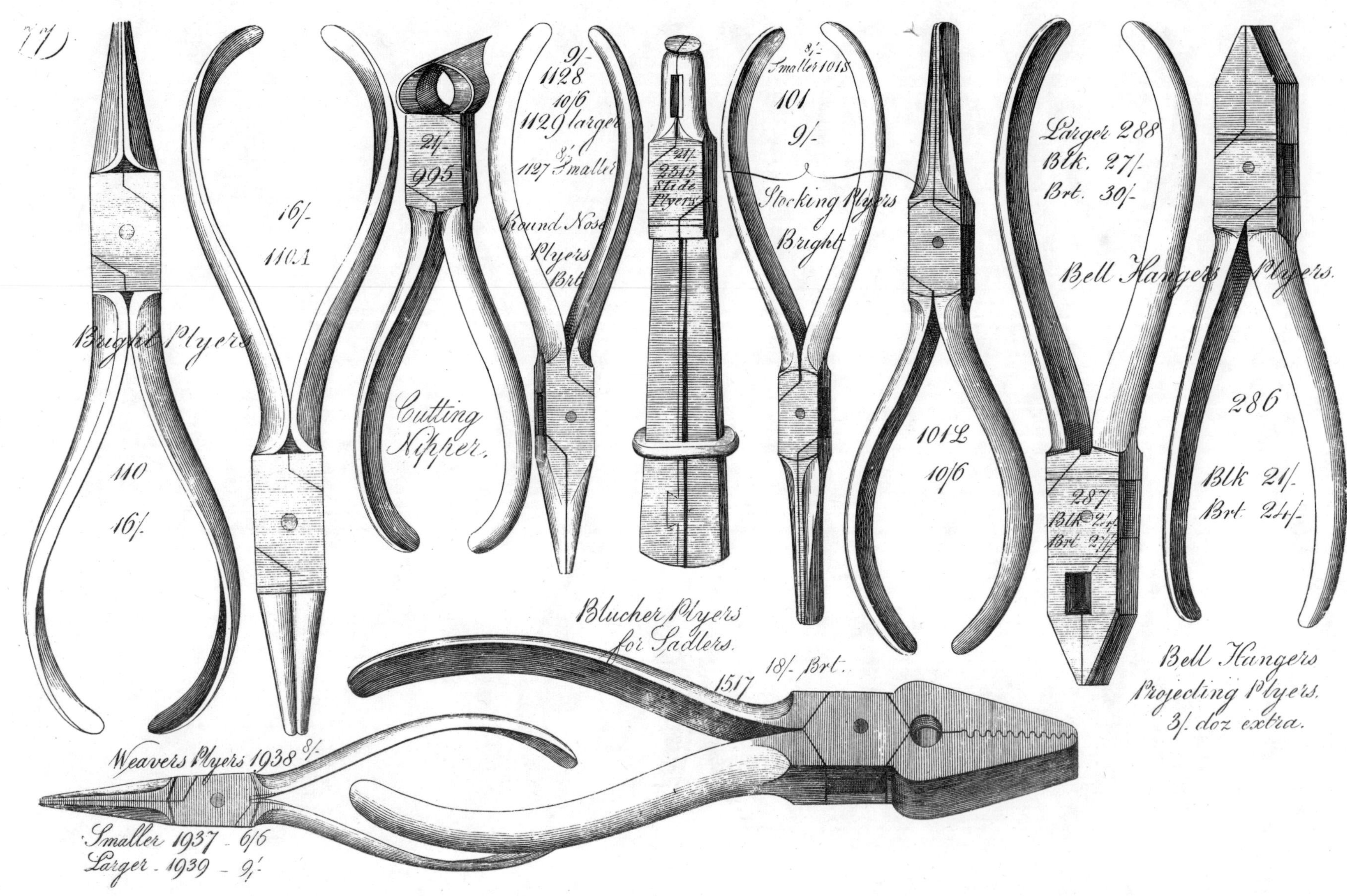
77
Bright Plyers
110
16/-
16/-
1101
095
21/-
Cutting Nipper.
9/-
1128
10/6
1129 larger
8/-
1127 smaller
Round Nose Plyers Brt.
21/-
2515
Slide Plyers
8/-
Smaller 1015
101
9/-
Stocking Plyers Bright
101L
10/6
Larger 288
Blk. 27/-
Brt. 30/-
Bell Hangers Plyers.
287
Blk. 21/-
Brt. 24/-
Bell Hangers Projecting Plyers.
3/- doz extra.
286
Blk. 21/-
Brt. 24/-
Blucher Plyers for Sadlers.
1517
18/- Brt.
Weavers Plyers 1938 8/-
Smaller 1937 - 6/6
Larger - 1939 - 9/-

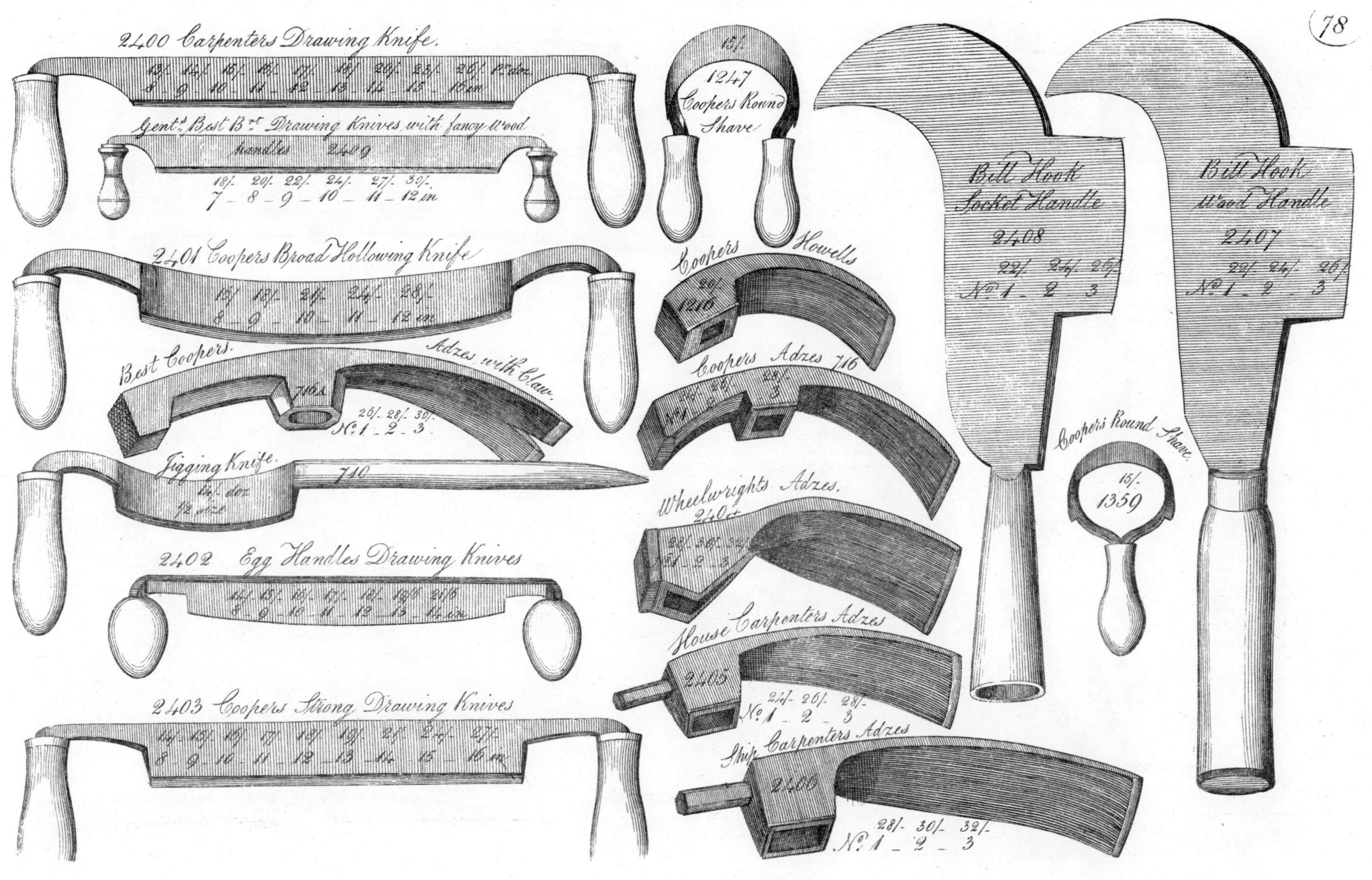
2400 Carpenters Drawing Knife.
Gents Best Brd Drawing Knives with fancy Wood handles 2409
2401 Coopers Broad Hollowing Knife
Best Coopers. Adzes with Claw.
Jigging Knife. 710
2402 Egg Handles Drawing Knives
2403 Coopers Strong Drawing Knives
1247 Coopers Round Shave
Coopers Howells 1210
Coopers Adzes 716
Wheelwrights Adzes. 2404
House Carpenters Adzes 2405
Ship Carpenters Adzes 2406
Bill Hook Socket Handle 2408
Bill Hook Wood Handle 2407
Coopers Round Shave. 1359

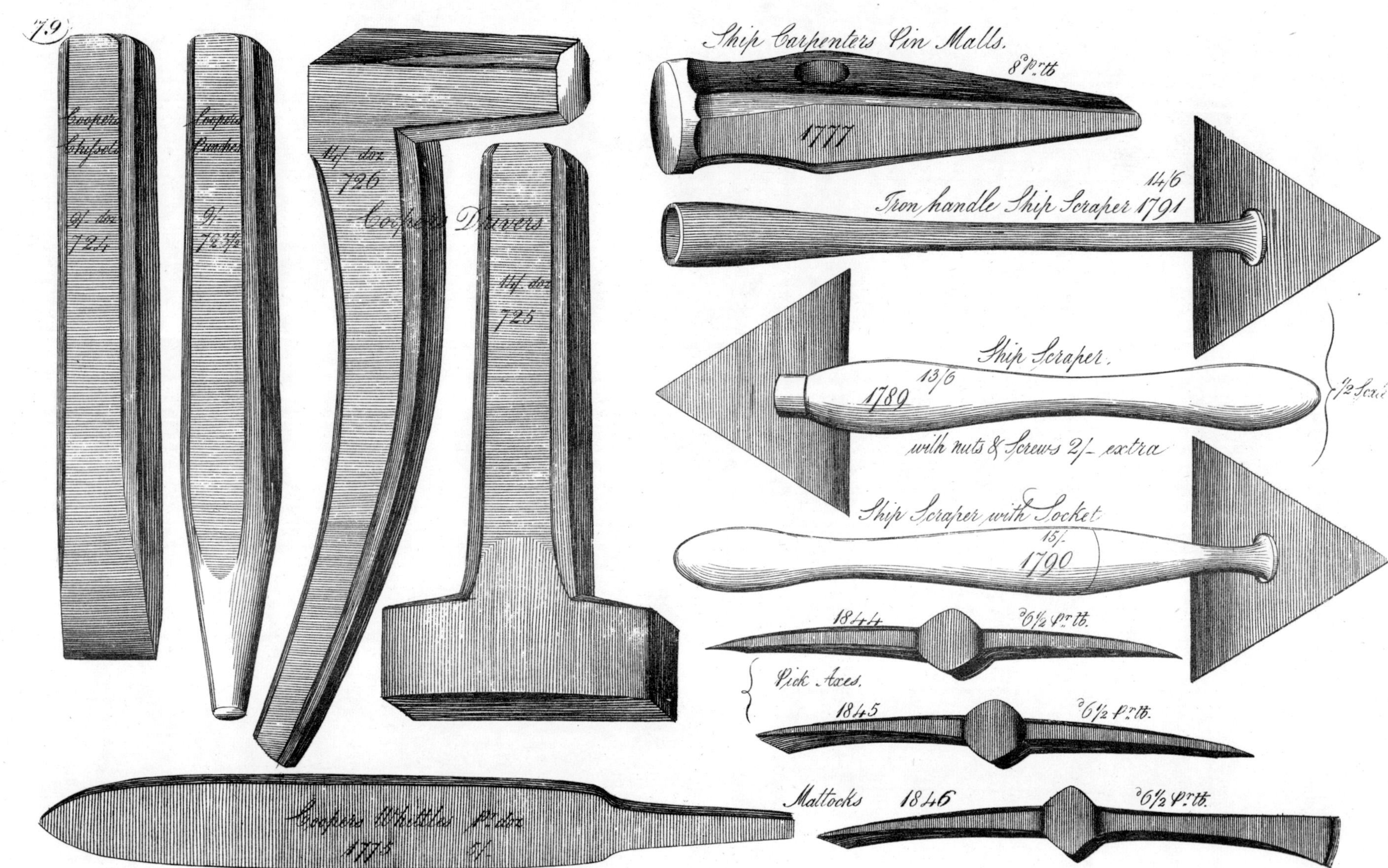
79
Coopers Chissels
9/ doz
724
Coopers Punches
9/
723 1/2
14/ doz
726
Coopers Drivers
14/ doz
725
Coopers Whittles P. doz
1775   5/-
Ship Carpenters Pin Malls.
8/ Pr. lb
1777
Iron handle Ship Scraper 1791   14/6
Ship Scraper.
1789   13/6
with nuts & Screws 2/- extra
1/2 Scale
Ship Scraper with Socket
15/-
1790
1844   6 1/2 Pr. lb
Pick Axes.
1845   6 1/2 Pr. lb
Mattocks   1846   6 1/2 Pr. lb

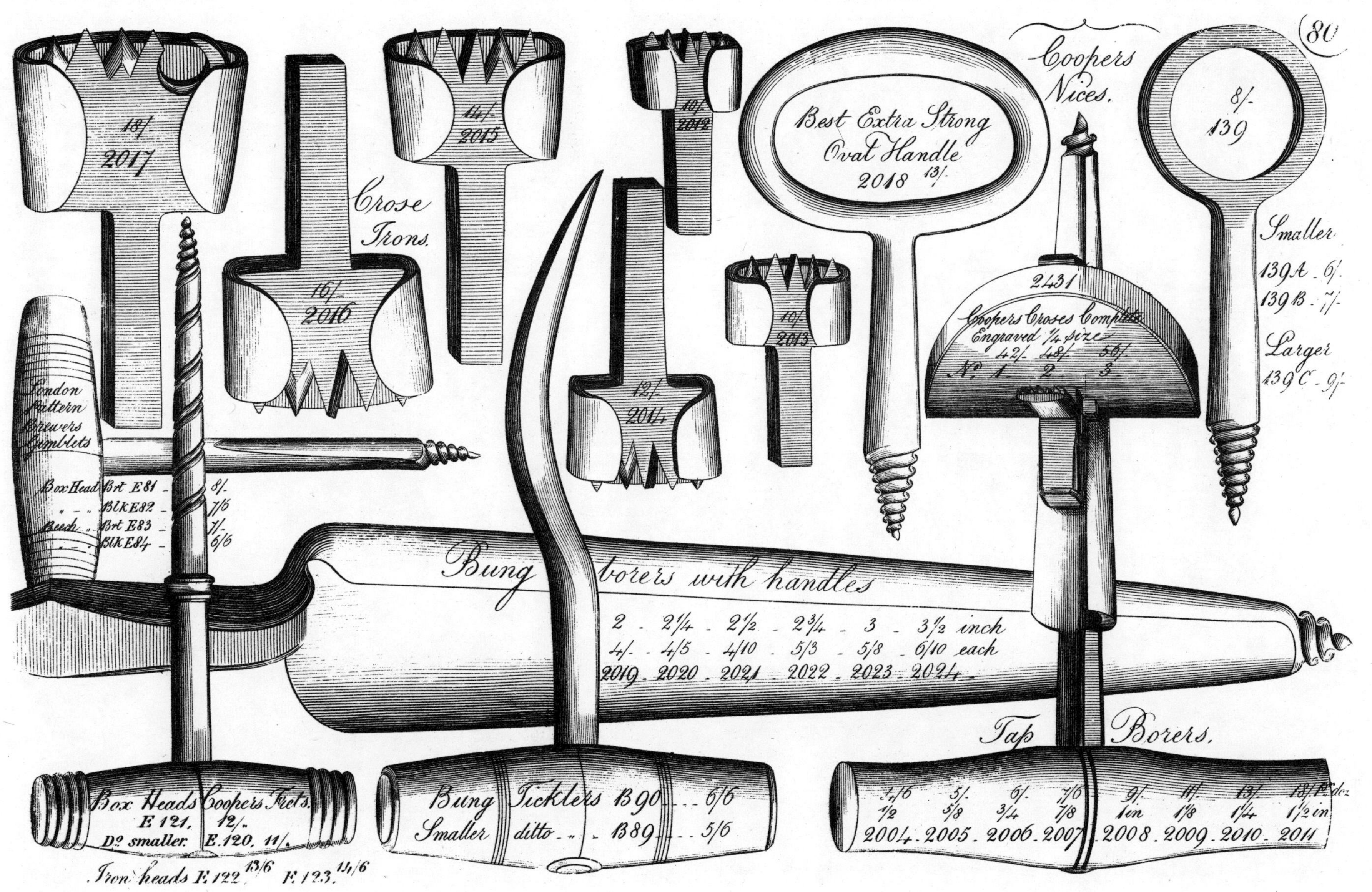
(80)
Coopers Nices.
Best Extra Strong Oval Handle 2018 13/
8/ 139
Smaller
139 A . 6/
139 B . 7/
Larger
139 C . 9/
18/ 2017
Crose Irons.
14/ 2015
10/ 2019
16/ 2016
10/ 2013
12/ 2014
London Pattern Brewers Gimblets
Box Head Brt E81 . 8/
" Blk E82 . 7/6
Beech Brt E83 . 7/
" Blk E84 . 6/6
2431
Coopers Croses Complete
Engraved 1/4 size
42/ 48/ 56/
No. 1 2 3
Bung borers with handles
2 - 2 1/4 - 2 1/2 - 2 3/4 - 3 - 3 1/2 inch
4/ - 4/5 - 4/10 - 5/3 - 5/8 - 6/10 each
2019 . 2020 . 2021 . 2022 . 2023 . 2024 .
Tap Borers.
Box Heads Coopers Frets.
E 121. 12/
Do smaller. E.120. 11/
Iron heads E.122 13/6 E.123 14/6
Bung Ticklers B90 ... 6/6
Smaller ditto ... B89 ... 5/6
3/6 5/ 6/ 7/6 9/ 11/ 13/ 18/ P.doz
1/2 5/8 3/4 7/8 1in 1/8 1/4 1/2 in
2004 . 2005 . 2006 . 2007 . 2008 . 2009 . 2010 . 2011

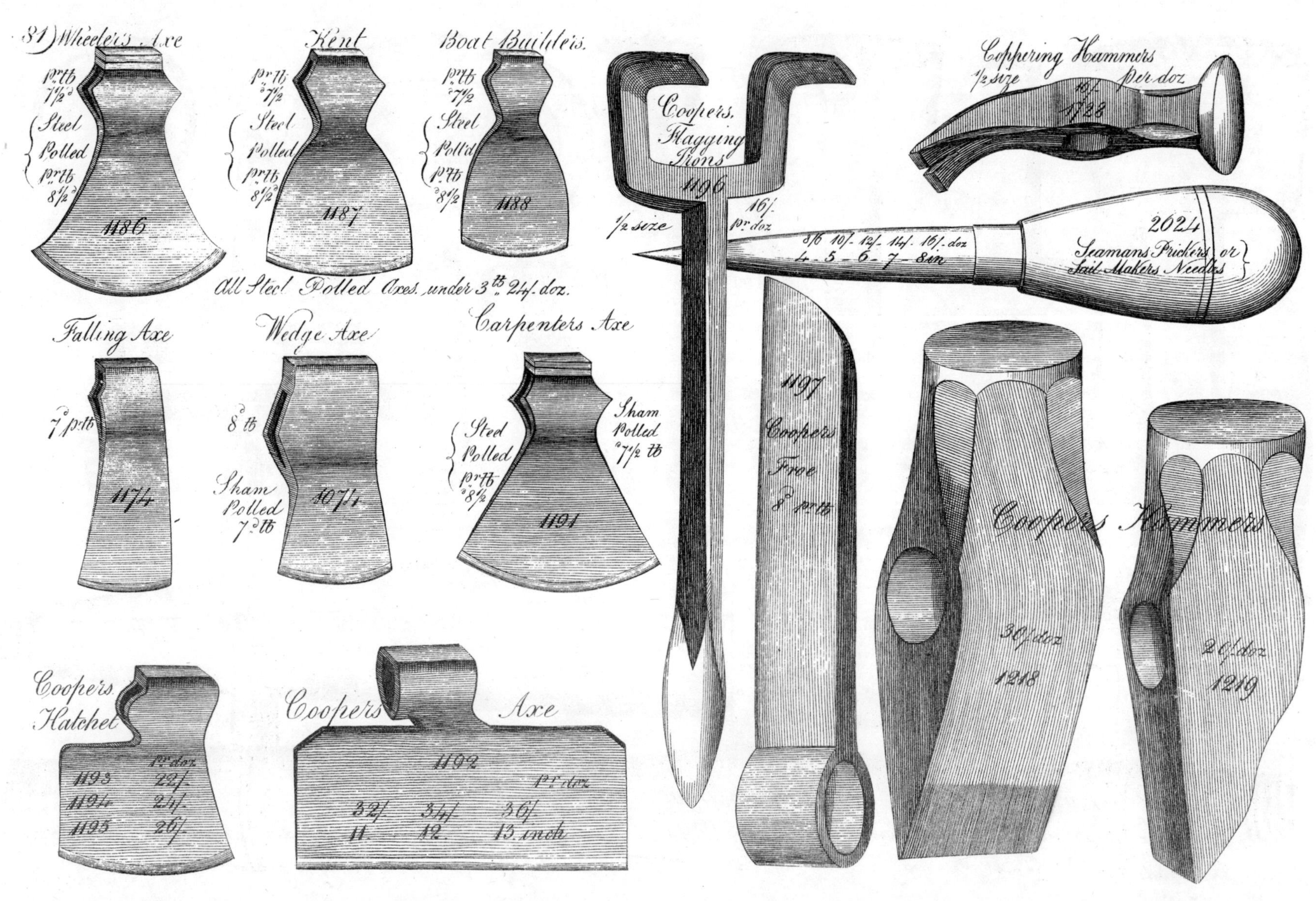
31) Wheeler's Axe
Pr.lb 7½d
Steel Polled
Pr.lb 8½d
1186

Kent
Pr.lb 7½d
Steel Polled
Pr.lb 8½d
1187

Boat Builders.
Pr.lb 7½d
Steel Polld
Pr.lb 8½d
1188

All Steel Polled Axes. under 3 lb 24/. doz.

Falling Axe
7 lb pr.lb
1174

Wedge Axe
8 lb
Sham Polled 7 lb
1071

Carpenters Axe
Steel Polled pr.lb 8½d
Sham Polled 7½ lb
1191

Coopers Hatchet
1193   pr. doz   22/.
1194   24/.
1195   26/.

Coopers   Axe
1192
pr. doz
32/.   34/.   36/.
11   12   13. inch

Coopers. Flagging Irons
1196
½ size   16/. pr doz

1197
Coopers Froe
8 pr.lb

Coppering Hammers
per doz
1728
½ size

2024
Seamans Prickers. or
Sail Makers Needles
8/6 10/. 12/. 14/. 16/. doz
4 - 5 - 6 - 7 - 8in

Coopers Hammers
30/. doz
1218

26/. doz
1219

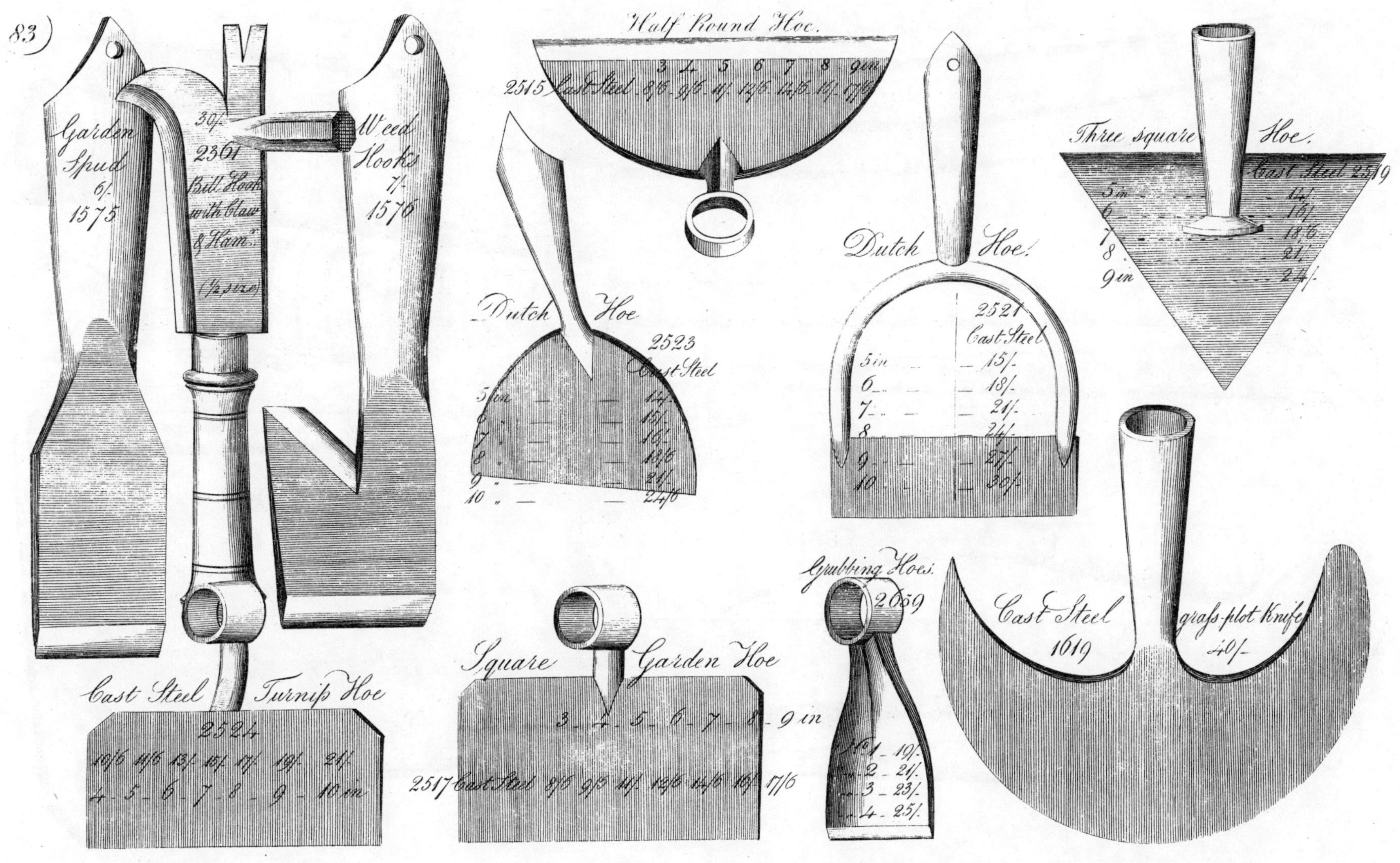

83
Garden Spud 6/ 1575
Garden Spud 6/ 1575
30/ 2361 Bill Hook with Claw & Ham" (½ size)
Weed Hooks 7/ 1576
Cast Steel Turnip Hoe
2524
10/6 11/6 13/ 15/ 17/ 19/ 21/
4 - 5 - 6 - 7 - 8 - 9 - 10 in
Half Round Hoe.
3 4 5 6 7 8 9 in
2515 Cast Steel 8/6 9/6 11/ 12/6 14/6 16/ 17/6
Dutch Hoe
5 in — 14/
6 — 15/
7 — 16/
8 — 18/6
9 — 21/
10 " — 24/6
2523 Cast Steel
Square Garden Hoe
3 - 4 - 5 - 6 - 7 - 8 - 9 in
2517 Cast Steel 8/6 9/3 11/ 12/6 14/6 16/ 17/6
Dutch Hoe!
2521 Cast Steel
5 in — 15/
6 — 18/
7 — 21/
8 — 24/
9 — 27/
10 — 30/
Grubbing Hoes.
2659
1 - 19/
2 - 21/
3 - 23/
4 - 25/
Three square Hoe.
Cast Steel 2519
5 in — 14/
6 — 16/
7 — 18/6
8 — 21/
9 in — 24/
Cast Steel 1619
grass-plot Knife.
40/

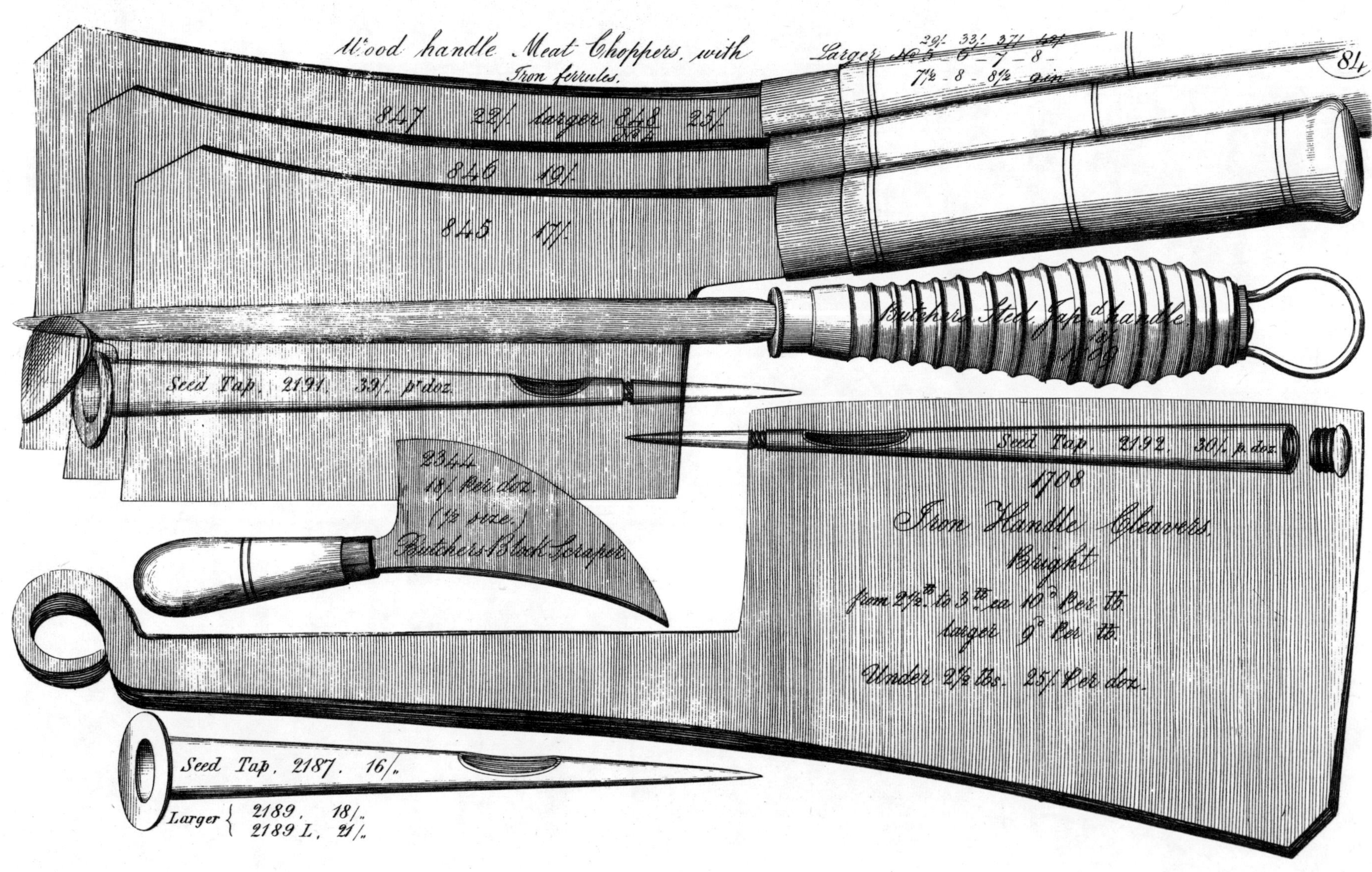

Wood handle Meat Choppers, with
Iron ferrules.
Larger No 5 29/. 33/. 37/. 42/. 6 - 7 - 8 -
7½ - 8 - 8½ - 9in.
847   22/   larger 848   25/
846   19/
845   17/
Butchers Steel Tap'd Handle
1729
Seed Tap. 2191. 39/ p' doz.
Seed Tap. 2192. 30/. p. doz.
1708
Iron Handle Cleavers,
Bright
from 2½℔ to 3℔ ea 10ᵈ Per ℔.
larger 9ᵈ Per ℔.
Under 2½ ℔s. 25/ Per doz.
2344
18/ Per doz.
(½ size.)
Butchers Block Scraper.
Seed Tap. 2187. 16/„
Larger { 2189.   18/„
        2189 L. 21/„

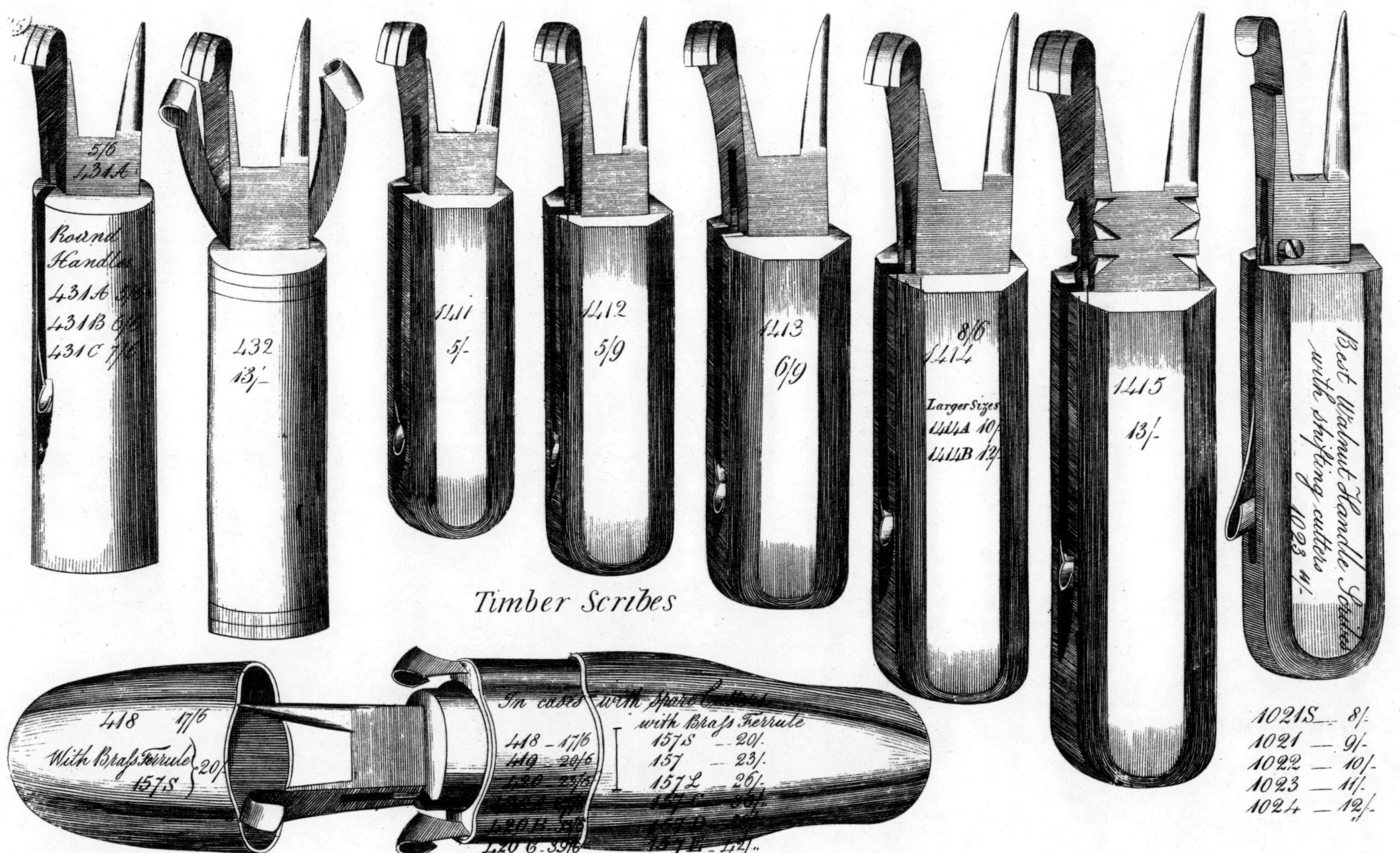
Round
Handles
431A 5/6
431B 6/6
431C 7/6
5/6
431A
432
13/-
1411
5/-
1412
5/9
1413
6/9
8/6
1414
Larger Sizes
1414A 10/
1414B 12/
1415
13/-
Best Walnut Handle fitted
with shifting cutter
1023 4/-
Timber Scribes
418 17/6
With Brass Ferrule 20/
157S
In cases with Spare Cutters
with Brass Ferrule
418 — 17/6
419 — 20/6
420 — 23/6
420B — 5/6
420 C. 39/6
157S — 20/.
157 — 23/.
157L — 26/.
1021S — 8/.
1021 — 9/-
1022 — 10/-
1023 — 11/-
1024 — 12/-

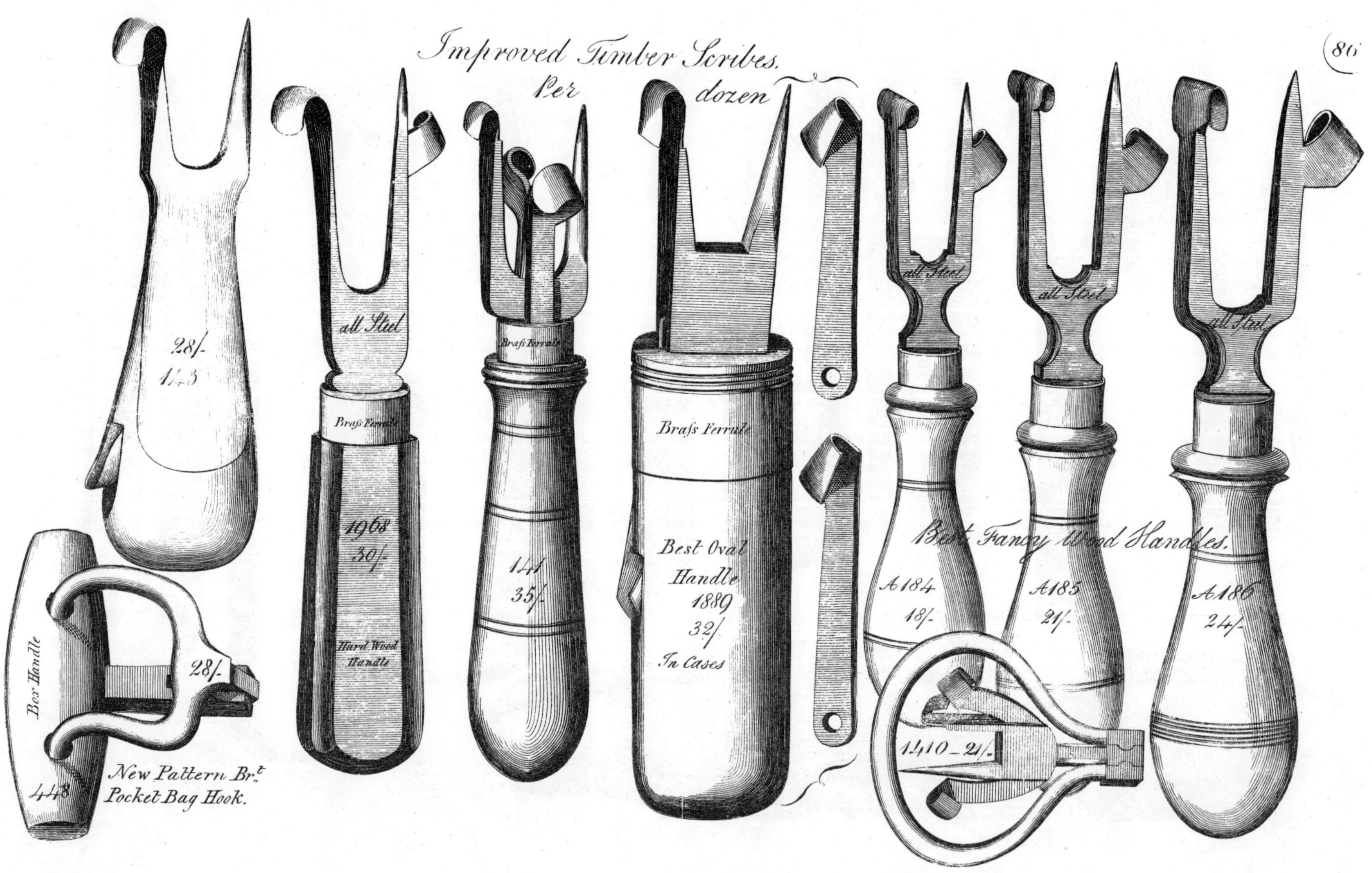

Improved Timber Scribes.
Per dozen
(86)
28/-
143
all Steel
Brass Ferrule
1968
30/-
Hard Wood Handle
Brass Ferrule
141
35/-
Brass Ferrule
Best Oval
Handle
1889
32/-
In Cases
all Steel
all Steel
all Steel
Best Fancy Wood Handles.
A184
18/-
A185
21/-
A186
24/-
1410 — 21/-
Box Handle
28/-
448
New Pattern Br.t
Pocket Bag Hook.

Ladies Netting Vices.

1185 54/-

Netting Vice. with Cushion.

Teeth Instruments in Cases.

867 7/6 ea

A size larger with a Brush 868 10/6

866 6/6 ea

865 5/6 ea

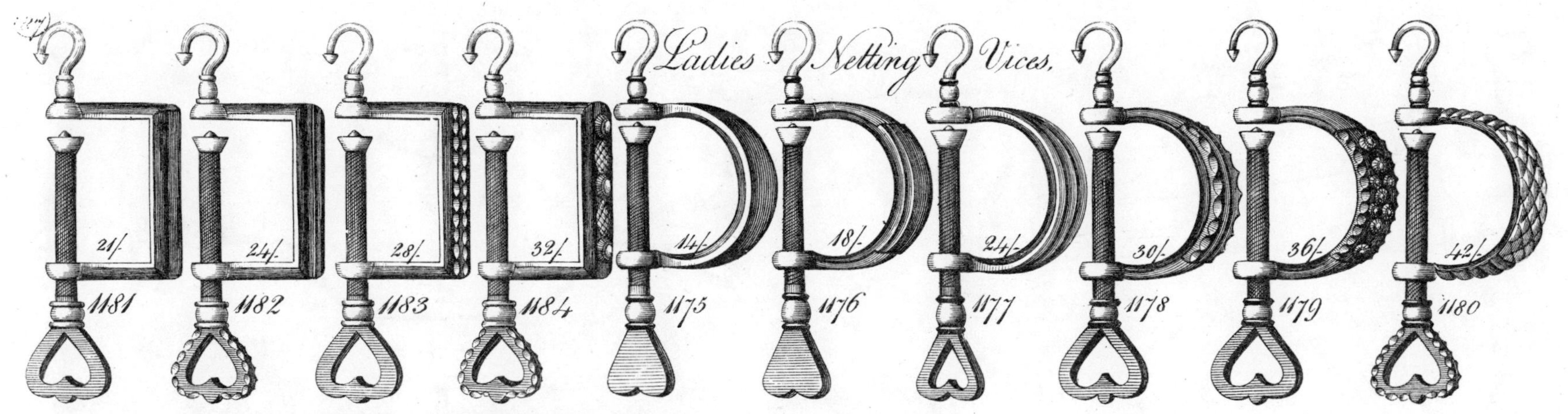

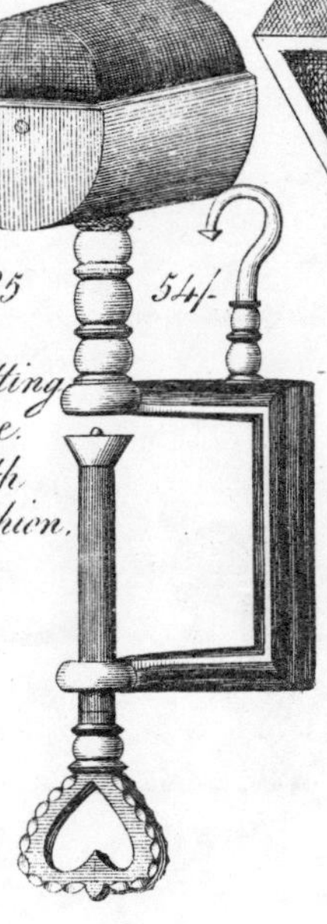

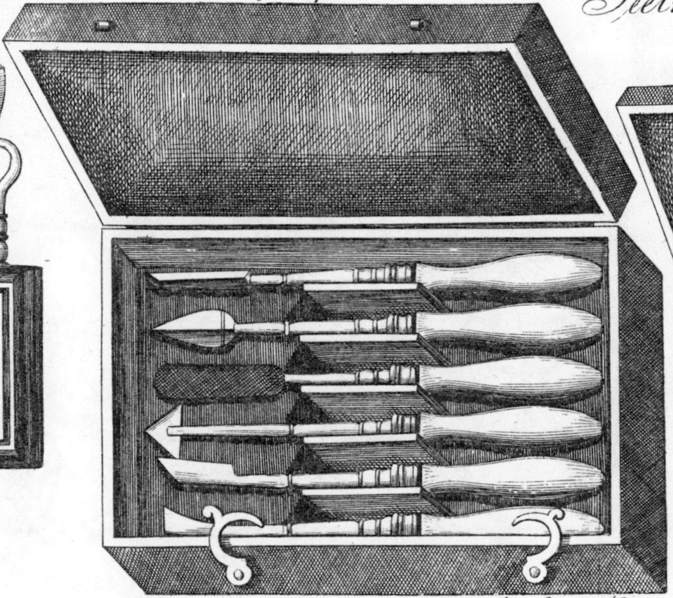

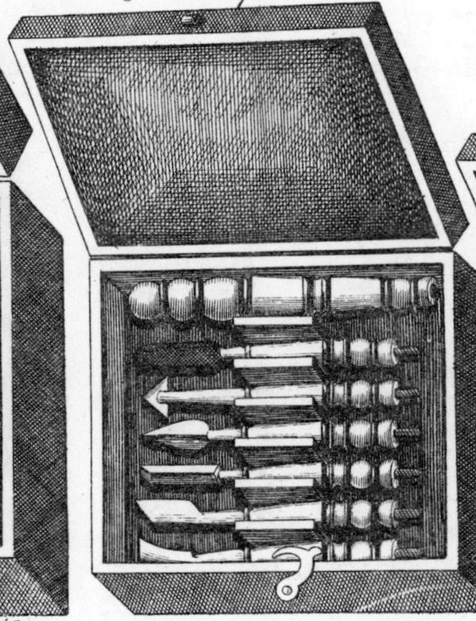

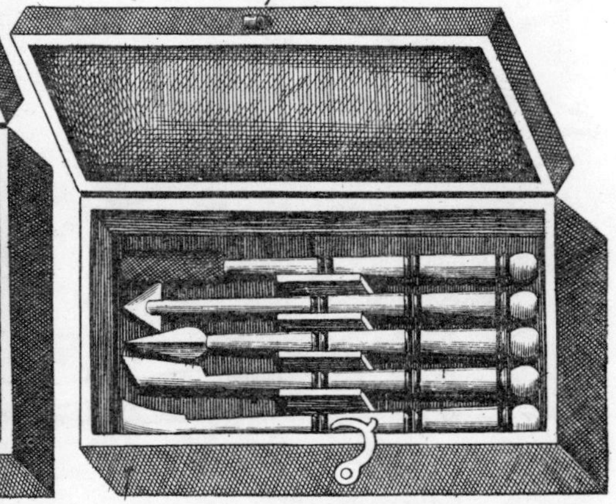

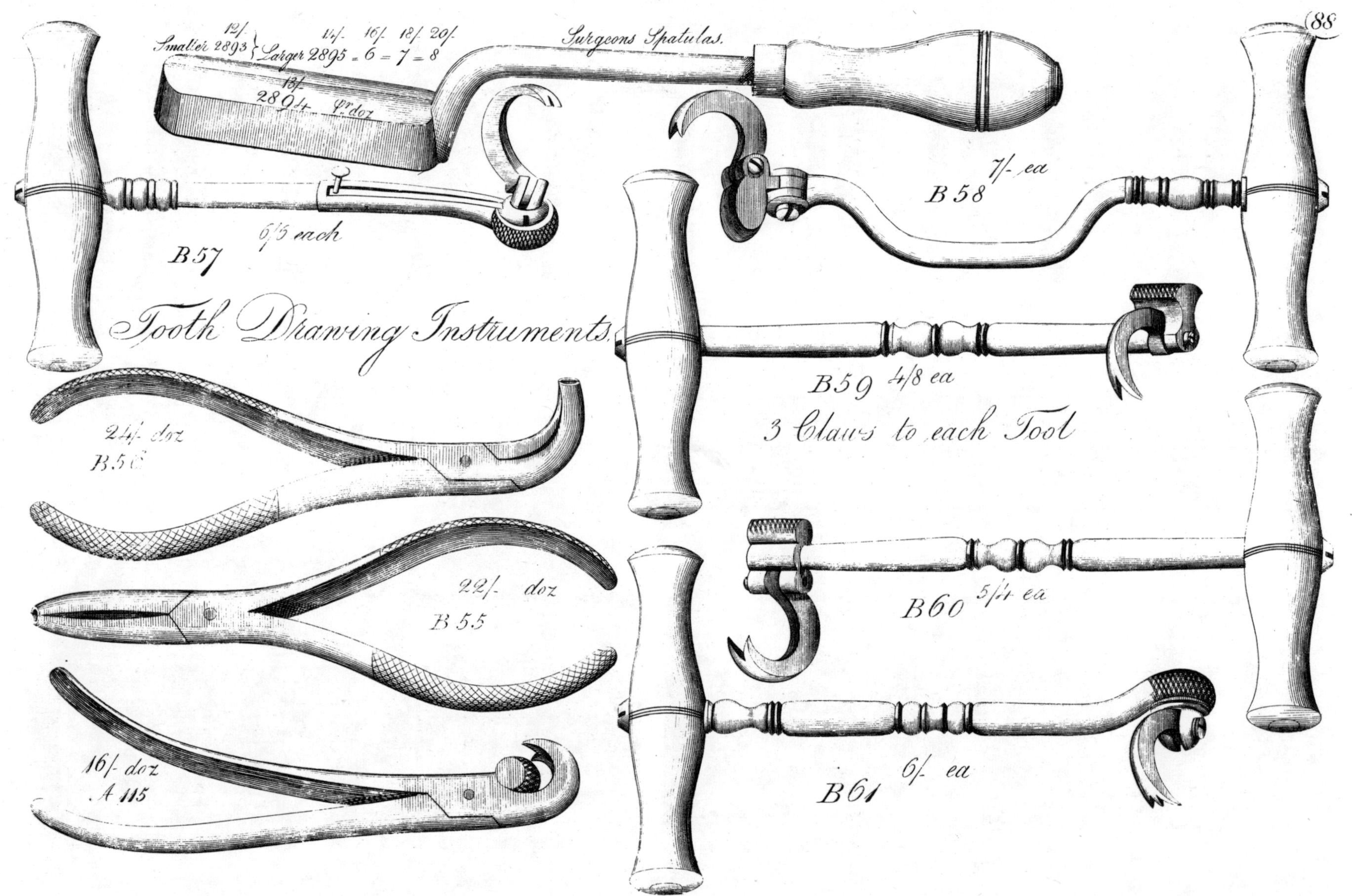

(88
12/
Smaller 2893
14/ 16/ 18/ 20/
Larger 2895 = 6 = 7 = 8
13/
2894 Pr doz
Surgeons Spatulas.
7/- ea
B 58
6/5 each
B 57
Tooth Drawing Instruments.
B 59 4/8 ea
3 Claws to each Tool
24/- doz
B 56
22/- doz
B 55
B 60 5/4 ea
16/- doz
A 115
B 61 6/- ea

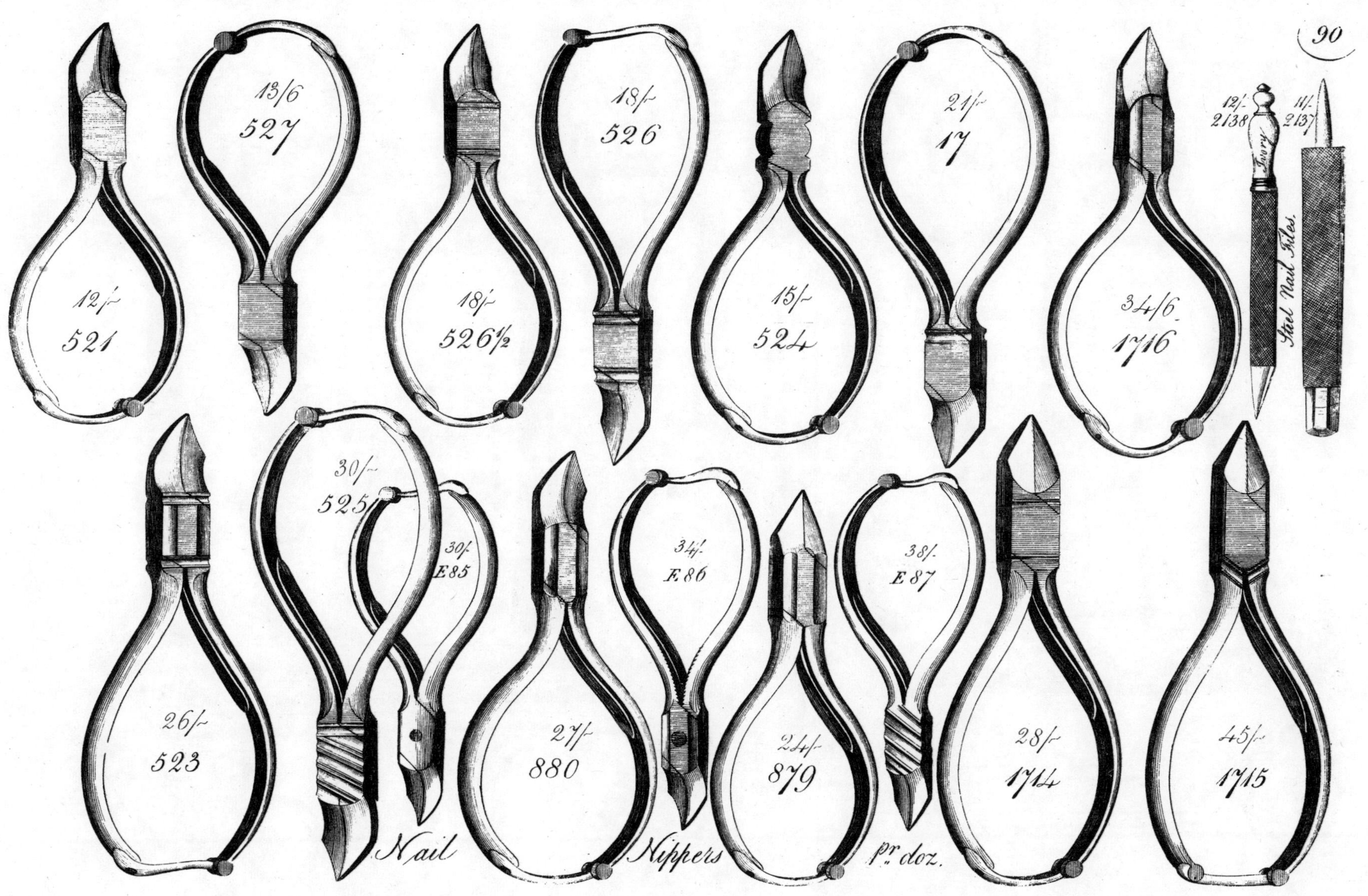
90
12/-
2138
11/-
2137
Ivory
Steel Nail Files.
13/6
527
18/-
526
21/-
17
12/-
521
18/-
526½
15/-
524
34/6
1716
30/-
525
30/-
E85
34/-
E86
38/-
E87
26/-
523
27/-
880
24/-
879
28/-
1714
45/-
1715
Nail Nippers pr doz.

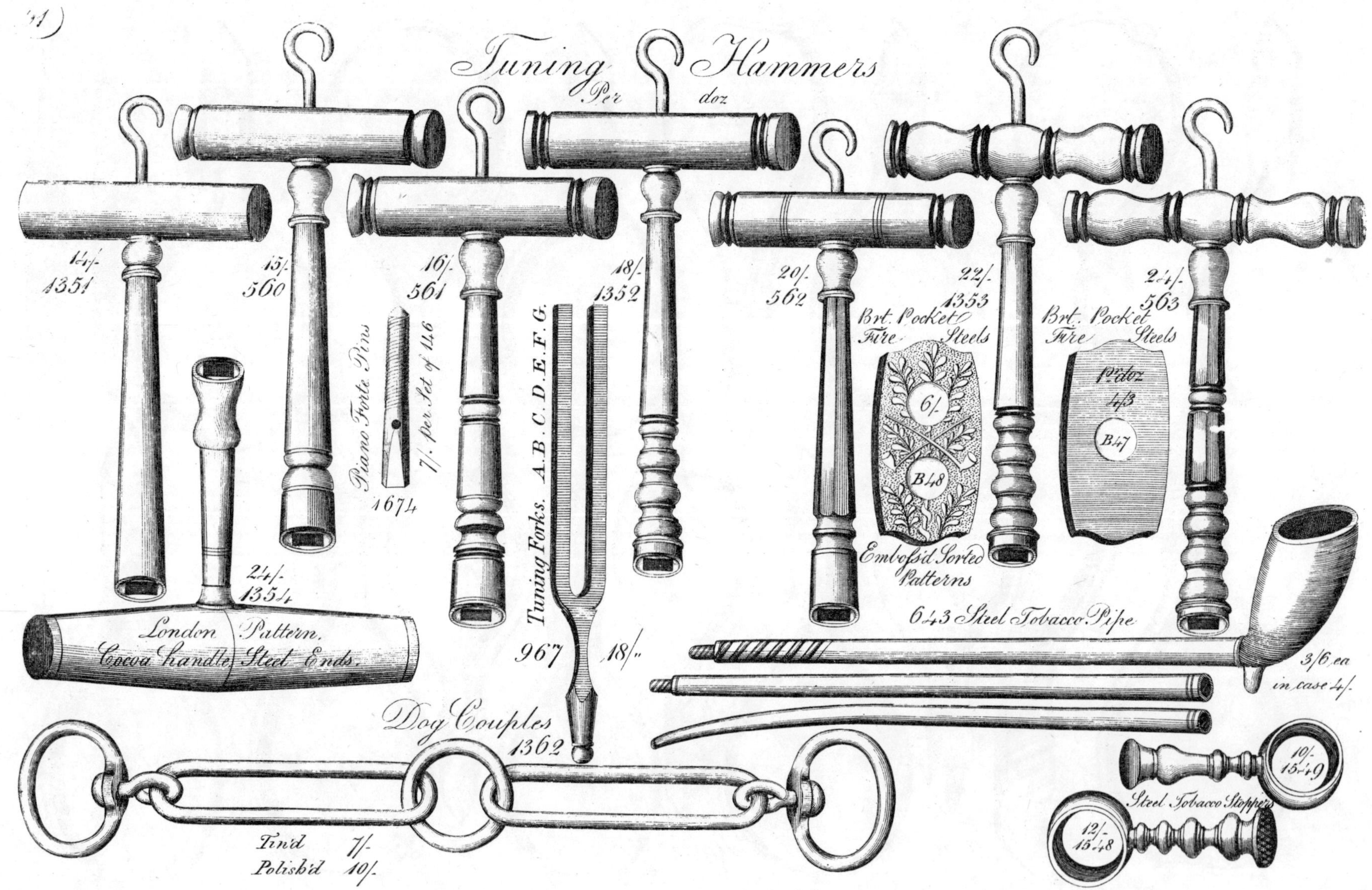
Tuning Hammers
Per doz
14/- 1351
15/- 560
16/- 561
7/- per Set of 116
Piano Forte Pins
1674
18/- 1352
Tuning Forks. A.B.C.D.E.F.G.
967   18/-
20/- 562
22/- 1353
Brt. Pocket Fire Steels
6/-
B48
Emboss'd Sorted Patterns
Brt. Pocket Fire Steels
1? doz 4/3
B47
24/- 563
643 Steel Tobacco Pipe
3/6 ea
in case 4/-
24/- 1354
London Pattern.
Cocoa Handle Steel Ends.
Dog Couples
1362
Tin'd   7/-
Polish'd 10/-
Steel Tobacco Stoppers
10/- 15-9
12/- 15-48

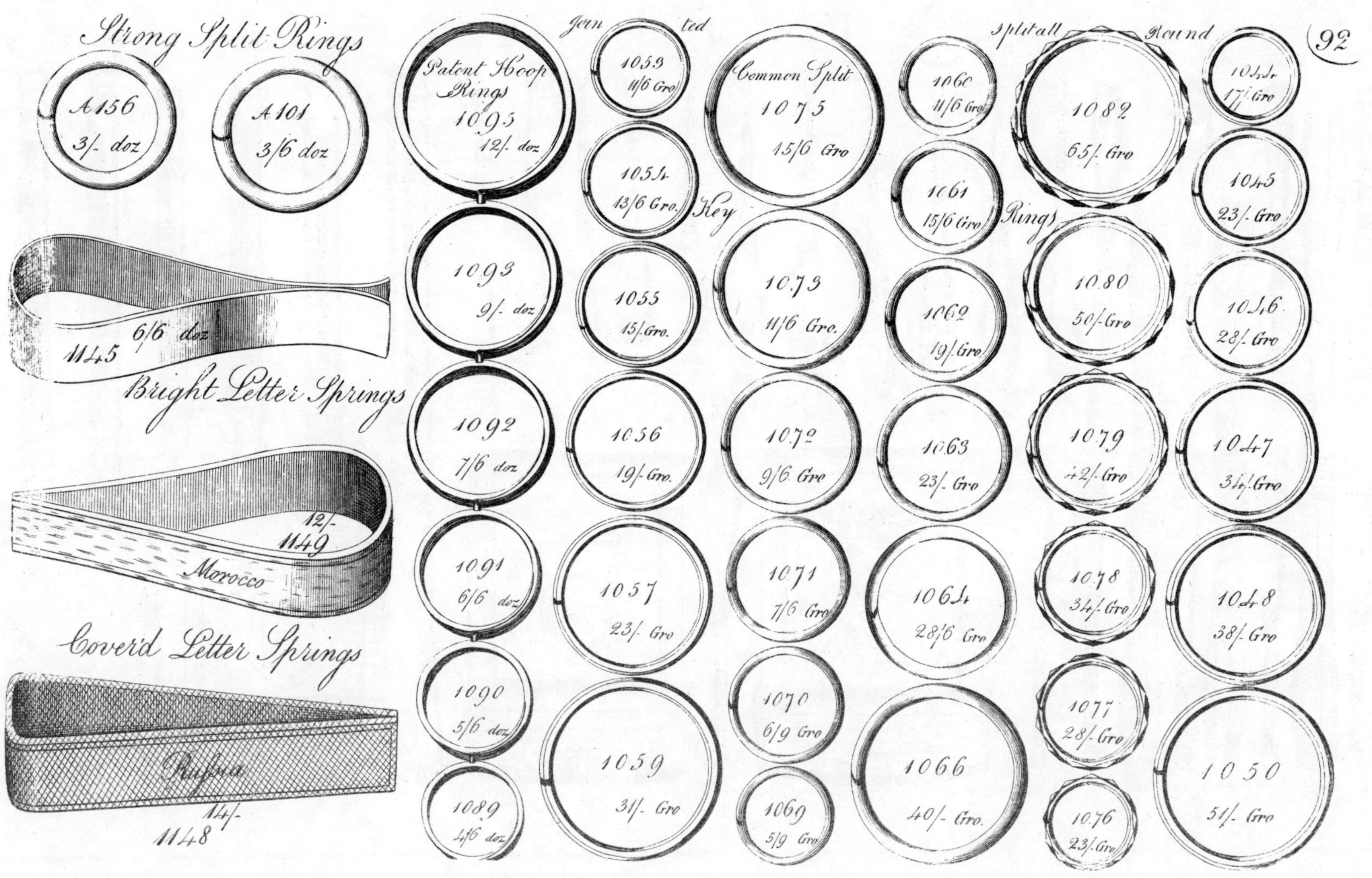
92
Strong Split Rings
A156
3/- doz
A101
3/6 doz
1145
6/6 doz
Bright Letter Springs
1149
12/-
Morocco
Cover'd Letter Springs
1148
14/-
Russia
Patent Hoop Rings
1095
12/- doz
1093
9/- doz
1092
7/6 doz
1091
6/6 doz
1090
5/6 doz
1089
4/6 doz
Join ted
1059
4/6 Gro
1054
13/6 Gro.
1055
15/. Gro.
1056
19/. Gro.
1057
23/. Gro
1058
31/. Gro
Key
Common Split
1075
15/6 Gro
1073
11/6 Gro.
1072
9/6 Gro
1071
7/6 Gro.
1070
6/9 Gro
1066
40/- Gro.
1060
11/6 Gro.
1061
15/6 Gro.
1062
19/. Gro
1063
23/. Gro
1064
28/6 Gro.
1069
5/9 Gro.
splitall Round
1082
65/. Gro
Rings
1080
50/. Gro
1079
42/. Gro
1078
34/. Gro
1077
28/. Gro
1076
23/. Gro
1044
17/. Gro
1045
23/. Gro
1046
28/. Gro
1047
34/. Gro
1048
38/. Gro
1050
51/. Gro

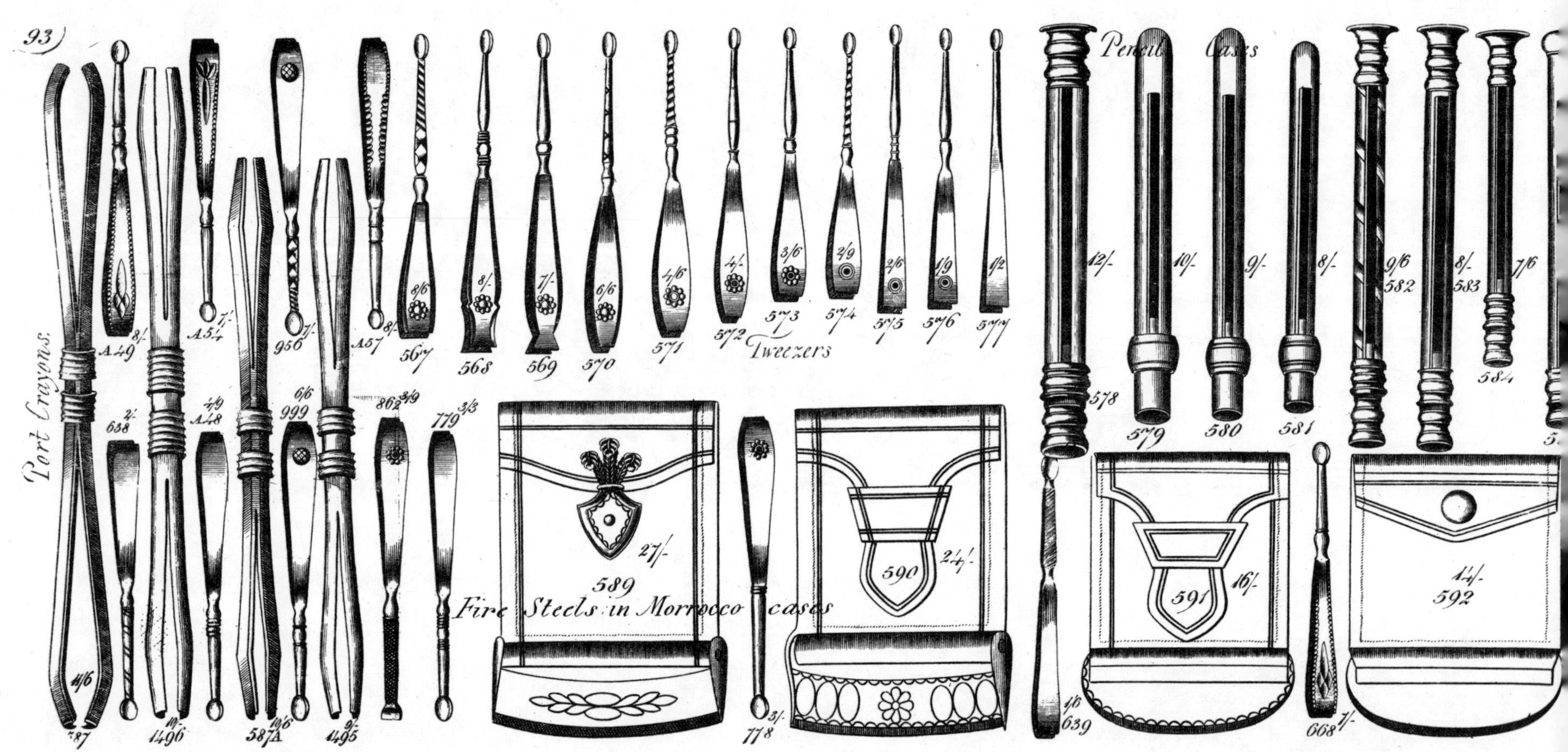

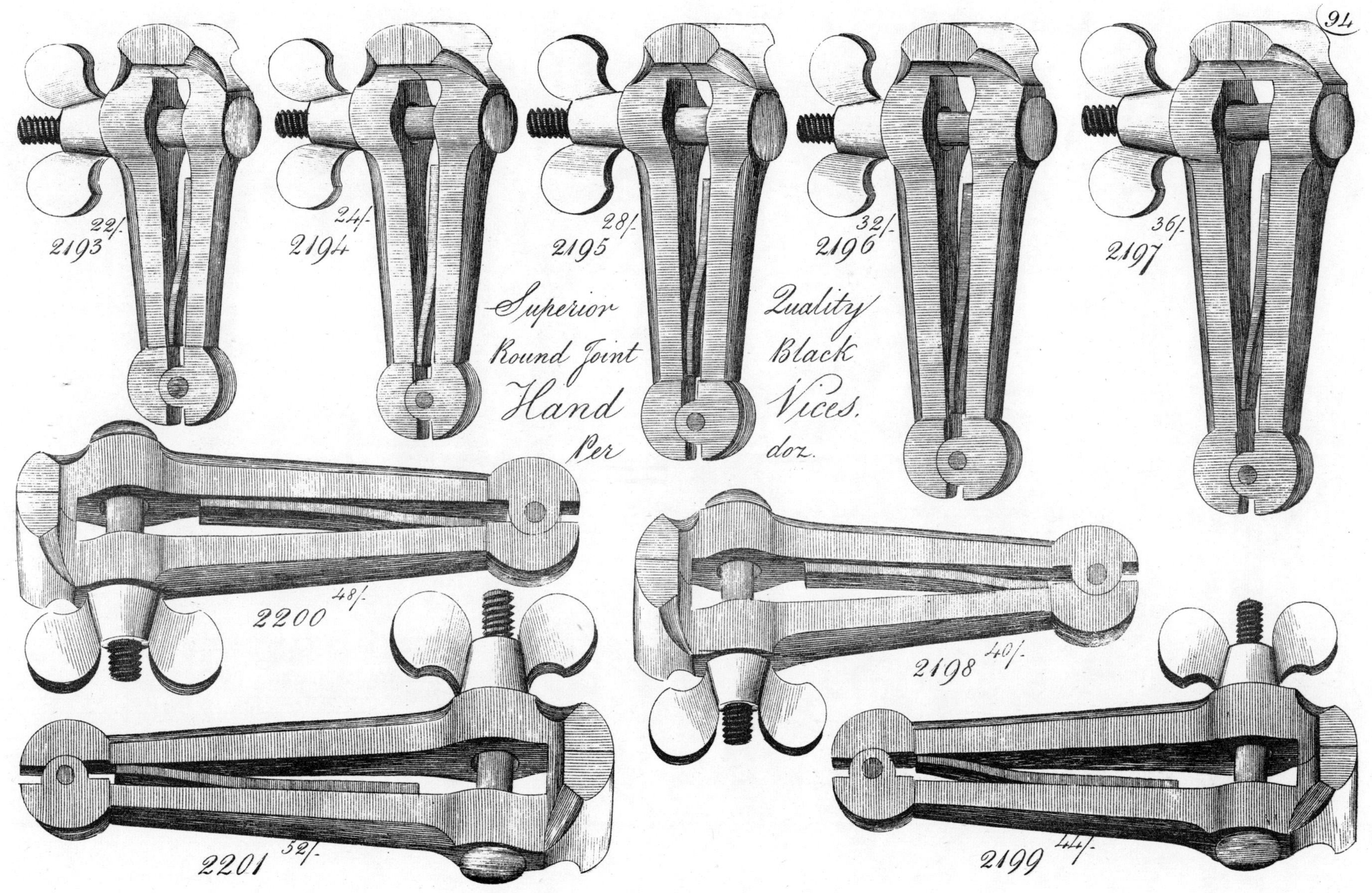

2193
22/-
2194
24/-
2195
28/-
2196
32/-
2197
36/-
Superior
Round Joint
Hand
Per
Quality
Black
Vices.
doz.
2200
48/-
2198
40/-
2201
52/-
2199
44/-

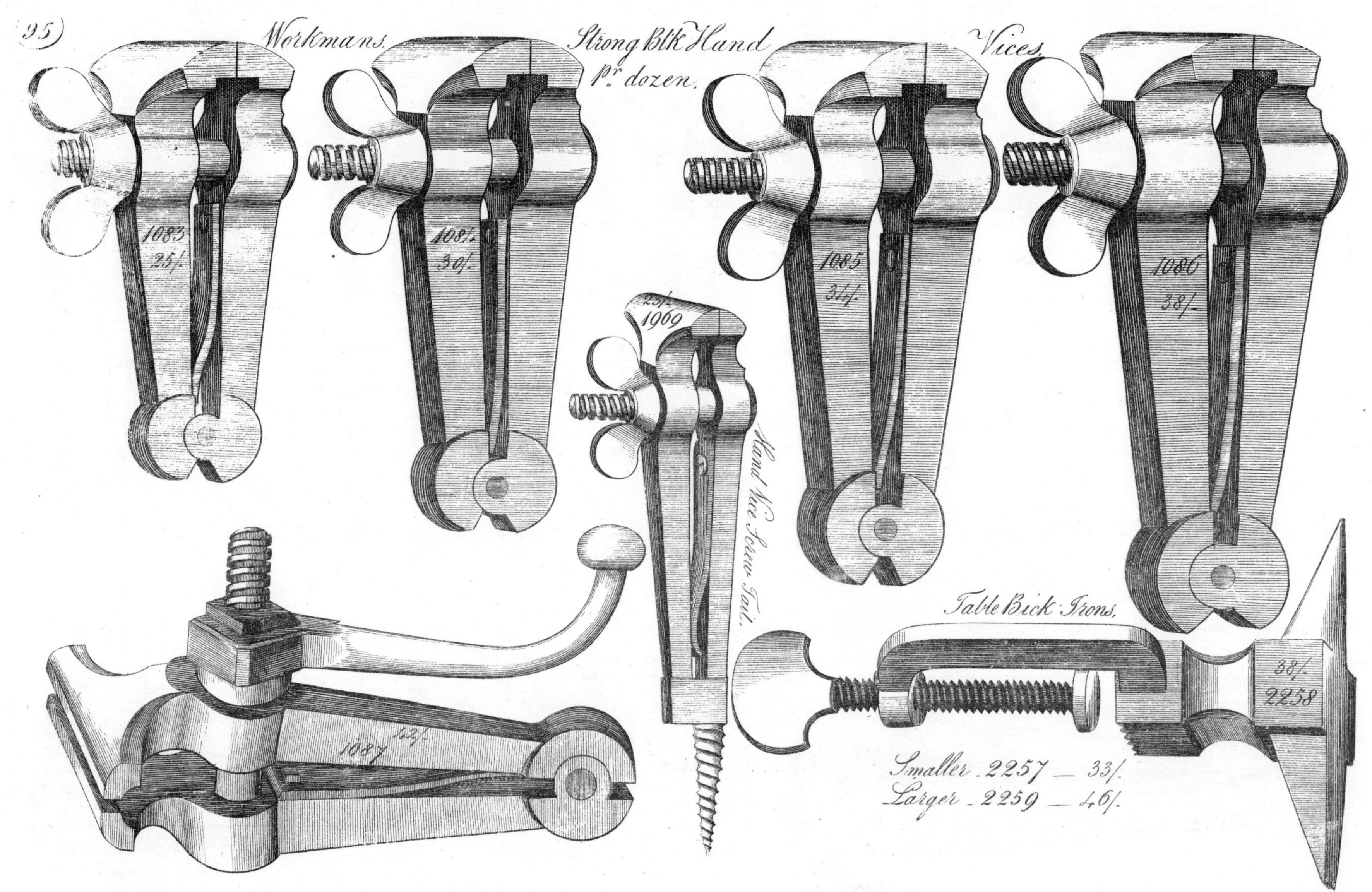
95)
Workmans. Strong Blk Hand Vices.
Pr dozen.
1083 25/
1084 30/
1085 34/
1086 38/
25/ 1969
Hand Vice Screw Tail.
1087 42/
Table Bick Irons.
38/ 2258
Smaller 2257 — 33/
Larger 2259 — 46/

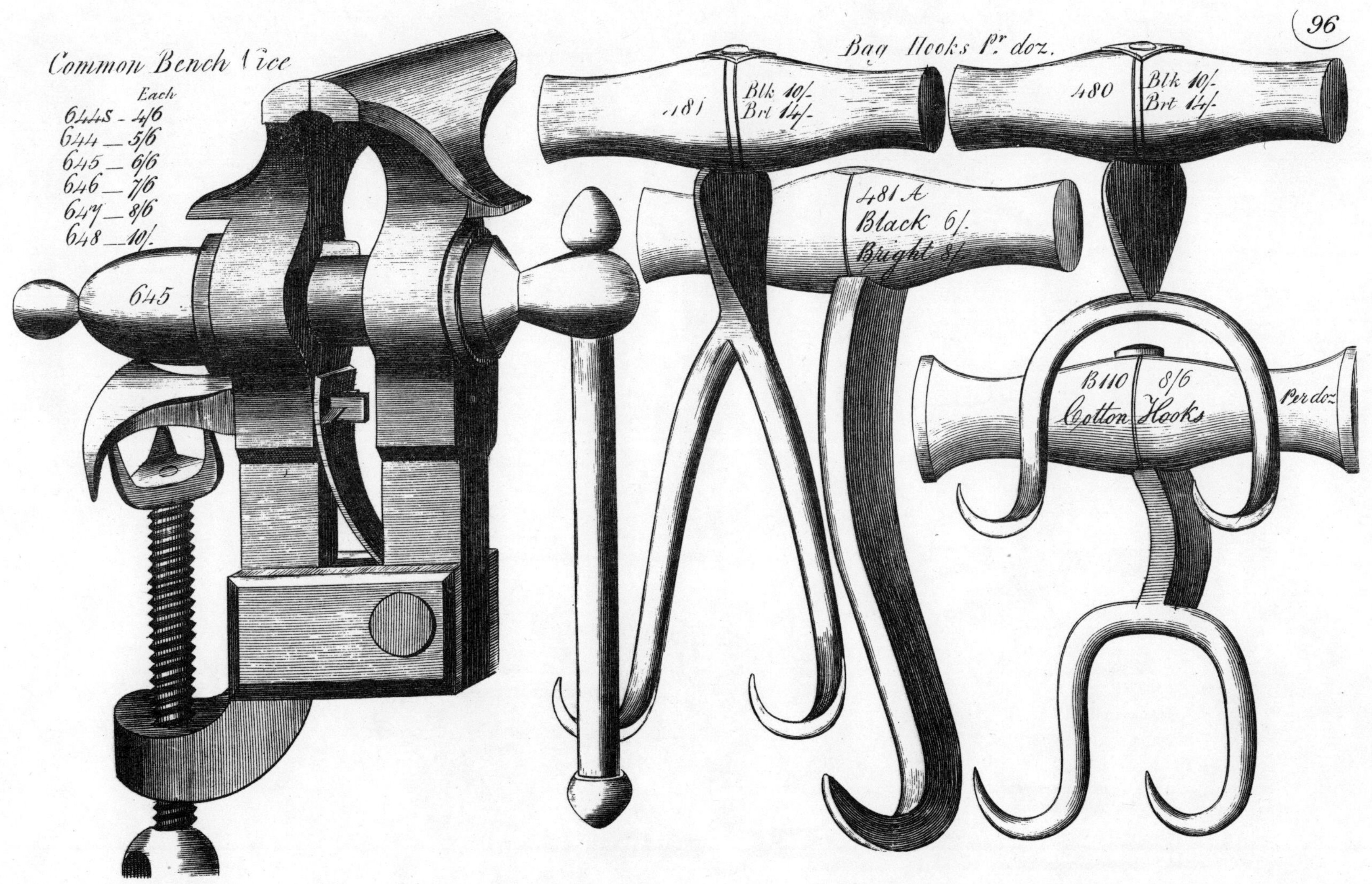

Common Bench Vice
Each
644S — 4/6
644 — 5/6
645 — 6/6
646 — 7/6
647 — 8/6
648 — 10/
645
Bag Hooks Pr. doz.
481
Blk 10/-
Brt 14/-
480
Blk 10/-
Brt 14/-
481 A
Black 6/.
Bright 8/
B 110
8/6
Cotton Hooks
Per doz.
96

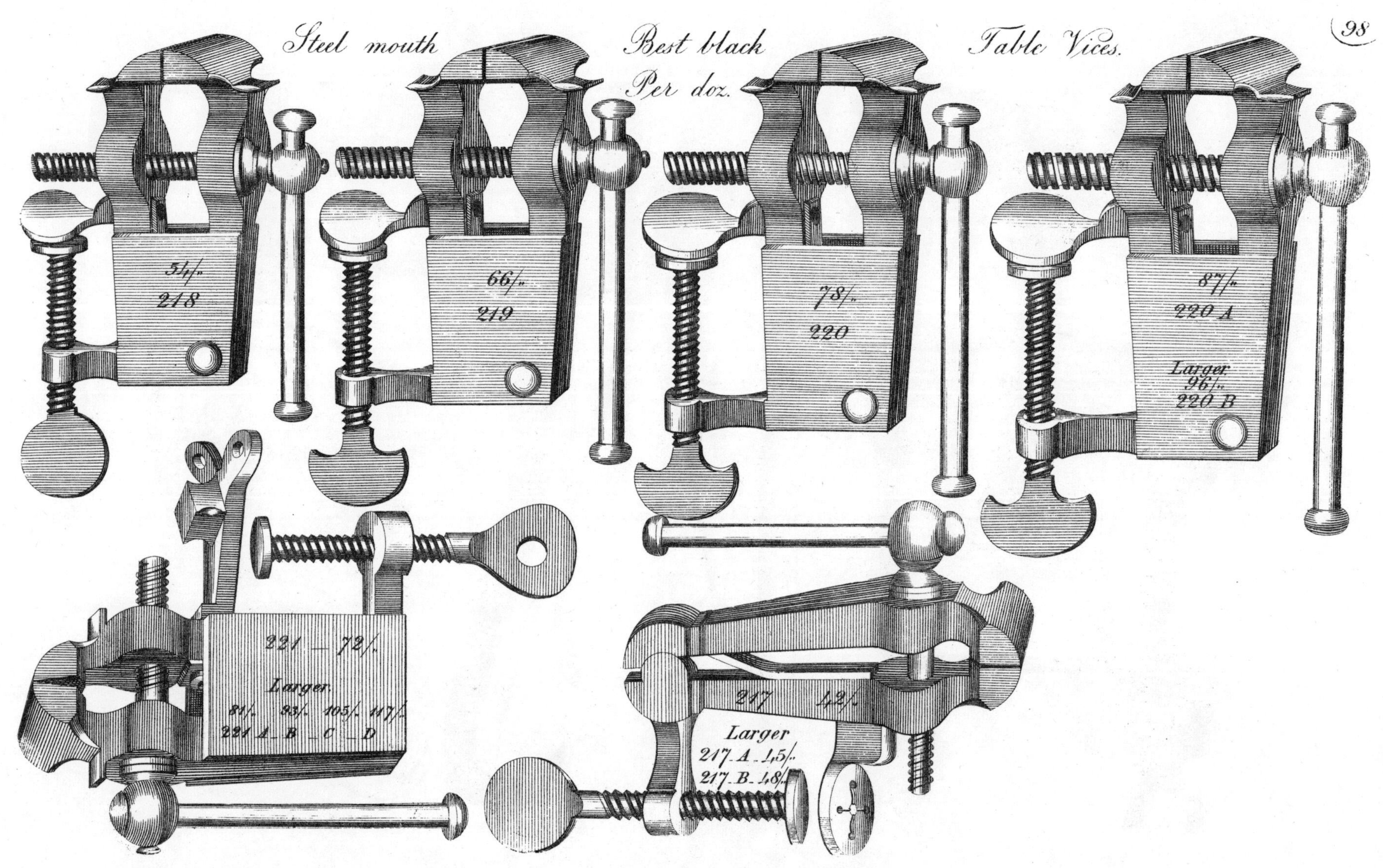
Steel mouth
Best black
Per doz.
Table Vices.
54/"
218
66/.
219
78/.
220
87/"
220 A
Larger
96/.
220 B
221 — 72/.
Larger
81/.   93/.   105/.   117/.
221 A   B   C   D
217   42/.
Larger
217 A   45/.
217 B   48/.

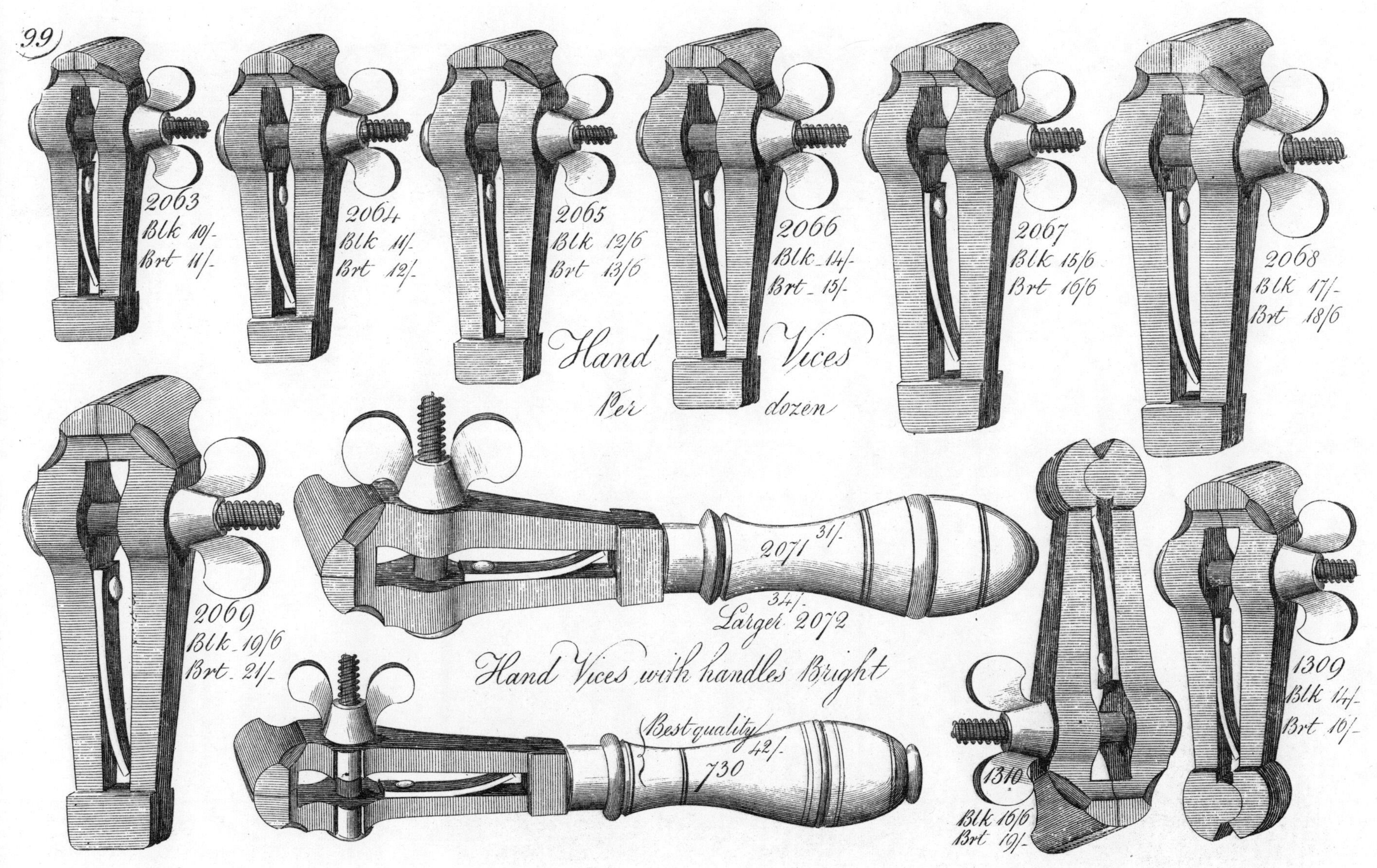
99
2063
Blk 10/-
Brt 11/-
2064
Blk 11/-
Brt 12/-
2065
Blk 12/6
Brt 13/6
2066
Blk 14/-
Brt 15/-
2067
Blk 15/6
Brt 16/6
2068
Blk 17/-
Brt 18/6
Hand Vices
Per dozen
2069
Blk 19/6
Brt 21/-
2071 31/-
Larger 2072 34/-
Hand Vices with handles Bright
Best quality 42/-
730
1309
Blk 14/-
Brt 16/-
1310
Blk 16/6
Brt 19/-

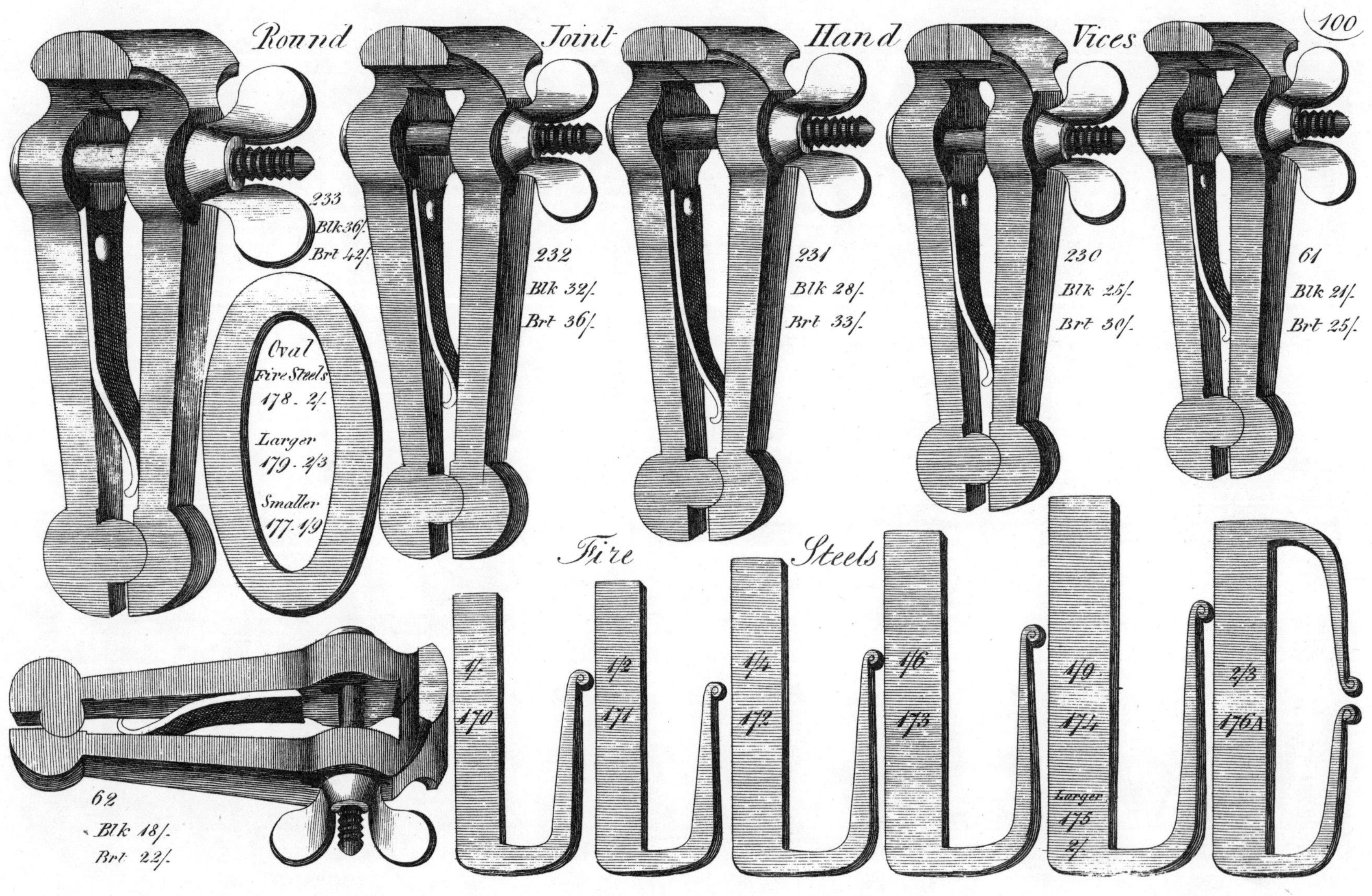

Round   Joint   Hand   Vices   100

233
Blk 36/.
Brt 42/.

Oval
Fire Steels
178 . 2/.

Larger
179 . 2/3

Smaller
177. 1/9

232
Blk 32/.
Brt 36/.

231
Blk 28/.
Brt 33/.

230
Blk 25/.
Brt 30/.

61
Blk 21/.
Brt 25/.

Fire   Steels

62
Blk 18/.
Brt 22/.

1/.
170

1/2
171

1/4
172

1/6
173

1/9
174

2/3
176A

Larger
175
2/.

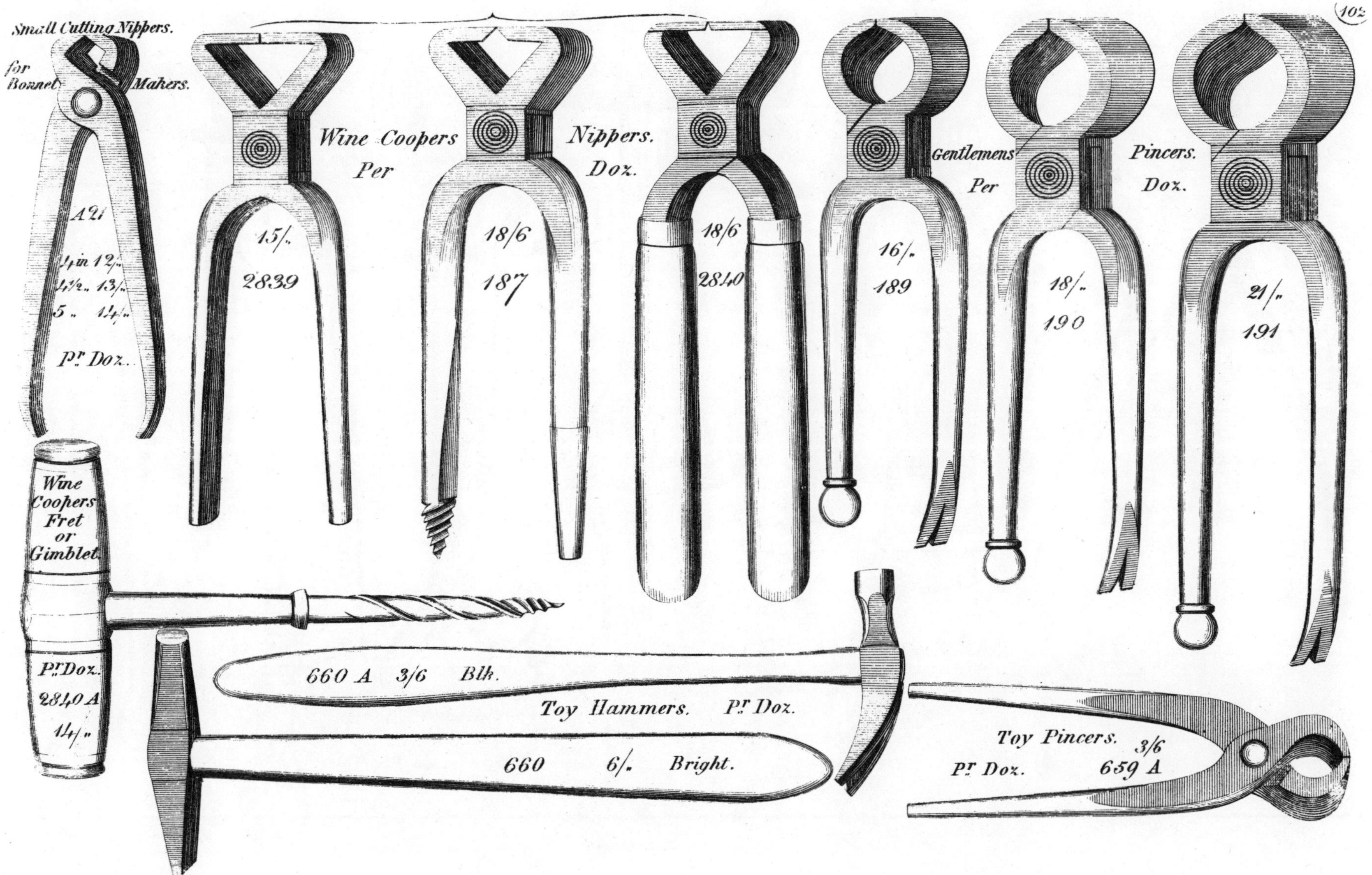
Small Cutting Nippers.
for Bonnet Makers.
A 2i
4 in 12/.
4 1/2 .. 13/.
5 .. 14/.
Pr Doz.
Wine Coopers
Per
15/.
2839
Nippers.
Doz.
18/6
187
18/6
2840
Gentlemens
Per
16/.
189
18/.
190
Pincers.
Doz.
21/.
191
Wine Coopers Fret or Gimblet.
Pr Doz.
2840 A
14/.
660 A   3/6   Blk.
Toy Hammers.   Pr Doz.
660   6/.   Bright.
Toy Pincers.   3/6
Pr Doz.   659 A

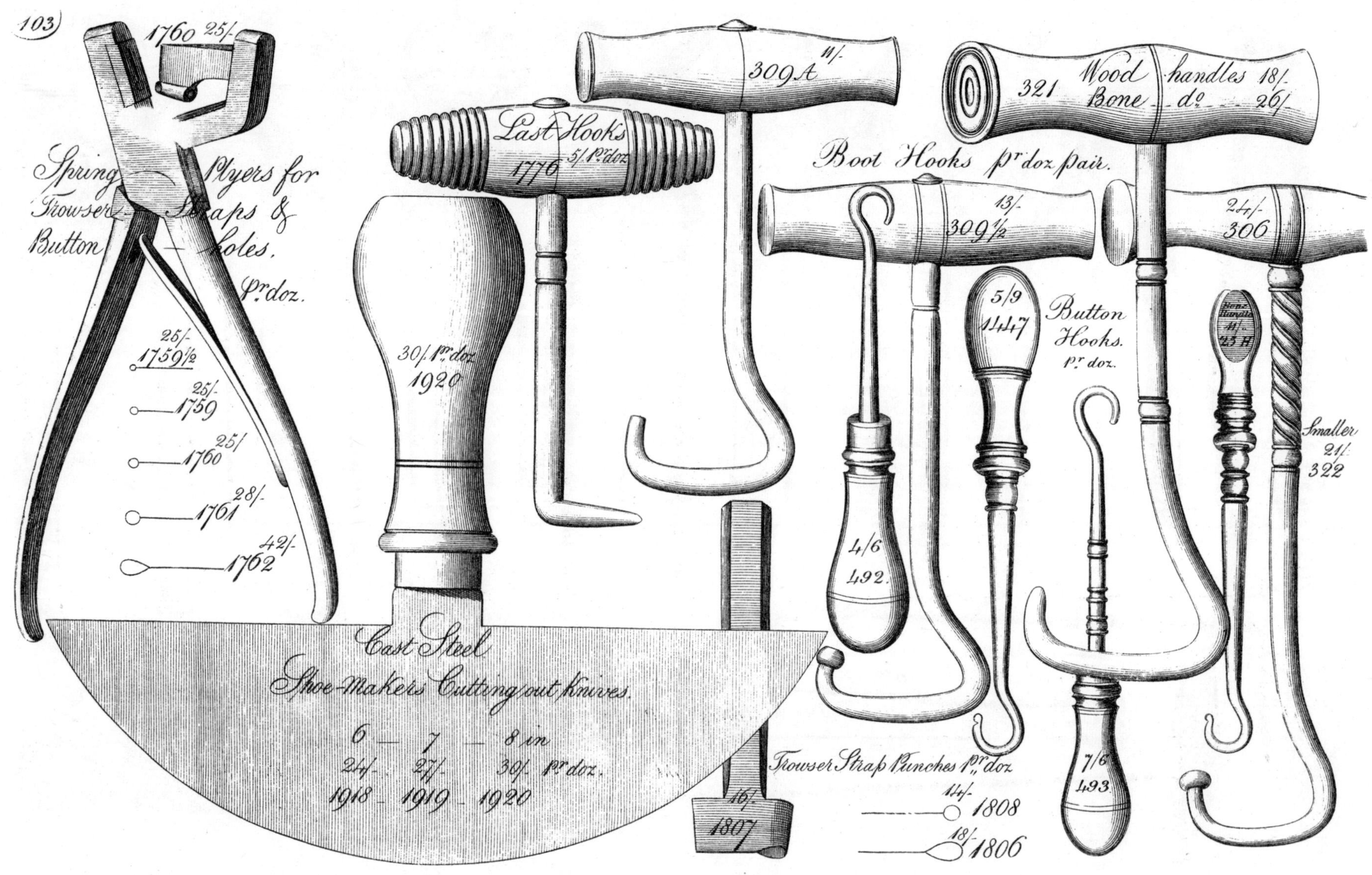

103
1760 25/
Spring Plyers for
Trowser Straps &
Button Holes.
Pr doz.
25/
1759½
25/
1759
25/
1760
28/
1761
42/
1762
Last Hooks
5/ Pr doz
1776
309A
11/
321 Wood handles 18/
Bone do 26/
Boot Hooks Pr doz pair.
13/
309½
24/
306
30/ Pr doz
1920
5/9
1447
Button
Hooks.
Pr doz.
Bone
Handle
4/
23 H
Smaller
21/
322
4/6
492.
Cast Steel
Shoe-Makers Cutting out Knives.
6 — 7 — 8 in
24/ — 27/ — 30/ Pr doz
1918 — 1919 — 1920
16/
1807
7/6
493
Trowser Strap Punches Pr doz
14/ 1808
18/ 1806

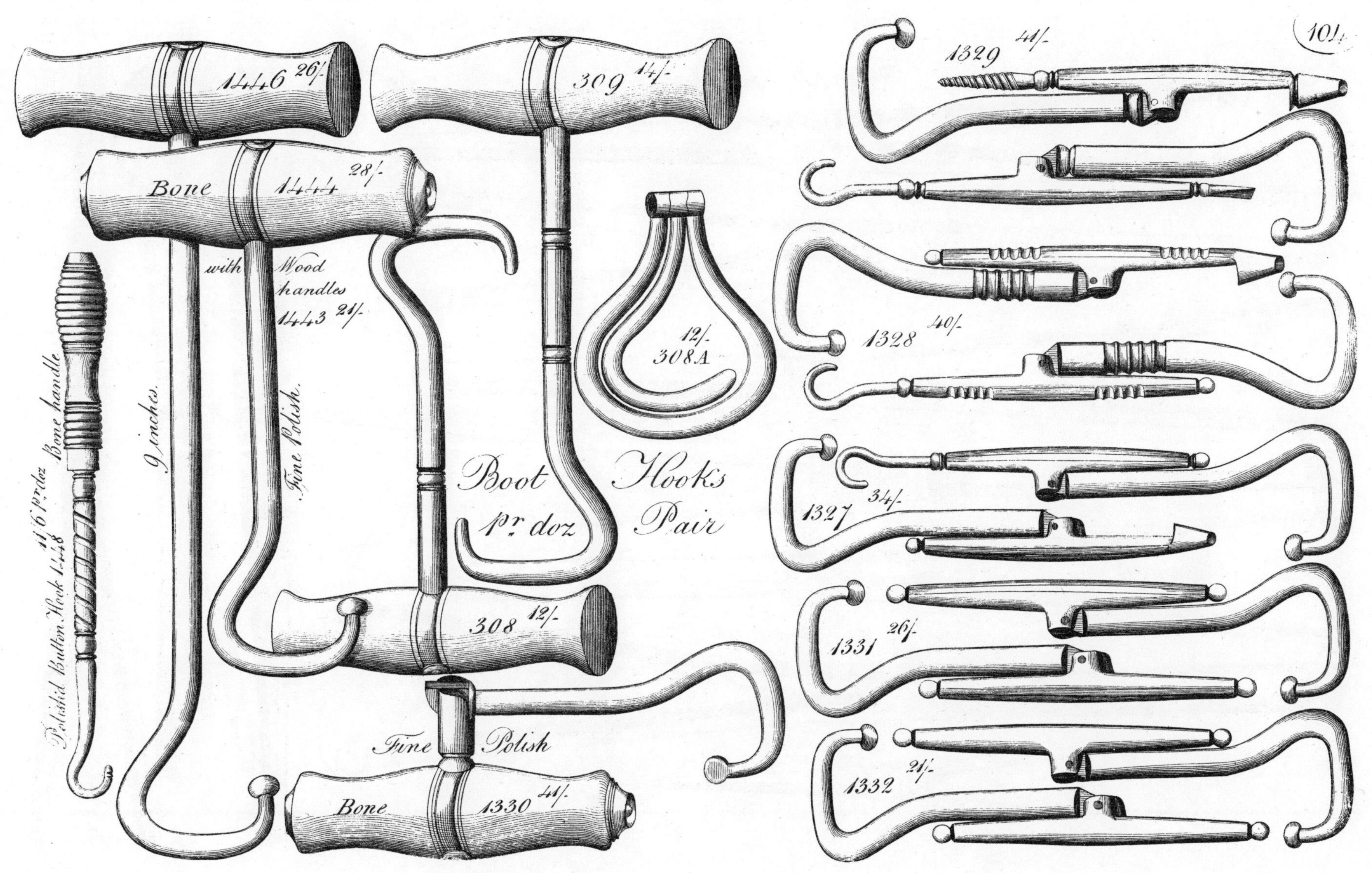

104
1329 41/
1446 26/
309 14/
Bone 1444 28/
with Wood handles 1443 21/
9 inches.
Fine Polish.
Boot pr doz Hooks Pair
12/ 308A
1328 40/
1327 34/
1331 26/
1332 24/
Polished Button Hook 1448 41/6 pr doz Bone handle
308 12/
Fine Polish
Bone 1330 41/

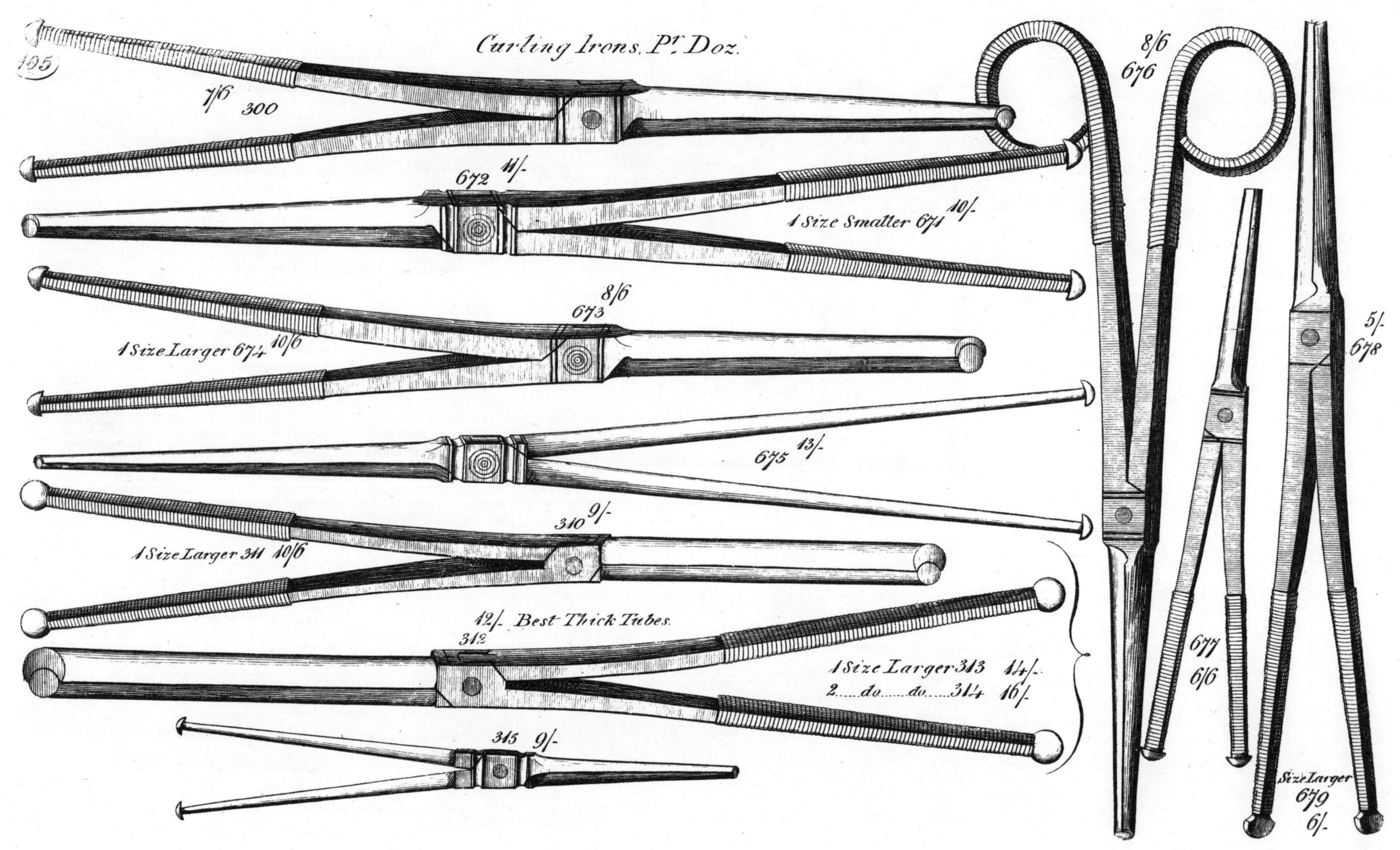

Curling Irons. P.r Doz.
105
7/6   300
672   11/-
1 Size Smaller 671   10/-
1 Size Larger 674   10/6
8/6   673
675   13/-
310   9/-
1 Size Larger 311   10/6
12/- Best Thick Tubes.
312
1 Size Larger 313   14/-
2 ....do....do..... 314   16/-
315   9/-
8/6   676
5/-   678
677   6/6
Size Larger 679   6/-

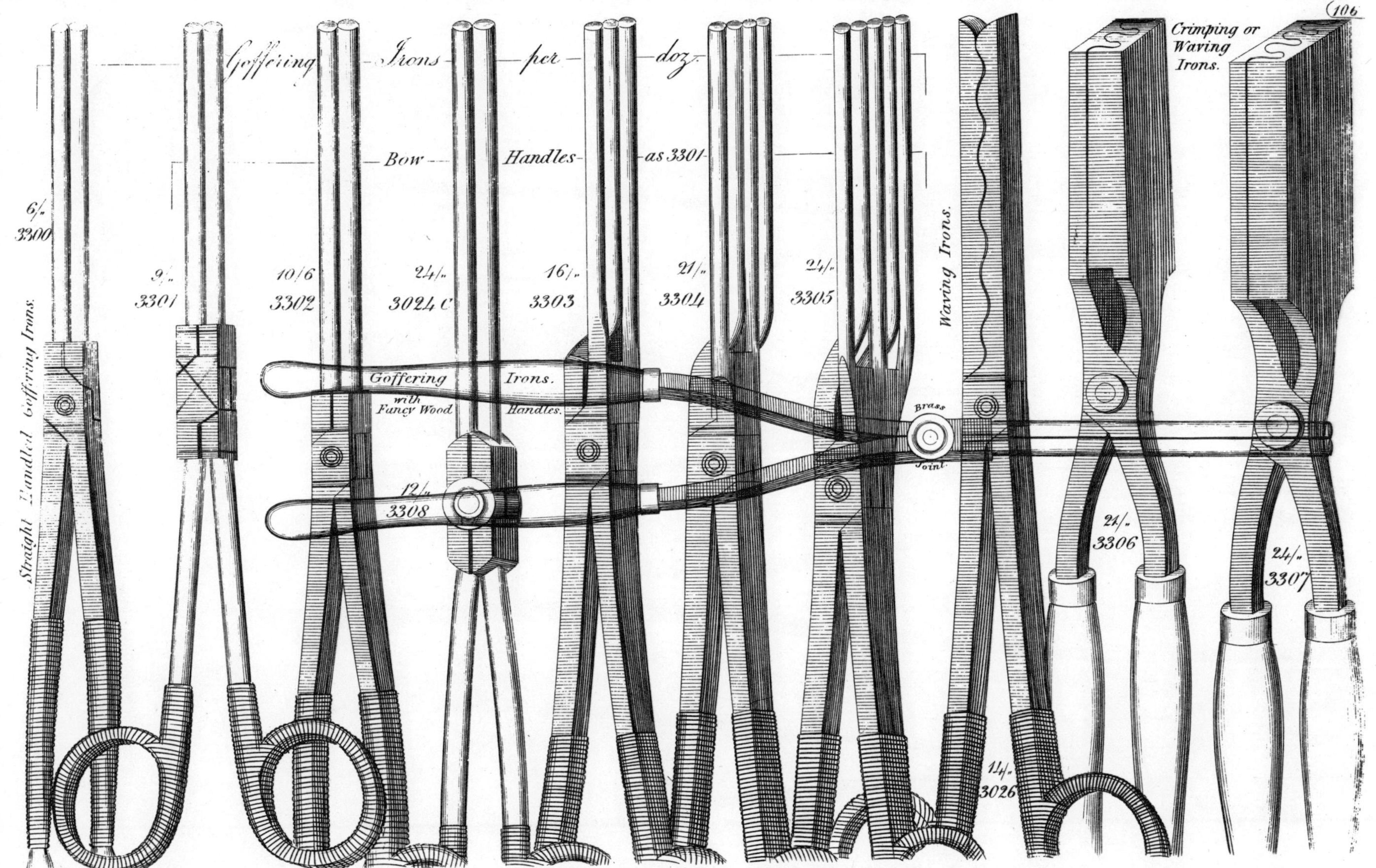
Goffering Irons per doz.
Bow Handles as 3301
Crimping or Waving Irons.
Waving Irons.
Straight handled Goffering Irons.
Goffering Irons with Fancy Wood Handles.
Brass Joint.
6/-
3300
9/-
3301
10/6
3302
24/-
3024 C
16/-
3303
21/-
3304
24/-
3305
12/-
3308
24/-
3306
24/-
3307
14/-
3026

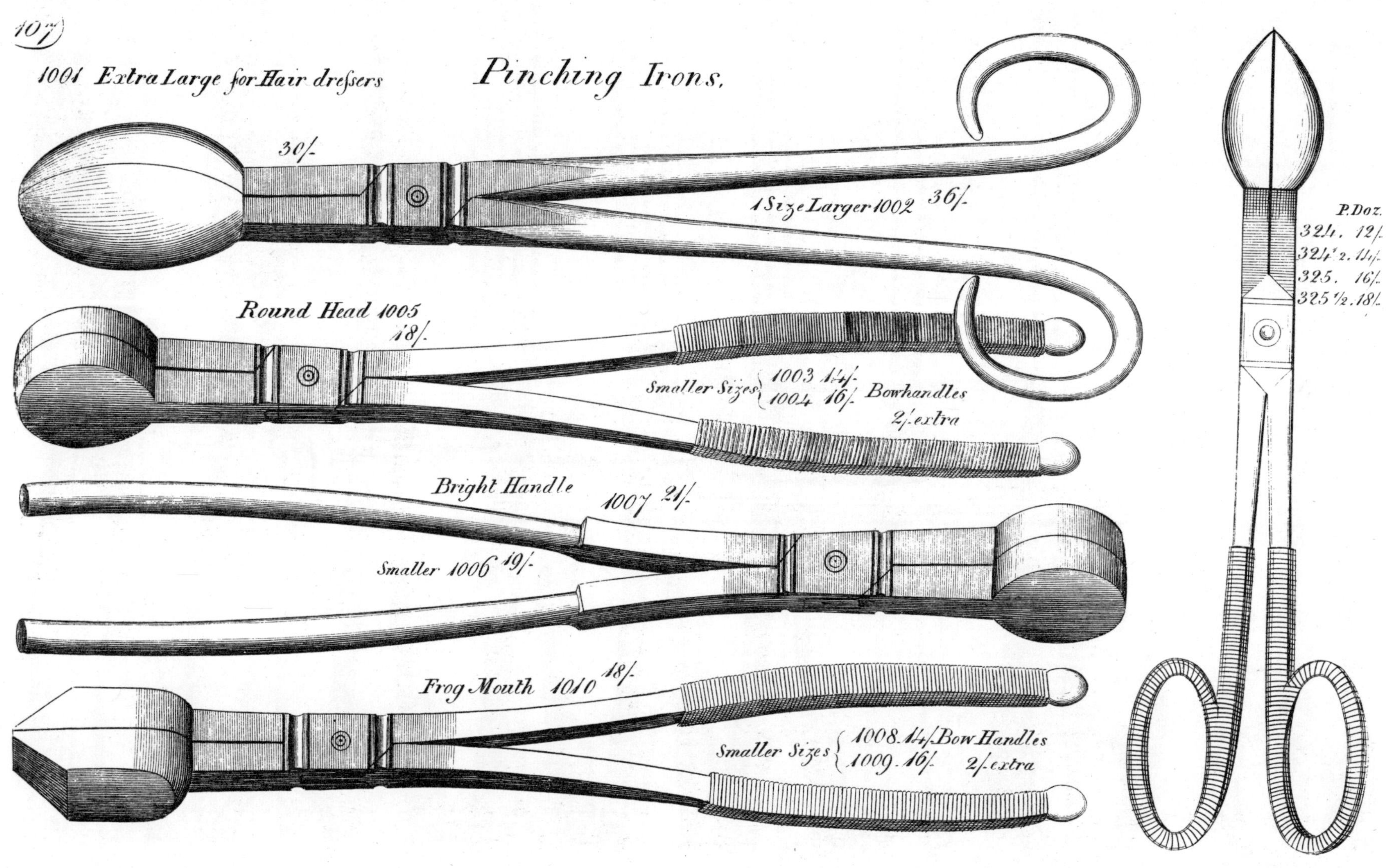

Pinching Irons.
1001 Extra Large for Hair dressers
30/-
1 Size Larger 1002 36/-
Round Head 1005
18/-
Smaller Sizes { 1003 14/- } Bowhandles
1004 16/- 2/- extra
Bright Handle 1007 21/-
Smaller 1006 19/-
Frog Mouth 1010 18/-
Smaller Sizes { 1008. 14/- Bow Handles
1009. 16/- 2/- extra
P. Doz.
324. 12/-
324½. 14/-
325. 16/-
325½. 18/-

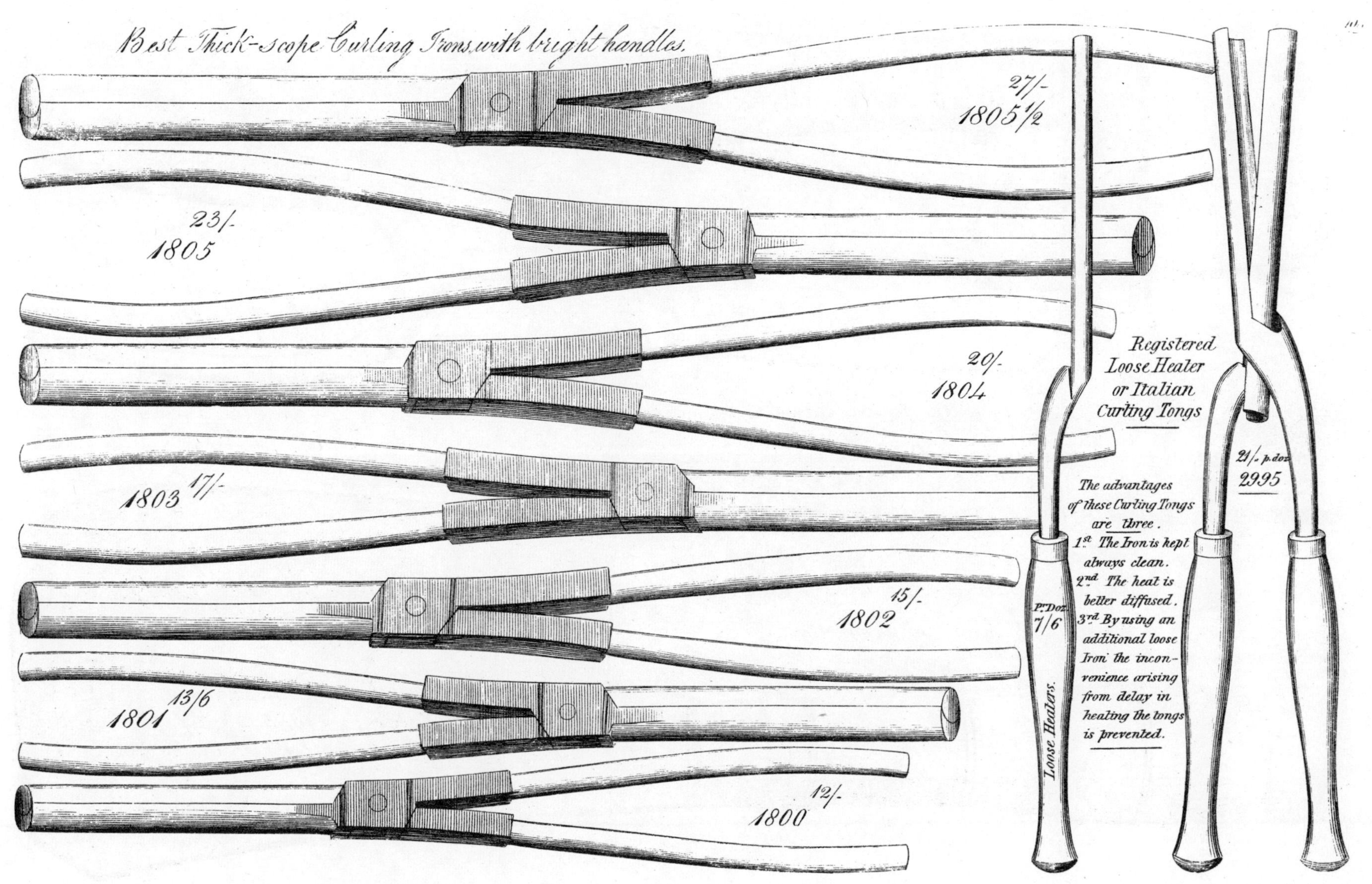

Best Thick-scope Curling Irons, with bright handles.
27/-
1805½
23/-
1805
20/-
1804
1803 17/-
15/-
1802
1801 13/6
12/-
1800
Registered
Loose Healer
or Italian
Curling Tongs
21/- p.doz
2995
The advantages
of these Curling Tongs
are three.
1st. The Iron is kept
always clean.
2nd. The heat is
better diffused.
3rd. By using an
additional loose
Iron the incon-
venience arising
from delay in
heating the tongs
is prevented.
Pr Doz
7/6
Loose Healers.

25/
1997

Flesh Forks Per doz.
No 289   290   291   292
Whole length 18 ..... 20 ..... 22 ..... 24 in
Bright 15/6 ..... 17/ ..... 20/ 25/

Cheese Knives with Beech handles &
Bright Iron Ferrules.

No 1996 . 1997 . 1998 . 1999
22/   25/   30/   36/ Pr doz
7   8   9   10 Inch

May be had Square at same prices.

London Pattern Meat Choppers.
24/ Pr doz
1852

1 Size smaller .... 1851 .... 22/
1 Size larger .... 1853 .... 27/
2 do do .... 1854 .... 30/

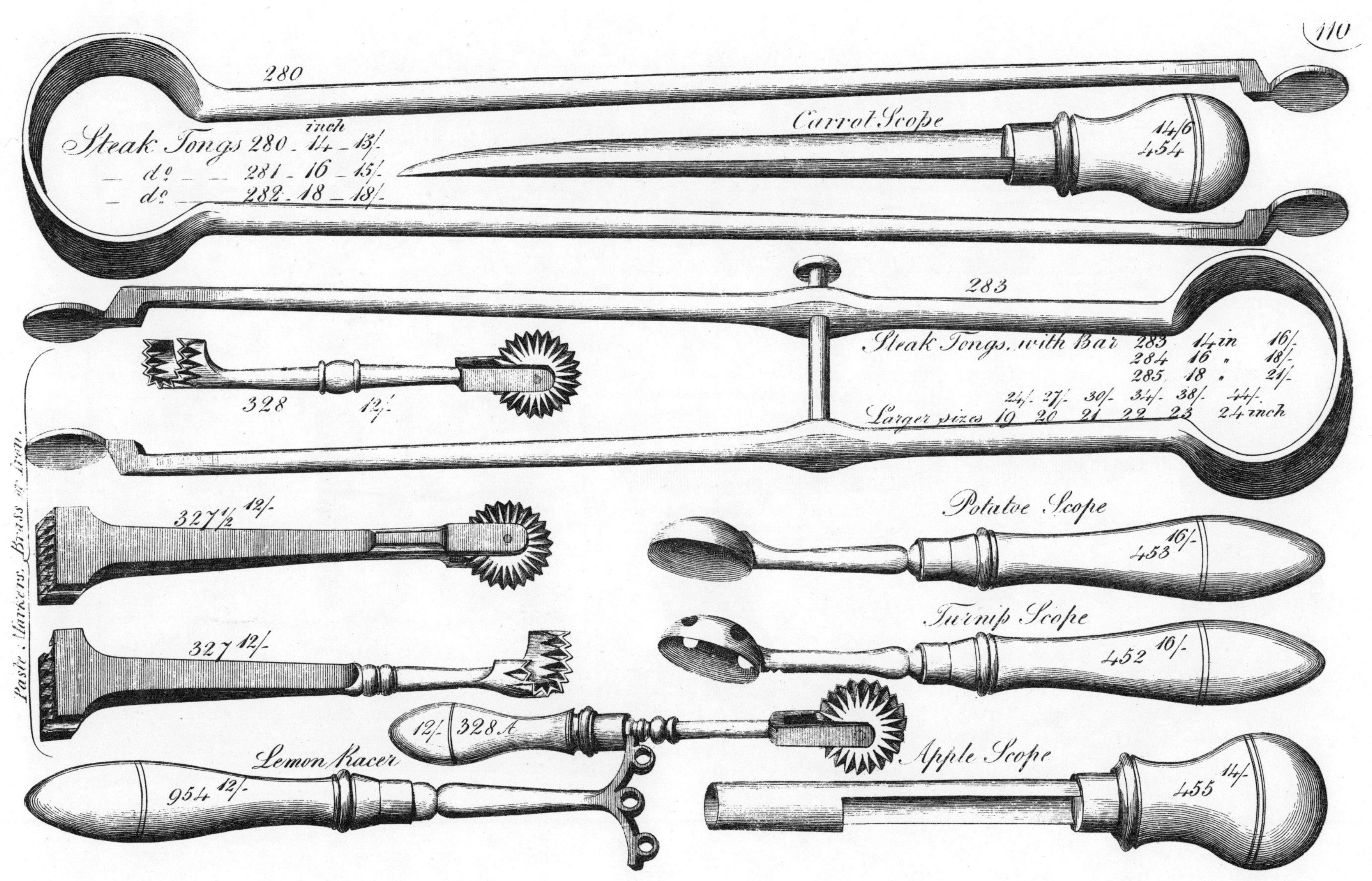
110
280
Steak Tongs 280 _ 14 _ inch 13/
do _ 281 _ 16 _ 15/
do _ 282 _ 18 _ 18/
Carrot Scope
14/6
454
283
Steak Tongs, with Bar   283   14 in   16/
284   16   "   18/
285   18   "   21/
Larger sizes   24/ 27/ 30/ 34/ 38/ 44/
19   20   21   22   23   24 inch
328   12/
327½ 12/
327 12/
Paste Markers. Brass & Iron.
Potatoe Scope
16/
453
Turnip Scope
452 16/
12/ 328A
Lemon Racer
954 12/
Apple Scope
455 14/

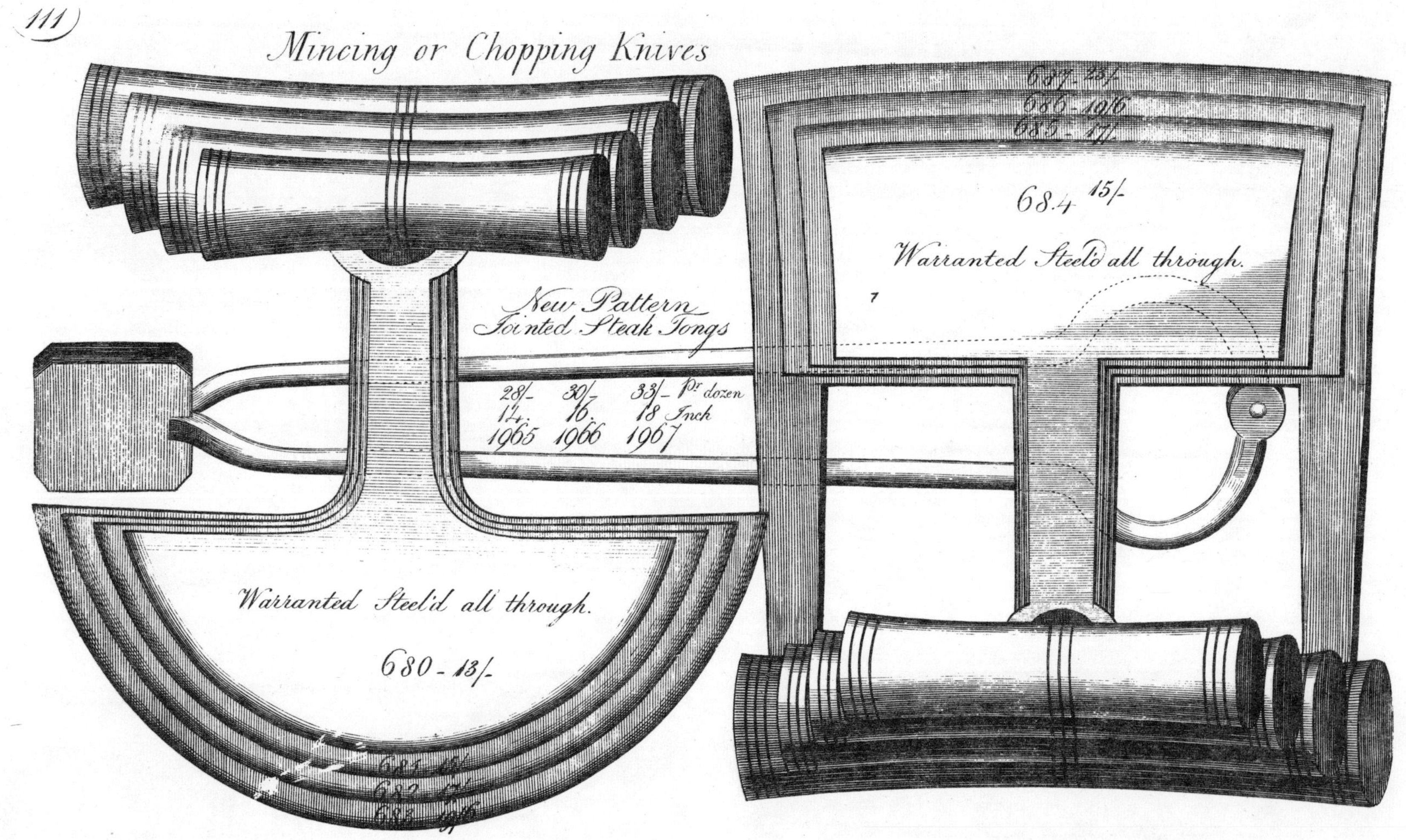
Mincing or Chopping Knives
New Pattern
Jointed Steak Tongs
28/-   30/-   33/- Pr dozen
14.   16.   18 Inch
1965   1966   1967
Warranted Steel'd all through.
680 - 13/-
687. 23/-
686. 10/6
685. 7/-
68.4 15/-
Warranted Steel'd all through.

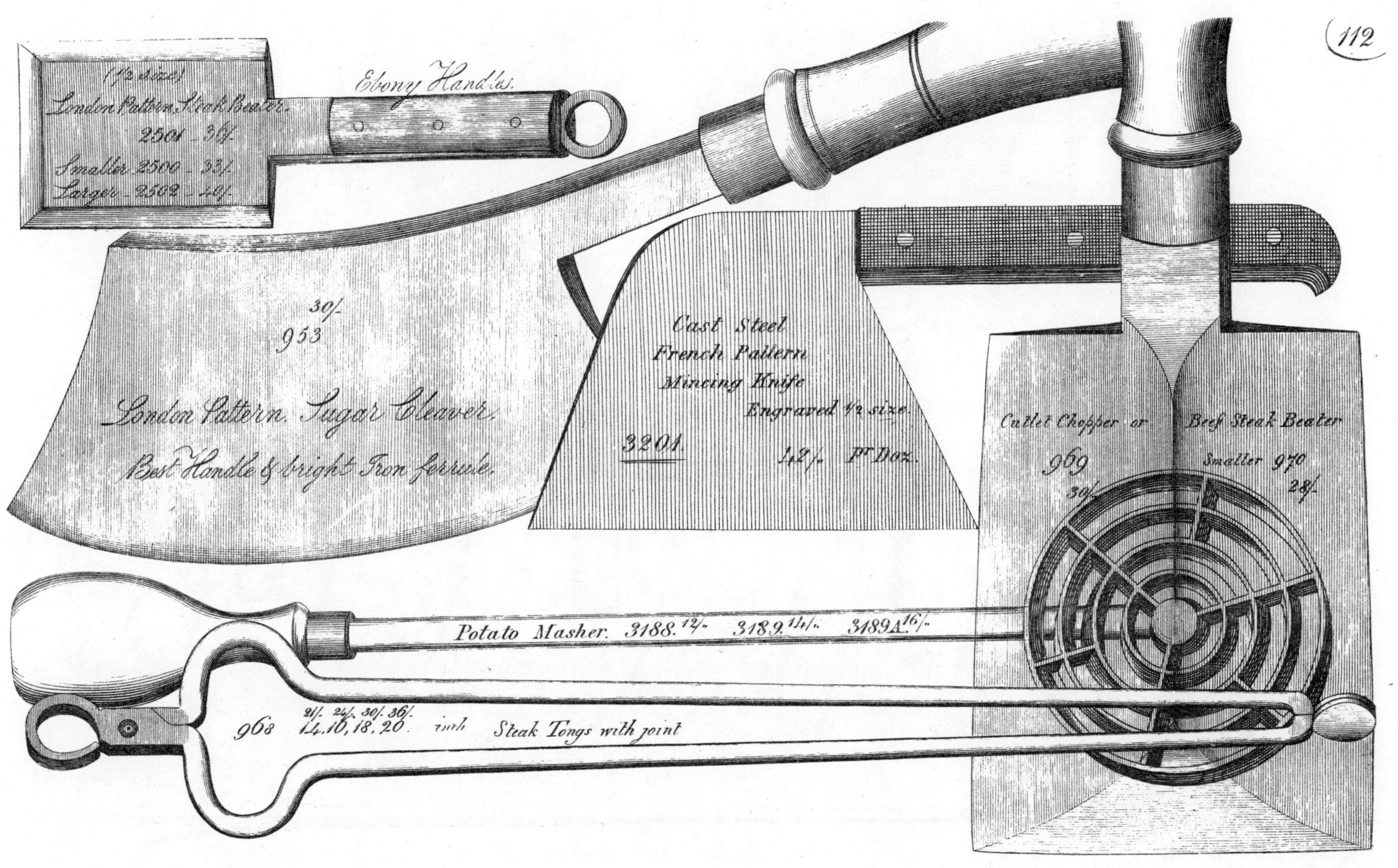
112
(½ size)
London Pattern Steak Beater.
2501 - 36/
Smaller 2500 - 33/
Larger 2502 - 44/
Ebony Handles.
30/
953
London Pattern Sugar Cleaver,
Best Handle & bright Iron ferrule.
Cast Steel
French Pattern
Mincing Knife
Engraved ½ size
3201
42/ Pr Doz.
Cutlet Chopper or Beef Steak Beater
969
30/
Smaller 970
28/
Potato Masher. 3188. 12/ 3189. 14/ 3189A 16/
968
21/. 24/. 30/. 36/
14. 16. 18. 20 inch Steak Tongs with joint

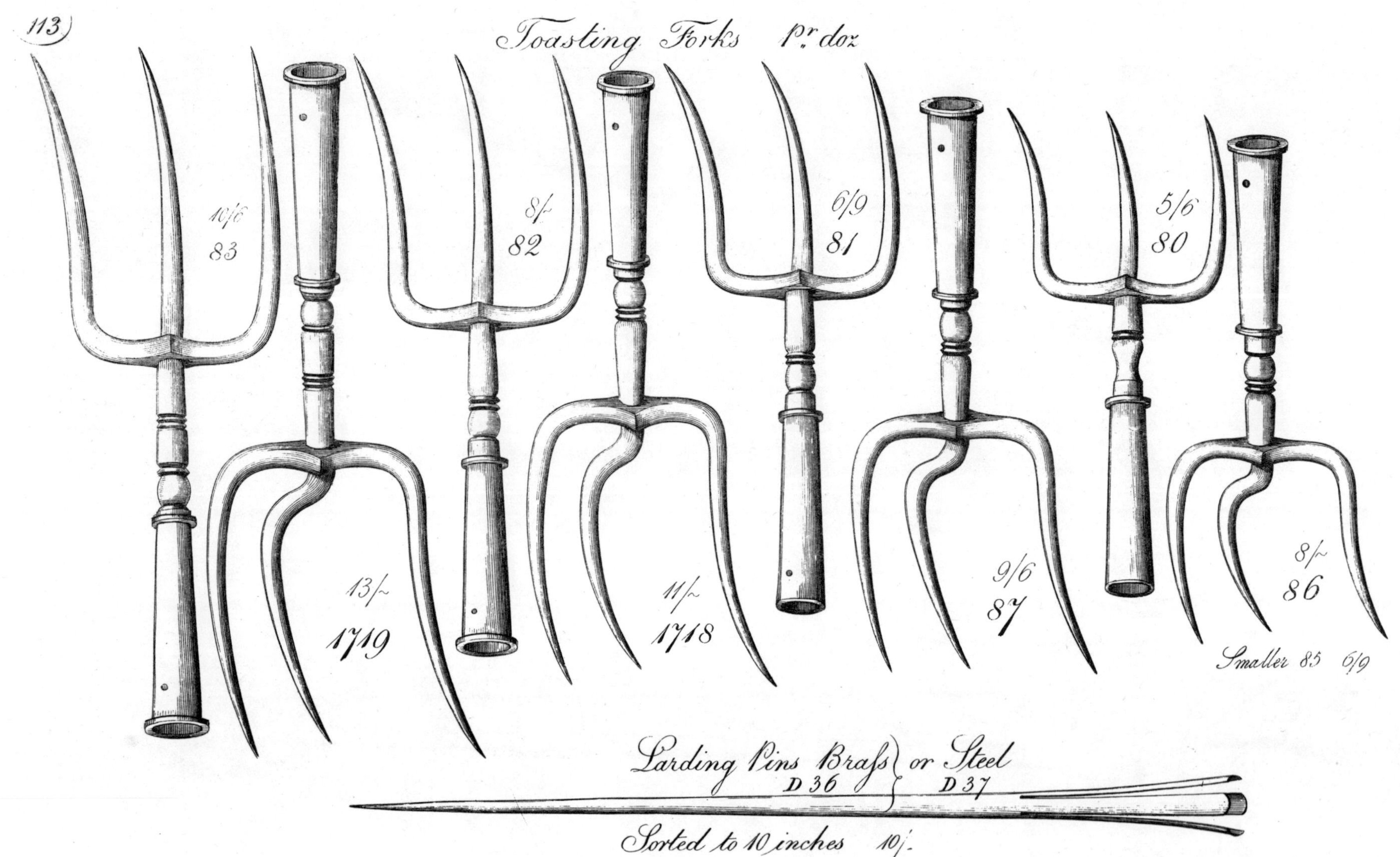

113)
Toasting Forks   Pr doz
10/6 83
8/ 82
6/9 81
5/6 80
13/- 1719
11/- 1718
9/6 87
8/ 86
Smaller 85 6/9
Larding Pins Brass or Steel
D 36   D 37
Sorted to 10 inches   10/-

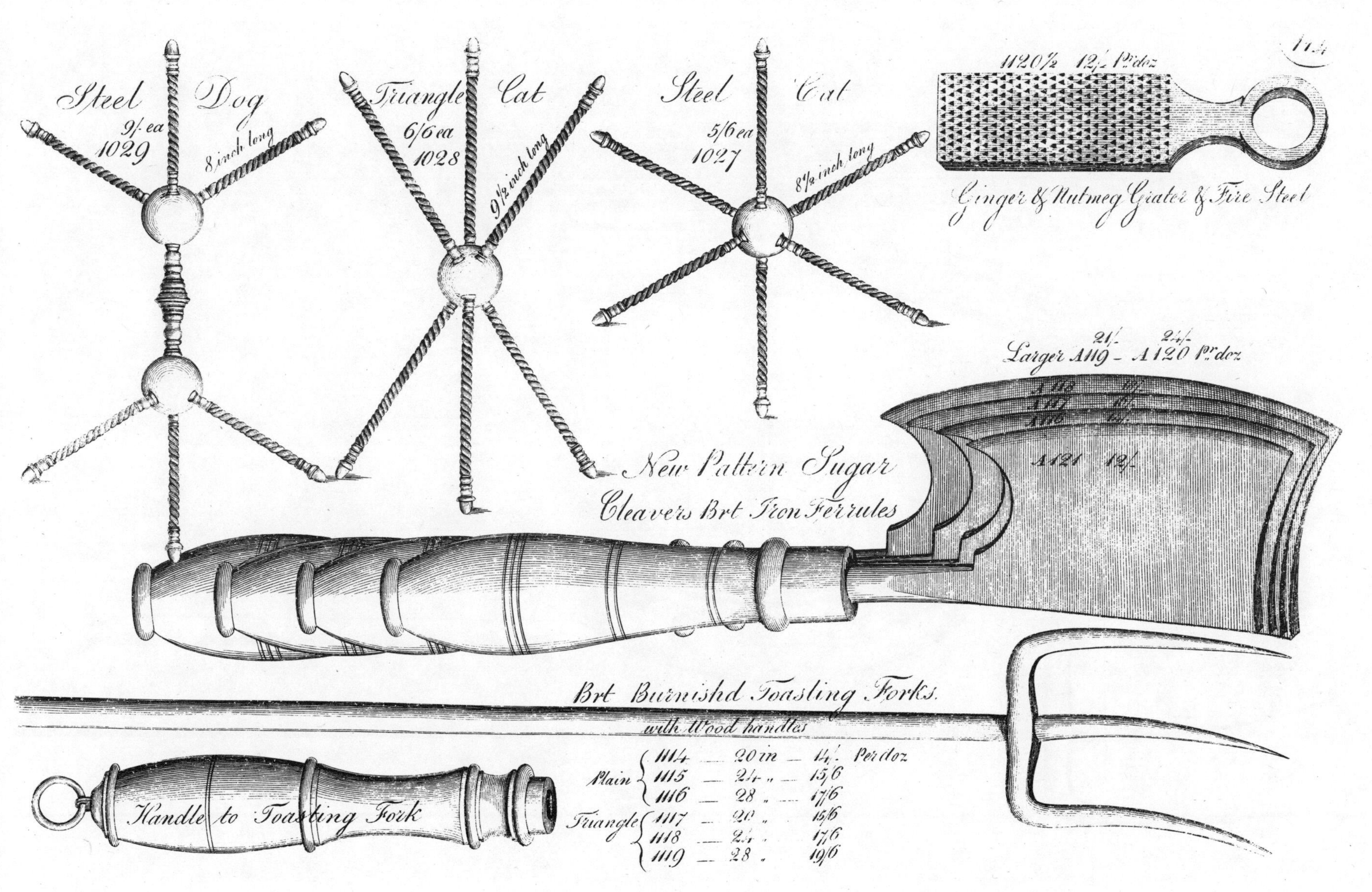
Steel Dog
9/ ea
1029
8 inch long
Triangle Cat
6/6 ea
1028
9½ inch long
Steel Cat
5/6 ea
1027
8½ inch long
1120½ 12½ P. doz
Ginger & Nutmeg Grater & Fire Steel
21/   24/
Larger 1119 - 1120 P. doz
1118   9/
1119   10/
1120   11/
1121   12/
New Pattern Sugar
Cleavers Brt Iron Ferrules
Brt Burnishd Toasting Forks.
with Wood handles
Handle to Toasting Fork
1114   20 in   14/   Per doz
Plain   1115   24 „   15/6
1116   28 „   17/6
Triangle 1117   20 „   15/6
1118   24 „   17/6
1119   28 „   19/6

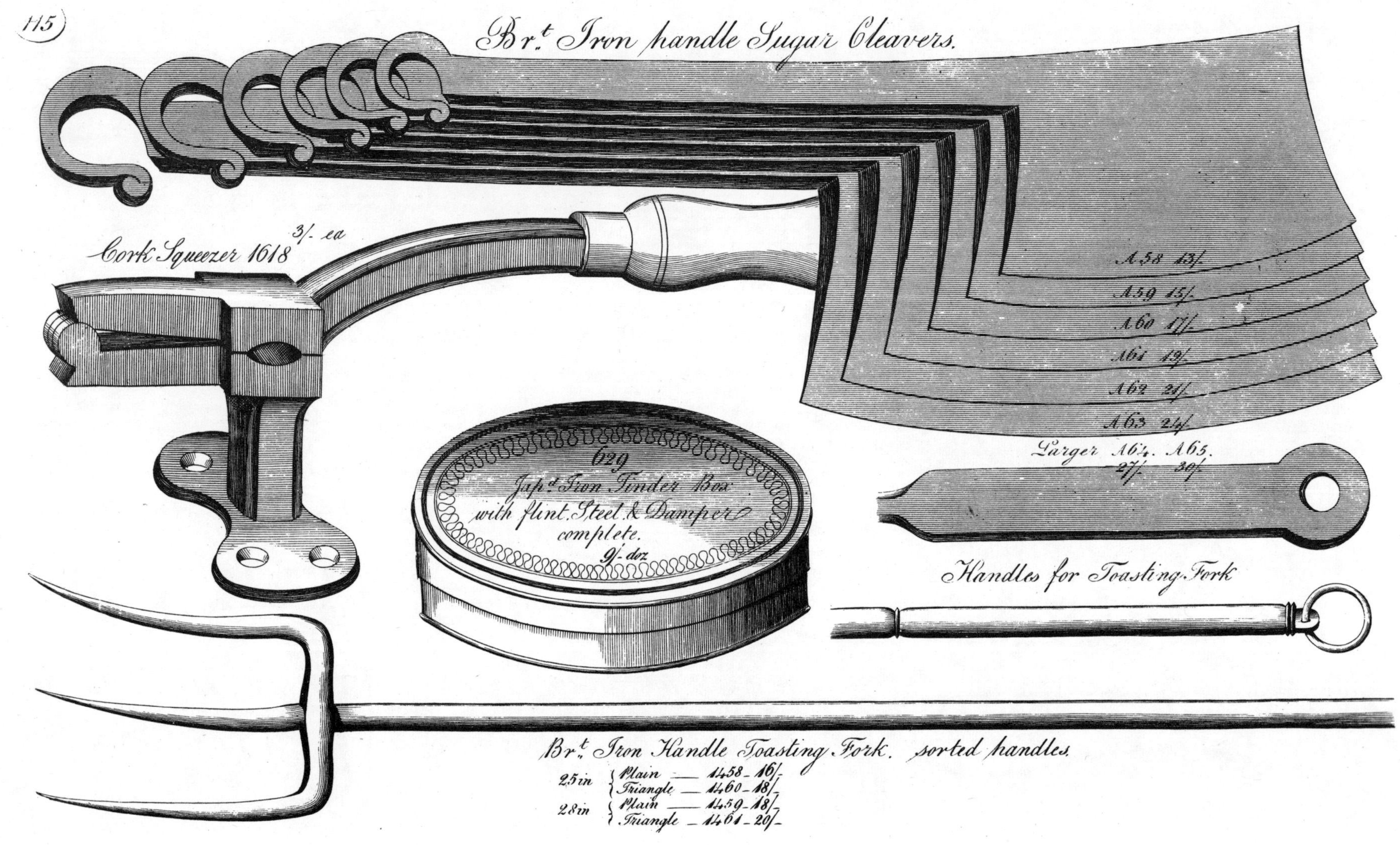
115
Brt. Iron handle Sugar Cleavers.
Cork Squeezer 1618   3/- ea
A58 13/
A59 15/
A60 17/
A61 19/
A62 21/
A63 24/
Larger A64. A65.
27/   39/
629
Japd Iron Tinder Box
with flint, Steel & Damper
complete.
9/- doz
Handles for Toasting Fork
Brt. Iron Handle Toasting Fork.   sorted handles.
25 in   Plain ____ 1458 _ 16/-
         Triangle _ 1460 _ 18/-
28 in   Plain ____ 1459 _ 18/-
         Triangle _ 1461 _ 20/-

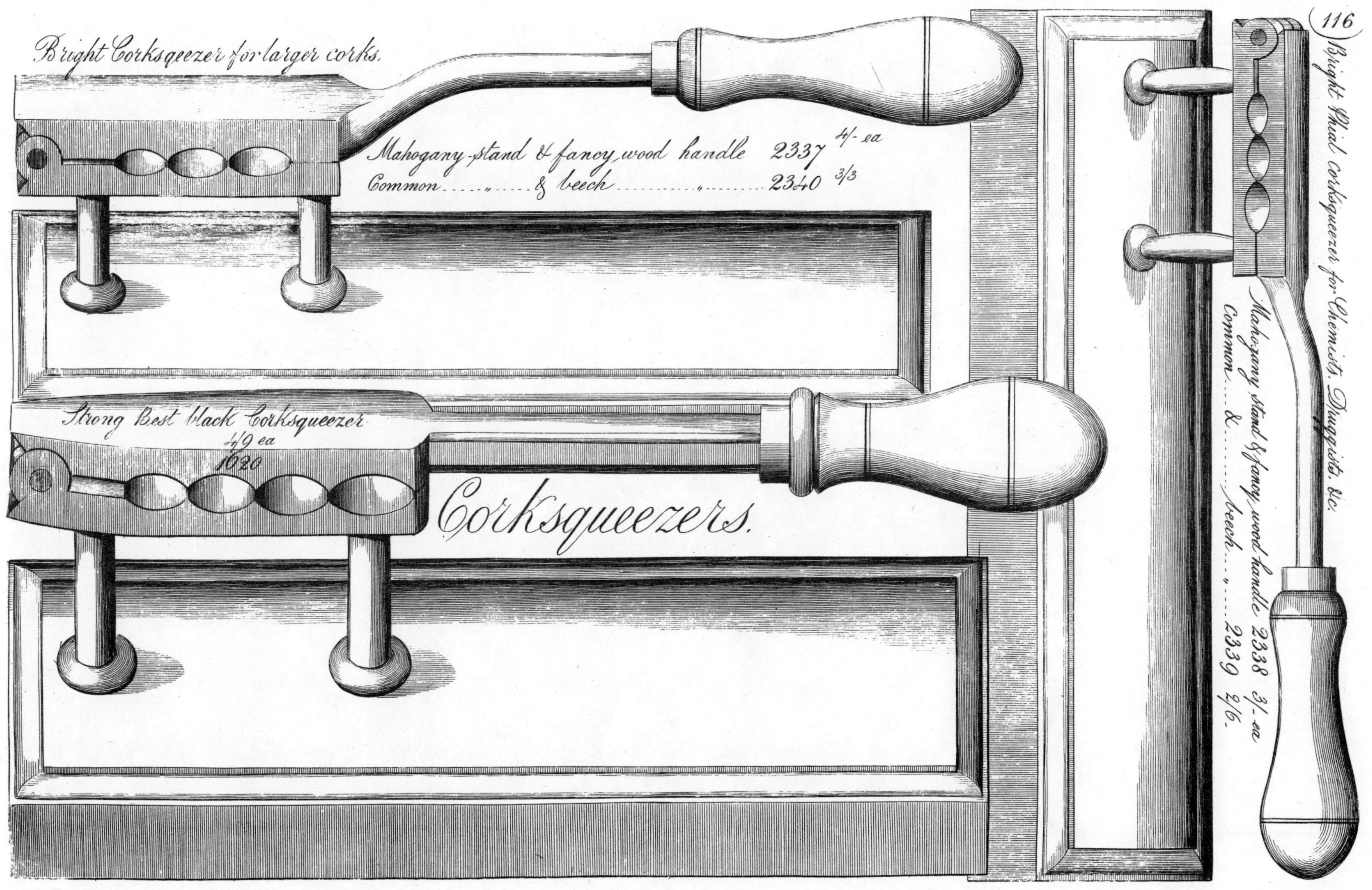
Bright Corksqeezer for larger corks.
Mahogany stand & fancy wood handle   2337   4/- ea
Common .... „ & beech .... „ 2340   3/3
Strong Best black Corksqueezer
4/9 ea
1020
Corksqueezers.
Bright Phial Corksqueezer for Chemists, Druggists &c.
Mahogany stand & fancy wood handle 2338 3/- ea
Common .... & beech .... „ 2339 2/6

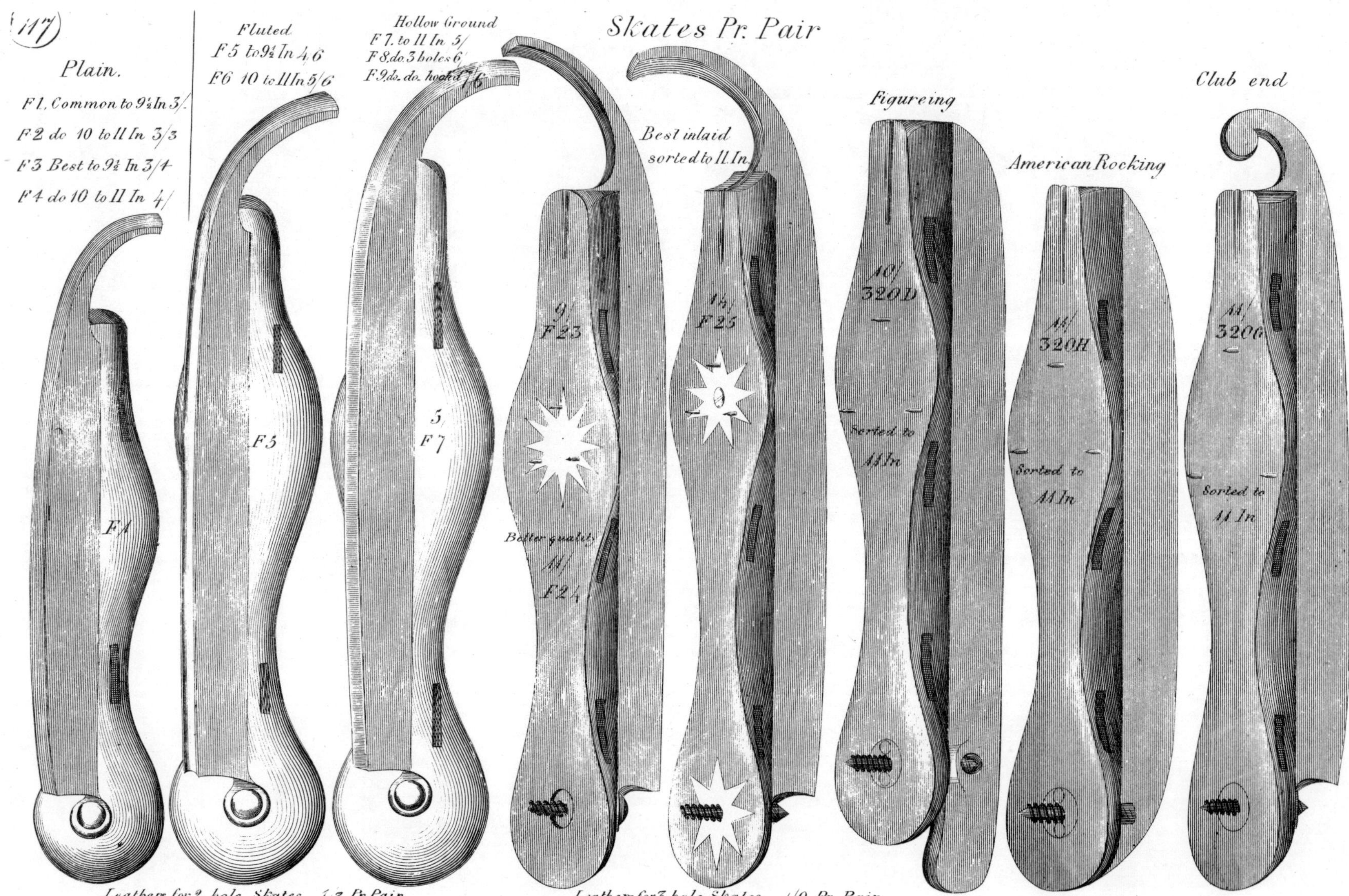
117
Plain.
F1. Common to 9½ In 3/
F2 do 10 to 11 In 3/3
F3 Best to 9½ In 3/4
F4 do 10 to 11 In 4/
Fluted
F5 to 9½ In 4/6
F6 10 to 11 In 5/6
Hollow Ground
F7 to 11 In 5/
F8 do 3 holes 6/
F9 do. do. hooked 7/6
Skates Pr. Pair
Best inlaid
sorted to 11. In.
Figureing
American Rocking
Club end
F4
F5
5/
F7
9/
F23
14/
F25
10/
320D
14/
320H
14/
320C
Better quality
14/
F24
Sorted to
44 In
Sorted to
44 In
Sorted to
44 In
Leathers for 2 hole Skates   1/3 Pr Pair
Leathers for 3 hole Skates   1/9 Pr Pair

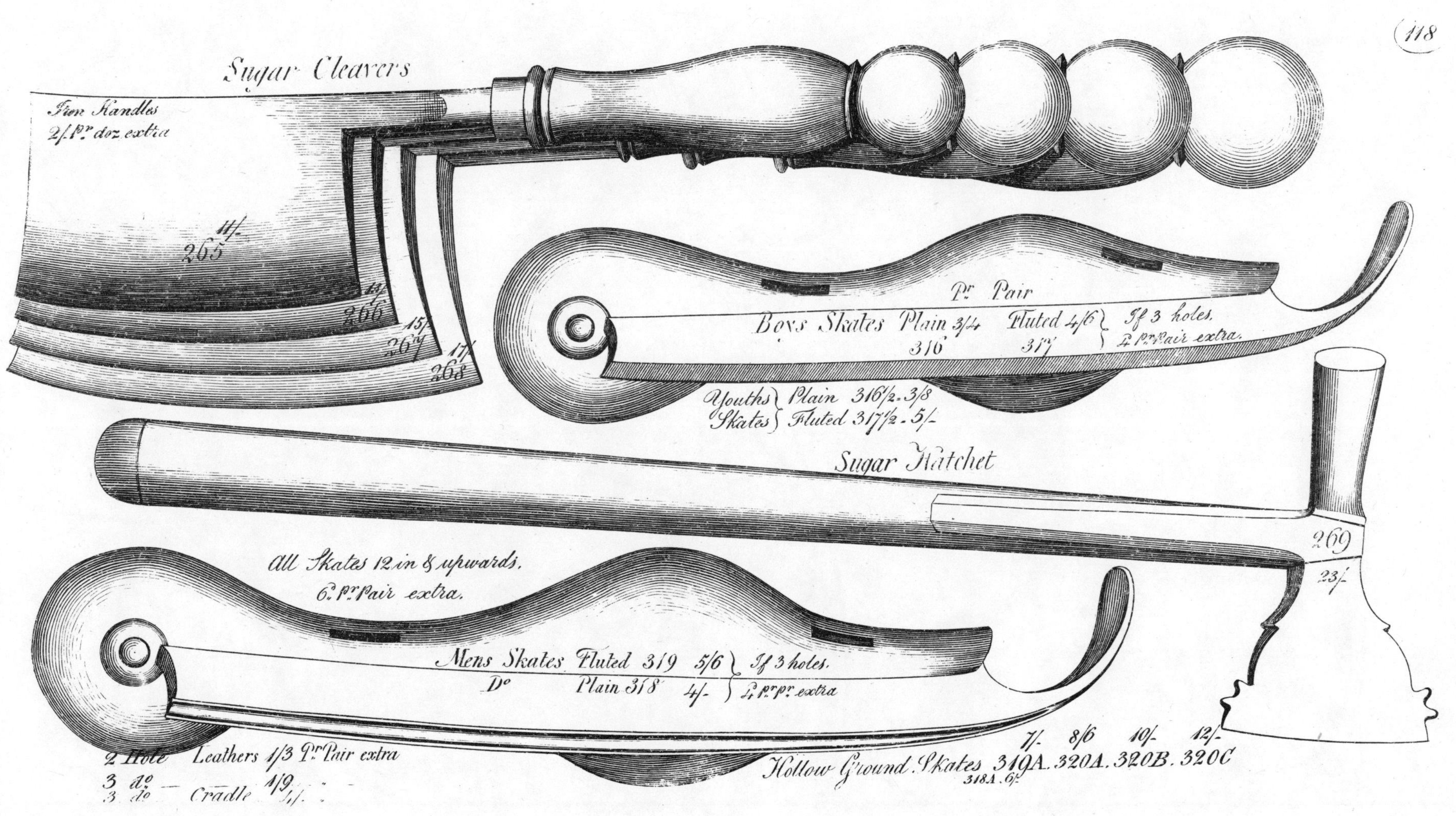
(118)
Sugar Cleavers
Iron Handles
2/ Pr doz extra
265
266
267
268
4/
4/
15/
16/
17/
Pr Pair
Boys Skates Plain 3/4   Fluted 4/6   If 3 holes.
316   317   4 Pr Pair extra.
Youths } Plain 316½. 3/8
Skates } Fluted 317½. 5/
Sugar Hatchet
269
23/
All Skates 12 in & upwards.
6 Pr Pair extra.
Mens Skates Fluted 319   5/6   If 3 holes.
Do   Plain 318   4/   4 pr pr extra
2 Hole   Leathers 1/3 Pr Pair extra
3 do
3 do — Cradle 1/9
7/   8/6   10/   12/
Hollow Ground Skates 319A. 320A. 320B. 320C
318A. 6/

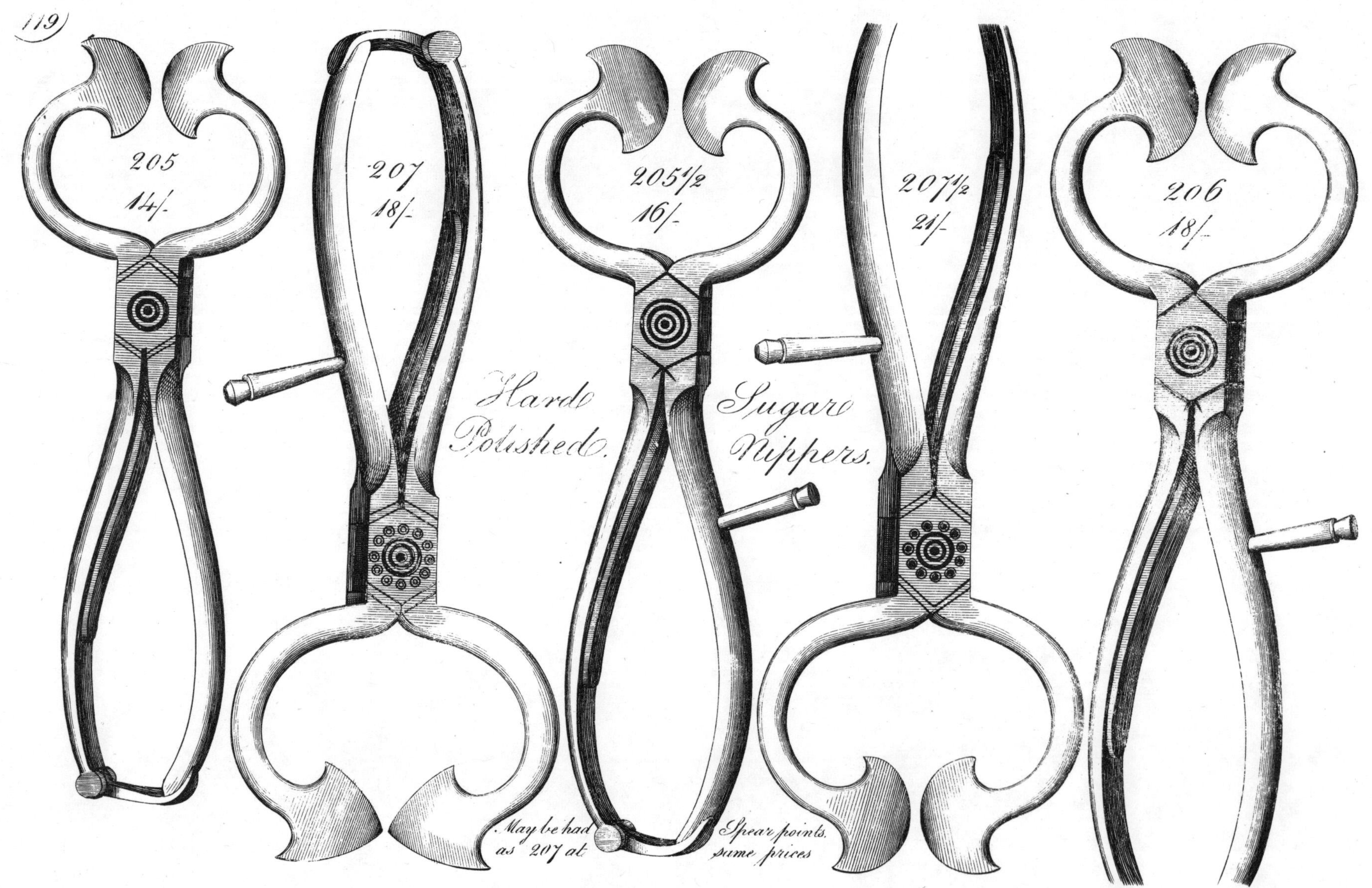
119
205
14/-
207
18/-
205½
16/-
207½
21/-
206
18/-
Hard
Polished.
Sugar
Nippers.
May be had
as 207 at
Spear points.
same prices

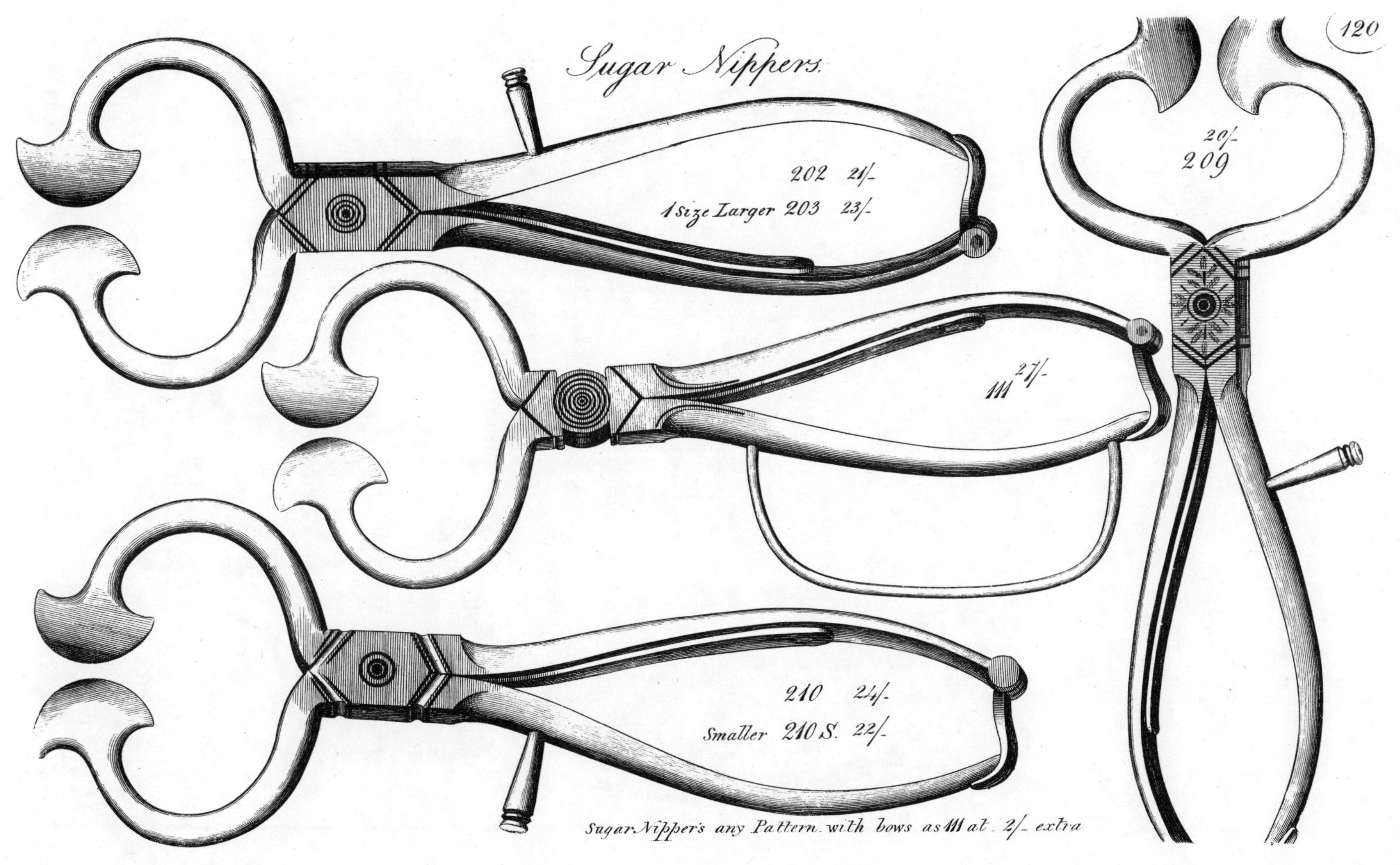

Sugar Nippers.
202   21/-
1 Size Larger 203   23/-
111   27/-
20/-
209
210   24/-
Smaller 210 S. 22/-
Sugar Nippers any Pattern with bows as 111 at 2/- extra

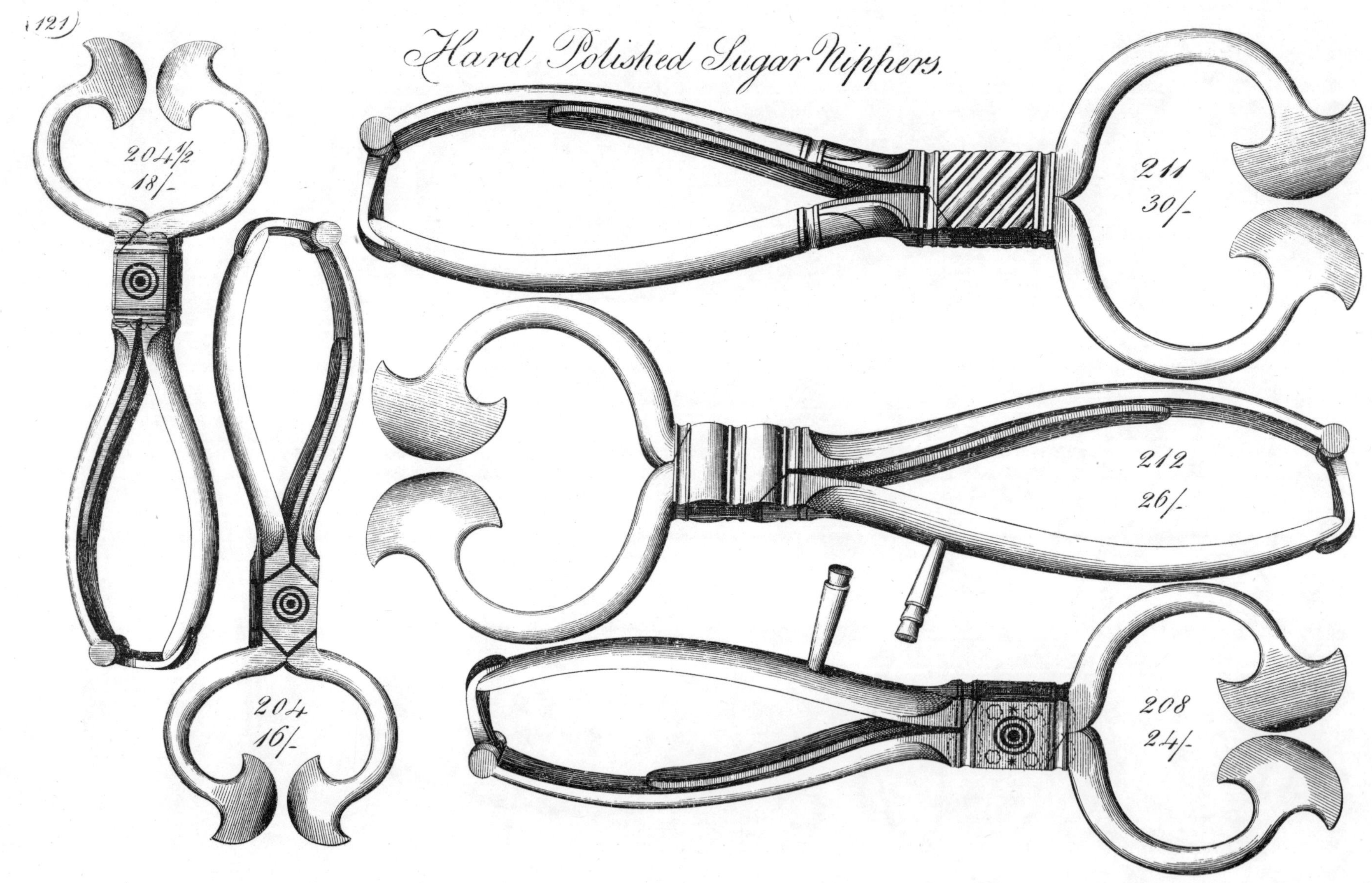

Hard Polished Sugar Nippers.
(121)
204½
18/-
204
16/-
211
30/-
212
26/-
208
24/-

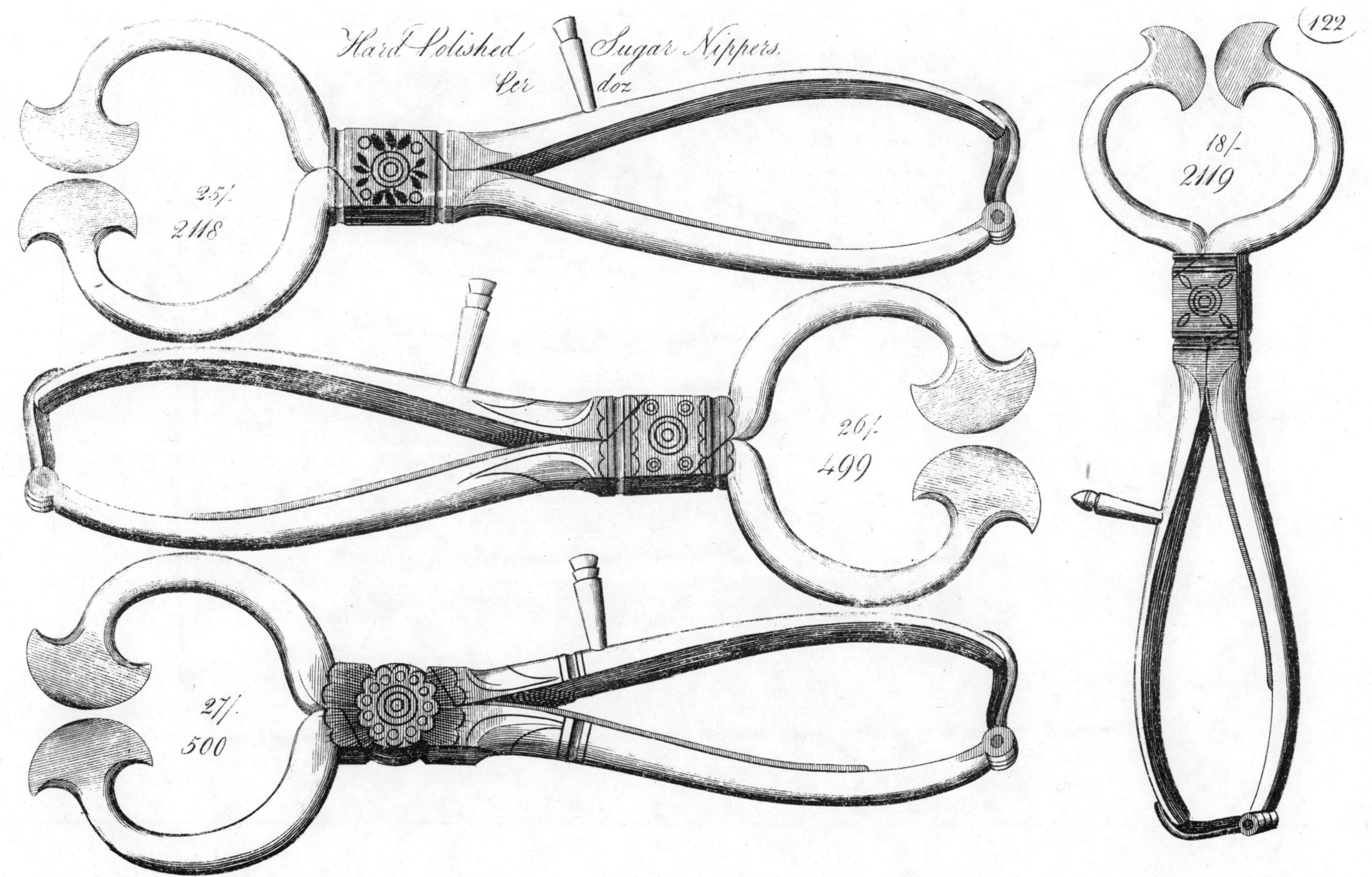

Hard Polished Sugar Nippers.
Per doz
25/-
2118
26/-
499
27/-
500
18/-
2119
122

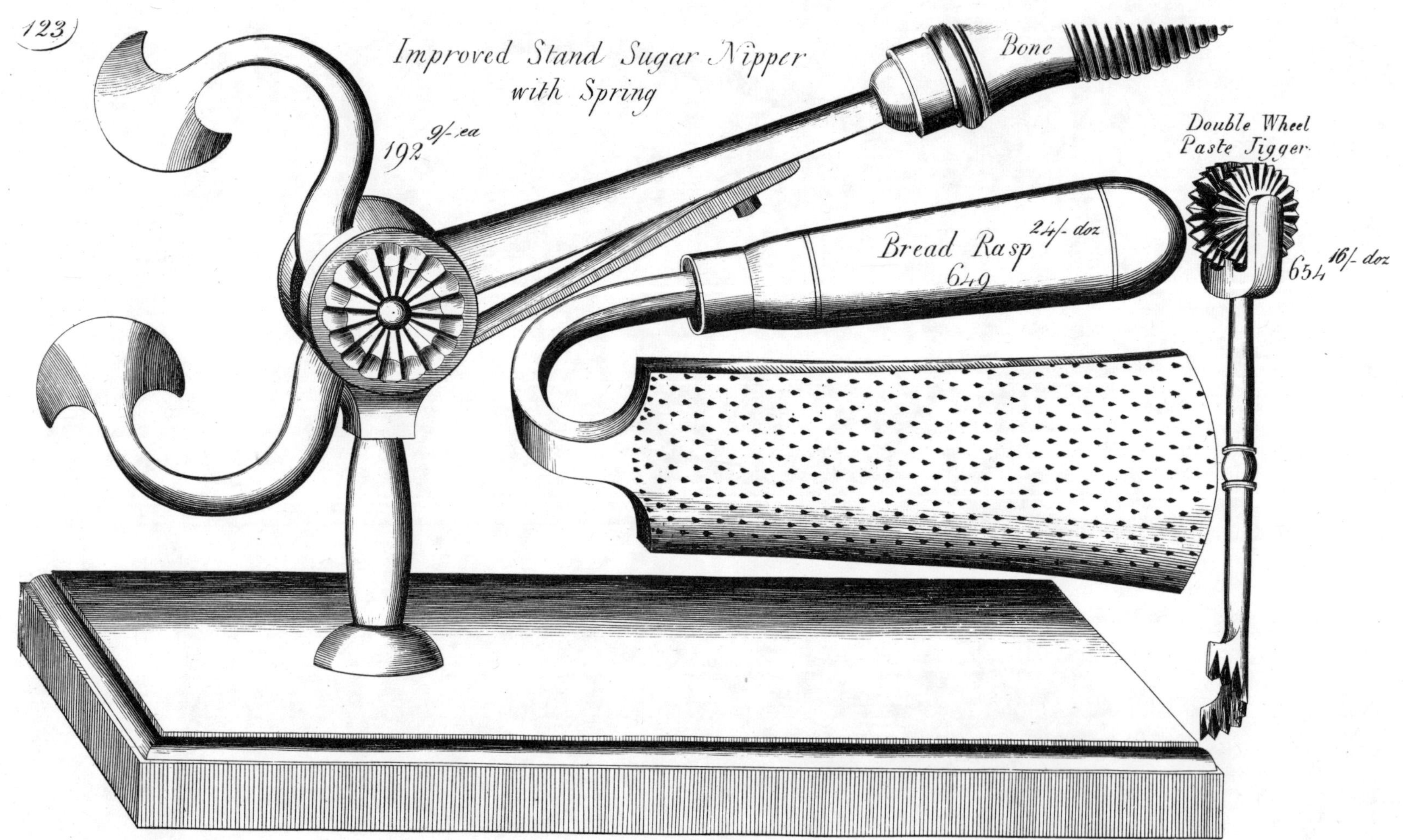
123
Improved Stand Sugar Nipper
with Spring
192 9/- ea
Bone
Double Wheel
Paste Jigger
Bread Rasp 24/- doz
649
654 16/- doz

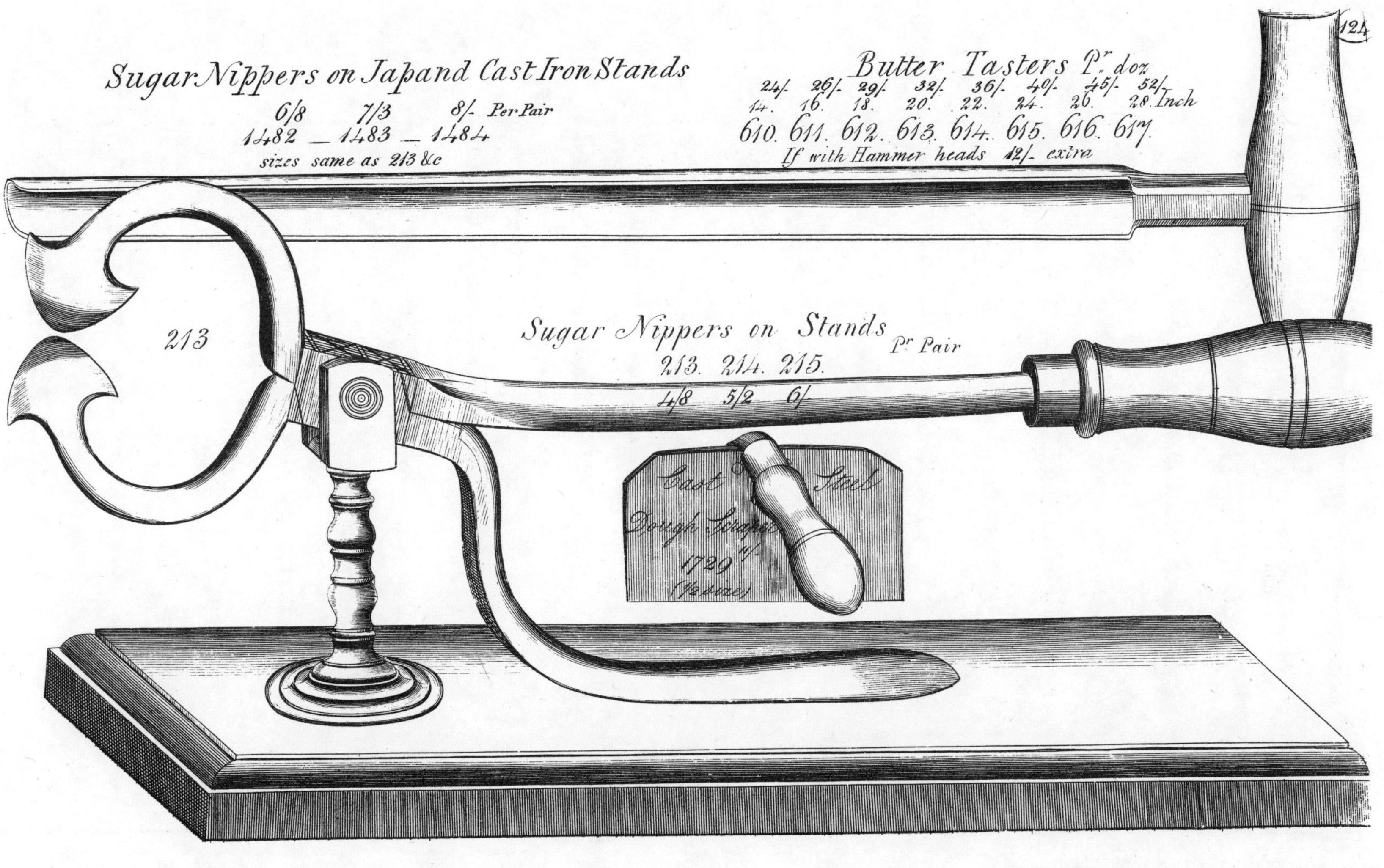
Sugar Nippers on Japand Cast Iron Stands
6/8   7/3   8/- Per Pair
1482 _ 1483 _ 1484
sizes same as 213 &c
Butter Tasters Pr doz
24/ 26/- 29/ 32/ 36/ 40/ 45/ 52/
14. 16. 18. 20. 22. 24. 26. 28 Inch
610. 611. 612. 613. 614. 615. 616. 617.
If with Hammer heads 12/- extra
213
Sugar Nippers on Stands Pr Pair
213. 214. 215.
4/8 5/2 6/
Cast Steel
Dough Scraper
1729
(full size)
124

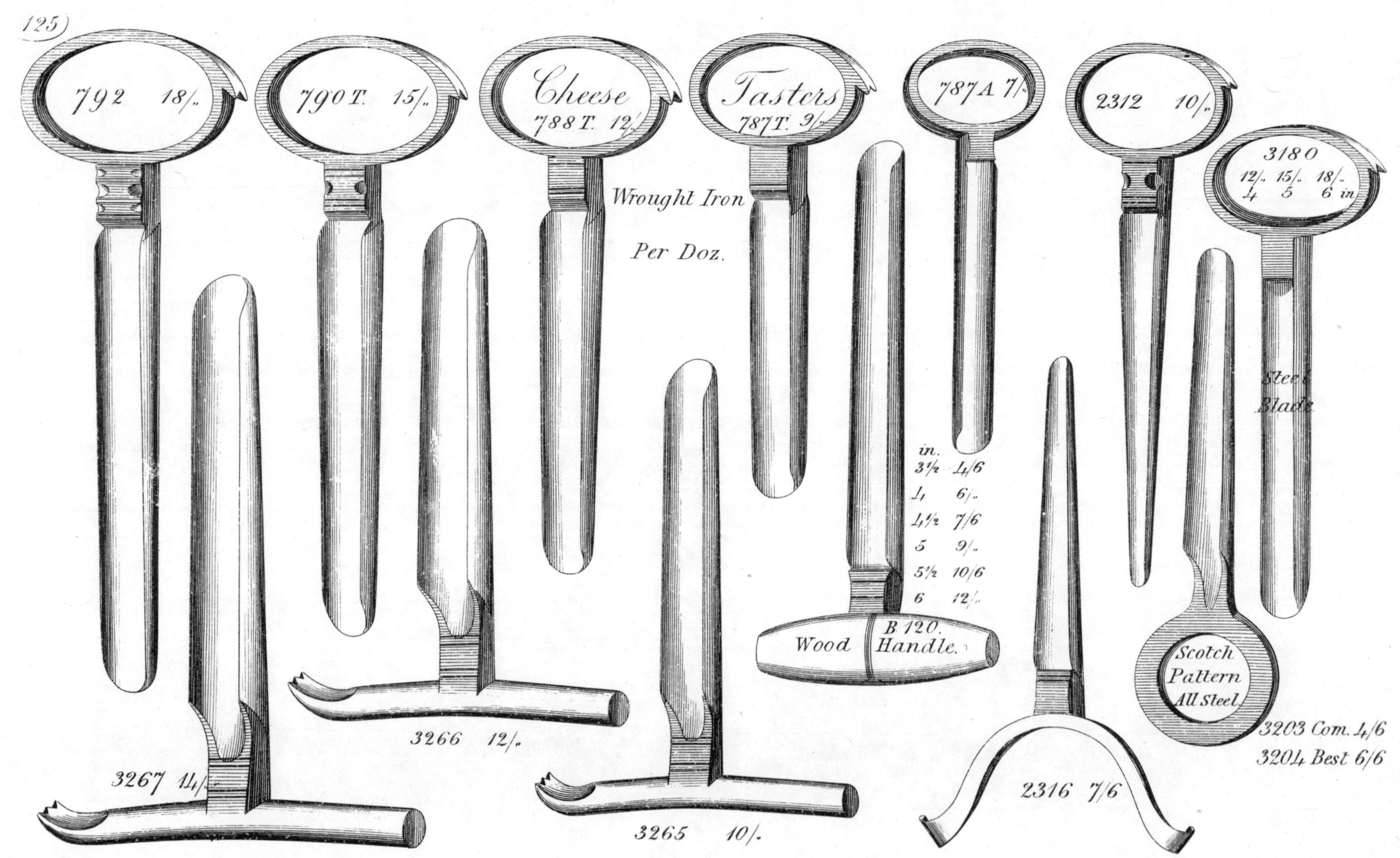
(125)
792   18/-
790 T.   15/-
Cheese
788 T.   12/-
Tasters
787 T.   9/-
787 A   7/-
2312   10/-
3180
12/-   15/-   18/-
4   5   6 in
Wrought Iron
Per Doz.
Steel Blade
in.
3½   4/6
4   6/-
4½   7/6
5   9/-
5½   10/6
6   12/-
Wood   B 120.
Handle.
Scotch
Pattern
All Steel
3267   14/-
3266   12/-
3265   10/-
2316   7/6
3203 Com. 4/6
3204 Best 6/6

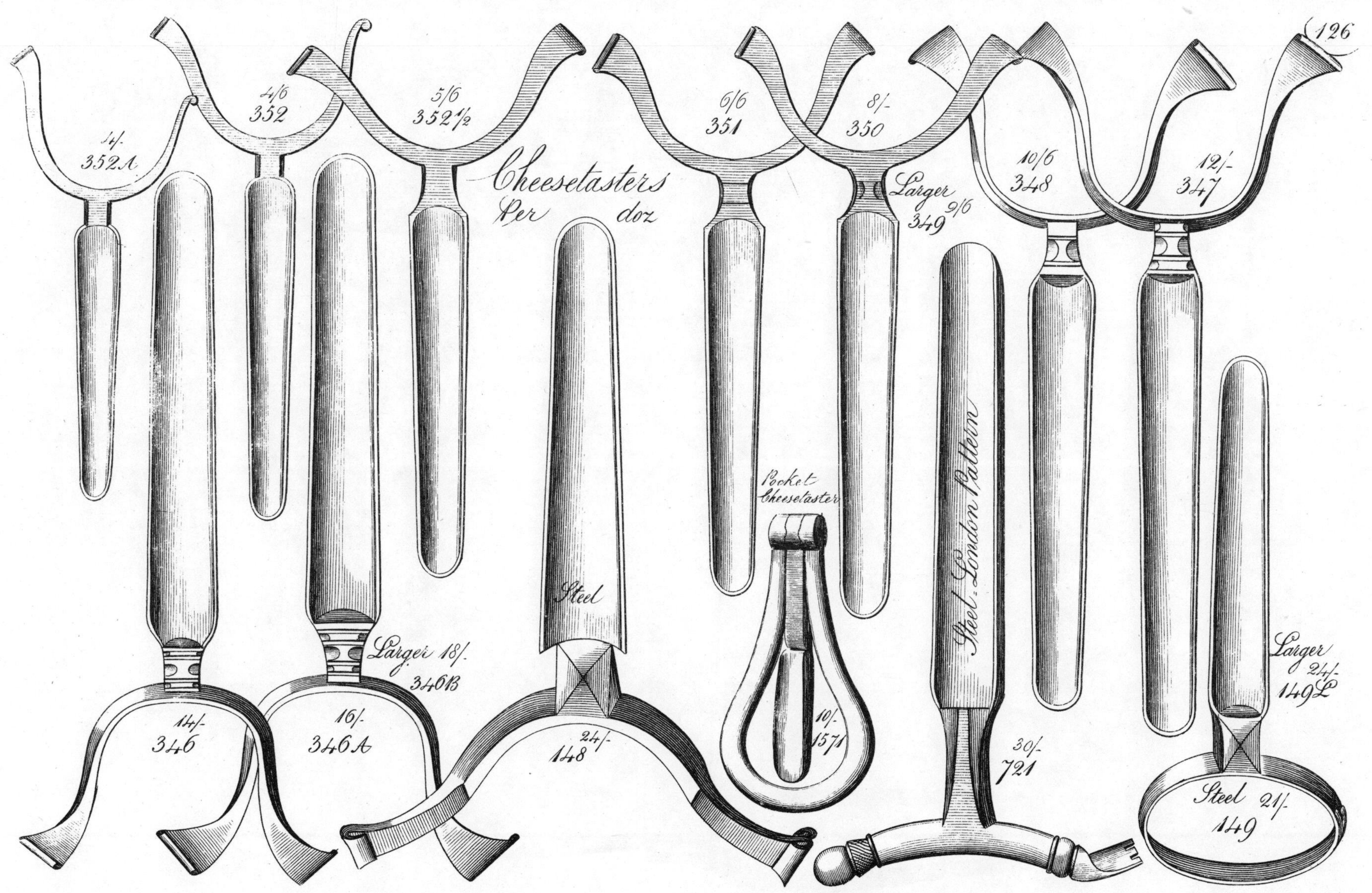
126
4/6
352
5/6
352 1/2
Cheesetasters
Per doz
6/6
351
8/-
350
Larger 9/6
349
10/6
348
12/-
347
4/
352A
Larger 18/-
346B
14/-
346
16/-
346A
Steel
24/-
148
Pocket Cheesetaster
10/-
1571
Steel London Pattern
30/-
721
Larger 24/-
149L
Steel 21/-
149

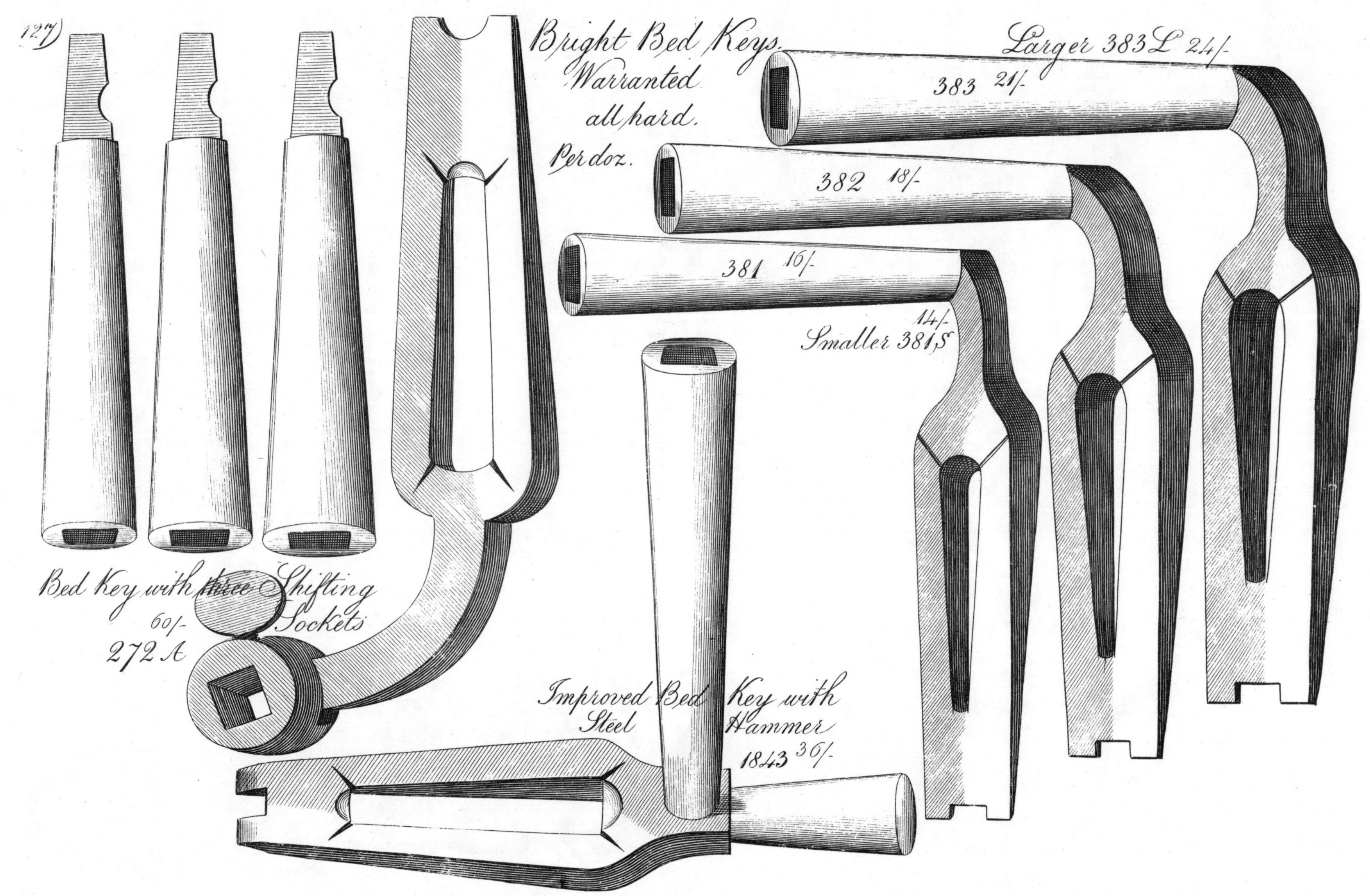
127
Bright Bed Keys.
Warranted
all hard.
Per doz.
Larger 383 L 24/-
383 21/-
382 18/-
381 16/-
14/-
Smaller 381 S
Bed Key with three Shifting
Sockets
60/-
272 A
Improved Bed Key with
Steel Hammer
1843 36/-

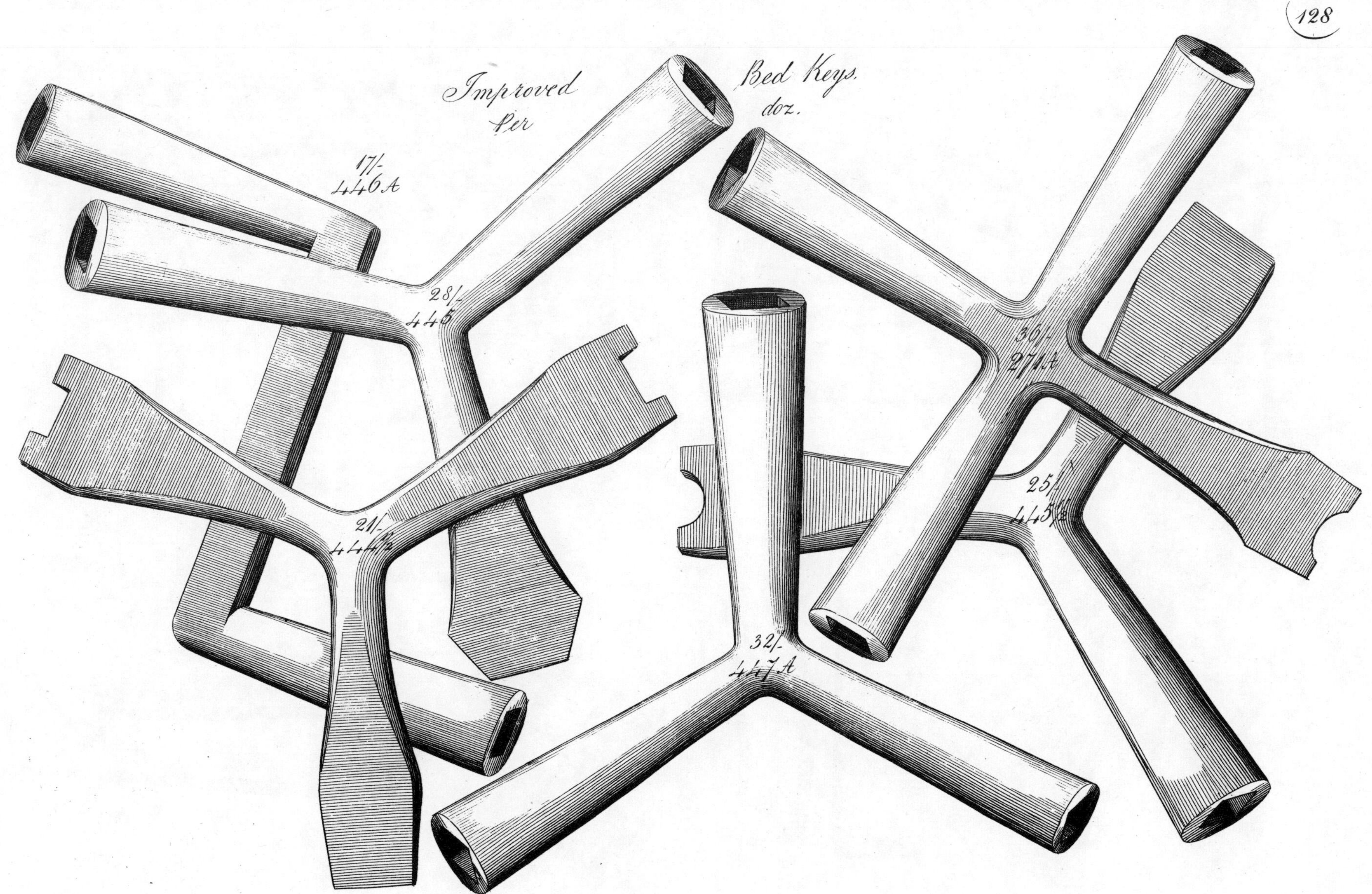

Improved Bed Keys.
Per doz.
17/-
446A
28/-
445
30/-
271A
21/-
444½
25/-
445½
32/-
447A

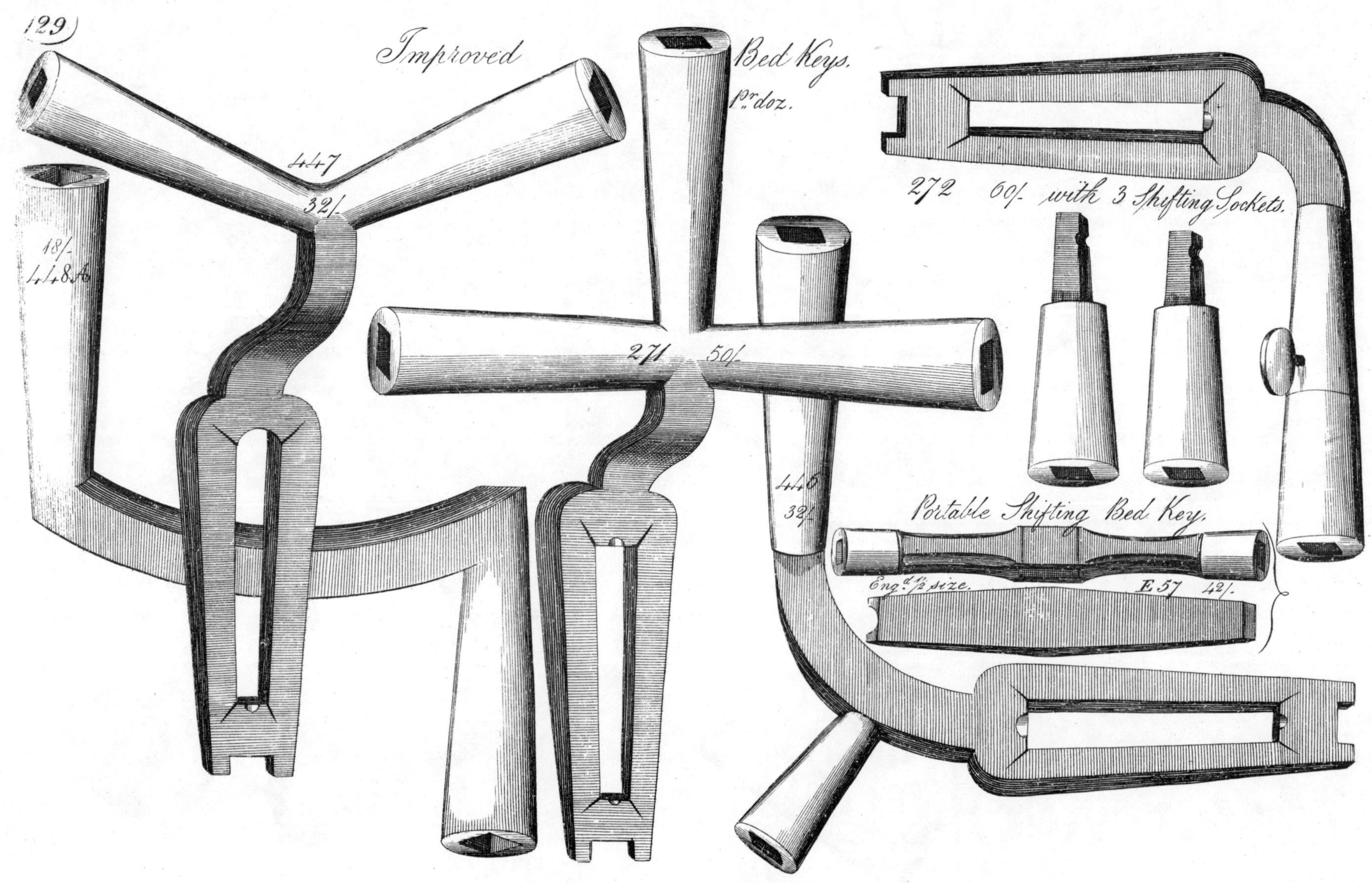
129
Improved Bed Keys.
Pr doz.
44 7
32/-
18/-
44 8A
272 60/- with 3 Shifting Sockets.
271 50/-
44 6
32/-
Portable Shifting Bed Key.
Eng.d 1/2 size.
E 57 42/-

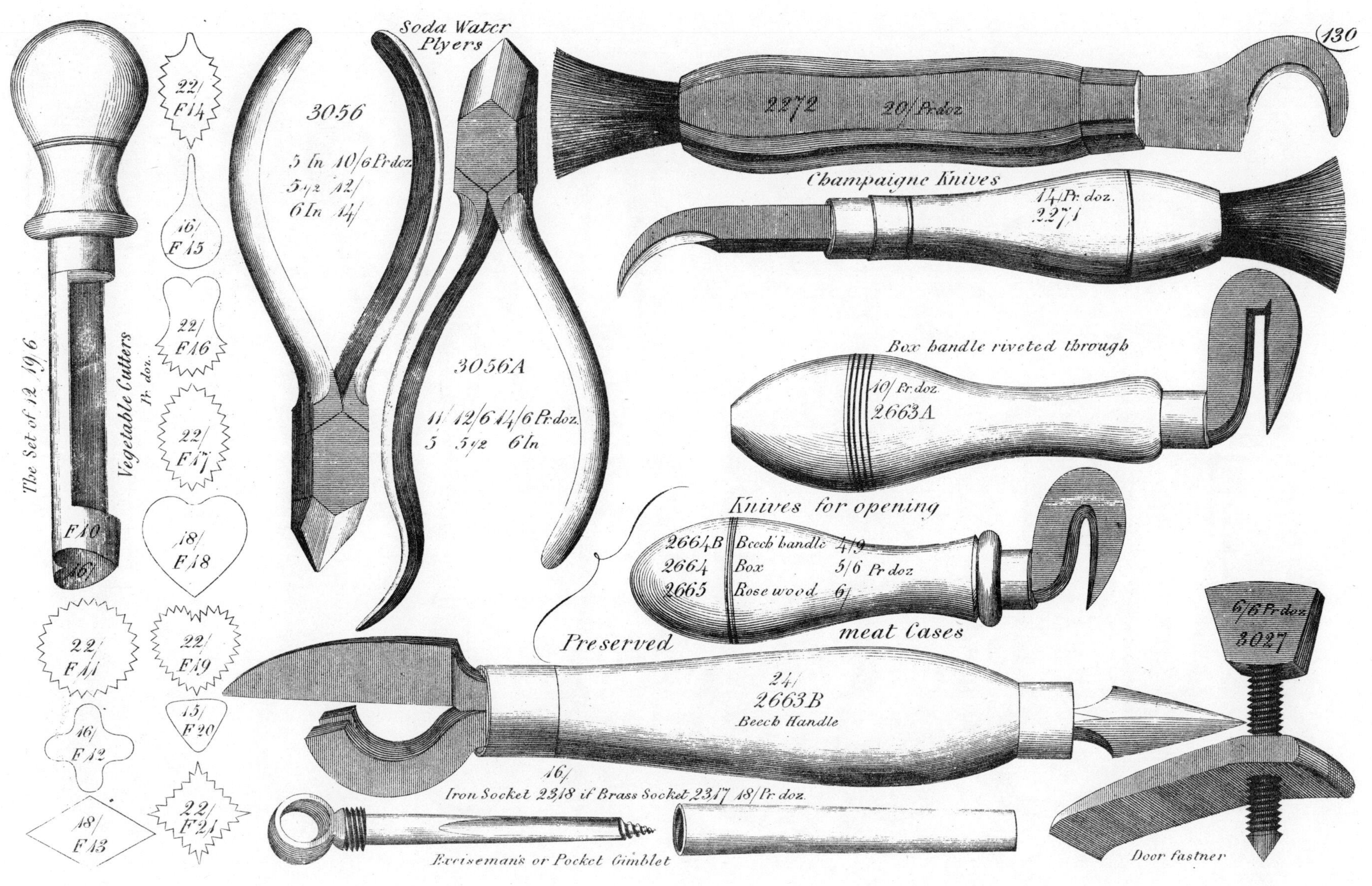
The Set of 12. 19/6
Vegetable Cutters
Pr. doz.
22/ F14
16/ F15
22/ F16
22/ F17
18/ F18
F10
16/
22/ F11
16/ F12
18/ F13
22/ F19
15/ F20
22/ F21
Soda Water Plyers
3056
5 In 10/6 Pr doz
5 1/2 12/
6 In 14/
3056A
11/ 12/6 14/6 Pr. doz.
5   5 1/2   6 In
2272   20/ Pr. doz.
Champaigne Knives
14/ Pr. doz.
2271
Box handle riveted through
40/ Pr. doz.
2663A
Knives for opening
2664B   Beech handle   4/9
2664   Box   5/6 Pr doz
2665   Rosewood   6/
Preserved
24/
2663B
Beech Handle
meat Cases
6/6 Pr. doz.
3027
16/
Iron Socket 23/8 if Brass Socket 23/7 18/ Pr. doz.
Exciseman's or Pocket Gimblet
Door fastner

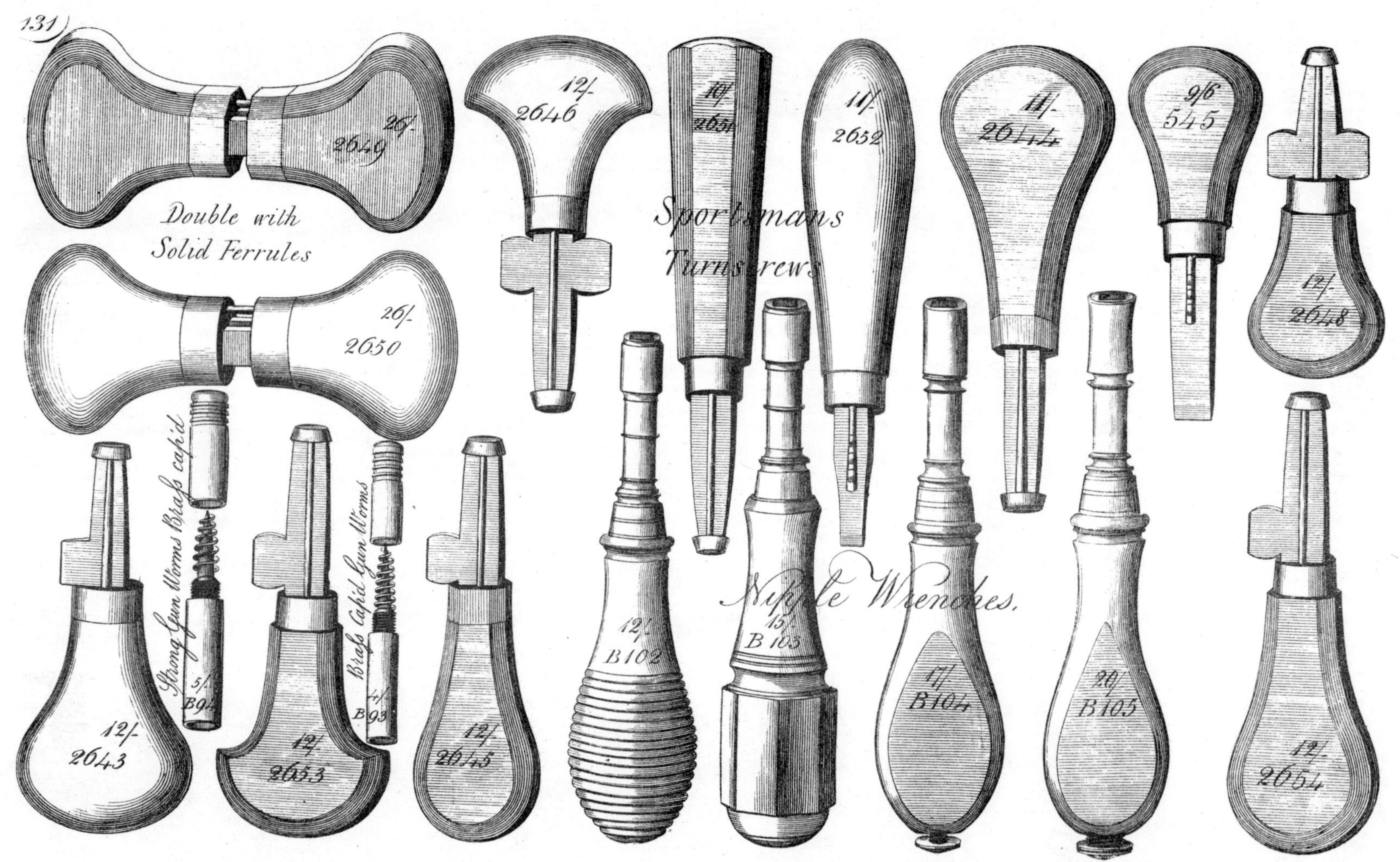

131)
Double with
Solid Ferrules
26/-
2649
26/-
2650
12/-
2646
Sportsmans
Turnscrews
10/-
2651
11/-
2652
11/-
2644
9/6
545
12/-
2648
Strong Gun Worms Brass cap'd
Brass cap'd Gun Worms
5/-
B92
4/-
B93
12/-
2643
12/-
2653
12/-
2645
12/-
B102
15/-
B103
Nipple Wrenches.
17/-
B104
20/-
B105
12/-
2654

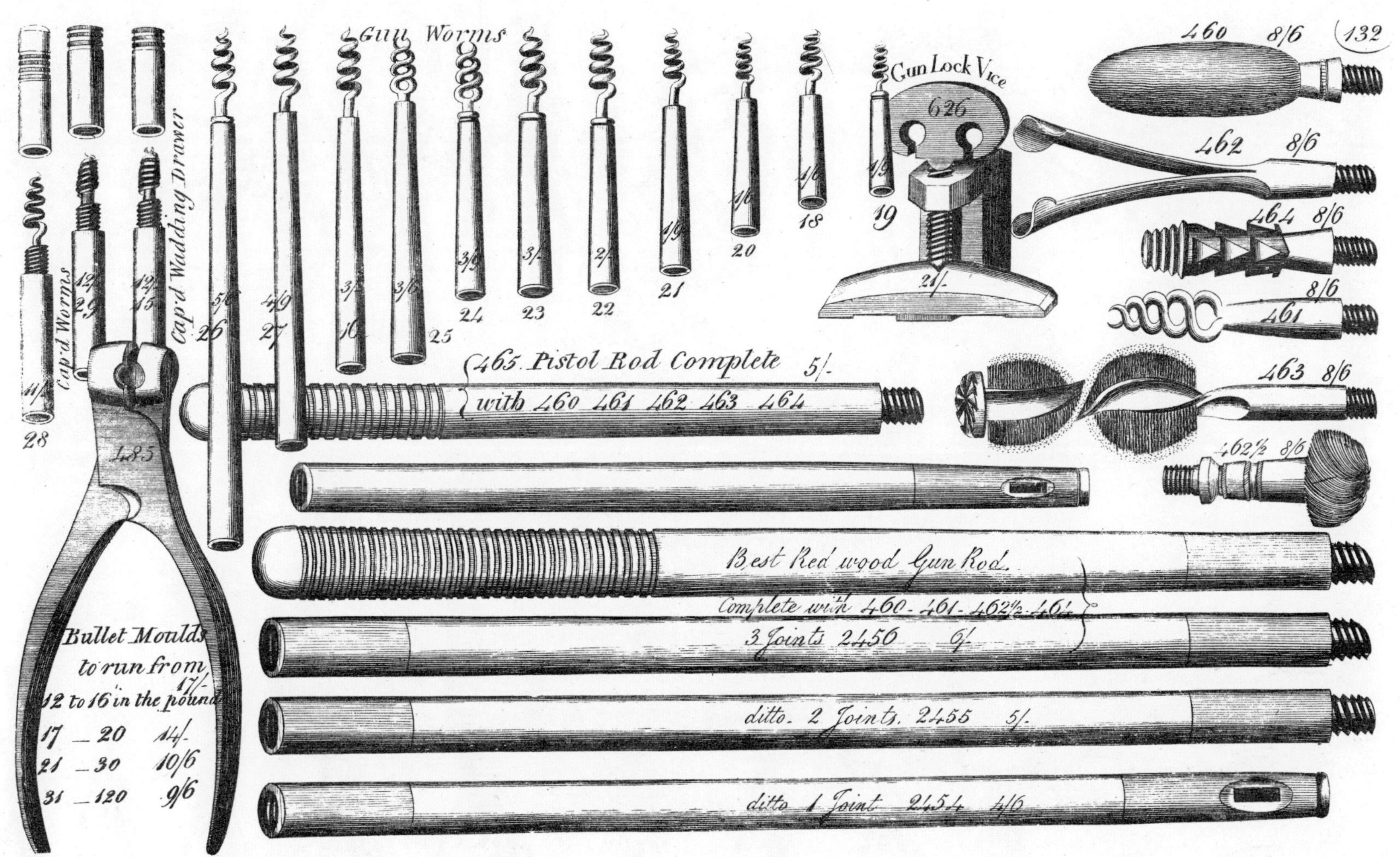
132
Gun Worms
Cap'd Worms
Cap'd Wadding Drawer
Gun Lock Vice
626
460 8/6
462 8/6
464 8/6
8/6
461
463 8/6
462½ 8/6
465. Pistol Rod Complete 5/-
with 460 461 462 463 464
Best Red wood Gun Rod.
Complete with 460. 461. 462½. 464.
3 Joints 2456 6/-
ditto. 2 Joints. 2455 5/-
ditto 1 Joint 2454 4/6
Bullet Moulds
to run from
12 to 16 in the pound 17/-
17 — 20 14/-
21 — 30 10/6
31 — 120 9/6
L85
11/4
19/6
19/6
20/-
15
28
5/6
4/6
3/6
3/6
3/6
3/-
2/6
1/9
1/6
1/6
1/9
26 27 10 25 24 23 22 21 20 18 19
21/-

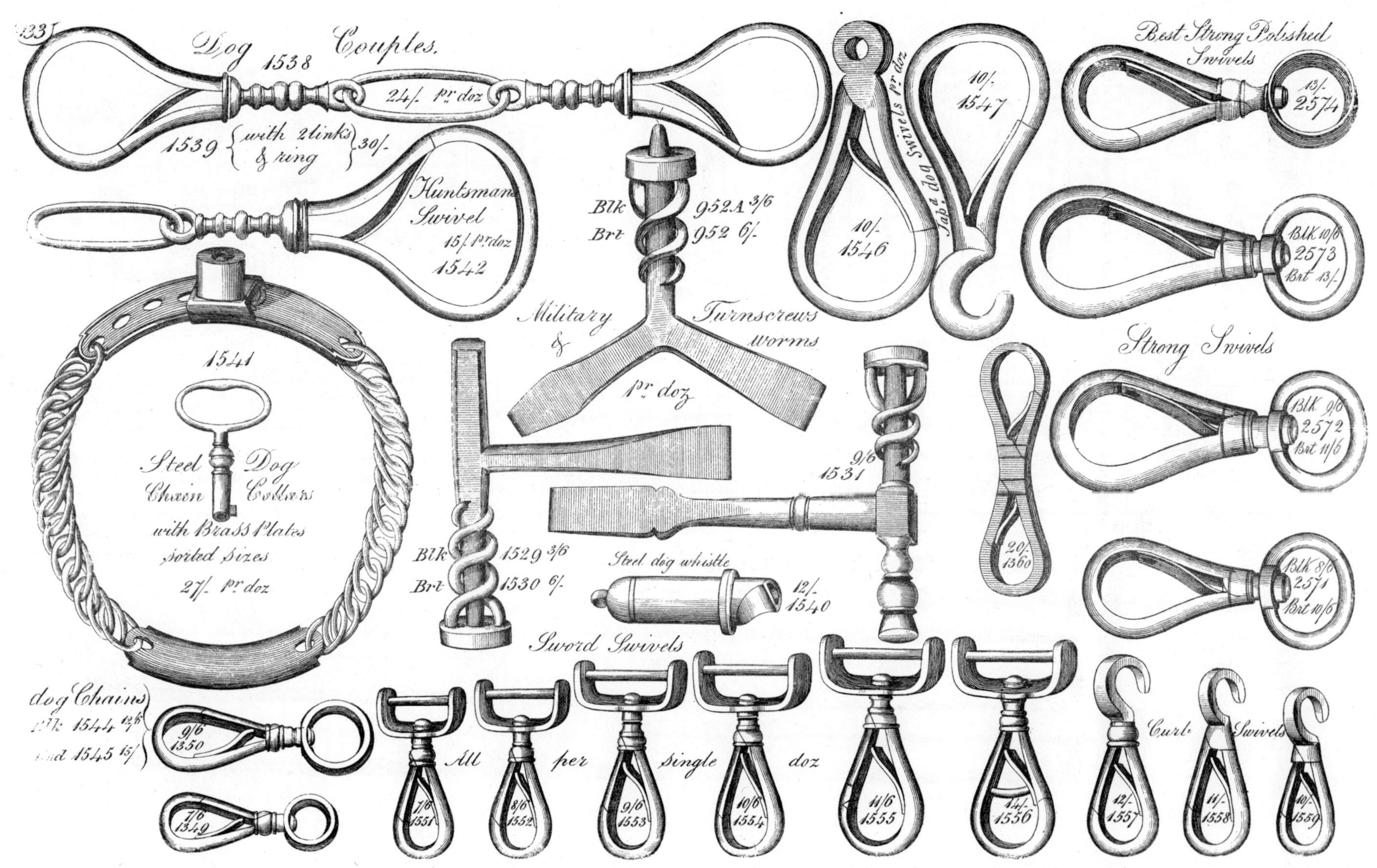
Dog Couples.
1538
24/- Pr doz
1539 {with 2 links & ring} 30/-
Huntsman Swivel
15/- Pr doz
1542
1541
Steel Dog Chain Collars
with Brass Plates
sorted sizes
27/- Pr doz
dog Chains
Blk: 1544 12/6
and 1545 15/-
9/6 1350
7/6 1349
Blk 952A 3/6
Brt 952 6/-
Military & Turnscrews worms
Pr doz
Blk 1529 3/6
Brt 1530 6/-
9/6 1531
Steel dog whistle
12/- 1540
Sword Swivels
All per single doz
7/6 1551
8/6 1552
9/6 1553
10/6 1554
11/6 1555
14/- 1556
Japd dog Swivels pr doz
10/- 1547
10/- 1546
20/- 1360
Best Strong Polished Swivels
13/- 2574
Blk 10/6 2573 Brt 13/-
Strong Swivels
Blk 9/6 2572 Brt 11/6
Blk 8/6 2571 Brt 10/6
Curb Swivels
12/- 1557
11/- 1558
10/- 1559

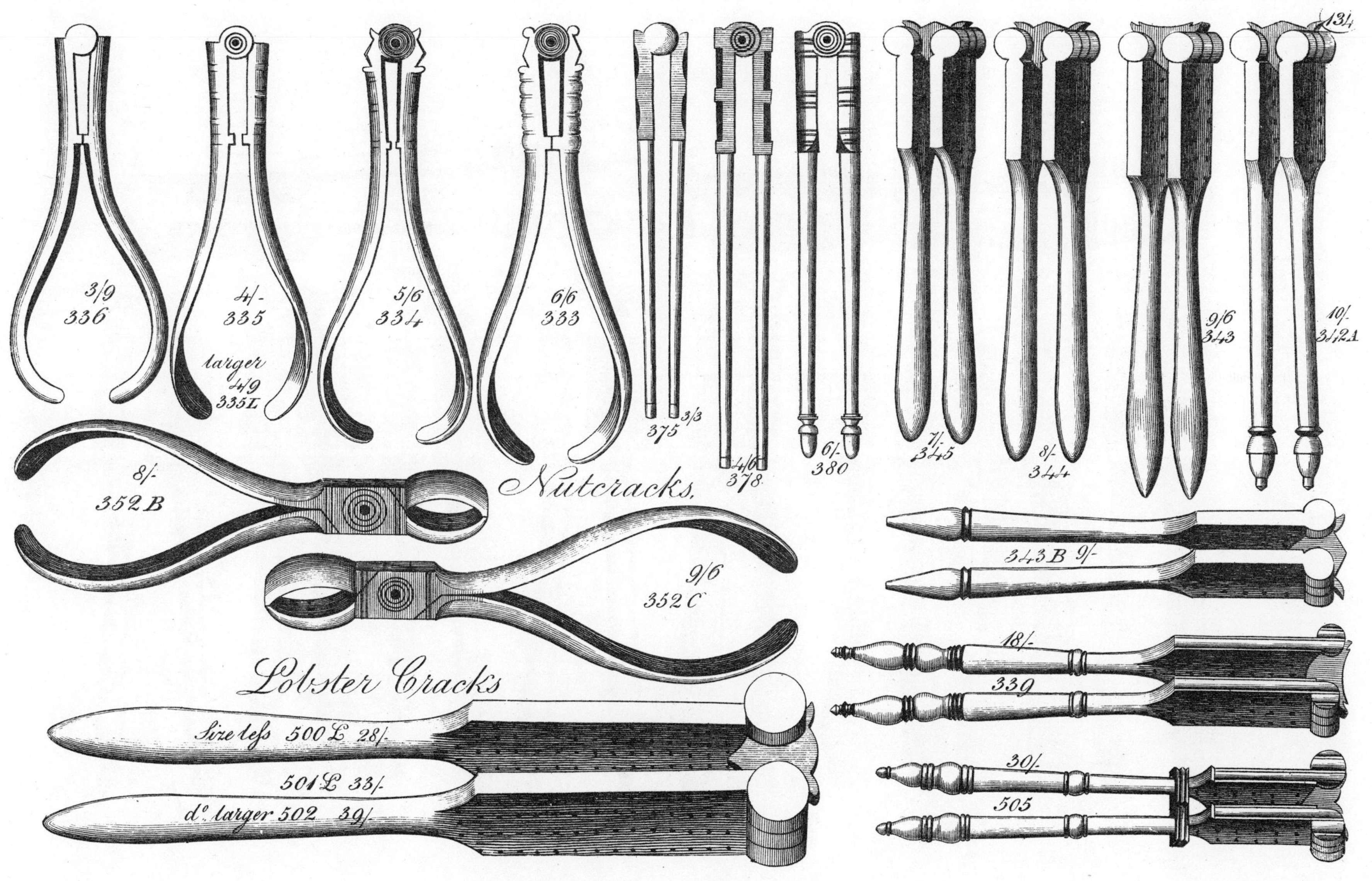
131
3/9 336
4/- 335
larger 4/9 335L
5/6 334
6/6 333
3/3 375
4/6 378
6/- 380
7/- 345
8/- 344
9/6 343
10/- 342A
Nutcracks.
8/- 352B
9/6 352C
343B 9/-
18/- 339
30/- 505
Lobster Cracks
Size less 500L 28/-
501L 33/-
do larger 502 39/-

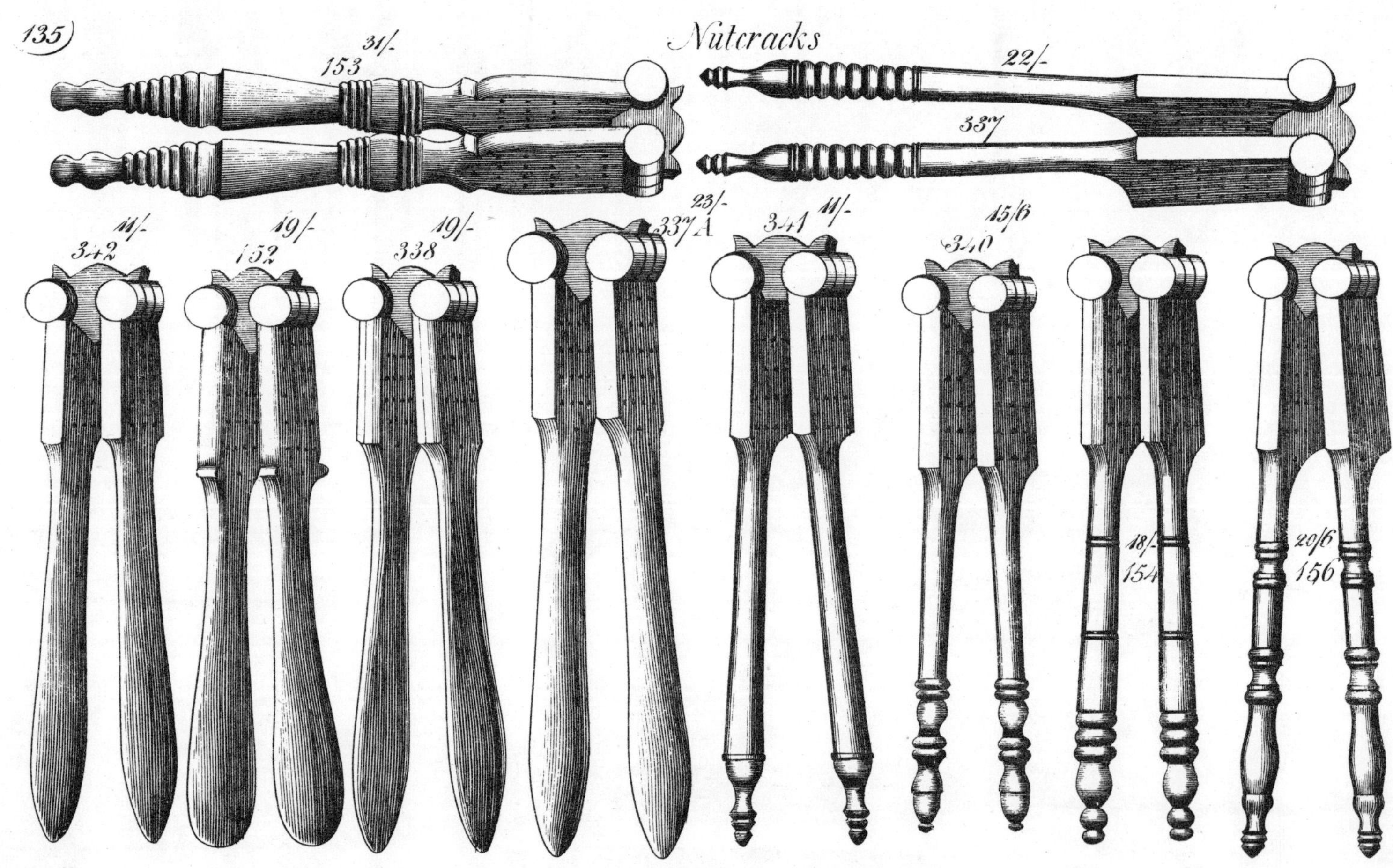
135)
Nutcracks
31/-
153
22/-
33"
11/-
342
19/-
152
19/-
338
23/-
33"/A
341
11/-
340
15/6
18/-
154
20/6
156

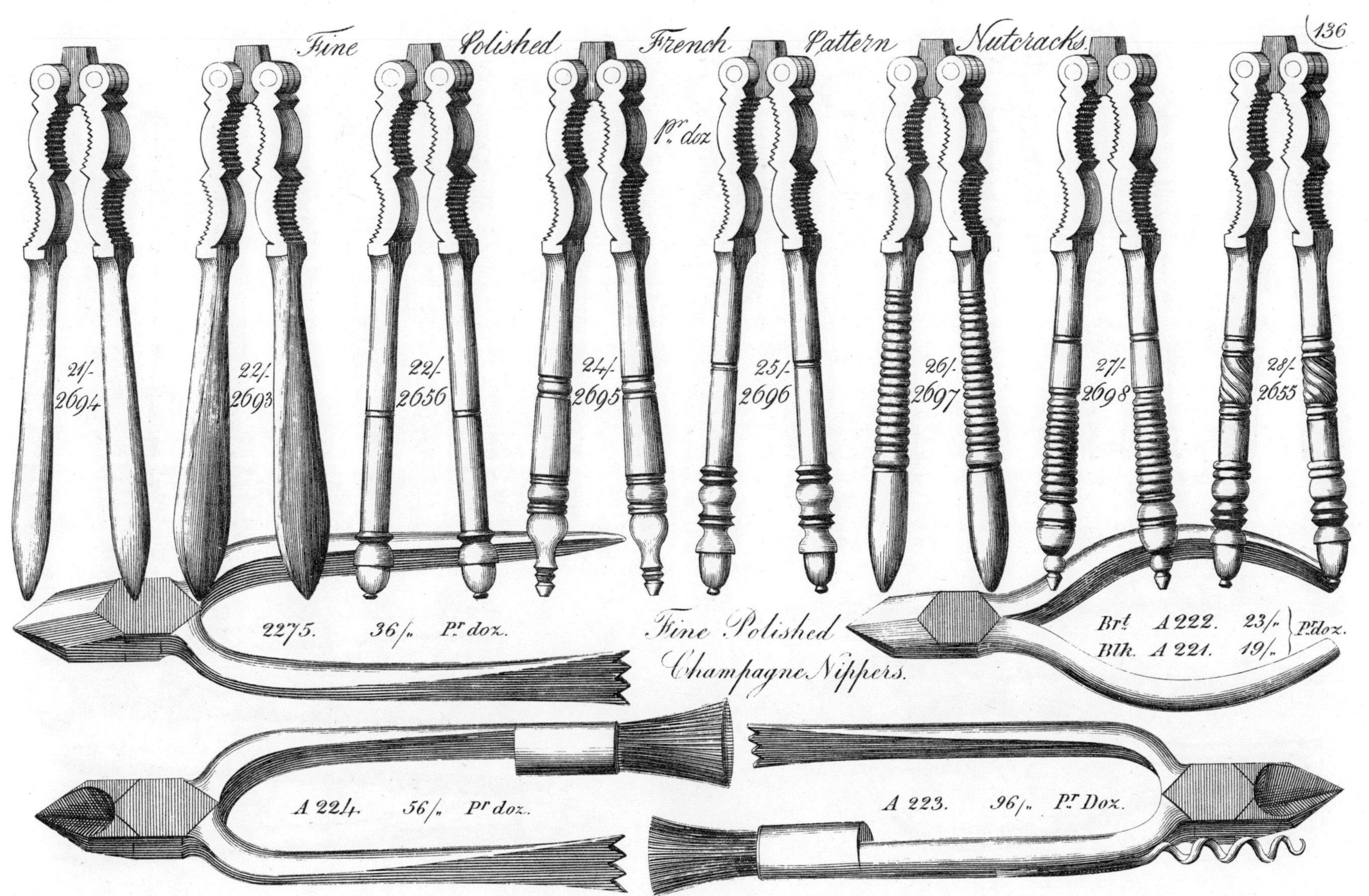
Fine Polished French Pattern Nutcracks.
Pr. doz
21/-
2694
22/-
2693
22/-
2656
24/-
2695
25/-
2696
26/-
2697
27/-
2698
28/-
2655
2275. 36/„ Pr. doz.
Fine Polished
Champagne Nippers.
Brt A 222. 23/„ Pr. doz.
Blk A 221. 19/„
A 224. 56/„ Pr. doz.
A 223. 96/„ Pr. Doz.

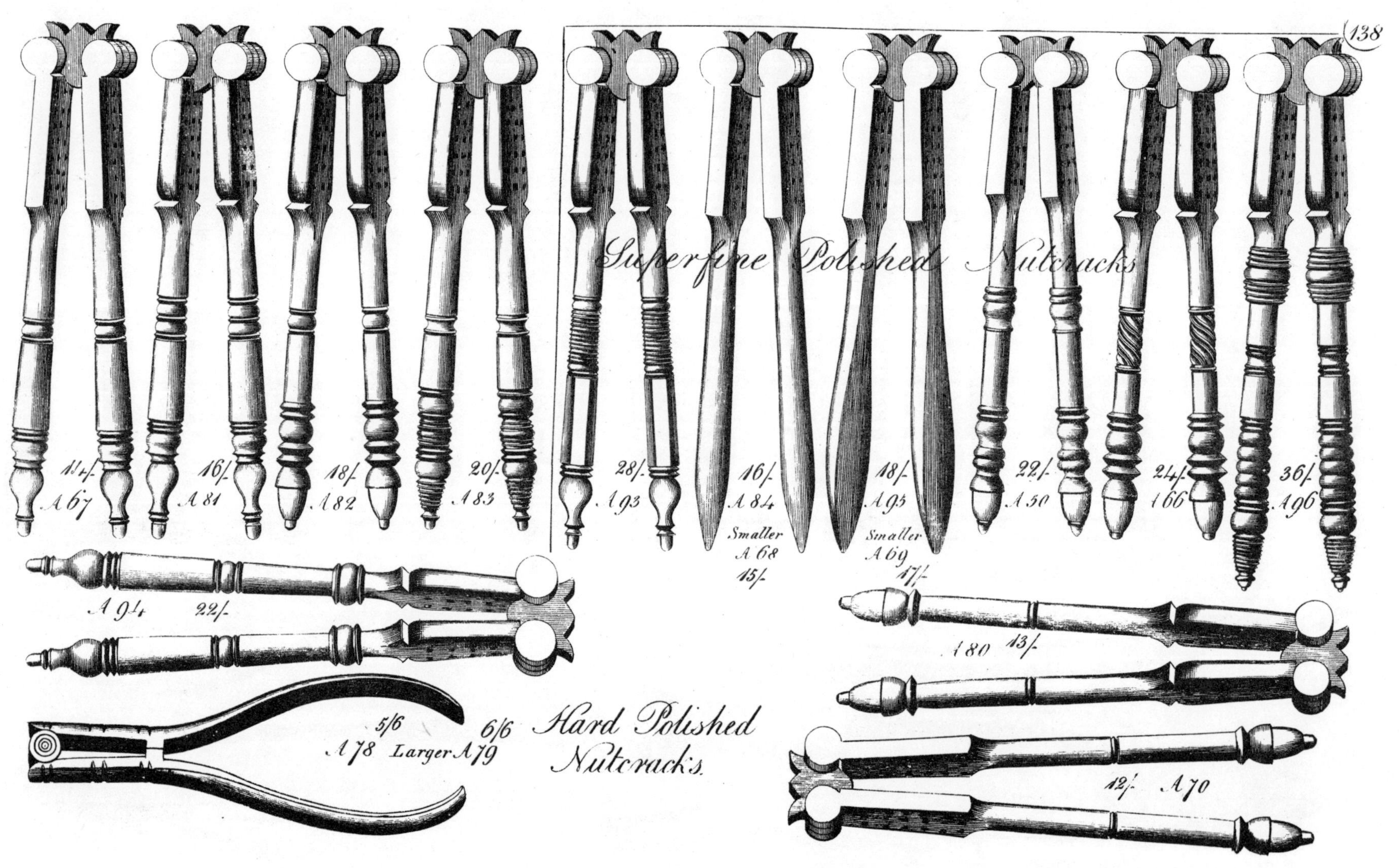
138
Superfine Polished Nutcracks
14/-
A 67
16/-
A 81
18/-
A 82
20/-
A 83
28/-
A 93
16/-
A 84
Smaller
A 68
15/-
18/-
A 95
Smaller
A 69
17/-
22/-
A 50
24/-
166
36/-
A 96
A 94   22/-
5/6   6/6
A 78 Larger A 79
Hard Polished
Nutcracks.
180 13/-
12/- A 70

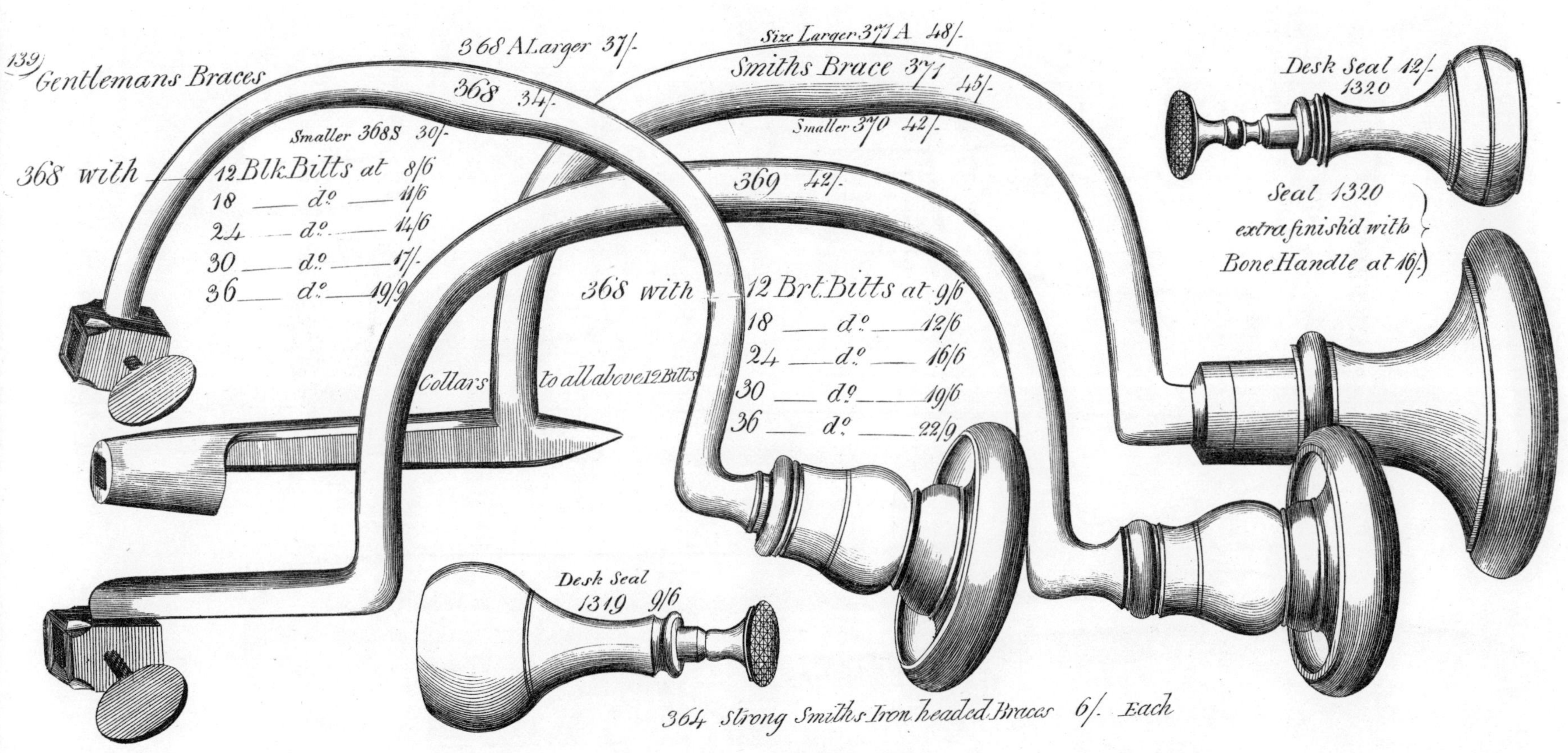

139) Gentlemans Braces
368 A Larger 37/-
368 34/-
Smaller 368 S 30/-
368 with ___ 12 Blk. Bitts at 8/6
18 ___ d.º ___ 11/6
24 ___ d.º ___ 14/6
30 ___ d.º ___ 17/-
36 ___ d.º ___ 19/9
Collars ___ to all above 12 Bitts
Size Larger 371 A 48/-
Smiths Brace 371 45/-
Smaller 370 42/-
369 42/-
368 with ___ 12 Brt. Bitts at 9/6
18 ___ d.º ___ 12/6
24 ___ d.º ___ 16/6
30 ___ d.º ___ 19/6
36 ___ d.º ___ 22/9
Desk Seal 12/- 1320
Seal 1320 extra finish'd with Bone Handle at 16/-
Desk Seal 1319 9/6
364 Strong Smiths Iron headed Braces 6/- Each

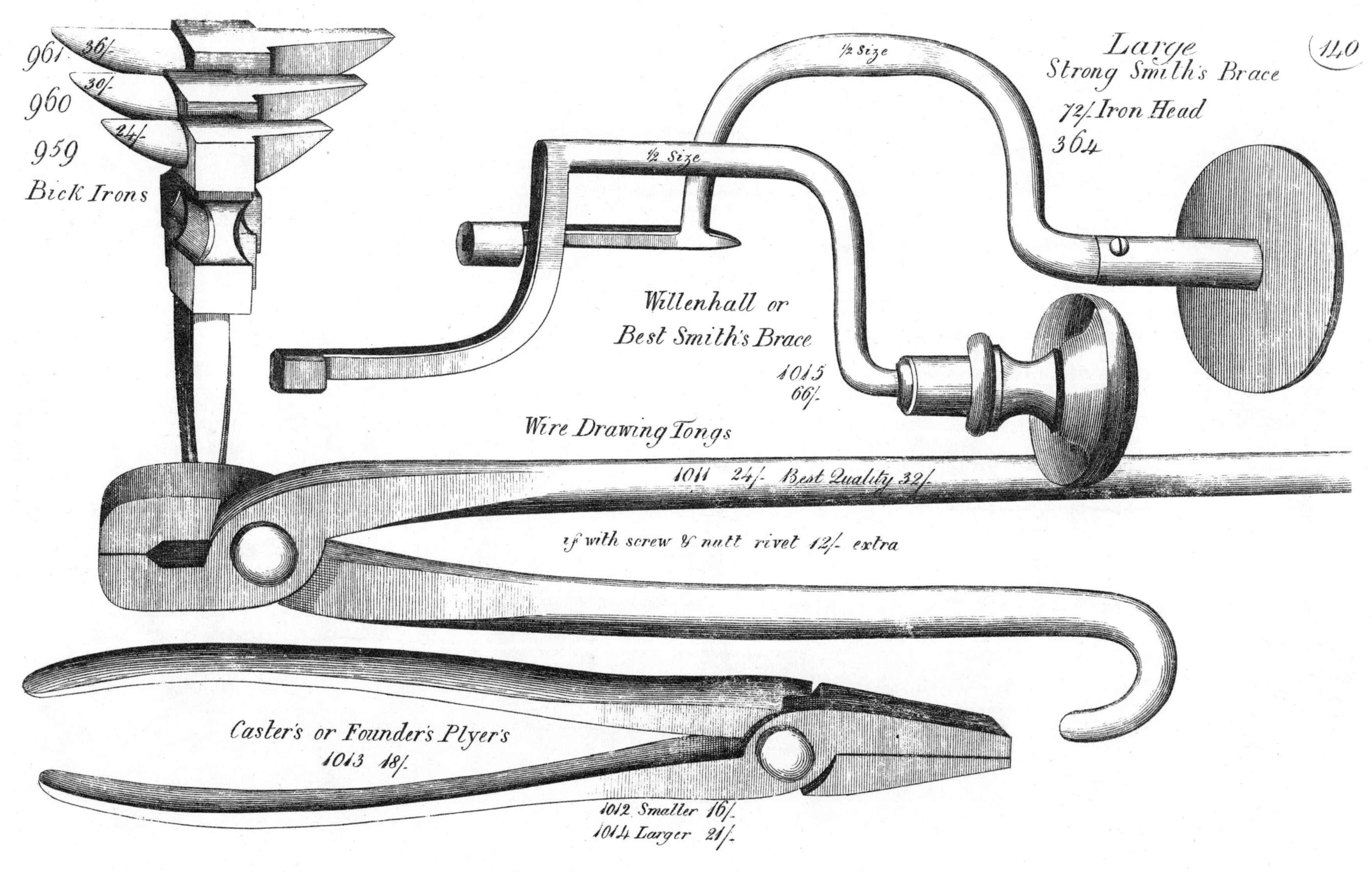
961 36/-
960 30/-
959 24/-
Bick Irons
1/2 Size
1/2 Size
Large
Strong Smith's Brace
72/- Iron Head
364
140
Willenhall or
Best Smith's Brace
1015
66/-
Wire Drawing Tongs
1011 24/- Best Quality 32/-
if with screw & nutt rivet 12/- extra
Caster's or Founder's Plyer's
1013 18/-
1012 Smaller 16/-
1014 Larger 21/-

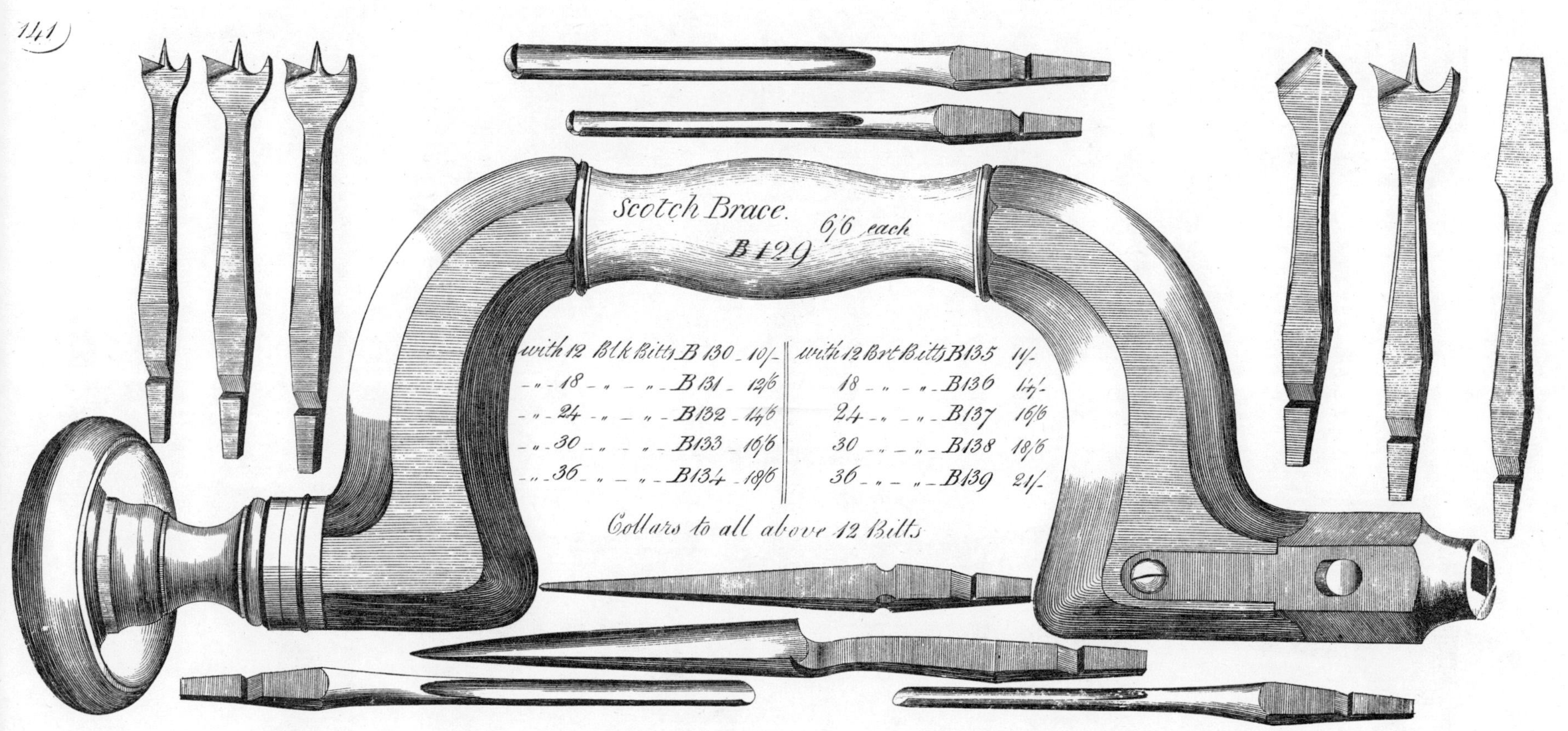
141
Scotch Brace.
B 129
6/6 each
with 12 Blk Bitts B 130 _ 10/-
_ " _ 18 _ " _ " B 131 _ 12/6
_ " _ 24 _ " _ " B 132 _ 14/6
_ " _ 30 _ " _ " B 133 _ 16/6
_ " _ 36 _ " _ " B 134 _ 18/6
with 12 Brt Bitts B 135 _ 11/-
18 _ " _ " B 136 _ 14/-
24 _ " _ " B 137 _ 16/6
30 _ " _ " B 138 _ 18/6
36 _ " _ " B 139 _ 21/-
Collars to all above 12 Bitts

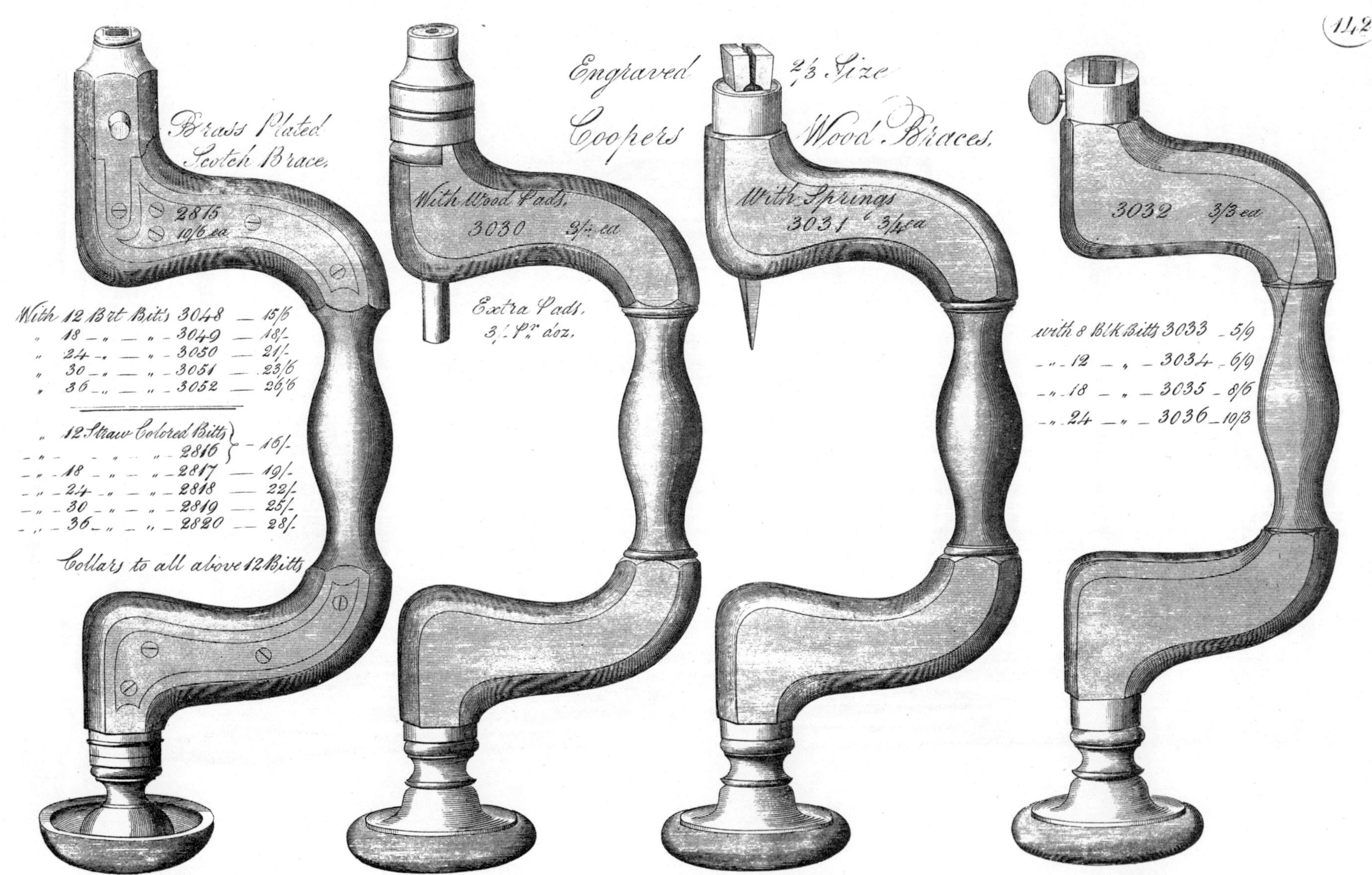
142
Brass Plated Scotch Brace.
2815
10/6 ea
Engraved Coopers
With Wood Pads.
3030   3/- ea
2/3 Size Wood Braces.
With Springs
3031   3/4 ea
3032   3/3 ea
With 12 Brt Bitts 3048 — 15/6
"   18 — "   — 3049 — 18/-
"   24 — "   — 3050 — 21/-
"   30 — "   — 3051 — 23/6
"   36 — "   — 3052 — 26/6
"   12 Straw Colored Bitts
2816   — 16/-
— " — 18 — " — " 2817 — 19/-
— " — 24 — " — " 2818 — 22/-
— " — 30 — " — " 2819 — 25/-
— " — 36 — " — " 2820 — 28/-
Collars to all above 12 Bitts
Extra Pads.
3/- P.r doz.
with 8 Blk Bitts 3033 _ 5/9
_ " _ 12 _ " _ 3034 _ 6/9
_ " _ 18 _ " _ 3035 _ 8/6
_ " _ 24 _ " _ 3036 _ 10/3

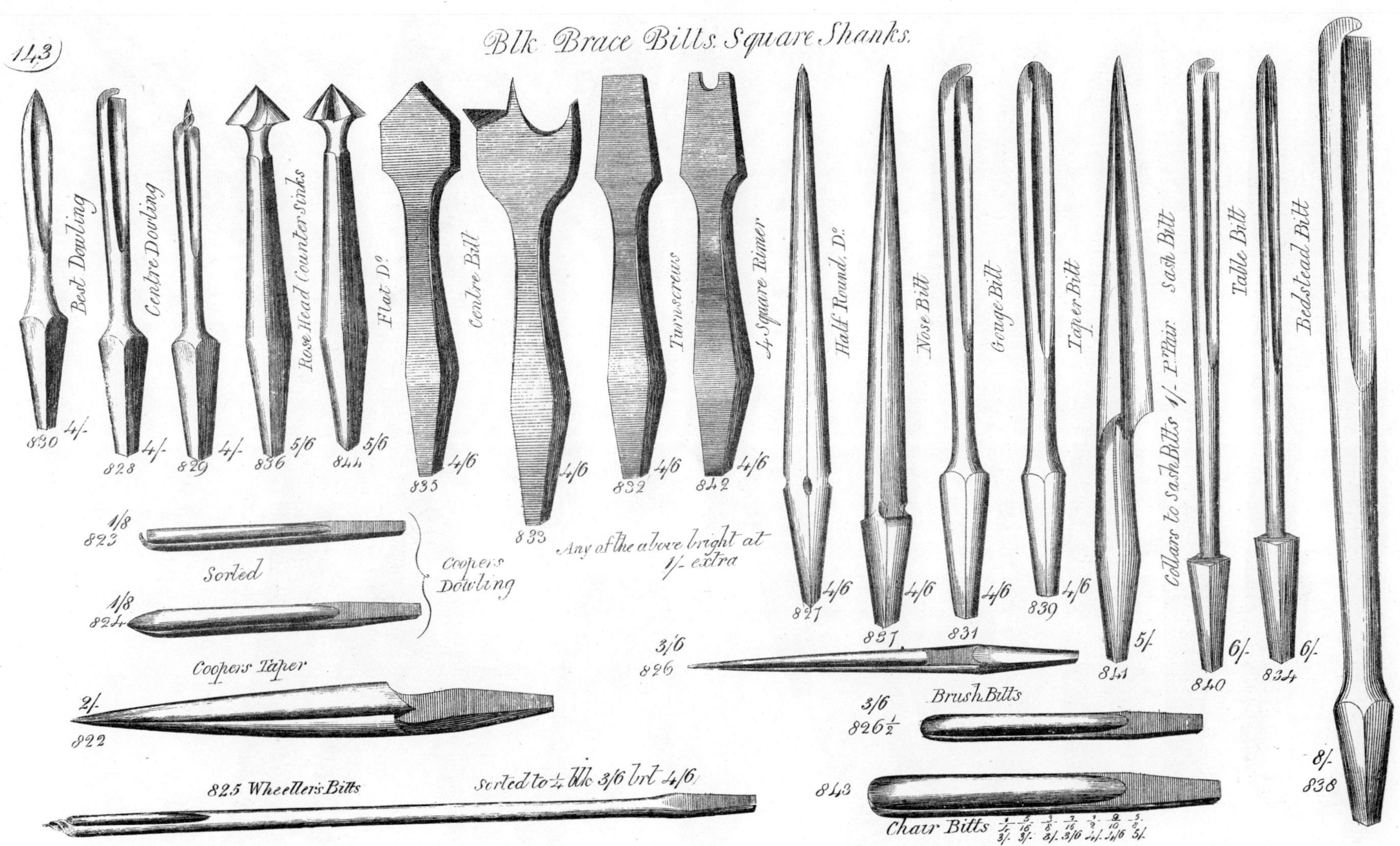
143
Blk. Brace Bitts. Square Shanks.
Best Dowling
Centre Dowling
Rose Head Counter sinks
Flat Do
Centre Bitt
Turnscrews
4 Square Rimer
Half Round. Do
Nose Bitt
Gouge Bitt
Taper Bitt
Collars to Sash Bitts 1/- P Pair. Sash Bitt
Table Bitt
Bedstead Bitt
830 4/-
828 4/-
829 4/-
836 5/6
844 5/6
835 4/6
833
832 4/6
842 4/6
4/6
827 4/6
837 4/6
831 4/6
839 4/6
841 5/-
840 6/-
834 6/-
838 8/-
1/8 823
Sorted
Coopers Dowling
1/8 824
Coopers Taper
2/- 822
825 Wheeller's Bitts
sorted to ½ blk 3/6 brt 4/6
Any of the above bright at 1/- extra
3/6 826
3/6 826½
Brush Bitts
843
Chair Bitts

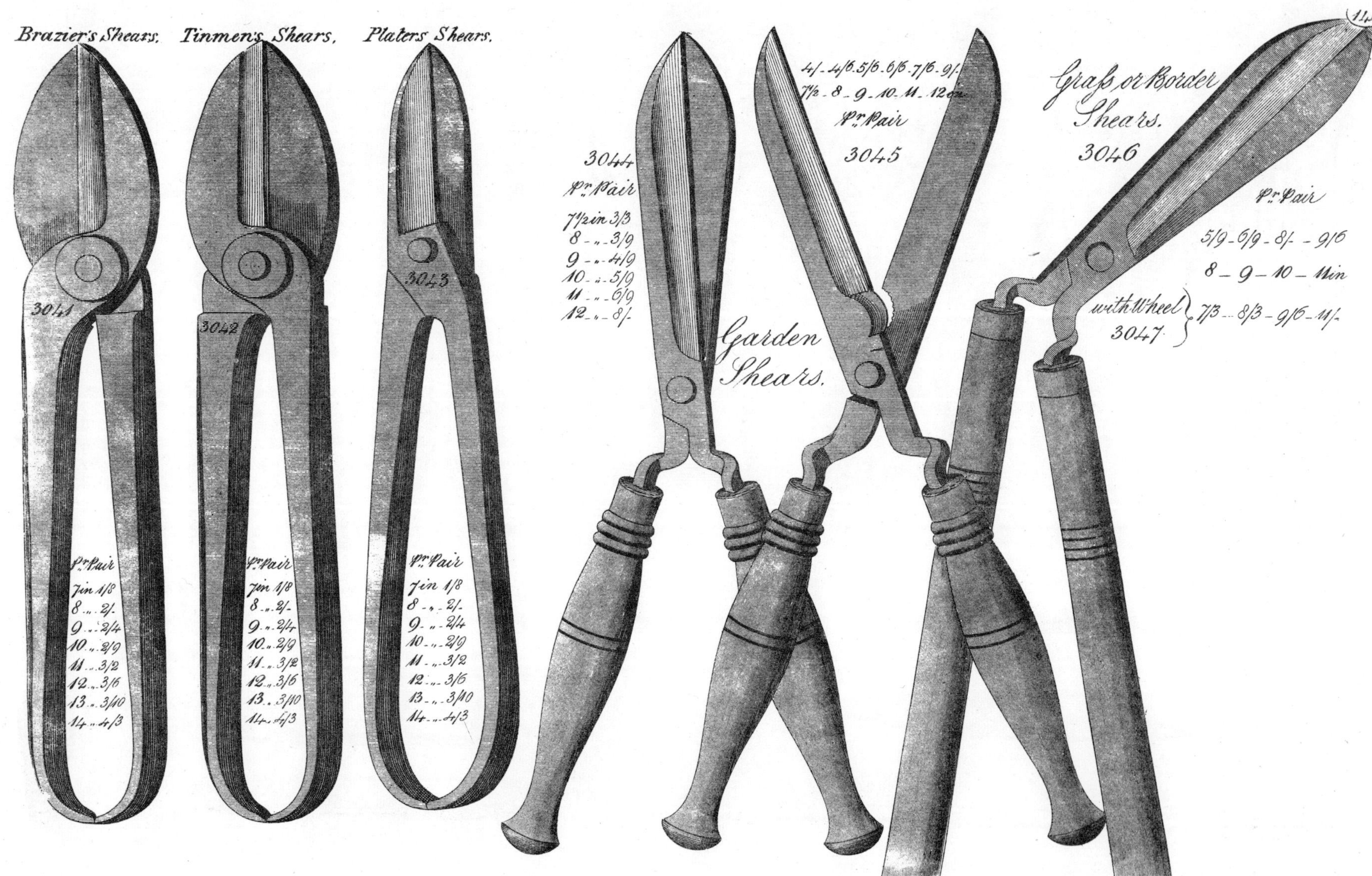
Brazier's Shears.
Tinmen's Shears.
Platers Shears.
Grass or Border Shears.
3046
3044
Pr Pair
3045
Garden Shears.
144
3041
3042
3043
Pr Pair
7½in 3/3
8 - „ - 3/9
9 - „ - 4/9
10 - „ - 5/9
11 - „ - 6/9
12 - „ - 8/-
4/- 4/6 5/6 6/6 7/6 9/-
7½ - 8 - 9 - 10 - 11 - 12 cu
Pr Pair
Pr Pair
5/9 - 6/9 - 8/- - 9/6
8 - 9 - 10 - 11in
with Wheel 3047
7/3 - 8/3 - 9/6 - 11/-
Pr Pair
7in 1/8
8 „ 2/-
9 „ 2/4
10 „ 2/9
11 „ 3/2
12 „ 3/6
13 „ 3/10
14 „ 4/3
Pr Pair
7in 1/8
8 „ 2/-
9 „ 2/4
10 „ 2/9
11 „ 3/2
12 „ 3/6
13 „ 3/10
14 „ 4/3
Pr Pair
7in 1/8
8 „ 2/-
9 „ 2/4
10 „ 2/9
11 „ 3/2
12 „ 3/6
13 „ 3/10
14 „ 4/3

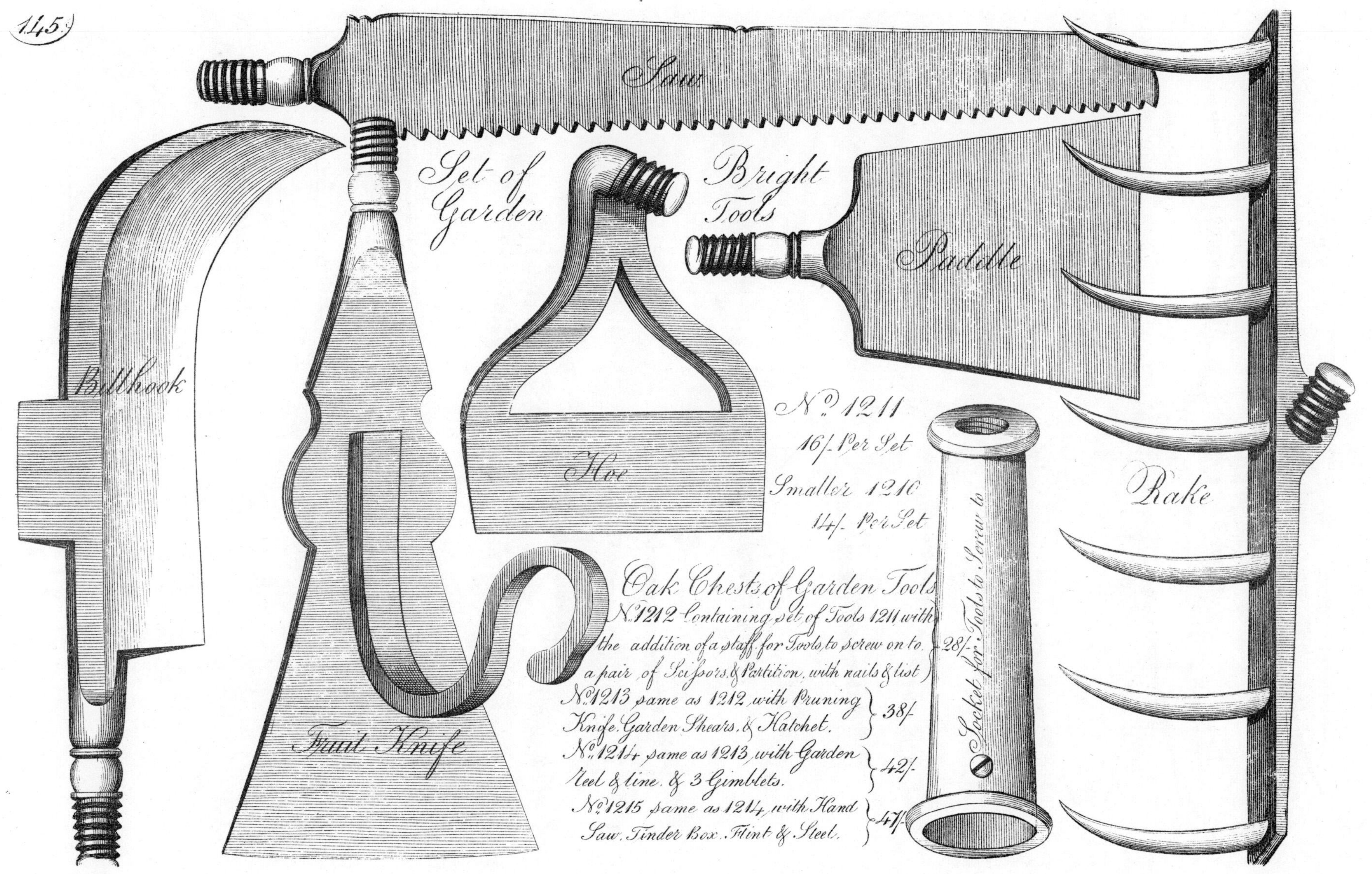
145
Saw
Set of Garden
Bright Tools
Paddle
Billhook
No. 1211
16/- Per Set
Smaller 1210
14/- Per Set
Hoe
Rake
Fruit Knife
Oak Chests of Garden Tools
No. 1212 Containing Set of Tools 1211 with
the addition of a staff for Tools to screw on to,
a pair of Scissors & Partition, with nails & list   28/-
No. 1213 same as 1212, with Pruning
Knife, Garden Shears, & Hatchet.   38/-
No. 1214 same as 1213, with Garden
Reel & line, & 3 Gimblets.   42/-
No. 1215 same as 1214, with Hand
Saw, Tinder Box, Flint & Steel.   47/-
Socket for Tools to screw to

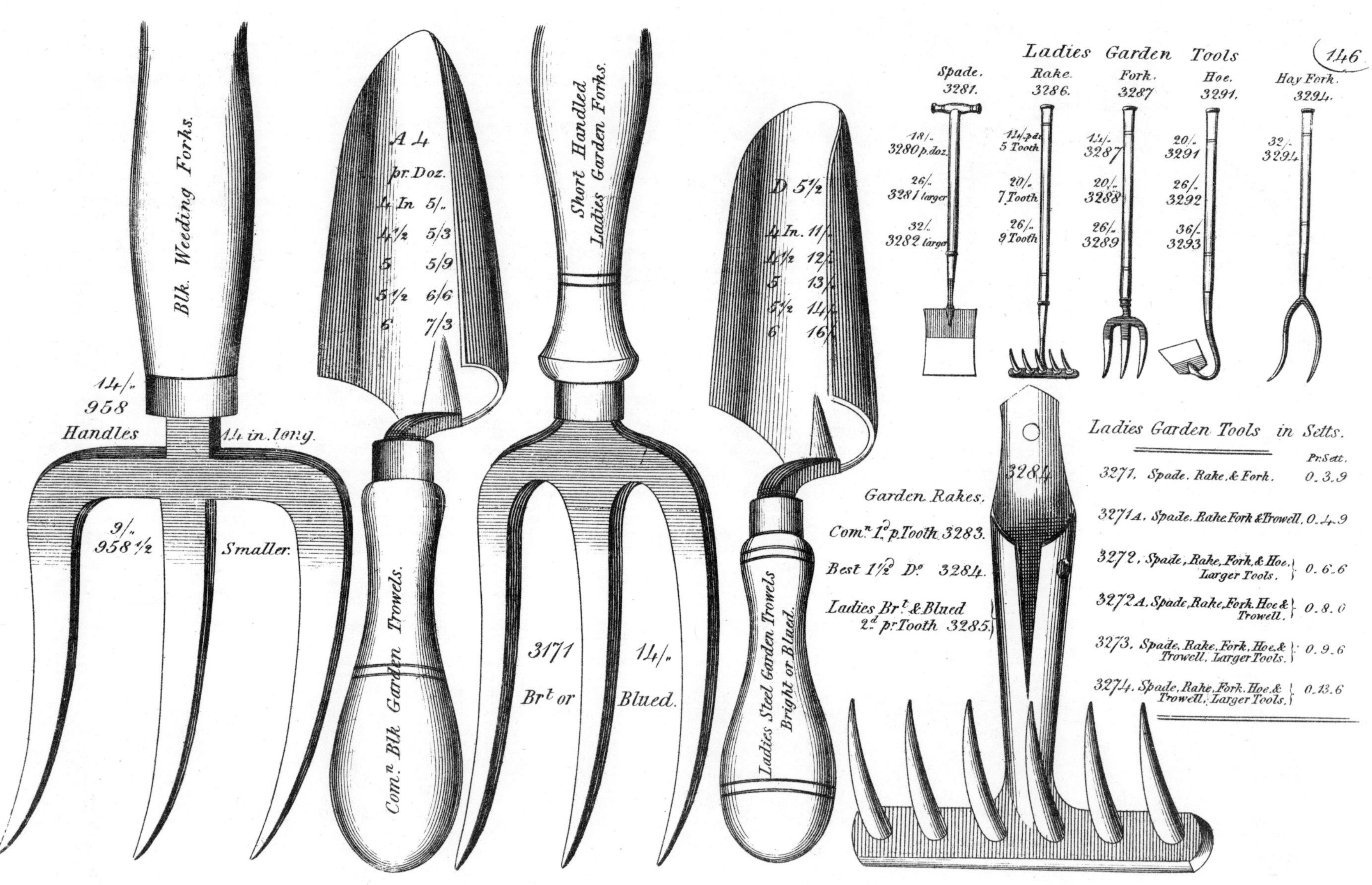
Blk. Weeding Forks.
14/-
958
Handles
14 in. long.
9/-
958 1/2
Smaller.
A 4
pr. Doz.
4 In 5/-
4 1/2 5/3
5 5/9
5 1/2 6/6
6 7/3
Com'n. Blk. Garden Trowels.
Short Handled
Ladies Garden Forks.
3171
Br't or
Blued.
D 5 1/2
4 In. 11/-
4 1/2 12/-
5 13/-
5 1/2 14/-
6 16/-
Ladies Steel Garden Trowels
Bright or Blued.
Garden Rakes.
Com'n 1'd p'Tooth 3283.
Best 1 1/2 D'o 3284.
Ladies Br't & Blued
2'd pr'Tooth 3285.
3284
Ladies Garden Tools
Spade.
3281.
Rake.
3286.
Fork.
3287
Hoe.
3291.
Hay Fork.
3294.
18/-
3280 p.doz.
26/-
3281 larger
32/-
3282 larger
14/- p.d.
5 Tooth
20/-
7 Tooth
26/-
9 Tooth
14/-
3287
20/-
3288
26/-
3289
20/-
3291
26/-
3292
36/-
3293
32/-
3294
Ladies Garden Tools in Setts.
Pr.Sett.
3271. Spade. Rake. & Fork. 0. 3. 9
3271A. Spade. Rake. Fork & Trowell. 0. 4. 9
3272. Spade, Rake, Fork, & Hoe. Larger Tools. 0. 6. 6
3272A. Spade, Rake, Fork. Hoe & Trowell. 0. 8. 0
3273. Spade, Rake, Fork, Hoe & Trowell. Larger Tools. 0. 9. 6
3274. Spade, Rake, Fork. Hoe & Trowell. Larger Tools. 0. 13. 6

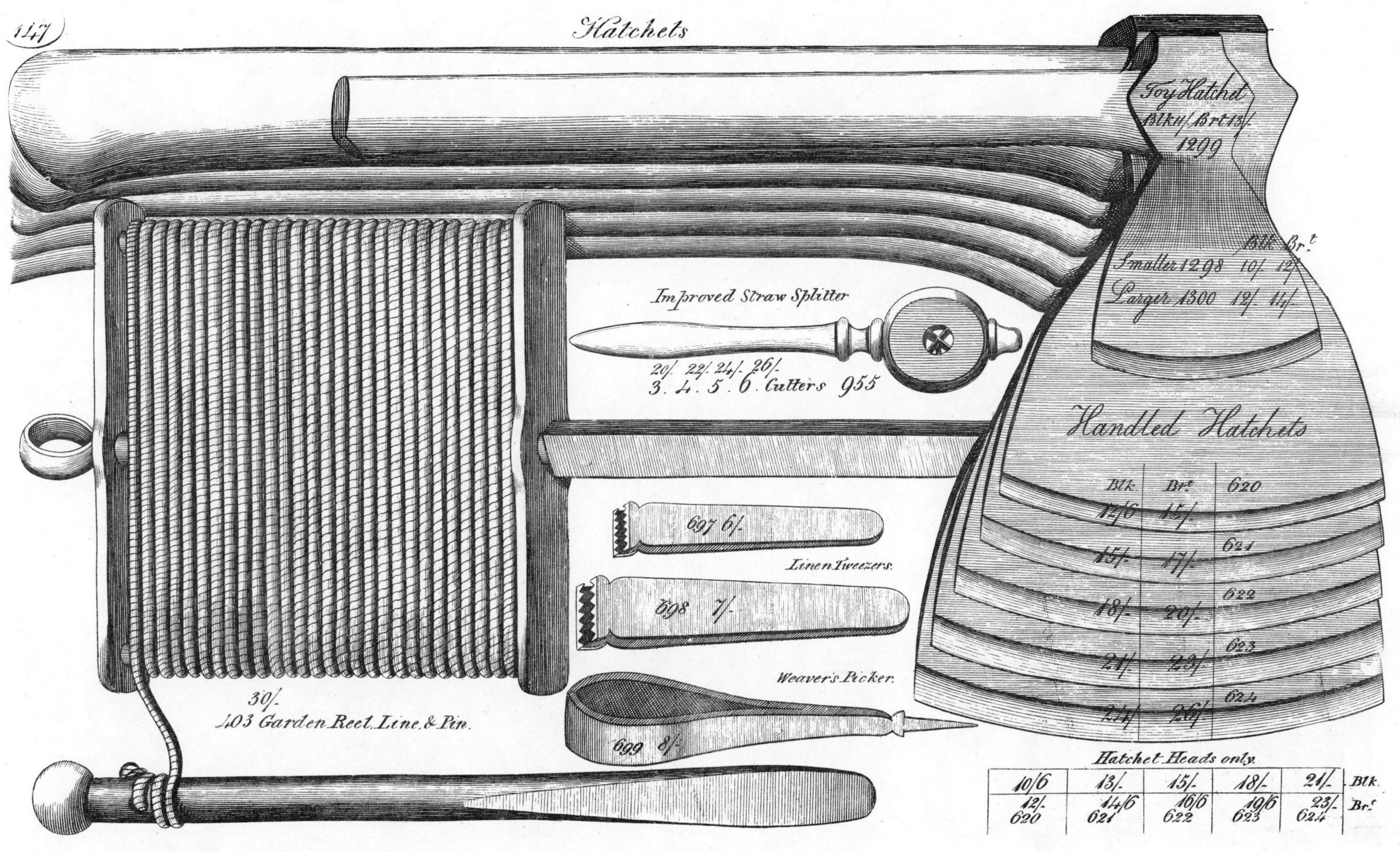

10/6	13/	15/	18/	21/	Blk.
12/	14/6	16/6	19/6	23/	Br.t
620	621	622	623	624	

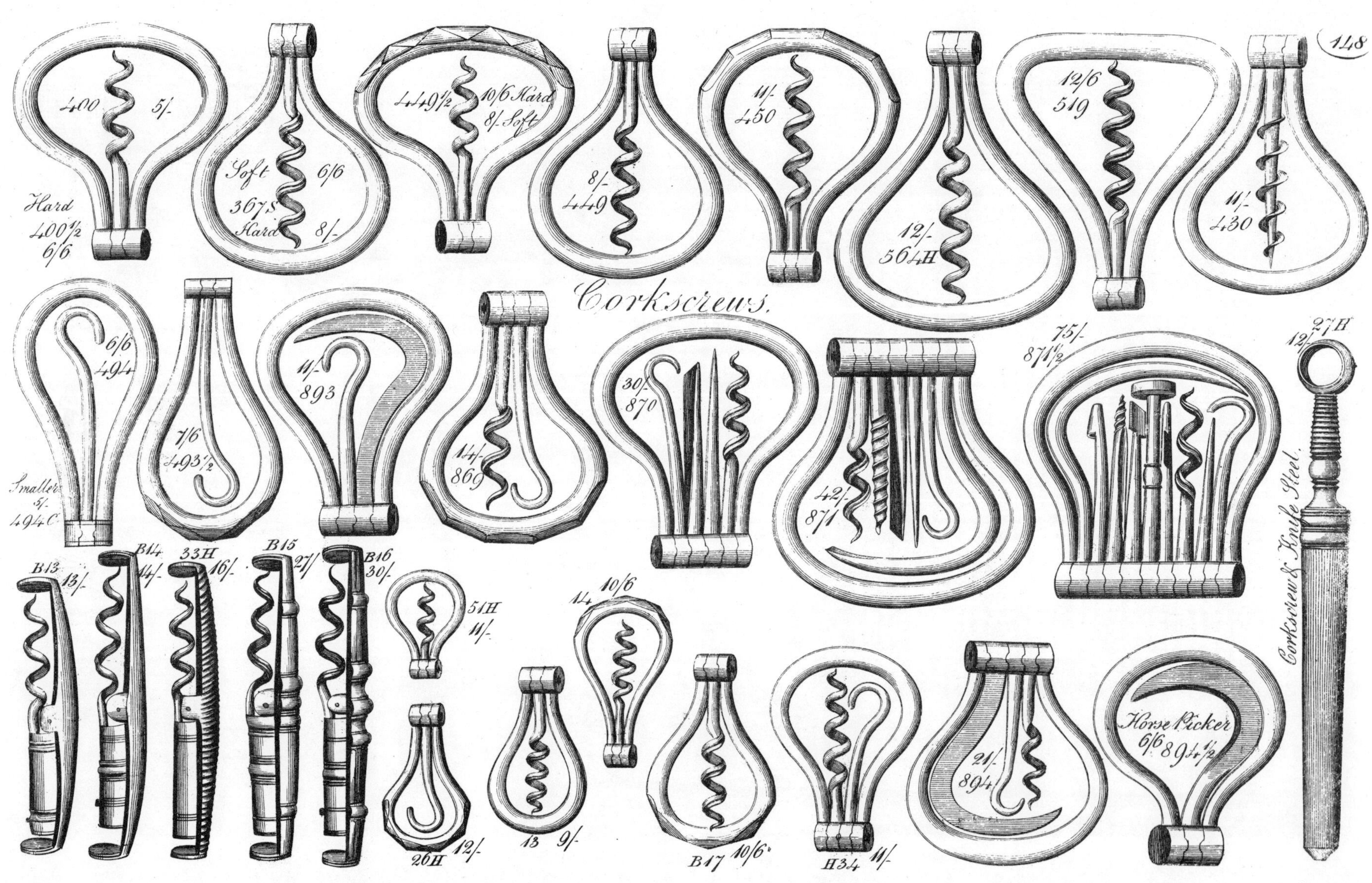
148
Corkscrews.
400   5/-
Hard 400½ 6/6
Soft 367S   6/6
Hard   8/-
449½   10/6 Hard   8/- Soft
8/- 449
11/- 450
12/6 564H
12/6 519
11/- 430
6/6 494
Smaller 5/- 494C
7/6 493½
11/- 893
30/- 870
14/- 869
42/- 871
75/- 87H½
27H 12/-
Corkscrew & Knife Steel.
B13 13/-
B14 14/-
33H 16/-
B15 27/-
B16 30/-
51H 11/-
26H 12/-
14/- 10/6
13 9/-
B17 10/6
H34 11/-
21/- 894
Horse Picker 6/6 8 9 4½

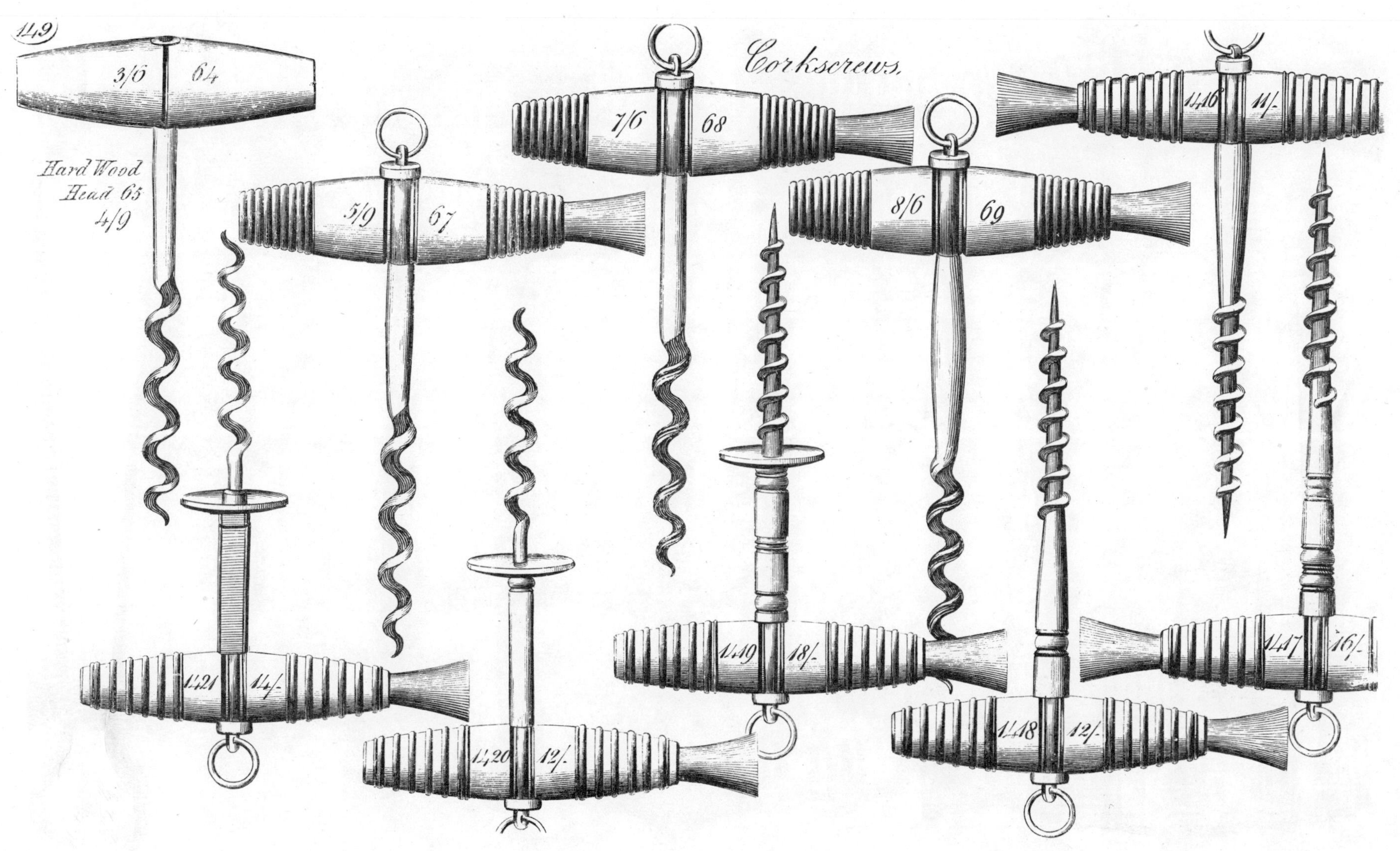
Corkscrews.
3/6 64
Hard Wood Head 65 4/9
5/9 67
7/6 68
8/6 69
1416 11/-
1421 14/-
1420 12/-
1419 18/-
1418 12/-
1417 16/-

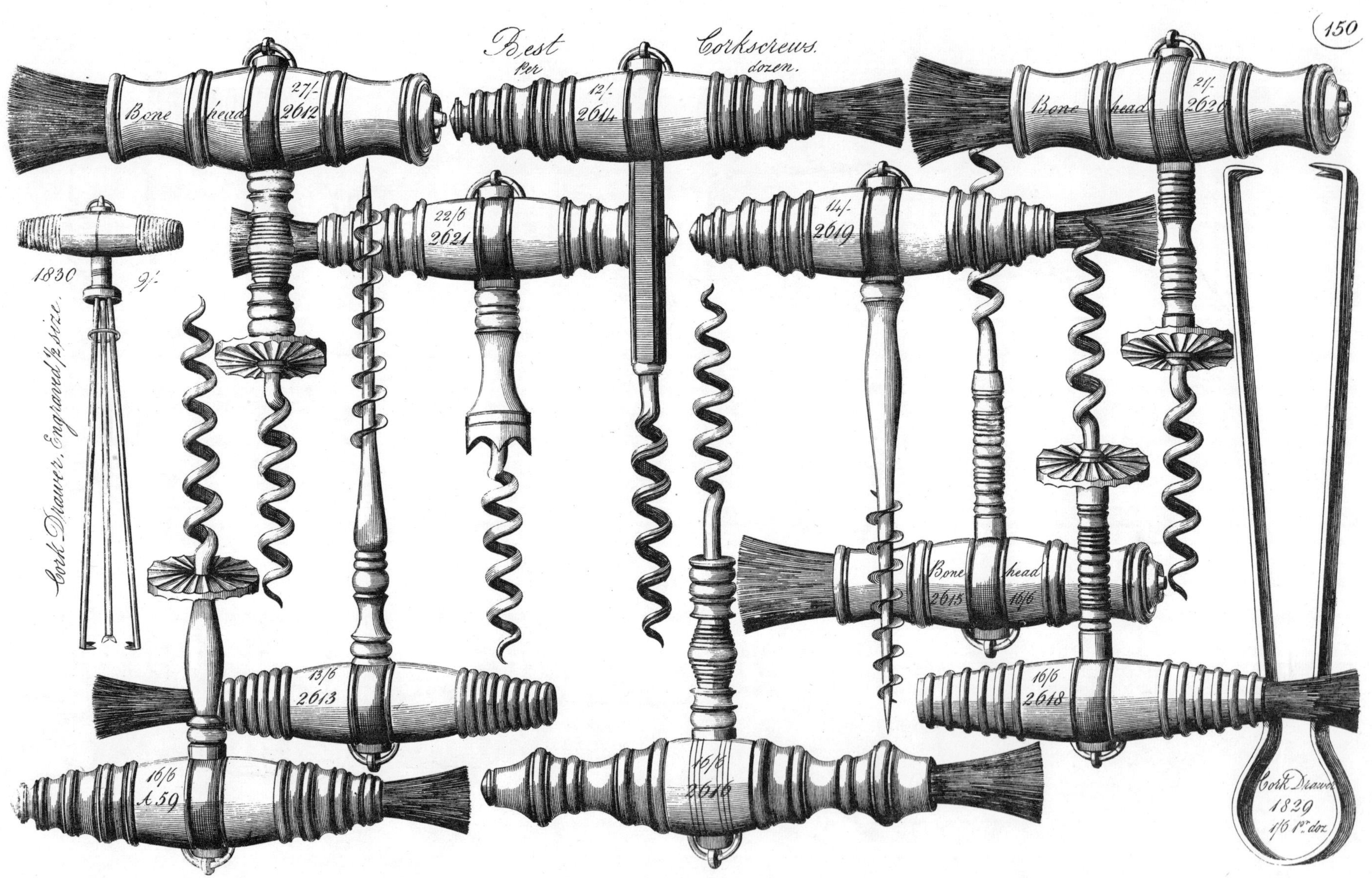

150
Best Corkscrews.
per dozen.
Bone head 27/- 2612
12/- 2614
Bone head 27/- 2620
1830 9/-
Cork Drawer, Engraved 1/2 size.
22/6 2621
14/- 2619
Bone head 2615 16/6
13/6 2613
Bone head 2617 16/6
16/6 2618
16/6 A 59
16/6 2616
Cork Drawer 1829 1/6 per doz.

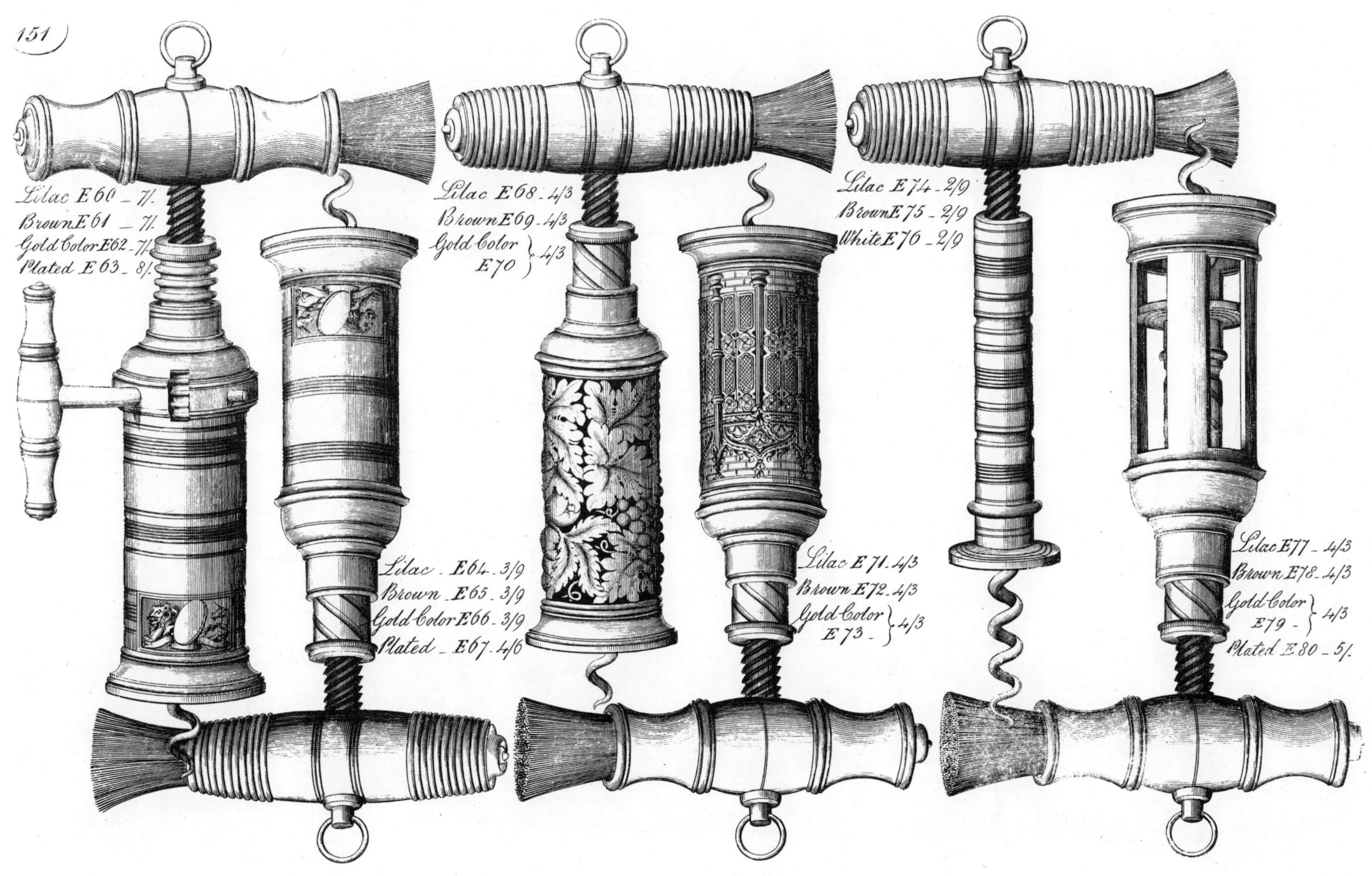
Lilac E60 — 7/.
Brown E61 — 7/.
Gold Color E62 — 7/.
Plated E63 — 8/.
Lilac E68 — 4/3
Brown E69 — 4/3
Gold Color E70 } 4/3
Lilac E74 — 2/9
Brown E75 — 2/9
White E76 — 2/9
Lilac — E64 — 3/9
Brown — E65 — 3/9
Gold Color E66 — 3/9
Plated — E67 — 4/6
Lilac E71 — 4/3
Brown E72 — 4/3
Gold Color E73 } 4/3
Lilac E77 — 4/3
Brown E78 — 4/3
Gold Color E79 } 4/3
Plated E80 — 5/.

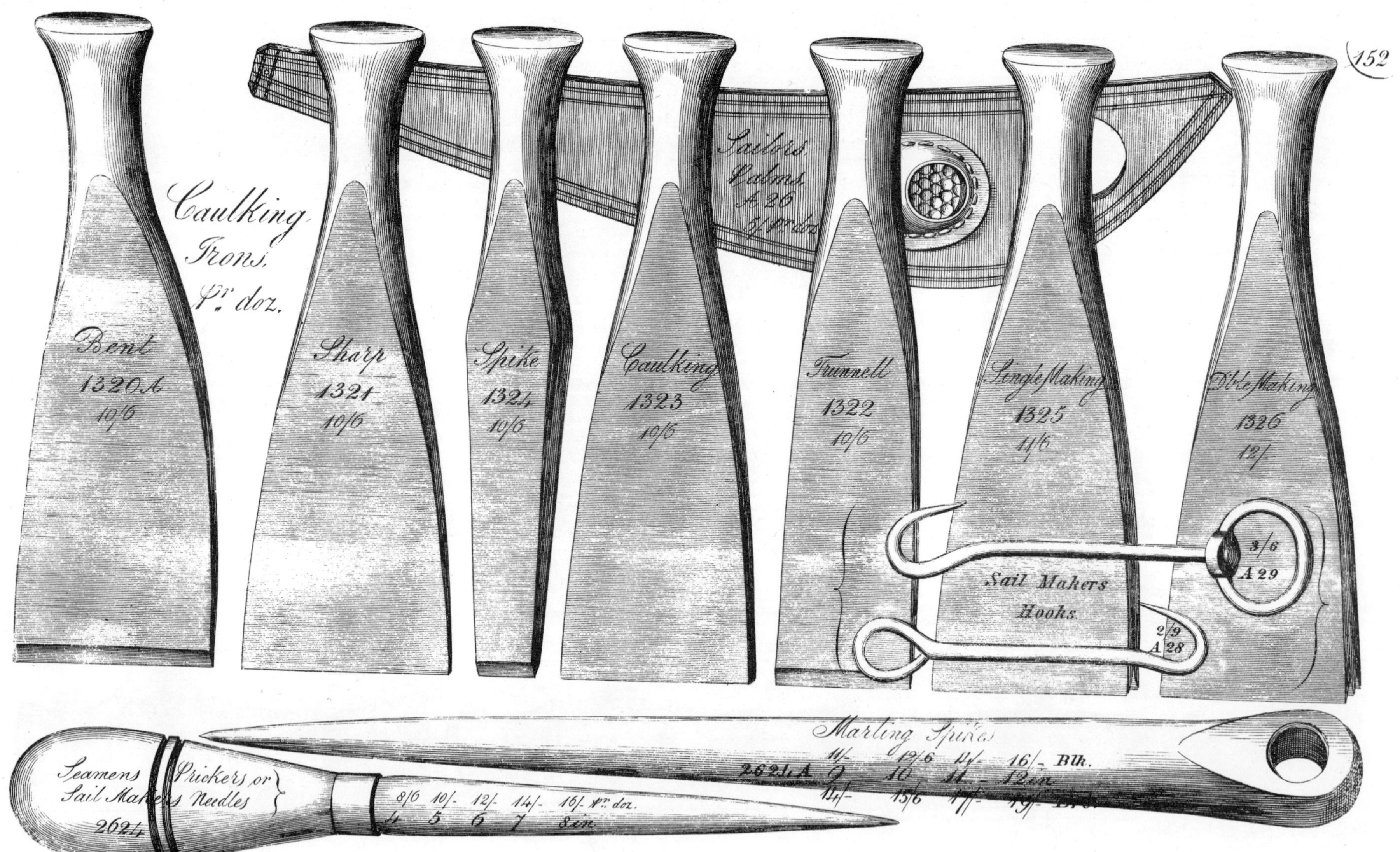
Caulking
Irons.
Pr. doz.
Bent
1320A
10/6
Sharp
1321
10/6
Spike
1324
10/6
Caulking
1323
10/6
Sailors
Palms
A 26
6/ pr doz
Funnel
1322
10/6
Single Making
1325
11/6
Dble Making
1326
12/-
Sail Makers
Hooks.
3/6
A 29
2/9
A 28
Seamens
Sail Makers
Prickers or
Needles
2624
8/6 10/- 12/- 14/- 16/- Pr. doz.
4   5   6   7   8 in.
Marling Spikes
11/-   12/6   14/-   16/-   Blk.
2621 A 9   10   11   12 in.
14/-   15/6   17/-   19/-

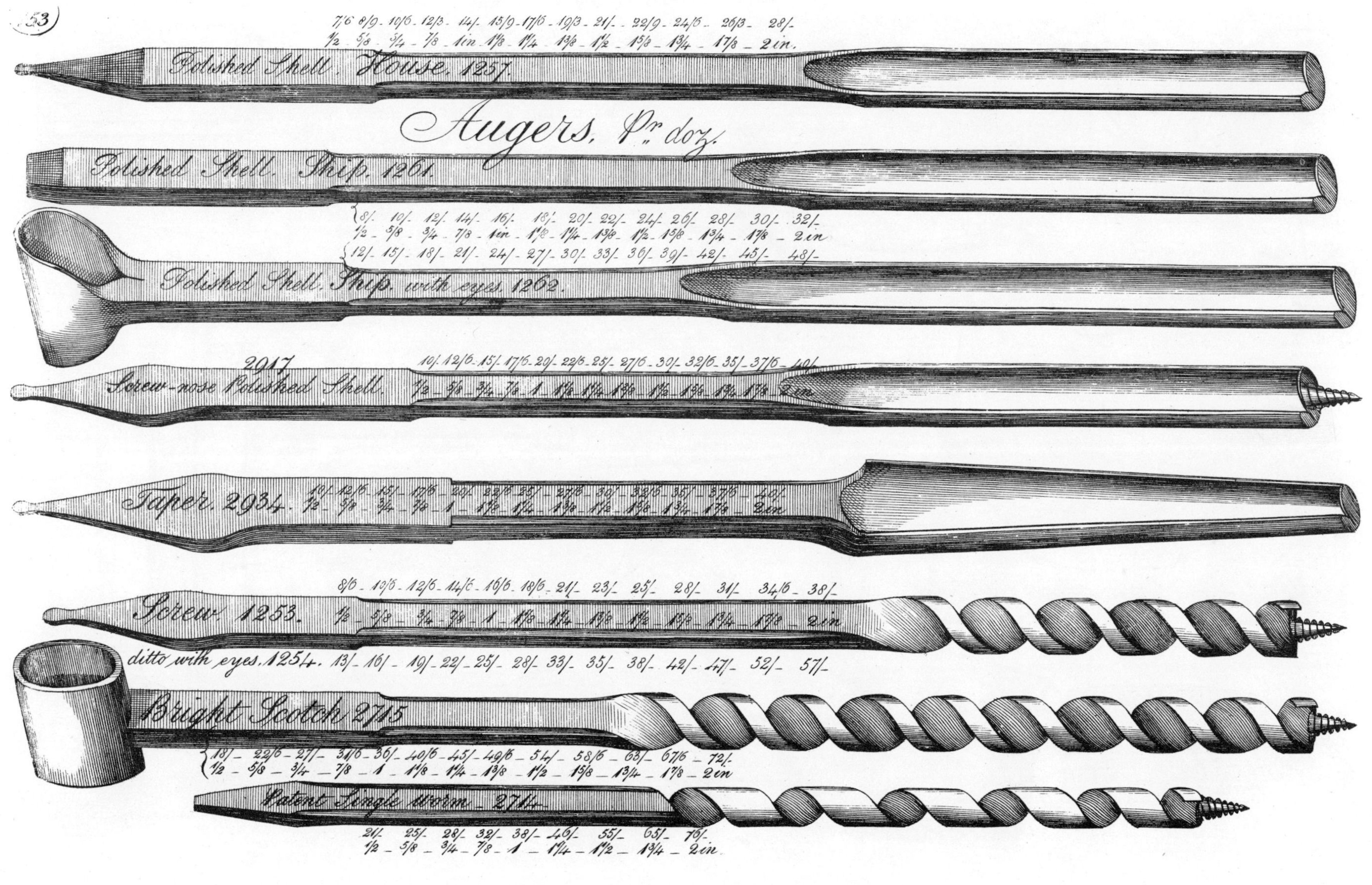
7/6 8/9 - 10/6 - 12/3 - 14/- 15/9 - 17/6 - 19/3 - 21/- - 22/9 - 24/6 - 26/3 - 28/-
1/2 5/8 3/4 - 7/8 - 1in 1⅛ - 1¼ - 1⅜ - 1½ - 1⅝ - 1¾ - 1⅞ - 2in
Polished Shell. House. 1257.
Augers. Pr doz.
Polished Shell. Ship. 1261.
8/- 10/- 12/- 14/- 16/- 18/- 20/- 22/- 24/- 26/- 28/- 30/- 32/-
1/2 - 5/8 - 3/4 - 7/8 - 1in - 1⅛ - 1¼ - 1⅜ - 1½ - 1⅝ - 1¾ - 1⅞ - 2in
12/- 15/- 18/- 21/- 24/- 27/- 30/- 33/- 36/- 39/- 42/- 45/- 48/-
Polished Shell. Ship. with eyes. 1262.
2917
10/- 12/6 - 15/- 17/6 - 20/- 22/6 - 25/- 27/6 - 30/- 32/6 - 35/- 37/6 - 40/-
Screw-nose Polished Shell.   1/2 - 5/8 - 3/4 - 7/8 - 1 - 1⅛ - 1¼ - 1⅜ - 1½ - 1⅝ - 1¾ - 1⅞ - 2in
Taper. 2934.   10/- 12/6 - 15/- 17/6 - 20/- 22/6 - 25/- 27/6 - 30/- 32/6 - 35/- 37/6 - 40/-
1/2 - 5/8 - 3/4 - 7/8 - 1 - 1⅛ - 1¼ - 1⅜ - 1½ - 1⅝ - 1¾ - 1⅞ - 2in
8/6 - 10/6 - 12/6 - 14/6 - 16/6 - 18/6 - 21/- 23/- 25/- 28/- 31/- 34/6 - 38/-
Screw. 1253.   1/2 - 5/8 - 3/4 - 7/8 - 1 - 1⅛ - 1¼ - 1⅜ - 1½ - 1⅝ - 1¾ - 1⅞ - 2in
ditto with eyes. 1254.   13/- 16/- 19/- 22/- 25/- 28/- 33/- 35/- 38/- 42/- 47/- 52/- 57/-
Bright Scotch 2715
18/- - 22/6 - 27/- 31/6 - 36/- 40/6 - 45/- 49/6 - 54/- 58/6 - 63/- 67/6 - 72/-
1/2 - 5/8 - 3/4 - 7/8 - 1 - 1⅛ - 1¼ - 1⅜ - 1½ - 1⅝ - 1¾ - 1⅞ - 2in
Patent Single Worm. 2714.
21/- 25/- 28/- 32/- 38/- 46/- 55/- 65/- 76/-
1/2 - 5/8 - 3/4 - 7/8 - 1 - 1¼ - 1½ - 1¾ - 2in

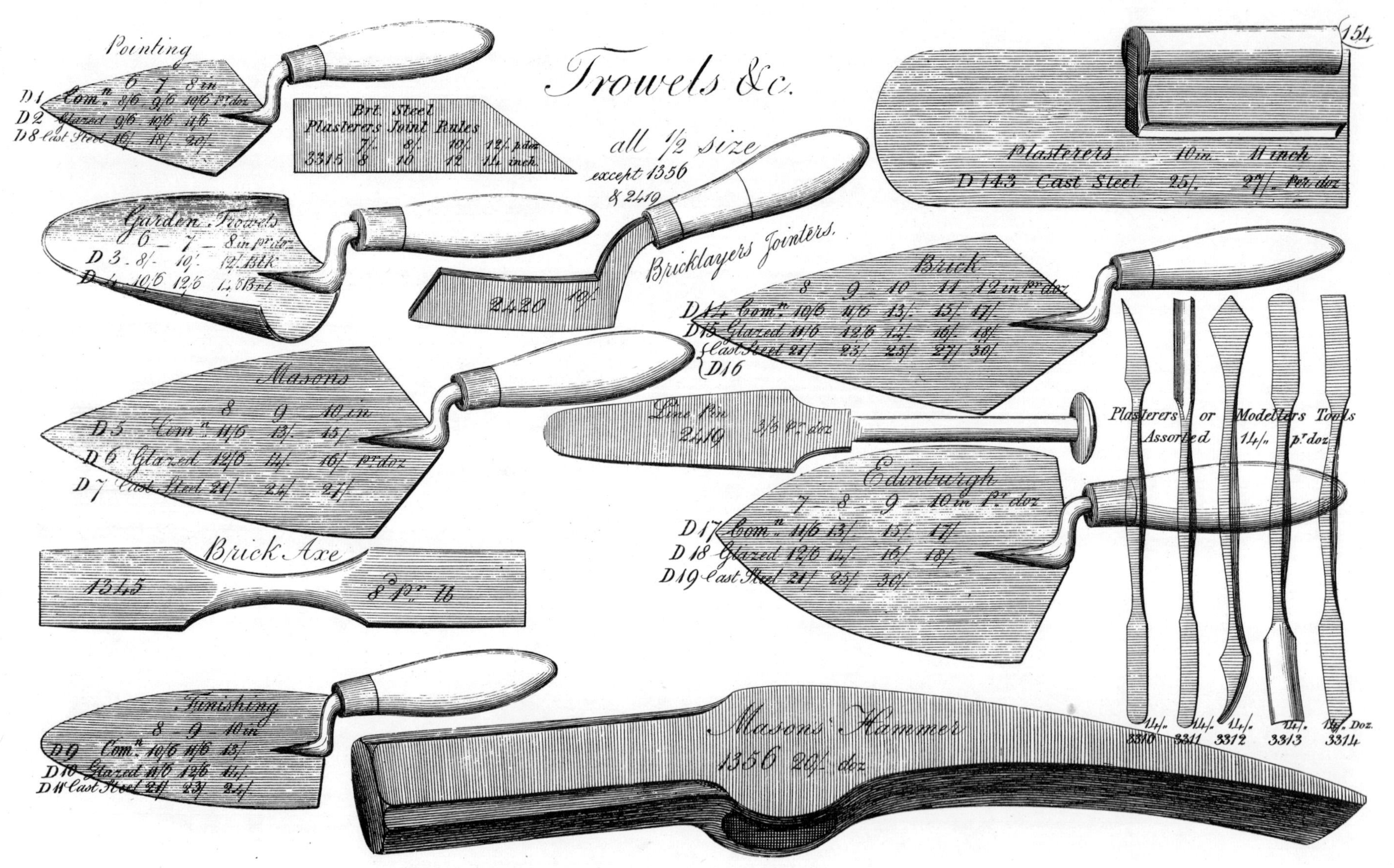
Trowels &c.
all ½ size
except 1356 & 2419
Pointing
D1 Comn 8/6 9/6 10/6 Pr doz
D2 Glazed 9/6 10/6 11/6
118 Cast Steel 16/ 18/ 20/
6 7 8 in
Brt. Steel Plasterers Joint Rules
7/ 8/ 10/ 12/ p doz
3315 8 10 12 14 inch
Garden Trowels
6 7 8 in pr dor
D3 8/ 10/ 12/ Blk
D4 10/6 12/6 12/6 Brt
Masons
8 9 10 in
D5 Comn 11/6 13/ 15/
D6 Glazed 12/6 14/ 16/ Pr doz
D7 Cast Steel 21/ 24/ 24/
Brick Axe
1345
8 pr lb
Finishing
8 9 10 in
D9 Comn 10/6 11/6 12/
D10 Glazed 11/6 12/6 14/
D11 Cast Steel 21/ 23/ 24/
Plasterers 10in 11 inch
D143 Cast Steel 25/ 27/ Per doz
Bricklayers Jointers.
2420 10/
Brick
8 9 10 11 12 in Pr doz
D14 Comn 10/6 11/6 13/ 15/ 17/
D15 Glazed 11/6 12/6 14/ 16/ 18/
Cast Steel 21/ 23/ 25/ 27/ 30/
D16
Line Pin 2419 3/6 pr doz
Edinburgh
7 8 9 10 in Pr doz
D17 Comn 11/6 13/ 15/ 17/
D18 Glazed 12/6 14/ 16/ 18/
D19 Cast Steel 21/ 23/ 30/
Plasterers or Modellers Tools
Assorted 14/ p doz
3310 3311 3312 3313 3314
14/ 14/ 14/ 14/ 14/ Doz
Masons' Hammer
1356 20/ doz

Plane Irons.

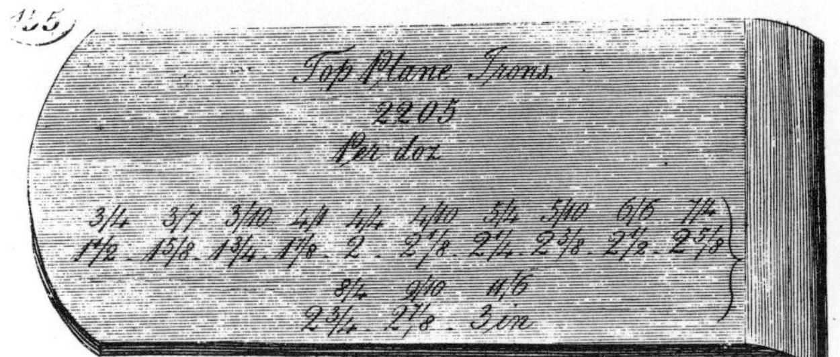

Top Plane Irons.
2205
Per doz
3/4 3/7 3/10 4/1 4/4 4/10 5/4 5/10 6/6 7/4
1/2 1 5/8 1 3/4 1 7/8 2 2 1/8 2 1/4 2 3/8 2 1/2 2 5/8
8/4 9/10 11/6
2 3/4 2 7/8 3 in

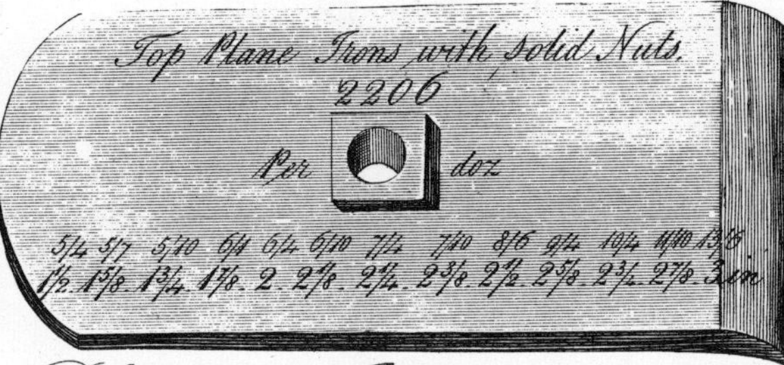

Top Plane Irons with solid Nuts.
2206
Per doz
5/4 5/7 5/10 6/4 6/4 6/10 7/4 7/10 8/6 9/4 10/4 11/10 13/4
1/2 1 5/8 1 3/4 1 7/8 2 2 1/8 2 1/4 2 3/8 2 1/2 2 5/8 2 3/4 2 7/8 3 in

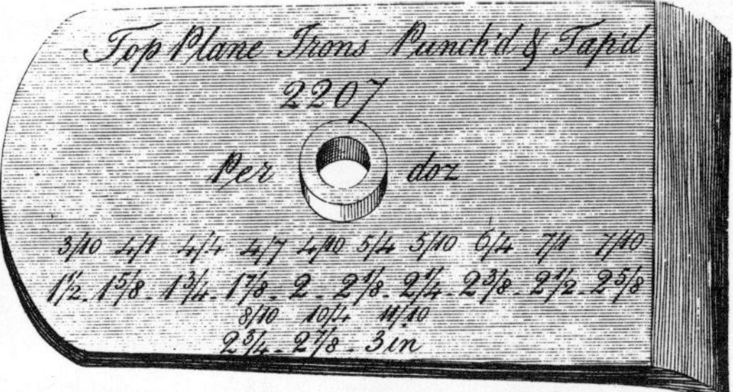

Top Plane Irons Punch'd & Tap'd
2207
Per doz
3/10 4/1 4/4 4/7 4/10 5/4 5/10 6/4 7/4 7/10
1/2 1 5/8 1 3/4 1 7/8 2 2 1/8 2 1/4 2 3/8 2 1/2 2 5/8
8/10 10/4 11/10
2 3/4 2 7/8 3 in

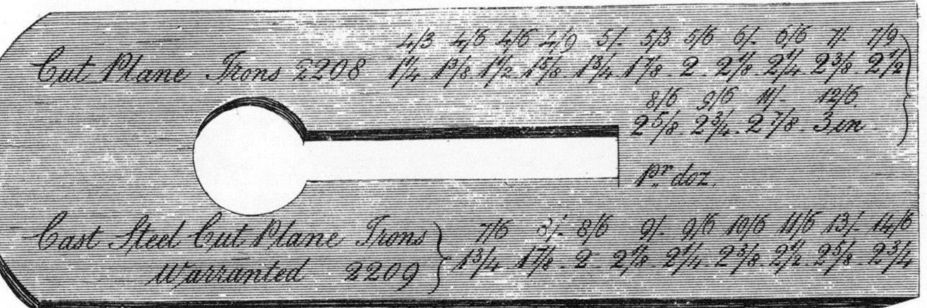

Cut Plane Irons 2208
4/3 4/5 4/6 4/9 5/ 5/3 5/6 6/ 6/6 7/ 7/9
1/4 1 3/8 1 1/2 1 5/8 1 3/4 1 7/8 2 2 1/8 2 1/4 2 3/8 2 1/2
8/6 9/6 11/ 12/6
2 5/8 2 3/4 2 7/8 3 in
Pr doz.
Cast Steel Cut Plane Irons
Warranted 2209
7/6 8/ 8/6 9/ 9/6 10/6 11/6 13/ 14/6
1 3/4 1 7/8 2 2 1/8 2 1/4 2 3/8 2 1/2 2 5/8 2 3/4

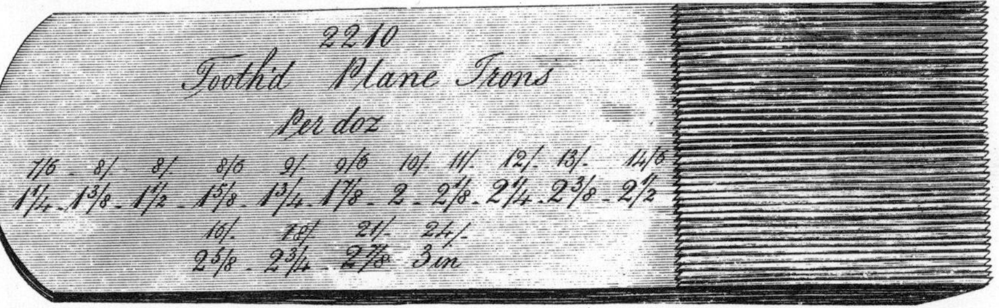

2210
Tooth'd Plane Irons
Per doz
7/6 8/ 8/ 8/6 9/ 9/6 10/ 11/ 12/ 13/ 14/6
1/4 1 3/8 1 1/2 1 5/8 1 3/4 1 7/8 2 2 1/8 2 1/4 2 3/8 2 1/2
16/ 18/ 21/ 24/
2 5/8 2 3/4 2 7/8 3 in

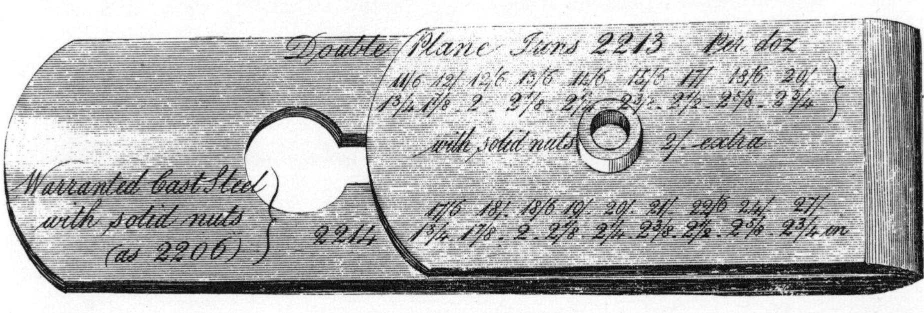

Double Plane Irons 2213 Per doz
11/6 12/ 12/6 13/6 14/6 15/6 17/ 18/6 20/
1 3/4 1 7/8 2 2 1/8 2 1/4 2 3/8 2 1/2 2 5/8 2 3/4
with solid nuts 2/- extra
17/6 18/ 18/6 19/ 20/ 21/ 22/6 24/ 27/
1 3/4 1 7/8 2 2 1/8 2 1/4 2 3/8 2 1/2 2 5/8 2 3/4 in
Warranted Cast Steel
with solid nuts
(as 2206) 2214

Single Plane Irons Pr doz
3/9 4/ 4/ 4/3 4/6 4/9 5/ 5/3 6/ 6/6 7/3 8/ 9/ 10/6 12/
2211 1 1/4 1 3/8 1 1/2 1 5/8 1 3/4 1 7/8 2 2 1/8 2 1/4 2 3/8 2 1/2 2 5/8 2 3/4 2 7/8 3 in
Cast Steel 2212 7/ 7/6 8/ 8/6 9/ 10/ 11/ 12/6 14/
Warranted 1 3/4 1 7/8 2 2 1/8 2 1/4 2 3/8 2 1/2 2 5/8 2 3/4

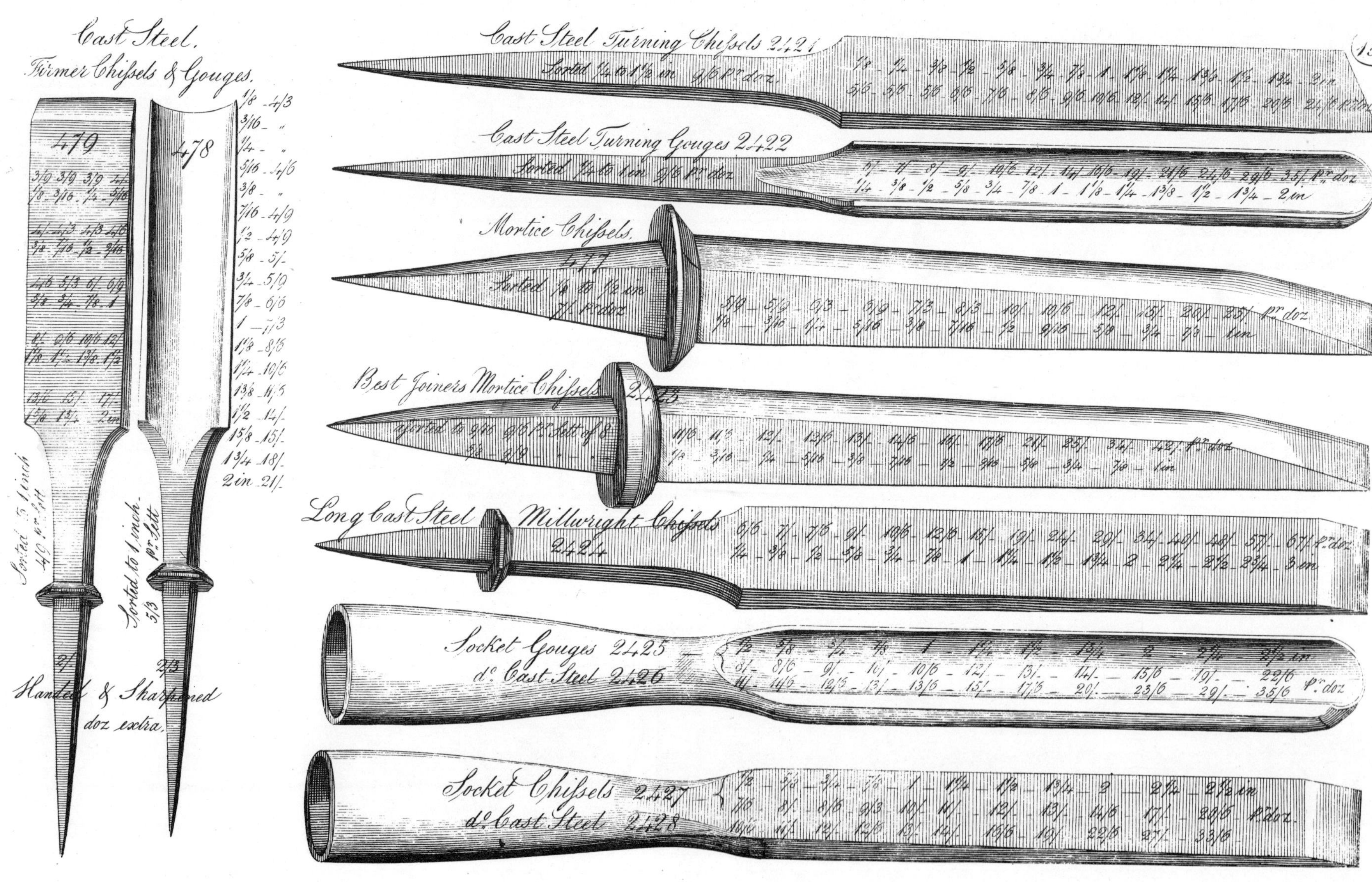
Cast Steel.
Firmer Chisels & Gouges.
479
478
Sorted 5 to 1 inch
Sorted to 1 inch
Handled & Sharpened
doz extra.
Cast Steel Turning Chisels 2421
Sorted ¼ to 1½ in
Cast Steel Turning Gouges 2422
Sorted ¼ to 1 in
Mortice Chisels.
Best Joiners Mortice Chisels 2423
Long Cast Steel Millwright Chisels 2424
Socket Gouges 2425
d⁰ Cast Steel 2426
Socket Chisels 2427
d⁰ Cast Steel 2428
156

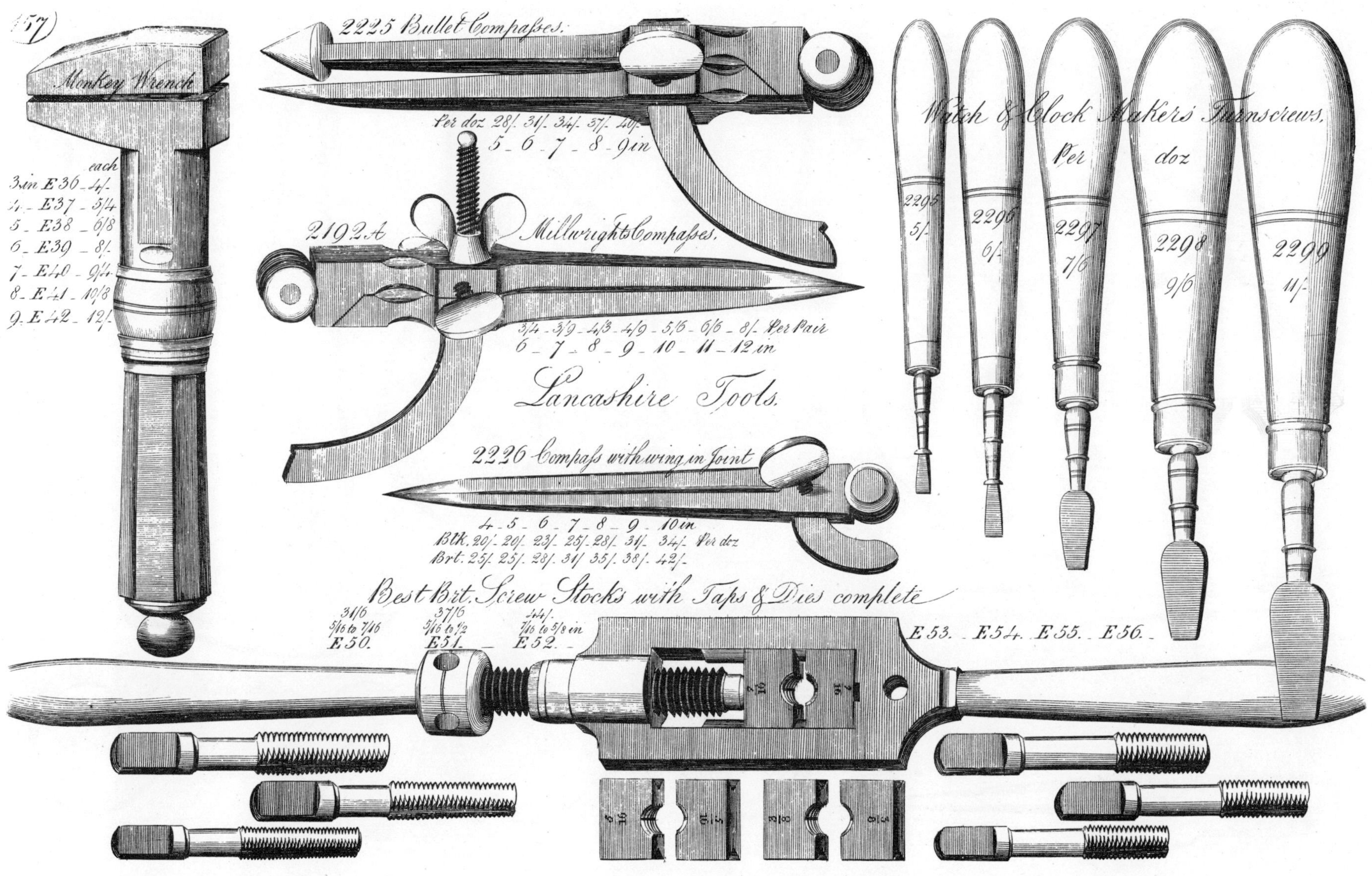
457
Monkey Wrench
each
3 in E 36 _ 4/-
4 _ E 37 _ 5/4
5 _ E 38 _ 6/8
6 _ E 39 _ 8/-
7 _ E 40 _ 9/4
8 _ E 41 _ 10/8
9 _ E 42 _ 12/-
2225 Bullet Compasses.
Per doz 28/. 31/. 34/. 37/. 40/.
5 - 6 - 7 - 8 - 9 in
2192 A
Millwrights Compasses.
3/4 - 3/9 - 4/3 - 4/9 - 5/6 - 6/6 - 8/. Per Pair
6 - 7 - 8 - 9 - 10 - 11 - 12 in
Lancashire Tools.
2226 Compass with wing in Joint
4 - 5 - 6 - 7 - 8 - 9 - 10 in
Blk. 20/. 20/. 23/. 25/. 28/. 31/. 34/. Per doz
Brt. 25/. 25/. 28/. 31/. 35/. 38/. 42/.
Watch & Clock Makers Turnscrews.
Per   doz
2295   2296   2297   2298   2299
5/.   6/.   7/6   9/6   11/.
Best Brt. Screw Stocks with Taps & Dies complete
31/6   37/6   44/.
5/16 to 7/16   5/16 to 1/2   7/16 to 5/8 in
E 50.   E 51.   E 52.
E 53.   E 54.   E 55.   E 56.

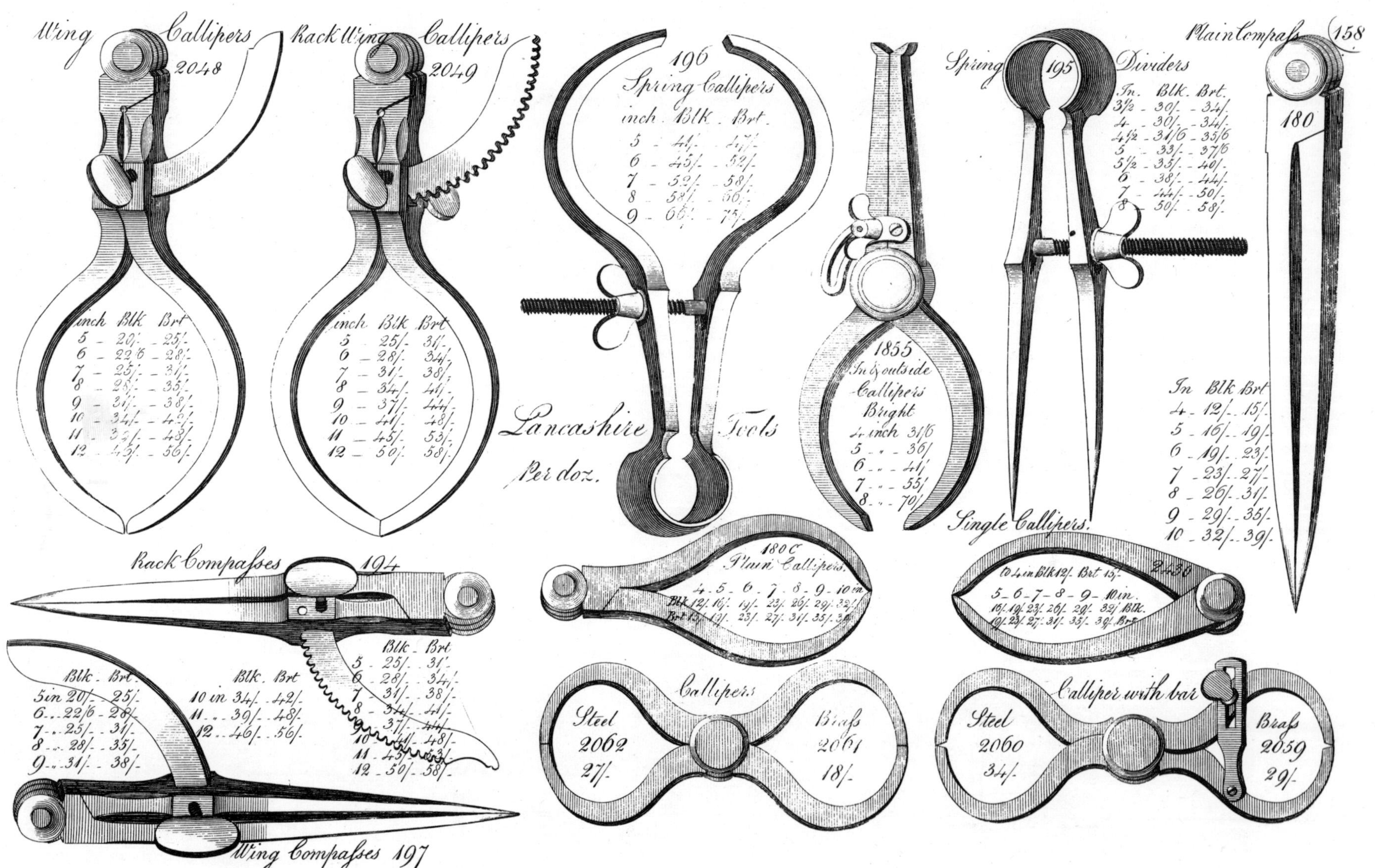

Wing Callipers 2048
Rack Wing Callipers 2049
196 Spring Callipers
inch Blk Brt
5 - 4/ - 4/7
6 - 4·5/ - 5·2/
7 - 5·2/ - 5·8/
8 - 5·8/ - 6·6/
9 - 6·6/ - 7·5/
inch Blk Brt
5 - 20/ - 25/
6 - 22/6 - 28/
7 - 25/ - 31/
8 - 28/ - 35/
9 - 31/ - 38/
10 - 34/ - 41/
11 - 39/ - 48/
12 - 45/ - 56/
inch Blk Brt
5 - 25/ - 31/
6 - 28/ - 34/
7 - 31/ - 38/
8 - 34/ - 41/
9 - 37/ - 44/
10 - 41/ - 48/
11 - 45/ - 53/
12 - 50/ - 58/
Lancashire Tools
Per doz.
Spring 195 Dividers
Plain Compass 158
In Blk Brt
3½ - 30/ - 34/
4 - 30/ - 34/
4½ - 31/6 - 35/6
5 - 33/ - 37/6
5½ - 35/ - 40/
6 - 38/ - 44/
7 - 44/ - 50/
8 - 50/ - 58/
180
1855 In & outside Callipers Bright
4 inch 31/6
5 - 36/
6 - 41/
7 - 55/
8 - 70/
In Blk Brt
4 - 12/ - 15/
5 - 16/ - 19/
6 - 19/ - 23/
7 - 23/ - 27/
8 - 26/ - 31/
9 - 29/ - 35/
10 - 32/ - 39/
Single Callipers
Rack Compasses 194
Blk Brt
5 in 20/ - 25/
6 - 22/6 - 28/
7 - 25/ - 31/
8 - 28/ - 35/
9 - 31/ - 38/
Blk Brt
10 in 34/ - 42/
11 - 39/ - 48/
12 - 46/ - 56/
Blk Brt
5 - 25/ - 31/
6 - 28/ - 34/
7 - 31/ - 38/
8 - 34/ - 41/
9 - 37/ - 44/
10 - 41/ - 48/
11 - 45/ - 53/
12 - 50/ - 58/
180 C Plain Callipers
4 - 5 - 6 - 7 - 8 - 9 - 10 in
Blk 12/ 16/ 19/ 23/ 26/ 29/ 32/
Brt 15/ 19/ 23/ 27/ 31/ 35/ 39/
4 in Blk 12/ Brt 15/
5 - 6 - 7 - 8 - 9 - 10 in
16/ 19/ 23/ 26/ 29/ 32/ Blk
19/ 23/ 27/ 31/ 35/ 39/ Brt
Wing Compasses 197
Callipers
Steel 2062 27/
Brass 2061 18/
Calliper with bar
Steel 2060 34/
Brass 2059 29/

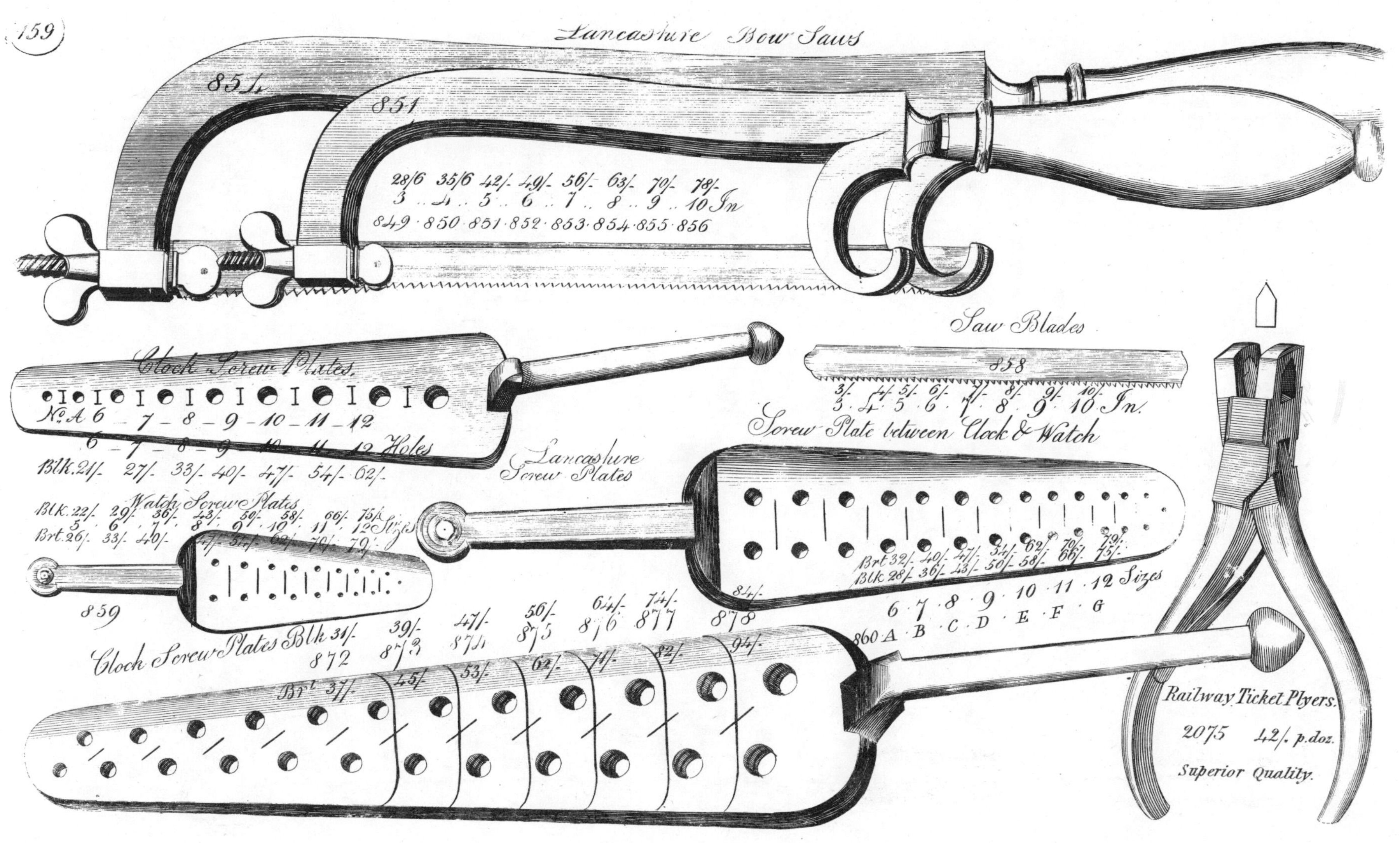

Lancashire Bow Saws
851
851
28/6 35/6 42/- 49/- 56/- 63/- 70/- 78/-
3 .. 4 .. 5 .. 6 .. 7 .. 8 .. 9 .. 10 In.
849 · 850 · 851 · 852 · 853 · 854 · 855 · 856
Saw Blades
858
3 4 5 6 7 8 9 10 In.
Screw Plate between Clock & Watch
Clock Screw Plates.
No A 6 7 8 9 10 11 12
6 7 8 9 10 11 12 Holes
Blk. 21/- 27/- 33/- 40/- 47/- 54/- 62/-
Watch Screw Plates
Blk. 22/- 29/- 36/- 43/- 50/- 58/- 66/- 75/-
5 6 7 8 9 10 11 12 Sizes
Brt. 26/- 33/- 40/- 47/- 54/- 62/- 70/- 79/-
859
Lancashire Screw Plates
Brt 32/- 40/- 47/- 54/- 62/- 70/- 75/-
Blk 28/- 36/- 43/- 50/- 58/- 66/- 75/-
84/-
6 7 8 9 10 11 12 Sizes
860 A B C D E F G
Clock Screw Plates Blk 31/- 39/- 47/- 56/- 64/- 74/- 82/- 94/-
872 871 877 878
Brt 37/- 45/- 53/- 62/- 74/- 82/- 94/-
Railway Ticket Plyers.
2075   42/. p.doz.
Superior Quality.

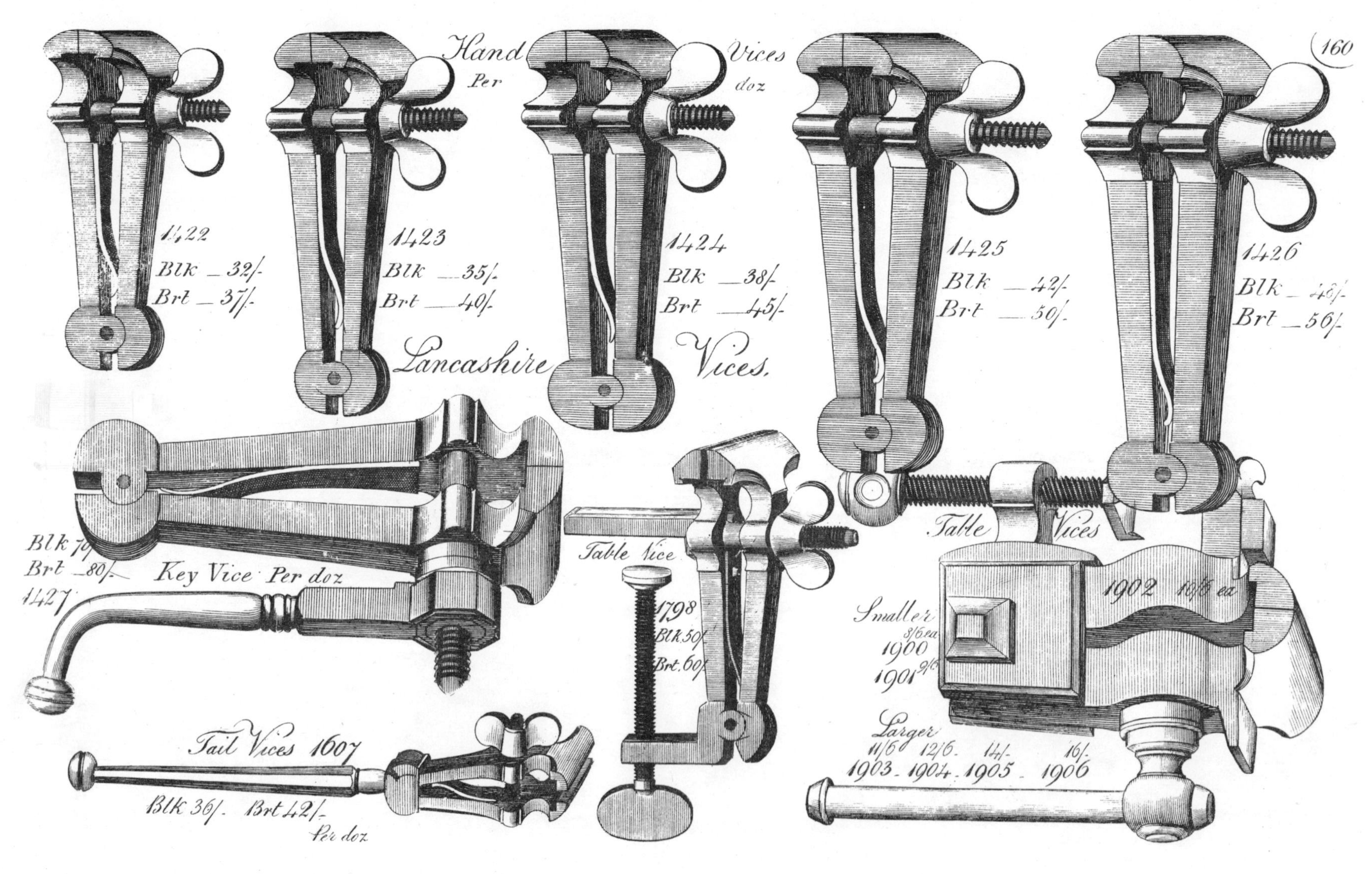
Hand Vices
Per doz
1422
Blk __ 32/-
Brt __ 37/-
1423
Blk __ 35/-
Brt __ 40/-
Lancashire
1424
Blk __ 38/-
Brt __ 45/-
Vices.
1425
Blk __ 42/-
Brt __ 50/-
1426
Blk __ 46/-
Brt __ 56/-
Blk 70/-
Brt __ 80/-
1427
Key Vice Per doz
Table Vice
1798
Blk 50/-
Brt 60/-
Table Vices
Smaller
3/6 ea
1900
1901 9/-
Larger
11/6 12/6 14/- 16/-
1903 - 1904 - 1905 - 1906
1902 19/6 ea
Tail Vices 1607
Blk 36/-   Brt 42/-
Per doz

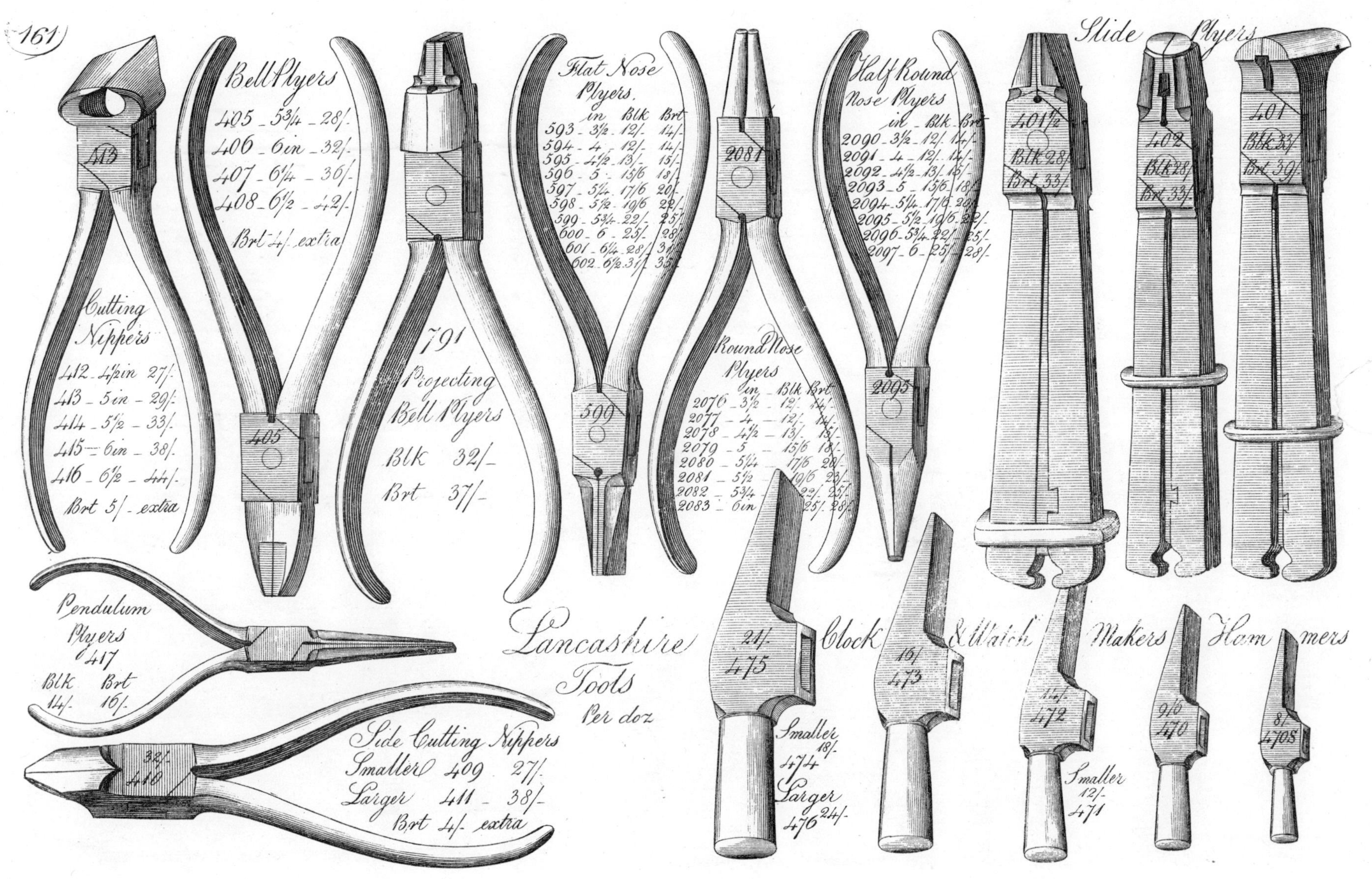
161

Bell Plyers
405 _ 5¾ _ 28/-
406 _ 6 in _ 32/-
407 _ 6¼ _ 36/-
408 _ 6½ _ 42/-
Brt 4/- extra

Cutting Nippers
412 _ 4½ in _ 27/-
413 _ 5 in _ 29/-
414 _ 5½ _ 33/-
415 _ 6 in _ 38/-
416 _ 6½ _ 44/-
Brt 5/- extra

Pendulum Plyers
417
Blk Brt
14/- 16/-

Side Cutting Nippers
Smaller 409 27/-
Larger 411 _ 38/-
Brt 4/- extra

791
Projecting Bell Plyers
Blk 32/-
Brt 37/-

Flat Nose Plyers.
in Blk Brt
593 _ 3½ _ 12/- 14/-
594 _ 4 _ 12/- 14/-
595 _ 4½ _ 13/- 15/-
596 _ 5 _ 15/6 18/-
597 _ 5½ _ 17/6 20/-
598 _ 5¾ _ 19/6 22/-
599 _ 5¾ _ 22/- 25/-
600 _ 6 _ 25/- 28/-
601 _ 6¼ _ 28/- 31/-
602 _ 6½ _ 31/- 35/-

599

Round Nose Plyers
in Blk Brt
2076 _ 3½ _ 12/- 14/-
2077 _ 4 _ 12/- 14/-
2078 _ 4½ _ 13/- 15/-
2079 _ 5 _ 15/6 18/-
2080 _ 5¼ _ 17/6 20/-
2081 _ 5½ _ 19/6 22/-
2082 _ 5¾ _ 22/- 25/-
2083 _ 6 in _ 25/- 28/-

2081

Half Round Nose Plyers
in Blk Brt
2090 _ 3½ _ 12/- 14/-
2091 _ 4 _ 12/- 14/-
2092 _ 4½ _ 13/- 15/-
2093 _ 5 _ 15/6 18/-
2094 _ 5¼ _ 17/6 20/-
2095 _ 5½ _ 19/6 22/-
2096 _ 5¾ _ 22/- 25/-
2097 _ 6 _ 25/- 28/-

2095

Slide Plyers
401½
Blk 28/-
Brt 33/-

402
Blk 28/-
Brt 33/-

401
Blk 33/-
Brt 39/-

Lancashire Tools
Per doz

Clock & Watch Makers Hammers

24/-
475

16/-
473

14/-
472

9/6
470

8/-
470S

Smaller 18/-
474
Larger 24/-
476

Smaller 12/-
471

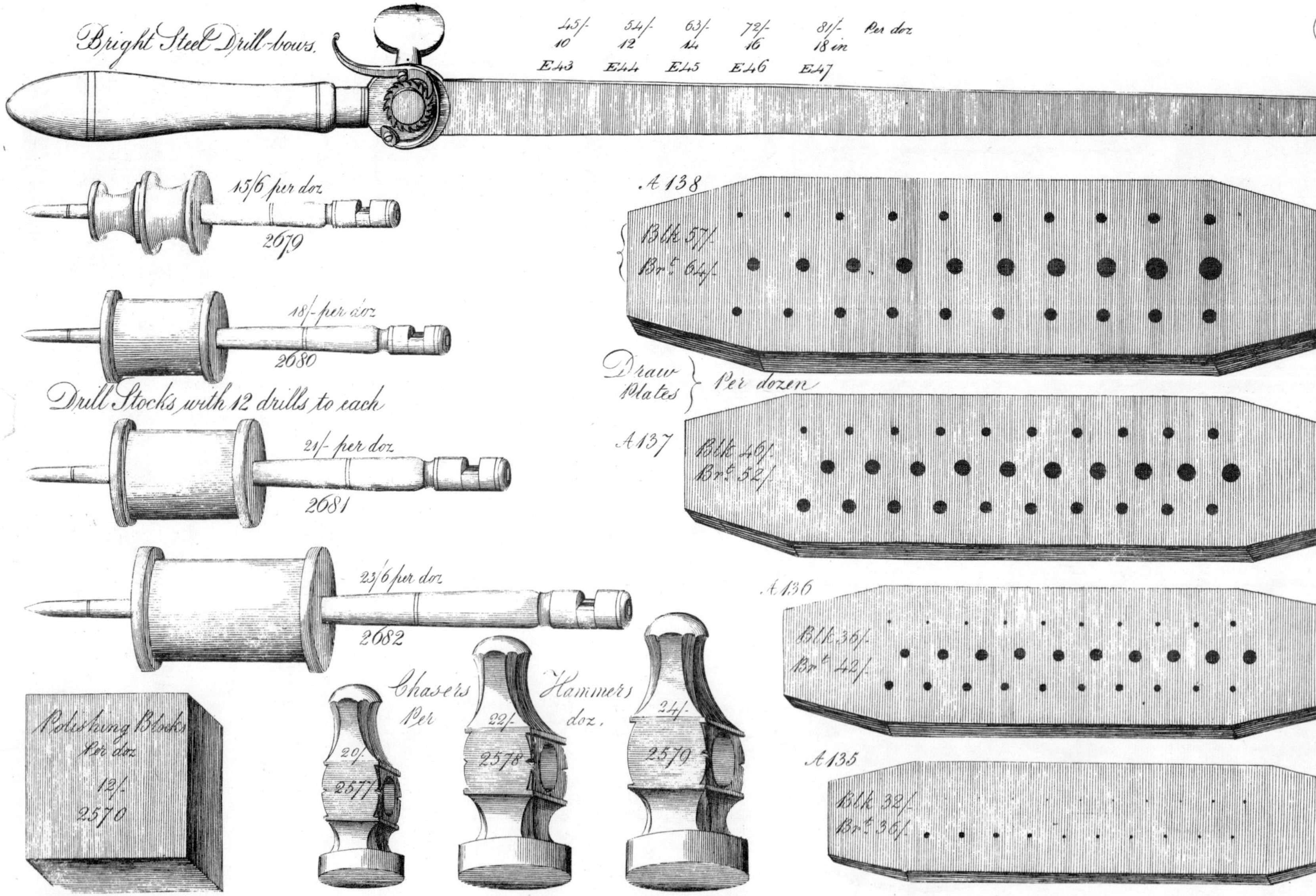

Bright Steel Drill-bows.

45/-	54/-	63/-	72/-	81/-	Per doz
10	12	14	16	18 in	
E43	E44	E45	E46	E47	

15/6 per doz
2679

18/- per doz
2680

Drill Stocks with 12 drills to each

21/- per doz
2681

23/6 per doz
2682

Polishing Blocks
Per doz
12/-
2570

Chasers
Per

Hammers
doz.

20/-
2577

22/-
2578

24/-
2579

A 138

Blk 57/-
Br.ᵈ 64/-

Draw Plates } Per dozen

A 137

Blk 46/-
Br.ᵈ 52/-

A 136

Blk 36/-
Br.ᵈ 42/-

A 135

Blk 32/-
Br.ᵈ 36/-

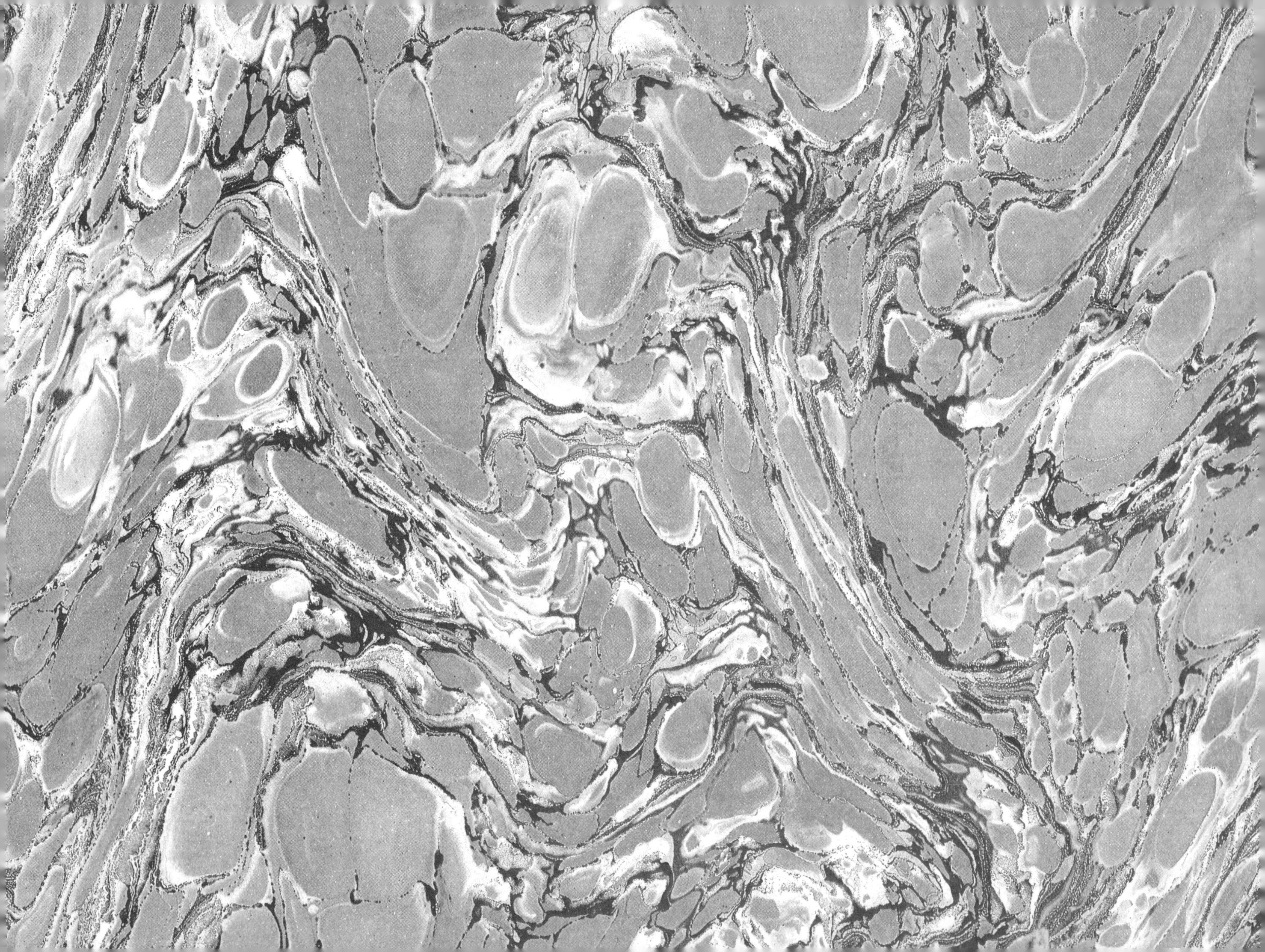